Fisherman's Companion

Material in this book has previously appeared in
The Complete Specimen Hunter, by Tony Miles
Beach Fishing, by John Holden
Tactical Fly Fishing for Trout and Sea Trout on River and Stream, by Pat O'Reilly
Stillwater Trout Tactics, by Bob Church and Charles Jardine
Fly Fishing for Salmon and Sea Trout, by Arthur Oglesby

All published by The Crowood Press

Fisherman's COMPANION

Consultant Editor: Bob Church

Contributors: Tony Miles • John Holden • Pat O'Reilly
• Bob Church • Charles Jardine • Arthur Oglesby

Produced exclusively for W. H. Smith Ltd by
The Crowood Press Ltd
Ramsbury, Marlborough
Wiltshire SN8 2HR

First published in 1991

British Library Cataloguing in Publication Data

Fisherman's companion.
1. Fishing (Field sports)
799.1

ISBN 1 85223 675 2

Photographic acknowledgements

All photographs by Trevor Housby except the barbel (Tony Miles) and the carp (Tim Paisley).

Typeset by Avonset, Midsomer Norton, Bath, Avon
Printed in Great Britain by
Butler & Tanner Ltd, Frome

Contents

Contents

PART THREE FLY FISHING

Foreword

As we move into the nineties, I have noticed that most serious anglers are taking on the role of all-round fishermen. By this I mean that they have come up through the ranks of coarse fishing and then, in the close season months, have dabbled at trout fly fishing. In most cases the result has been a very successful change over. In my opinion, this is due to the watercraft learned while coarse fishing. Why else do such anglers have so much more success than someone starting fly fishing from scratch?

Once you can fish the fly, you may find yourself in Wales, Scotland or Ireland on holiday, where you can try for wild brown trout, perhaps sea trout, or even the mighty salmon. I can remember a few family summer holidays at Looe in Cornwall, sea fishing for blue shark, pollack, ling and conger. At Poole, where I caught tope and various rays, I even broke the British record for a small-eyed ray. I could never have dropped into the sea-fishing style so easily had I not already fished for pike, carp and eel in those earlier freshwater fishing years.

In this book we have brought together some of the best angling writers who are experts in their own particular fields.

Tony Miles covers all the important coarse fishing species – very few angling writers could have done this job. On second thoughts, I would describe Tony as a writing angler rather than as an angling writer, and there is a big difference. Over the years he has built up a vast experience and likes to fish for all the different species. I would add that he would only try for one species at a time though, and then he sets himself certain weight targets which he tries to achieve. This type of fishing is known as either specimen hunting or specialist angling. In this country there are many clubs or groups which cater for this type of angler. They are very well organized, publishing their own magazines and holding various social occasions – there must be one near to you, so enquire at your local tackle shop.

John Holden is such a good instructive writer that your beach sea fishing must be improved after reading this chapter. As you will see, he not only covers tactics, baits and various species so well, but even more importantly he describes the technical approach to tackle and casting which is the first thing that must be mastered.

Pat O'Reilly takes you river fly fishing for trout. If you are a newcomer to this branch of the sport, all the basics on kit and approach are covered in detail.

That great game fisherman Arthur Oglesby covers the mighty salmon and the sea trout. Most certainly, no one is better qualified for this job. Arthur has spent a lifetime fishing for and studying those species. He reflects on all the excitement a man can feel when he catches the King of Fish – the salmon.

Angling artist and entomologist Charles Jardine covers the life cycles of all the important aquatic foods on which stillwater trout feed. This really is an excellent reference and a chapter which must be studied closely and memorized. If you can learn to observe the trout's feeding behaviour on any fishing day, you are more than half-way to catching your limit bag.

For my part, I have taken you through a typical trout season from March to October. I have described all the best-known tactics for the appropriate time of year. Stillwater trout fly fishing is the fastest growing branch of our sport, with many waters springing up all over the country during the past fifteen years. For me, the ultimate is still a trip to the west of Ireland where I take a boat out on either Lough Mask (my favourite), Lough Carra or the mighty Lough Corrib. I have fished many places throughout the world, but the wild west of the Emerald Isle is still the place for me.

Enjoy this book and learn to become the complete all-round angler – you will never regret it.

Bob Church
Northampton, 1991

PART ONE

COARSE FISHING

Tony Miles

Introduction

Don't be confused by the name. 'Coarse' refers not to the anglers or their skills but to the fish themselves, historically considered less worth eating and therefore less prized in fishery-value terms than their more protected 'game' brethren. We have grown out of that. Now we appreciate sporting quality at least as much as table value – not least in monetary terms, since a live specimen carp, which will never be killed by a fisherman, is worth many times the price of a salmon of the same weight on the slab.

As to the skills required to tempt these wily and often educated creatures, coarse they are certainly not. Refinement and sophistication play a greater part in the approach of the coarse fisher than in any other branch of the sport. And gameness? Ask a carp man or a barbel hunter whether the lack of an adipose fin has any effect on fighting quality.

Coarse fishing is where most of us started. Perhaps it was at a very early age, with jamjar and bent pin for sticklebacks or minnows. This was largely because of transport. There can scarcely be anywhere that is not within the reach of a canal, a stream or a farm pond. With more years and greater mobility, trips further afield can be undertaken – or to the famous lakes, shrouded in mystery; to the powerful rivers where the big barbel live; to the Broads for pike; to the pits for giant bream. All-night sessions are organized – week-long sessions even, at home or abroad.

Beware. It can become addictive. Watch for the gleam in the eye. Happy the angler whose wife or girlfriend understands his passions – or, better still, shares it.

We may become obsessed by tackle. In recent years high tech has played a greater part in coarse fishing than in any other branch of our sport. Modern developments in tackle, rigs, bite detection and rigs, as well as techniques, have certainly given us an edge on the hardest-fished waters. It may be the latest rods that tempt us, or this year's model of the old reel.

It nevertheless remains true that for many species – and many anglers – a piece of crust free-lined off an old centrepin on an old cane rod will give just as much if not more aesthetic pleasure than all the modern wizardry. It is not the machine that matters but the operator. And stealth, mobility and watercraft will always outfish blind obedience to scientific progress.

It may be that in our angling middle age we are seduced by the spots of the brownie, the gleam of the rainbow, the silver of the salmon. Or perhaps it is the monsters of the salt that draw us. And why not? Fishing is a broad church, and skills learned with the coarse rod will stand in good stead for any form of fishing.

But coarse fishing will not release you for good. You will return to trot for chub and dace, to tempt the canny roach, to tackle the savage pike. You will be back to stalk the margins for carp and explore the lily pads for bubbling tench. The magic does not go. If you haven't yet started, try it now. The following chapters will guide your path.

1

Tackle

There is such a bewildering array of excellent fishing tackle around these days, that it is extremely difficult to give anything except very general advice, especially on rods and reels. Different anglers are looking for different things, and I can only recommend what I use. I would make the point that I consider tackle to be of relative unimportance when compared with the art of watercraft and location. The best gear in the world won't catch a fish that isn't there, or one that has been scared a mile downstream because you are incapable of walking to the water's edge without sounding like a water buffalo. Having said that, the correct tool for the job will often help catch fish that would be otherwise impossible.

RODS

All the rods I use are from the Tricast range, for no other reason than that they are strong, and their action suits me. For light legering work, say small-stream roach and perch fishing, or light chubbing, I delight in using my 14-ounce special leger, with spigoted quivertip. It is a delightful tool, and even a one-pound fish gives me a good scrap. For slightly heavier work, such as feeder fishing, bream fishing, big chub, tench, and barbel fishing, the eleven-foot, 1¼-pound Avon is my choice. It has slightly more backbone than many rods of similar test-curve rating, but a nice through-action for all that.

For the general run of pike and carp fishing, I use my eleven-foot 2¼-pound test-curve rods, which are still through-action blanks. These suffice for carping, and live and deadbaiting up to medium range, as well as being used for pike fishing from a boat. Where I want to carp fish at longer range, or hurl a deadbait further than usual, I revert to my twelve-foot ER blanks, which are of 2½-pound test. These are slightly more steeply tapered than the others, but in no way can they be classed as fast-taper blanks. I find ultra-fast rods no fun to fish with whatsoever.

REELS

As I play fish from the clutch, an efficient and reliable clutch mechanism is absolutely imperative. For this reason, I have used ABU Cardinal 54s for years, for all but carp and pike fishing, when I revert to the greater, heavier line capacity of ABU 755s. The only line I ever use is Maxima, which has never let me down, although I did use Sylcast at Cassien, and was very impressed with it. I always carry spools loaded with 4, 6, 8 and 12-pound BS, together with 100-yard spools of 1, 2 and 3-pound BS for making up lighter hooklinks.

HOOKS AND SUNDRIES

I use only two types of hook: Au Lion d'Or in sizes 2 to 8, and Drennan Super Specialists in the smaller sizes. In the smaller sizes, I have had Au Lion d'Or hooks straighten, but never in the heavier patterns which I believe are the most reliable on the market.

It goes without saying that all shot I use nowadays is lead free, and I have long since dispensed with the use of keep-nets. I always carry two or three carp sacks, in which fish can be kept quite happily, and without damage, while awaiting a photograph.

My tackle bag will contain all the paraphernalia of the modern specimen hunter, but one item is extra. That is a large plastic sack, in which to place litter on my departure. I get completely paranoid about rubbish being deposited in the countryside. It is totally beyond my comprehension how a man will cheerfully carry lager cans or luncheon-meat cans to the water side, and then leave them on the bank when he goes home. It is absolutely senseless. If you can carry full tins easily enough, why not empty ones, which are considerably lighter? If we all ensured that the swim we were fishing was rubbish free on our departure, even though some of the litter may not have been ours, the problem may be brought under control.

2
Barbel

SUMMER FISHING

Small Streams

In this section, I am principally concerned with the fishing of small rivers and streams with a fairly low stock density of barbel, but where individual very big specimens exist. The two rivers with which I am most familiar for this type of barbel fishing are the Wensum and the Cherwell, and so the approach I shall be discussing is one that has worked for me on those rivers. Doubtless, it would be applicable to other rivers of similar characteristics.

Location

With a small barbel stock in what could be many miles of river, it is absolutely vital to locate the fish first before contemplating fishing. The best way to do this is to spend a day in the summer, in sunny conditions and with the river low and clear, walking the banks, looking for fish with the aid of polarizing glasses. The only problem with this is that where there is a substantial amount of cover, streamer weed for instance, very many fish will be missed as they will be lying concealed under the foliage. So the method I adopt these days is to select perhaps half a mile of river for a day's

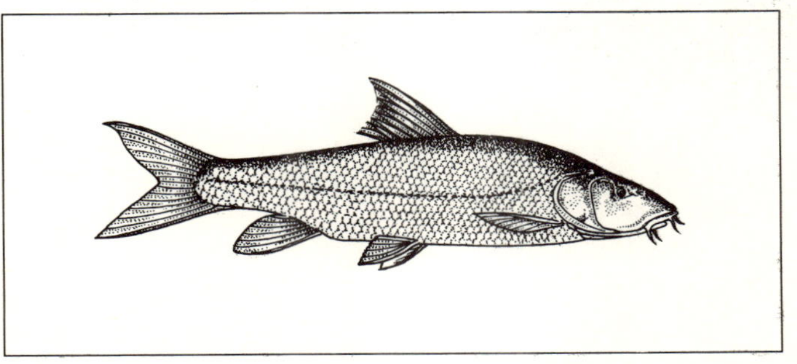

Barbel.

fishing, and then walk the entire length first, carrying a rod and bait dropper, and a bucket of hemp.

Every area I come to where there is clean gravel I put several droppers of hemp, and this is particularly important where such an area is adjacent to a large weed bed. By the time I have walked the entire stretch, I may have baited twenty or more areas, but so great is the pulling power of hempseed on barbel that I am confident that if barbel are anywhere near any of the baited areas, they will move in and start to feed. Once all the areas have been baited to my satisfaction, I then spend a further few hours continually commuting from swim to swim just looking, until barbel are located. Having found one or two, the serious business of catching them can begin, but with a lot more confidence than if I were fishing blind.

It is sometimes appropriate to create new feeding areas. I'm thinking here of perhaps a long unbroken bed of streamer, where every twenty yards or so it pays to cut away a few tresses to expose the gravel, obviously close to the near bank so that they can be easily observed. It is important not to go mad with this. You don't want to be dragging masses of weed out – a gap

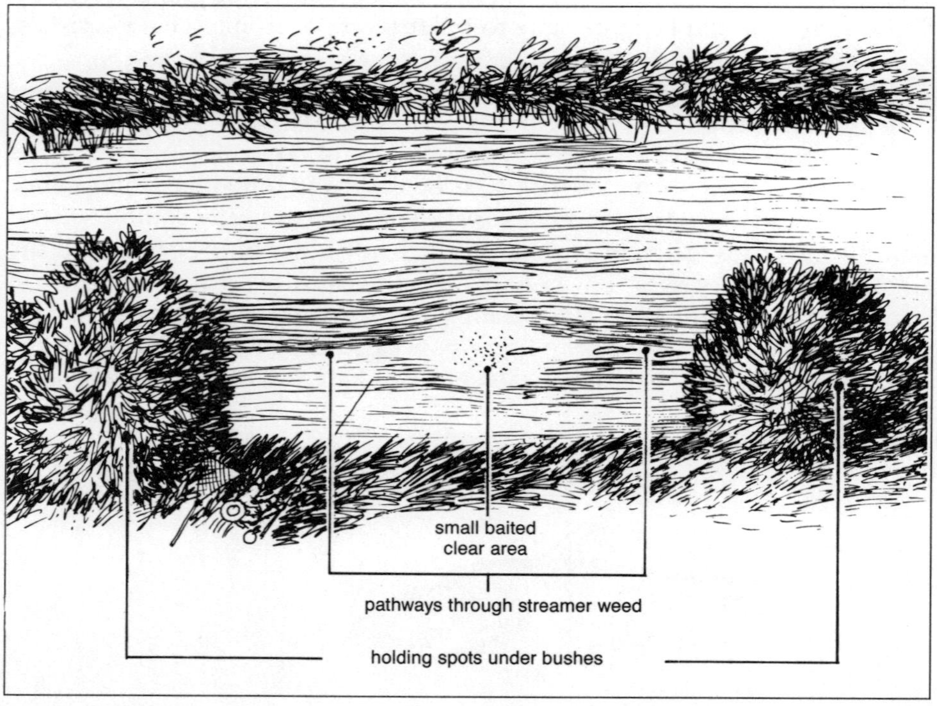

Selecting your swim.

of a couple of feet wide by two yards long is ample. I use a screw-in scythe blade that can be attached to my extending landing-net handle; with this it is simple to cut away individual tresses without causing widespread damage. Having prepared several areas like this, bait and observe them as before. When it comes to fishing, obviously use tackle strong enough to land the barbel despite the snags. I repeat: do not undertake mass weed removal. The fish will feed far more confidently in a small gap than they will in a large open area, where they will naturally feel far more vulnerable.

During the above combined location and pre-baiting process, I always include a limited amount of corn in each dropper-load of hemp. The purpose of this is that the sweetcorn grains, being highly visible, tell me immediately which areas are attracting fish. This does not mean that the fish will be barbel of course, but it is a good start point, as a swim that is attractive to roach, chub, and the like, will also be one that attracts barbel.

Baits and Rigs

There is no doubt whatever that hemp is the premier bait for attracting barbel and inducing them to feed. They become totally addicted to it, and there seems no limit to the amount they will eat. Having said that, however, it is a mistake I believe to introduce too much at once. I have found it far more beneficial to introduce a modest amount to start with, and then regularly top it up as the barbel eat it. In that way, there is always hemp in the swim. My normal approach would be between six and ten droppers to start with, followed by another three or four every hour or so,

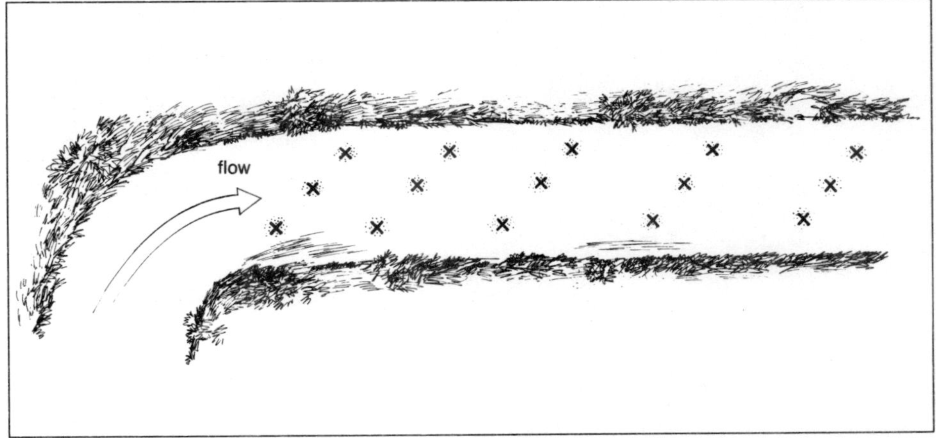

A suitable swim for systematic baiting.

or after a fish was landed. Obviously, you should use your common sense about this. If there is very heavy barbel activity in the swim, it would pay to introduce more hemp on each topping up. Conversely, if there were say just one big fish making regular visits, the initial baiting could be sufficient for the whole day.

Without doubt, fishing particles is an extremely efficient method of taking barbel in the summer, but their use does create other problems, particularly with fish that have been fished for regularly. Having watched barbel feeding at close quarters on many occasions, it is a matter of wonderment to me how we ever manage to catch one at all. Recently, I watched a group of Wensum fish feeding on corn and casters, and their approach was to flash over the gravel, fanning vigorously with their fins. This had the effect of lifting the loose offerings from the river bed, when they were taken confidently. Anything that did not behave naturally in this way, such as a bait attached to a heavy hook, was left well alone. So we have the problem of making our hookbaits behave as do the free offerings, without sacrificing the essential strength of gear that will enable us successfully to land any barbel we hook.

The first thing we can try is the use of the hair rig, with a fine hair of about half an inch. This at least will give the bait a limited amount of free movement which may be sufficient to fool the barbel. The only problem with this is that where there are nuisance fish pecking at the baits, such as dace and gudgeon, the use of the hair can be self-defeating, as the bait is

Buoyant baits.

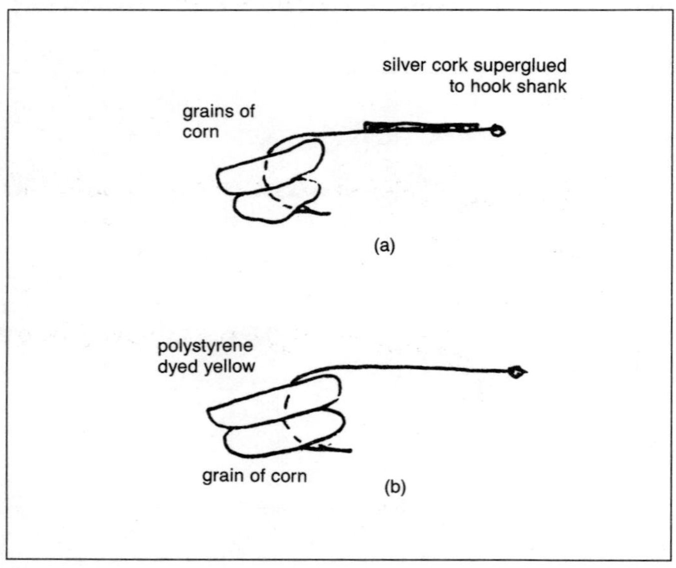

continually pulled off the hair. The baits can be superglued, of course, but I find this very tiresome, and I will now only use a hair-rigged bait if there are only barbel in my swim. Better, in my experience, is the use of either buoyant baits, or baits attached to hooks which have been counter-balanced. I always carry a chunk of polystyrene with me, and this comes in useful in making buoyant baits. I think it is worth going to the trouble of dyeing appropriately-shaped pieces to match the hookbait, round yellow bits for corn, cigar-shaped brown bits for casters, and so on. I'm not sure that it makes that much difference, but I certainly find it aesthetically more pleasing.

If you require a bait that rests on the bottom and rises with the free offerings when the fish create turbulence, rather than a permanently buoyant offering, then you have to go to slightly more trouble. It is worth spending some time at home, fitting hooks with just sufficient cork slivers so that they just, and only just, sink. The hook is then virtually weightless in water with the result that the bait then behaves as if it were unfettered. The last refinement, of course, is to use an ultra-soft hook length material, such as Dacron, Kryston, or dental floss dyed brown. Where fish are being particularly circumspect, a bait that has produced me an extra fish or two is hemp, superglued on a longish hair, in a caddis-case arrangement.

In low clear water, there are many occasions when the barbel will steadfastly avoid the hookbait, no matter how natural we try to make the terminal rig. In these situations a large natural bait fished over the hemp is often different enough to induce confident takes. There is nothing better than a large lively lobworm or, failing that, a bunch of maggots. That standard barbel bait, luncheon meat, will take fish under these conditions also, but in my experience it is not a very effective bait in clear water in the daytime. More than once, I have actually seen barbel flee in terror if a piece of meat was in a swim. At night or in coloured water those same barbel will take luncheon meat with confidence. Don't ask me to explain why.

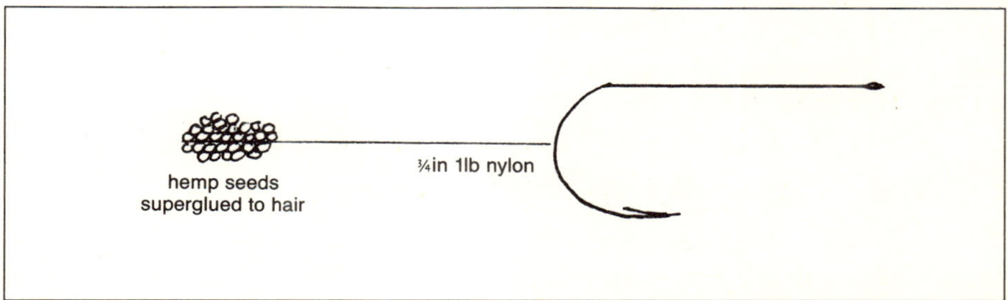

Hair-rigged hair cluster.

Fishing at Night

Without a doubt, where it is allowed, night fishing offers the best chance of most consistent barbel sport in low summer conditions, and I often spend the bulk of the daytime hours simply preparing swims for the evening and night fishing, when I will fish several hours into the darkness. Generally speaking, you will have more room after dark, and this allows you to have several swims on the go, which is a definite advantage. Unlike barbel in clear water in the day, the fish will tolerate the introduction of a hookbait after dark, provided that it is introduced very quietly and gently. For this reason, when I am preparing swims for an after-dark barbel assault, I will always do so in areas no more than a rod length out from the bank. Thus, the bait can be lowered into the swim, rather than cast and so causing disturbance. It doesn't matter that the barbel may not naturally feed in those areas. By introducing enough hemp, they will move in after dark if they haven't done so during the day, due to bank-side disturbance for instance. My usual procedure is to spend a few hours in the afternoon baiting perhaps six areas. As explained earlier, I start off with about ten droppers of hemp with a little corn, and then periodically visit each swim until late evening, continually topping up the bait. If I am lucky, I'll have seen barbel feeding in at least some of the swims.

As the light fades, I will lower a bait to rest on the hemp. This is where a lump of meat on a size 4 has proved its worth time and again. Provided the bait has been introduced gently, I will expect a bite very quickly. The fish have been feeding confidently on the hemp all day, and will not be suspicious if you have made no noise. If there has been no bite within, say, ten minutes, I assume that no barbel are in the swim, and move to swim number two. But before doing so, and bearing in mind the patrolling nature of barbel feeding behaviour, I top up the swim with another dropper of hemp to last until my return, an hour or so later. In this way I will constantly rotate the swims, perhaps visiting each five or six times in a night. It is very active fishing, and extremely effective. The large number of barbel I have caught, when the bite has come literally seconds after the bait has touched bottom, tells me that the basic thinking behind the technique is sound.

Fishing More Heavily Stocked Rivers

When there is a large stock of barbel, and particularly where they are the predominant species, such as in the Severn, lower Dorset Stour, Hampshire Avon and certain parts of the Kennet, barbel appear to take on different characteristics. It is sometimes difficult to believe that they are the same fish as those that are so shy and retiring on rivers such as the Cherwell. Possibly the competition for food and the fact that they have become used to anglers' baits accounts for it.

In the above-mentioned rivers, I doubt whether you could sit anywhere and be more than twenty yards from barbel, and so the problem of location is not nearly so all-important. If the swim you select has been picked with care and is one in which you feel the barbel will happily feed, then the fish can be encouraged to come to you by the judicious use of feed. The methods already explained will still work, of course, hemp being the universal barbel attractor, but the swimfeeder can also be considered. For this kind of barbel fishing the swimfeeder is a deadly tool if used properly. Depending on the prevailing circumstances, there are many variations in its use.

Obviously, the standard approach of straightforward maggot fishing has caught countless barbel, and is one that I use myself. It is a method, however, that I tend to reserve for clear-water conditions in the winter. During the summer, although the method is sound enough, it is also the most efficient method I know of attracting eels, and therefore is counter-productive. My use of the feeder in the summer is more linked to filling the feeder with hemp, and using it with the holes opened out sufficiently to allow the hemp to filter out. This is especially good in streamy swims where the hemp grains can wash out and downstream in a narrow band. Maggots and hemp are both fished in blockend feeders, but I also use inverted Drennans, open at one end to accept groundbait plugs. These can be used to hold casters, tares, corn or anything else that takes your fancy. Hemp and casters in particular are a deadly combination, and the way I fish them is as follows.

I do my preliminary baiting as before, putting in about six droppers of hemp and three of casters, and then fish over it with an opened-out blockend containing hemp, with two casters on a size 12. I like to fish a longish tail, about three feet, and it is important that the feeder is fished free-running. Most summer barbel fisheries are well endowed with weed and, as barbel are such strong fighters, the use of a fixed swimfeeder is inviting irretrievable snagging. When I caught my best Stour fish of ten pounds nine ounces, by the time the barbel had run through two beds of streamer the feeder was about forty yards up the line! In the case of very heavy weed, it is a worthwhile precaution to fish the feeder on a rotten bottom. I must admit to not being entirely happy with this, as I do not like the thought of littering the river bed with swimfeeders. In heavy weed conditions, I would rather content myself with the more responsible use of straightforward legering tactics, reverting to the bait dropper for the entire loose feeding.

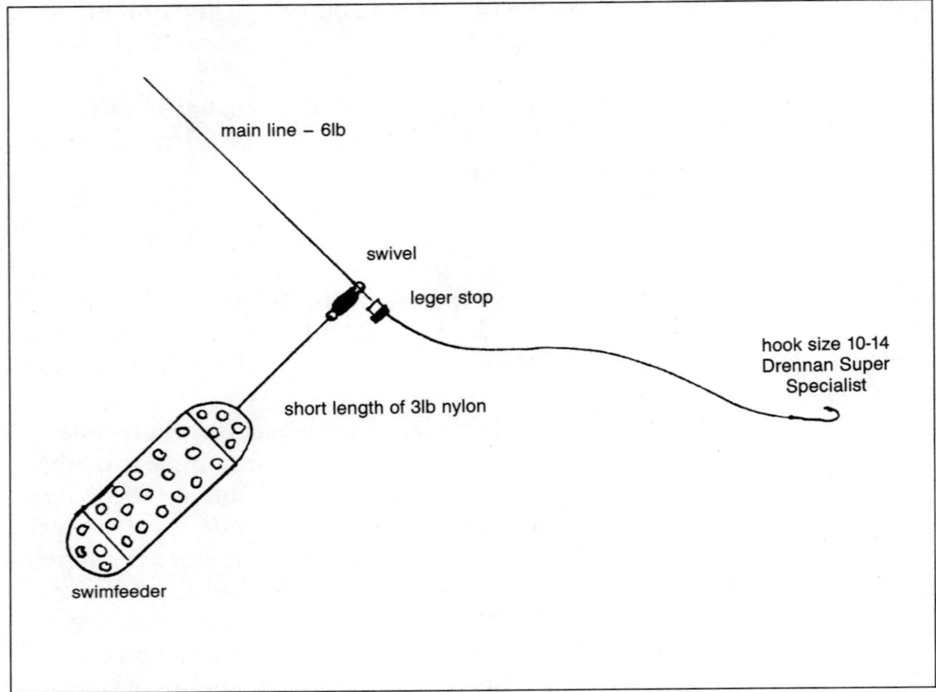

Fishing feeder in heavy weed.

Reading the River

So far in this summer section I have been discussing situations where the barbel themselves can be observed, but of course there are many occasions when this is not possible. The river may normally be too coloured for visual location, like the Thames, or it may be more coloured or higher than usual, or the stretch you fish may be too deep for effective spotting. In these circumstances, you have to revert to other means of locating the fish, and this is where the ability to read the river comes in so handy. I would refer the reader to the coverage of this topic in the chapter on chub, where it is covered extensively. Everything I say about chub location applies to barbel. Particularly important are the areas around streamer weed beds which barbel love, and steady gravelly glides of smooth surface, either downstream of more turbulent areas or in crease-type swims.

In a sluggish water such as the Thames or lower Severn, location is much more difficult and, to be truthful, much of it is trial and error. In this kind of water, I believe the swimfeeder has an important role to play, using gallons of maggots. By adopting this tactic you can be slightly out with your choice of swim, but the amount of bait should eventually draw fish to you. There are clues you can read to lessen the odds, however, and on the Thames especially, any narrowing of the river or bend is worth thorough investigation, as is a cabbage patch. Thames barbel have a special affinity with these beds of sunken lilies. That excellent Thames angler, John Everard, swears by cabbages as one of the most important factors in barbel location, and I know that he has taken many fish from alongside the near-bank cabbages, fishing orthodox baits over a carpet of hemp.

On the river Severn, I would state that it is virtually impossible to use too much bait. Few of us are in a position to use five or six gallons of maggots for a day's fishing, but on more than one occasion my friend Joe Taylor, a tackle dealer from Bicester, has fished the Severn this way. Some of his catches have been fabulous, and he has obviously attracted fish to his swim from a very long way downstream. The same tactic works on the Kennet, another river prolific in barbel.

Taking Care of the Fish

This small section is by way of a plea. If you have any regard for the fish at all, please do not retain barbel in keep-nets. I have little time for keep-nets generally these days, but they are manifestly unsuitable for barbel. That pronounced leading edge of the dorsal fin will get caught in the net mesh, even if you use micromesh, with the attendant risk of damaging the fish when you remove it. The sorry state of some Severn barbel in particular is a sad indictment of some anglers' lack of thought.

I do, however, recommend retaining barbel for a short while after capture, in a soft, well-perforated carp sack, which must be placed in deep, well-oxygenated water. Barbel always fight to their last gasp, and returning them immediately is fraught with the danger of their turning belly up with exhaustion and actually drowning. The faster the river, the more this will be likely, as the fish will lack the energy to fight the strong flow. When you do put them back, always hold them head upstream in a clean steady current, and wait until you can feel them moving strongly before releasing them. A final word about carp sacks: they are perfectly safe receptacles, and I have been using them for years with specimen fish of all species without a single loss, and without any fish ever suffering damage. Like everything else, however, they must be used with common sense. When you are using them to retain barbel temporarily, make sure that they are positioned so that the barbel is facing upstream. It is also important that they are pegged out in such a way that the fish has plenty of room.

WINTER FISHING

Barbel have always been regarded as a summer quarry, but to me they have always been a much more exciting and predictable proposition in the winter months. That is when I prefer to fish for them.

There are two major factors that control the feeding behaviour of winter barbel, and those are the height and colour of the river, and the water temperature. Let us look at these two points in order. A river that is high and coloured – and all subsequent comments will apply equally to a summer or autumn flood – gives us ideal conditions for voracious barbel feeding, unless it is very cold, or the conditions have been caused by melting snow. Barbel are very similar to roach in their liking for murky conditions, although roach will tolerate lower temperatures more happily.

As far as temperature is concerned, evidence gathered principally by my old mate Trefor West, who nowadays fishes solely for barbel and has probably caught more winter fish than most anglers alive today, suggests that barbel activity declines rapidly at below about 40°F. It is, however, dangerous to rely completely on the thermometer reading without giving some consideration to the conditions prevailing on the days prior to fishing. For instance, a reading of 41°F, where the temperature is dropping rapidly following frosts, is likely to be less beneficial than a reading of 39°F, where it is rising rapidly following warm rain after a long freeze-up. So it is also a matter of intelligent interpretation of all the factors involved. Steadily rising water temperature, coupled with high coloured water, add up to ideal winter barbel conditions, but even if the water is at normal winter level and is clear, the conditions are still acceptable provided the temperature is suitable. The clarity of the water is what determines the best approach to the fishing.

High, Coloured Water

These are the conditions when roving tactics with large baits such as luncheon meat, cheese paste or sausage-meat paste really come into their own. Luncheon meat and bacon grill are my favourites for this fishing. The barbel are actively foraging around and, because of this, the smell of the bait will attract them from a long way off. It pays to be mobile, as barbel bites will often occur immediately after moving swims. This happens so often that I now spend only a short time in a swim without a bite before moving on. Returning to that swim later will often yield an immediate pull, and this tells me that if there is a barbel nearby, it will take the bait without hesitation. As I mentioned earlier in the summer night-fishing section, setting up your stall in one swim and fishing it all day will produce fish, but not as many, I've found, as if you fish the swim on and off through the day, fishing several others at the same time in the same way.

Most barbel rivers will have a good push of water, so during high water conditions you will be fishing in quite strong flows. A roving approach will also see you fishing in many varied flows, or you may have to fish across a strong current, so it is important that the terminal rig is heavy enough to achieve correct bait presentation, and has the ability to be altered quickly and easily. If it is cold or wet, or after dark, you do not want anything too fiddly. The terminal rig I use is illustrated. The snap-link swivel makes weight change a simple task. I keep the whole range of leger weights in my coat pocket, and this will include some that have been flattened for extra holding power.

As far as I am concerned, the most exciting barbel fishing of all is after dark in the winter, when the conditions are high and coloured. Trefor and I have often fished right through a winter's night and we have had some tremendous sport. If you have never tried it, you don't know what you're missing. The approach to the fishing is the same as during the daylight, a

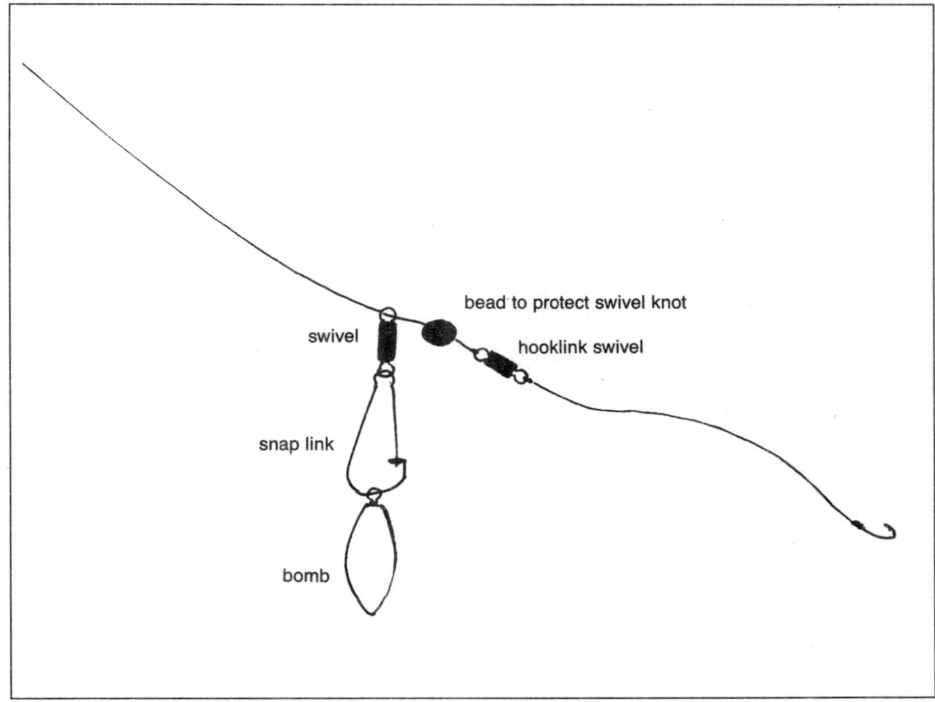

Link-swivel rig.

mobile one of moving from swim to swim. Bites are tremendous, the rod usually hammering round wildly. For this fishing, I usually dispense with the quivertip and revert to a Betalight directly on the rod top, coupled with touch legering. For me, there is nothing in angling to compare with the excitement of a sudden heavy pull of the line on my index finger after dark, as a barbel powers away with the bait.

Presentation

Bait presentation is an interesting topic, and one that I now know is a very variable factor depending on the river I am fishing. On most rivers of my acquaintance, the barbel prefer the bait to be totally stationary, and the terminal rig is chosen with this object in mind. The Wensum is the classic example of this. Moving a barbel bait is absolutely taboo and is guaranteed to drive the fish out of the swim instantly. Inducing a bite, therefore, which is so deadly a method for Wensum chub, is a non-starter for the barbel.

On the Royalty, on the other hand, static baits are very inferior indeed to moving ones, and there are days when you will not get a bite on a bait presented still on the bottom. All anglers who enjoy consistent sport on the Royalty use moving baits, and this fishery more than any other produces barbel equally well to trotting tactics as it does to legering. It is my firm belief that for barbel fishing generally, trotting is an inferior method, and the Royalty is the exception. A deadly method is to leger upstream, with sufficient weight to give a slow bumping down in the current. If there is room, it even pays to walk slowly backwards downstream allowing the bait a long travel. It is a difficult technique to master, as contact with the weed beds gives false bites. Experience soon tells you what is the real thing, however, the compensation being that the bites to this presentation are usually savage and unmistakable. Anyone who complains of small barbel bites on the Royalty, where the fish have undoubtedly seen it all in their time, should give this method a try.

Winter Fishing in Clear Water

Providing it is not too cold, clear-water conditions at normal winter level need be no bar to good barbel sport. You simply need to adopt a different approach to the fishing. For after dark, I will fish in the same way as explained for coloured water, with large meat baits. The only difference to the approach would be that, because I expect the fish to be less active than if the conditions were perfect, I would pre-bait the swims I intended fishing with hemp if that were practical. In high coloured water this is not necessary as the fish are actively looking for food.

During the daylight hours, as in the summer, meat is not a very good bait to use in clear water. This is when swimfeeder fishing with maggots is undoubtedly the most effective method. The more maggots you introduce, the more likely you are to achieve success, and I fish a large blockend and cast as often as every ten minutes to keep a constant flow of bait through the swim. It is important to maintain the same line of feed, and I weight my feeders with extra lead to ensure that they are not rolled around by the current. This is one circumstance where a naturally moving bait can produce good results. The barbel will be expecting the maggots to be wafting around with the current, and so I usually fish a tail length of about three feet to allow this freedom of movement.

When the river is clear and cold, the only method liable to produce a bite is the feeder. In these conditions, it pays to fish a much more static bait on a short tail, and restrict the number of times you refill the feeder. One thing to watch for is that cold water makes maggots very comatose and it may be necessary to open up the holes in the feeder to allow them to escape quickly enough for the method to be effective. If the water is that cold, however, you would be better off chub or pike fishing!

3

Bream

GRAVEL PITS AND OTHER STILLWATERS

Many times over the last few years have I cursed the day I first became obsessed with giant bream, as they surely must be one of the most difficult and unpredictable of all specimen fish. In this context, it is appropriate to remind ourselves that I am discussing here bream of over ten pounds in weight, which are by no means as common as press reports might suggest. Over the last eight seasons, I have spent a large proportion of each summer fishing for double-figure bream, in the company of men who have enjoyed considerable success with the species, and at two of the premier big bream waters in this country, TC pit and Queenford Lagoon. We are all agreed that, although we are slowly getting one or two things together, none of us can claim to understand big bream behaviour. This is what makes the fishing so fascinating, and it is that very unpredictability that keeps us going back for more time and time again.

Catching a double-figure bream from a gravel pit is therefore a task requiring lots of patience, hours of inactivity, and an unswerving

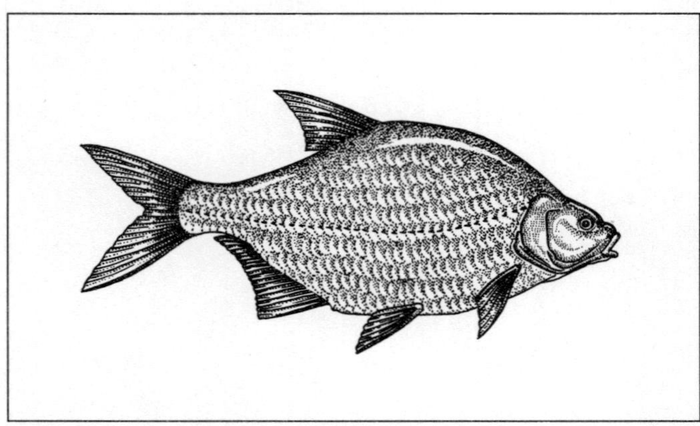

The bream, Abramis brama.

determination not to be beaten. But, while there is no denying that the fishing is extremely slow at the best of times, there are many facets of gravel-pit breaming to get right if you are at least to lessen the odds as far as possible. Let's look at location first of all.

Location of the Fish

The most obvious method of locating the fish, of course, is to see them rolling, and fish in the vicinity. If the rolling is a regular feature on your water, and it occurs at all hours, it may be possible even to plot patrol routes. This I know has been carried out successfully on one or two of the Cheshire meres by men such as Graham Marsden, but I certainly know of no gravel pit where a patrol route has been established by watching bream roll. The reason for that is quite simple: from my experience and that of many of my friends, the incidence of bream rolls on gravel pits is so infrequent an occurrence that it is simply not viable to rely on visual location. If they do happen to show themselves on any particular day, then

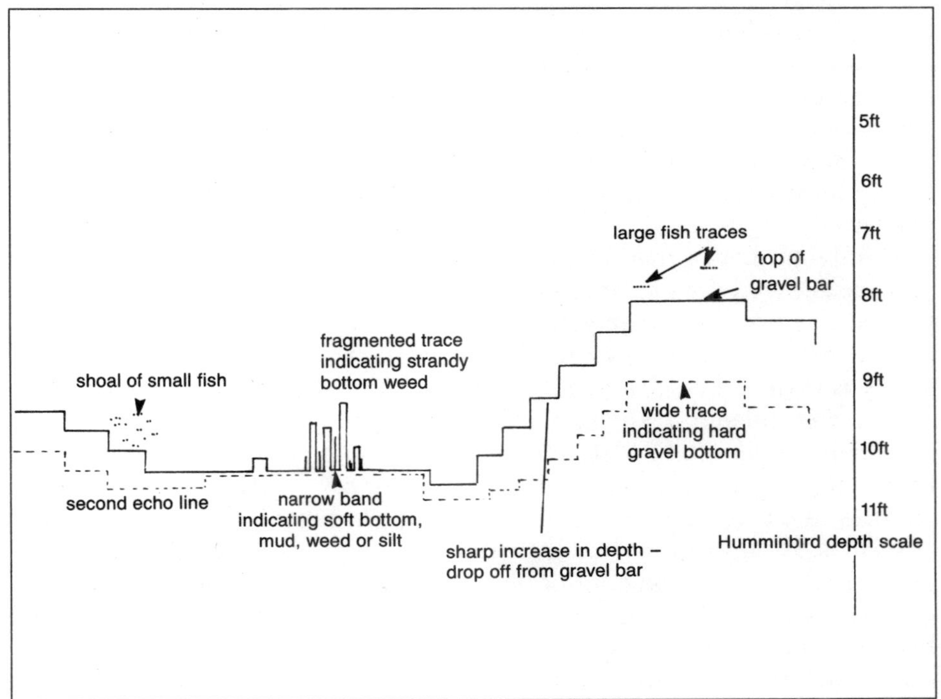

A typical Humminbird trace.

advantage can be taken, but normally we have to rely on the more painstaking method of mapping the contours of the pit, and interpreting how they and the other characteristics of the water will affect the location and feeding behaviour of the fish.

Mapping the Water

The information I am looking for is as follows. Where are the gravel bars, and how extensive are they? Where are the drop offs, and how steeply shelving are they? Are there any gravel plateaux in otherwise deep water? Where are the major weed beds, and how extensive are they? What about bottom weed – where is it bad, where is it sparse and where is there none? If there is an area which is weed free, in an otherwise weedy pit, how extensive is this area? What does the bottom consist of? Where is it hard gravel, where is it soft or hard packed mud, and where is it soft silt? It goes without saying that the more complete a picture you can build up of the pit bottom, the more likely you are to be successful in pin-pointing the feeding areas of the bream.

So how do we go about mapping a gravel pit? Firstly, there are bank-side features that tell us some useful preliminary information. Where the natural bank is gently shelving it indicates a similarly sloping bottom running out into the pit. Thus you can expect deep water in the margins if the bank drops away steeply. Points and promontories extending out into the lake show the presence of gravel bars. In the body of the water itself, regular diving by water-birds in one spot could indicate the location of a shallow plateau.

Mainly, however, mapping of a gravel pit is a long laborious job, unless you are allowed the use of a boat with an echo sounder.

If you do not possess an echo sounder, but you are allowed the use of a boat at your water, a very useful implement is a very long-handled rake. All of us in the Queenford syndicate have rakes adapted with handles up to sixteen feet in length. The best way to make one is to obtain one of those extendable poles used for cleaning out swimming pools, and adapt the end of it to take a garden leaf rake. We all have our own methods of finding the features of a particular swim and I will explain mine.

First of all, I set up a sliding float using a big, easily visible float and a heavy lead, so that I can comfortably map the water well out to maximum casting distance. The stop knot is made with power gum. Firstly, I set the float at a comparatively shallow setting, say about six feet, and then cast it out to maximum range. As most pits have a maximum depth of about twenty feet, the probable result is that the float will disappear from sight. Then I slowly retrieve the float, a few feet at a time, until it has been

3 Bream

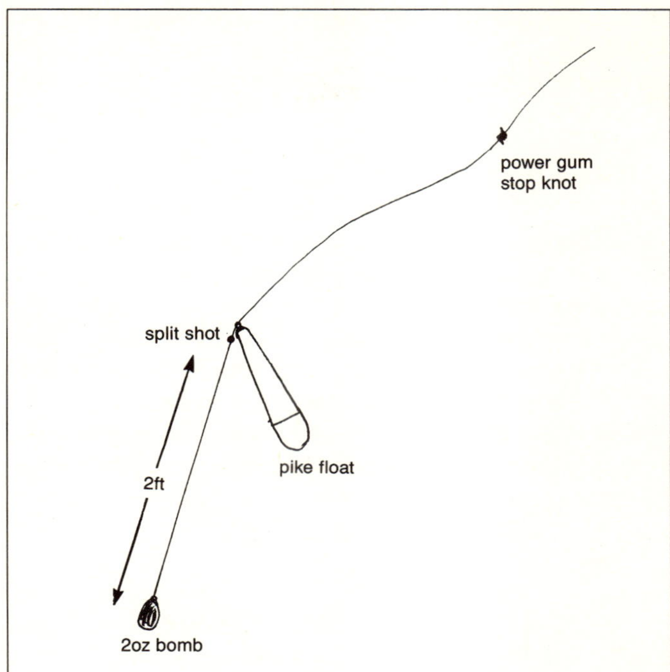

Depth-finder float.

completely recovered. If there are any areas of six feet or less, the float will suddenly pop up, and you have located one interesting feature. A word of warning: as you will almost certainly be crossing weed on some of the retrieve, it is important to use a big buoyant float, otherwise the weed will give you all sorts of false information.

Assuming that no shallow area has been located, repeat the procedure with the float set at eight feet, and so on. In this way, you can very easily locate any depth changes in the area in front of you. That is phase one of the mapping process. Phase two is to mark those areas where you wish to investigate further. I do this by dropping in marker buoys alongside the float as each area is found. I make these out of squares of polystyrene, attached to strong line and a heavy lead.

Once the areas have been marked, it is then time to go out once more on the boat, and probe around with the rake. By using the buoy as a focal point, it is then simple to establish the general features around it. First of all, I find the extent of the feature, and see where it starts to drop off and how fast. By using the rake-head end of the pole first, I can quickly establish the extent and nature of any bottom weed, and then by inverting it and using the flat metal end, I can tell whether the bottom is hard gravel, silt or mud.

In the case of silt or mud, some sediment will stick to the end of the pole, showing the exact composition.

By adopting this general procedure all round the lake, you can find many useful areas and, over a period of time, most of the water within casting range can be investigated. Obviously, a group of friends working in harmony and sharing information can do the job that much quicker. That is why such spectacular results have come from Queenford Lagoon. All those of us in the syndicate agreed from the start to have a totally open exchange of information and it has paid off handsomely.

On a gravel pit, where big bream are the quarry, you really are at a disadvantage if you are not allowed the use of a boat, and under these circumstances you are limited to the range at which you can comfortably introduce your groundbait. When Trefor and I were fishing TC pit, we never used a boat and fished quite easily at up to fifty yards, introducing bait by catapult. There is no doubting, however, that this is nowhere near as efficient.

Promising Features

Having discussed how we find the various features of a gravel pit, it is time to consider what we are actually looking for. To identify good bream features, the most important characteristic, from my experience and that of all my friends, is that the area should be naturally free of bottom weed. A little silkweed is acceptable, but heavy bottom weed is not. So often have we all cleared tremendous-looking features of weed, and fished them without a bite over the years, that we are now convinced that the bream search out preferentially the weed-free areas.

Gravel bars and humps, and the drop offs associated with those features, are probably the most reliable areas to fish, followed by flat, apparently barren, areas of hard-packed mud or silt. The most exciting results from Queenford have come from weed-free plateaux in the middle of deeper water with dense bottom weed, which leads us to believe that the bream swim along the surface of the weed rather than through it as do tench, and stop to feed temporarily, and in an opportunist manner, whenever the weed is sparse.

Baits and Groundbaiting Techniques

There is not really that much to say about hookbaits for large bream, except that if you used only sweetcorn, bread, maggots or worms, you would not go far wrong. Over the last ten years, during which I have put in considerable time bream fishing, most of the fish I have caught, or seen caught, have accepted these standard offerings. The bait *par excellence* has been proved to be a large lively lobworm, either fished on its own, or as a cocktail bait with flake, corn, maggots or casters. Very many of the Queenford fish have fallen to the lobworm/sweetcorn combination, using as many as four grains of corn and a big lob on a size 4 or 6 hook. Large bream like a big mouthful and an extra refinement has been to inject air into the lob with a syringe, to make it waver around very attractively just off bottom, while being effectively anchored by the corn. This trick is obviously useful if there is a light covering of silkweed, as it prevents the worm from being obscured. Running lobs a close second are a large piece of breadflake or, even better, flake/maggot cocktail. The latter has produced many TC fish, as it has from Wilstone and Startops reservoirs.

Sweetcorn is a bit of an enigma. All of us in the Queenford syndicate include quantities of sweetcorn in our groundbait, because the bream obviously eat it in bulk. This is evident from the amount of corn in the sacks after many of the captures. And yet, not one bream has yet to fall to a hookbait consisting solely of corn, although we have all tried. Recently, many of us have been experimenting with double-hook rigs purposely, using lobs or lob/corn cocktail on one hook, and solely corn, corn/flake or corn/maggot on the other. Every bream has taken the lobworm, suggesting that they are selecting the worms preferentially. The problem with the corn must obviously be one of presentation.

Groundbaiting

Groundbaiting is a vitally important part of big bream fishing, and it is extremely difficult to ascertain what is the correct approach to adopt in gravel pits, particularly in those waters containing a smallish head of very big fish. We have all tried very heavy baiting campaigns, and very sparse ones. We have used mounds of cereal bait, and at other times solely particle feed, and it is fair to say that we are no nearer to knowing what is the correct approach. One thing, however, that I do believe is clear, from my experience of TC and Queenford, is that the feed should contain a good amount of an acceptable particle bait. If bream do visit the swim, a bed of particles may hold them long enough for a couple to pick up the hookbaits. There are many particles that can be used, and the best are casters, squatts and corn. We all placed great faith in hemp in our groundbaits for some time but careful observation has led us to the belief that the bream do not touch it. Very often indeed, as stated earlier, captured bream have regurgitated loads of corn, but never once can that be said of hempseed. And usually, hemp and corn had been used together in the feed. So I have now dispensed with hemp in my feed. The same comments apply to tares and maple peas which I have also tried extensively.

These days, my base feed consists invariably of a bucket full of pure breadcrumbs, sweetened with molasses. I use the liquid molasses that is obtainable from horse- and cattle-feed suppliers, which makes a lovely crumbly brown mix. To this I then add my particles. At TC pit, this was usually casters or squatts, but for the breaming I am doing nowadays at Queenford, corn is my choice. Very many gravel pits contain large numbers of small perch, and the introduction of casters, squatts or any other maggot does have the disadvantage that it can promote a perch invasion. As perch are particularly active at the hour either side of dawn, which has also proved to be a good time for the bream to bite, disturbing the swim by striking at bites from perch has to be avoided if at all possible.

Invariably, groundbaiting for gravel-pit bream is carried out once a day, usually late in the evening in readiness for the night to come. Undoubtedly, it is best carried out from a boat if possible, between two swim markers for absolute accuracy. There is little point baiting one area and fishing elsewhere. If I am fishing a session of several days, I will usually cut down the amount of feed if nothing has happened after the first couple of nights. As I've said before, gravel-pit bream are nomadic wanderers, no matter how much feed you use in an attempt to hold them, and I do not want bream finding an enormous mound of bait in my swim when they eventually do arrive. I actually believe that this acts as a deterrent. Remember, we are not talking about a large number of small- to medium-sized bream which can clear a terrific amount of food, but a small head of big individuals. All I require is a modest carpet of bait, sufficient to encourage the bream to tarry for a night or two, but not so extensive that there are long odds against one of my hookbaits being picked up.

Fishing Techniques

Of all specimen fish, bream are undoubtedly one of the most nocturnal, and this, plus the many hours of inactivity that are an unavoidable part of gravel-pit bream hunting, means that legering, coupled with audible bite indication, is the only really viable approach for long sessions. It obviously would be possible to fish after dark with a driftbeater float fitted with a Betalight, but in all honesty I think that it would be totally impractical.

The main problem is that it is difficult to concentrate on a Betafloat for more than two or three hours, before your eyes start playing tricks. This is true even at comparatively short range so if you try fishing further out, perhaps on a windy night with a good chop on the water, the problem is going to be magnified many times over. Add to this the factors of drifting weed, with which all pits are plagued on occasions, and small plucks from nuisance fish, and you begin to get an idea how frustrating any attempt at float fishing would be. Fishing with the Optonic and bobbins, small plucks register as bleeps and perhaps a very small lift of the bobbin. Also, line bites, which are such an important indicator of the possible onset of bream feeding, give a very distinctive signal on bobbins or butt indicators. If the bobbin shoots to the butt and then drops again just as fast, a liner is responsible, and the urge to strike has to be resisted. Striking at that point could alarm the fish just as they are starting to investigate the baited area. If you were using a float, it is now clear that it would be impossible to tell what was responsible for that sudden disappearance of the Betalight. Was it an optical illusion, drifting weed, a small pull from small fry, a liner, or indeed a genuine bream bite? There is no way of knowing. From all of the foregoing, you will have got the impression, correctly, that I am not in favour of float fishing at night for gravel-pit bream!

There is one circumstance where float fishing could be viable, and that is where a swim is located where the bream are found to feed in daylight. At

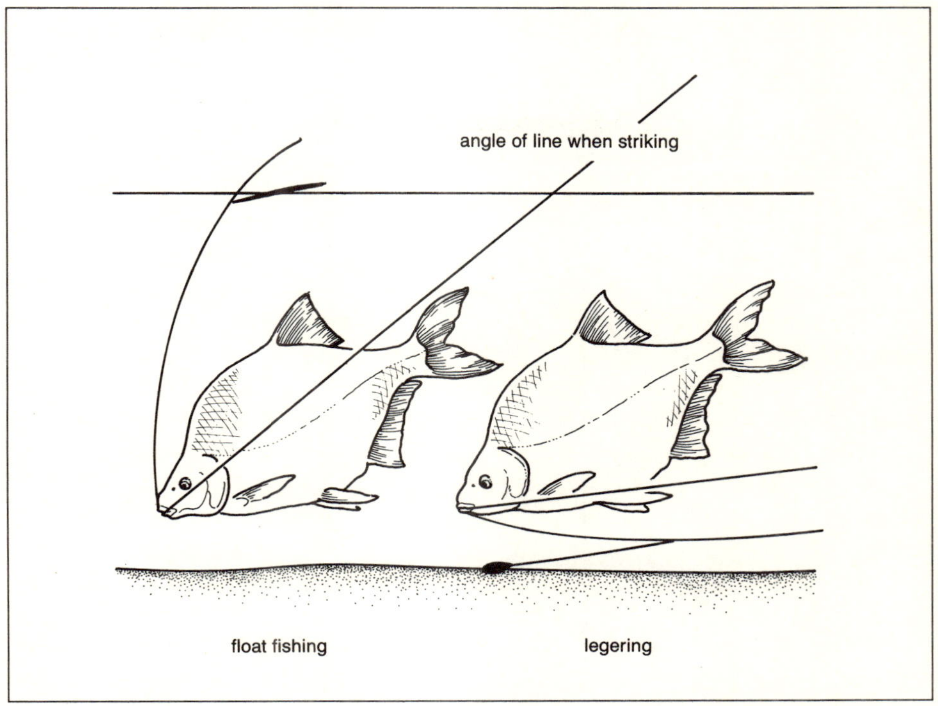

Angle of line when striking.

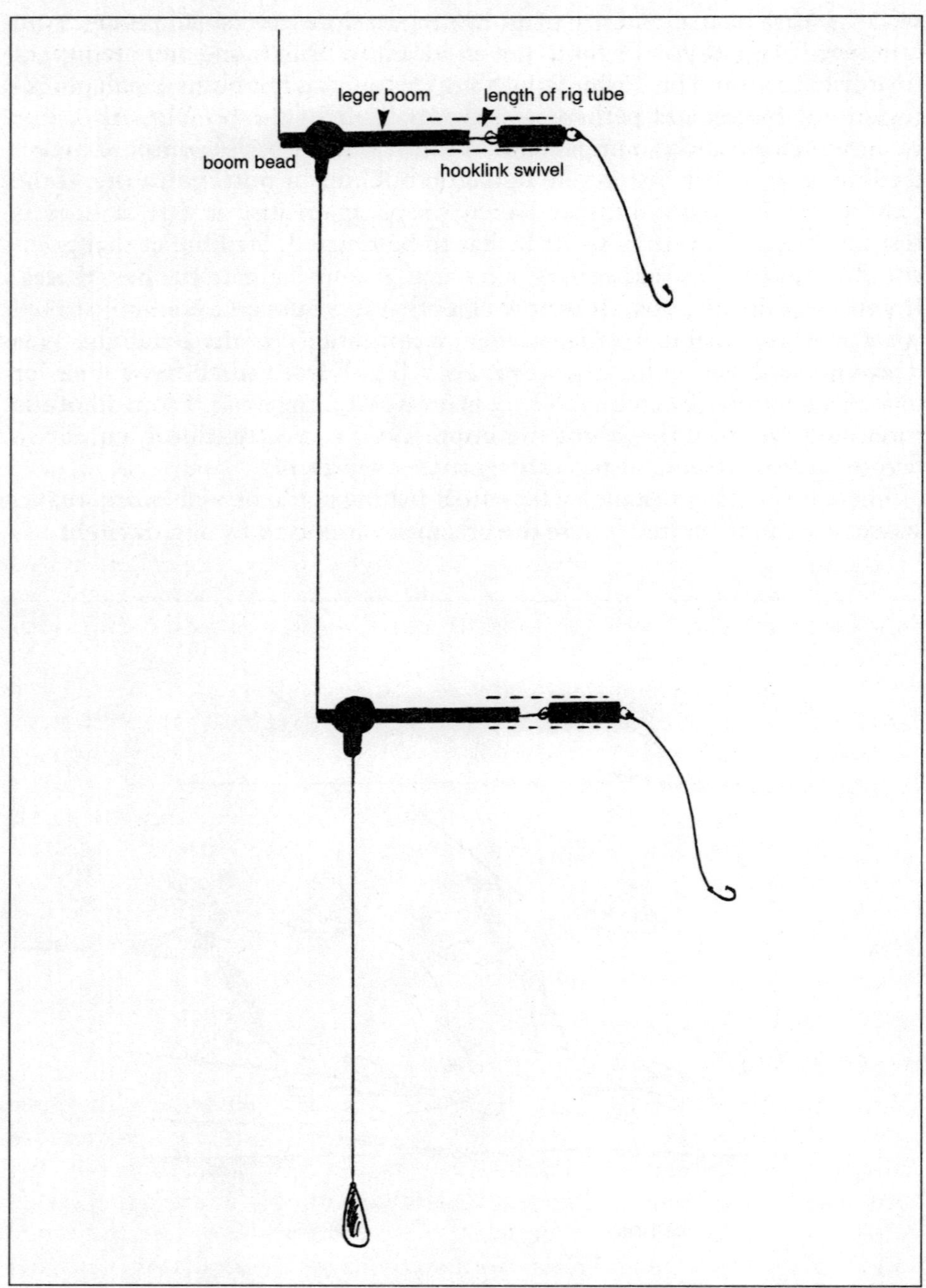

Double-hook rig.

TC pit there were two such areas, both very shallow gravel plateaux fairly close in. The bream would not feed when there was any bank-side disturbance, but if an angler fished quietly on his own, each of these swims often produced fish around midday or early afternoon. Laying on or fishing lift-style with a driftbeater would be my choice for this fishing.

Legering

My standard legering approach is with the fixed paternoster, usually incorporating a lead of about 1½ ounces. Big gravel-pit bream give very positive bites against this amount of resistance. If maggots, casters or flake/maggot cocktail are the choice of bait, a loaded feeder would replace the lead. I have used both long and short hooklinks with equal success, although I do not use very long hooklinks now to avoid the possibility of deep hooking. Generally speaking, I settle for a link of about six inches if I'm fishing over a hard bottom, but if I am faced with soft mud or silt, a longer tail with flake or air-injected lobs is usually more appropriate.

Because gravel-pit breaming can be so slow, I can see nothing wrong with a double-hook rig to present a bait alternative. Obviously, the two hooklengths should be spaced out sufficiently apart so that it is impossible for them to tangle one another.

One of the most important features is being able to hit the correct spot after dark. When bream eventually do visit your swim, perhaps after weeks of waiting, it is possible to take two or three fish in quick succession and you must take maximum advantage of the situation. It is worth taking the trouble of marking the line at the appropriate place so you know when the bait is in the correct spot. If polystyrene swim markers are used, they can be picked out easily with a powerful torch to aid casting direction. One of my colleagues at Queenford equips his swim markers with those little starlights, which give off a surprising amount of light for several hours after dark, and act as a focal point for night casting.

Bite Detection

Bite detection is another vital component. It is a mistake to be in too much of a hurry to strike at a bite from a gravel-pit bream, for two reasons. Firstly, early striking results in many missed bites, and secondly, it is important to differentiate between real bites and liners, as explained earlier. The two methods of bite detection are the use of bobbins or butt indicators, both equipped with Betalights. Both methods are as good as one another, and it is down to personal preference which one you adopt. Personally, I prefer bobbins. Whichever you use, it is important that they be heavy enough to register drop-back bites and liners efficiently. The characteristic of a line bite is the bobbin shooting to the butt ring and then dropping back again, as the line comes free from the fish that caused it. If the bobbin is too light, it could stay in the butt ring, tempting you into an unwarranted strike. My bobbins are loaded with two swan shot apiece, to which more can be added if drift becomes a problem. Similarly, butt indicators can be loaded with lead wire. Whichever you use, do not be in a hurry to strike. What I do is fish with my anti-reverse off and wait for the reel to start rotating before I strike.

My first double from TC taught me the value of patience. For two hours that night, liners occurred regularly, the bobbins rising to the butt and falling back again almost as fast. The real bite was so different. The bobbin inched its way to the butt ring but this time did not fall back. I allowed it to pull off the line, and when the reel started to backwind, I hit it. This restraint in striking bream bites is so important that we all deliberately position ourselves far enough from our rods so that we must physically move forward before we can strike. In this way, most liners will have shown themselves for what they are before, in our excitement, we have struck prematurely, and possibly instinctively.

Having landed your bream, it is important to handle it with care. Like barbel, bream will not tolerate careless handling, and there are too few big ones to risk losing them needlessly. If a fish has been landed at night, there is nothing wrong with keeping it in a large carp sack in deep water until morning. I have done this many times, as have my friends, and we have had no problems whatever. The fish have suffered no damage, as they invariably do in keep-nets. I implore you, do not cram big bream into inadequate keep-nets. This will inevitably lead to deaths.

RIVER BREAM

As most anglers are aware, most rivers contain bream, and in the sluggish waterways such as the Norfolk rivers the methods of catching them differ little from those used in lakes. So in this section I shall discuss the surprisingly big bream that are available on the more stream-like rivers which would normally be associated with chub or barbel. All the rivers I regularly fish for the latter species have produced big bream from time to time. I do not mean big in the context of gravel pits, but fish of seven and eight pounds which I consider big by any standards for smaller streams.

In recent seasons, I have caught good bream from the Leam, Cherwell, Wensum and Dorset Stour, all accidentally on chub or barbel baits. The best of these went a little over seven pounds and gave me a tremendous scrap. This seems to be typical of small-stream bream, in that they fight much harder than their stillwater counterparts. In the days of the Coventry Specimen Group, many of us fished quite deliberately for Cherwell bream which rarely exceeded five pounds in weight, but which were a very worthwhile quarry and fought the equal of any chub. More recently, I have had a seven pounder from the Wensum and was convinced that I was attached to a small barbel. The latter river, in fact, could well hold a few doubles and I know that two or three nine pounders have been reported.

Small-river bream seem to inhabit many of the gentler swims inhabited by chub, although they do appear to shun the shallower areas. Particularly favoured are smooth-flowing glides, and crease-type swims over even gravel or hard-packed mud. This is especially true if the glide runs alongside marginal rushes and is slightly deeper than average. Straightforward quivertipping with breadflake, maggots, lobs or redworms will take fish regularly, provided that you keep a constant stream of feed going down. Mashed bread is as good as anything. For a stream containing a reasonable head of fish, the swimfeeder is tailor-made and, providing that you don't skimp on the bait, a good bag of fish can result. As with barbel, if you are going to fish the feeder with maggots, you must use plenty of maggots to get the best out of the fishing. Bites are often impressive, with the tip thumping round like a chub bite. If you are deliberately seeking bream, however, it would pay to scale down your tackle, use a softer tip than normal and strike at any movements. Delicate bites from river bream are common.

Perhaps surprisingly, in view of their lethargic reputation, river bream love to inhabit weir-pools, generally being found in the run out of the weir or the back eddies at the side of the main push of water. I know, however, of good bream having been caught from the white water of Thames weir-pools.

River bream love cabbage patches and these are without doubt my favourite swims. In the days when I used to fish the upper Great Ouse at Beachampton, I spent a lot of time fishing for the bream there. Those bream were magnificent, unlike the flaccid creatures you often see from stillwaters. The biggest I ever caught went just over six pounds, although I saw a catch of fish just above Dick Walker's stretch one day that included a fish of eight pounds ten ounces. Most of my fish came from a swim which was known as the small cabbage patch. The method of fishing was to prebait at the edge of the cabbages in late evening, with mashed bread and chopped worms, and then return at the crack of dawn to start fishing. The method would be laying on with a simple quill, cocked by a single swan shot, a foot from a size 6 hook baited with a lob.

4

Carp

I would offer a cautionary note to younger anglers who are taking up carp fishing, many of whom these days, mistakenly in my view, have never fished for anything else. When you read the writings of successful men like Andy Little, try to put what they have to say into the proper perspective. Remember, these men are at the very top, and are fishing for the biggest and most intensely pursued carp in the country. That ultra-cult, amino acid-laced bait you have just read about, or the new all-singing, all-dancing, anti-eject rig that has just produced another thirty at Savay, may well have been necessary. But your club lake down the road which may contain doubles and an occasional twenty, could well be taken apart with free-lined flake or float-fished lobs. Don't laugh – it's a fact. Without meaning to be in any way derogatory, I have to say that many carp men these days fish with little or no original thought whatsoever, being content to follow the latest fashion slavishly. Often, they miss the obvious.

These days, big carp are available to any anglers who wish to fish for them. Waters as diverse as small secluded estate lakes, canals, large

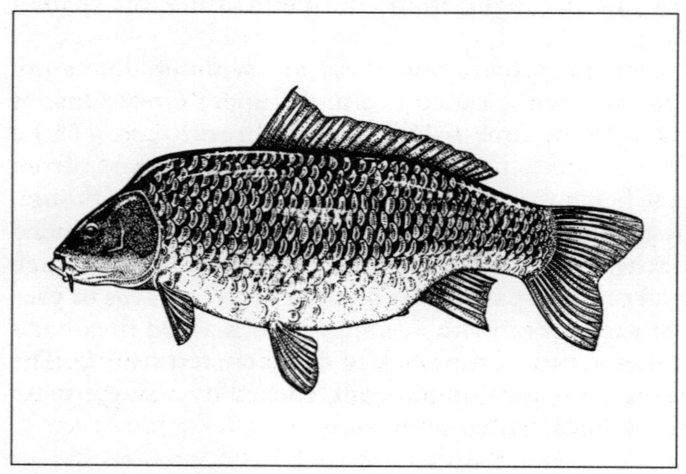

Common carp.

windswept gravel pits and many rivers, contain fish of twenty, thirty and even forty pounds, and many of these waters are open to anyone. As with all specimen hunting, location of the quarry is essential to consistent success, so I will look at this important topic first.

LOCATION

On many waters, the most reliable method of carp location is visual, seeing the fish rolling, bubbling or simply swimming with dorsals partly out of the water. For this reason a pair of powerful binoculars is an essential part of the equipment. Even if the fish themselves cannot be seen, evidence of their presence is available through localized patches of coloured water or movements of weed beds as the fish pass through them. An isolated sighting of a carp does not necessarily mean that you have located a feeding area, of course, as the fish may simply be passing through, but it does indicate where such an area may be, especially if you are able to follow the direction of the carp's movement. Location of carp by looking for coloured areas is an extremely reliable method of finding fish that you can be reasonably certain are feeding and I always fish with great confidence under these conditions. Obviously, this will generally apply to soft-bottomed lakes rather than gravel pits.

One drawback to this method of location is that when there is a fair wind on the water, a colouring effect may be general, due to the wave action. The wind, however, can be your greatest ally in location since carp, more than any other fish, move very quickly in response to the onset of any wind or change in wind direction. This applies to larger waters in the main. In very small estate lakes, I have found little evidence that wind direction makes any significant difference. In the larger lakes and gravel pits, however, it certainly does, and if a steady breeze has been blowing for a day or so, I would always look for the carp off the downwind bank. In a soft-bottomed lake, this bank will usually be more heavily coloured, especially if it is comparatively shallow and this always seems to encourage carp feeding. It is an exciting sight to see carp rolling, and head and tailing in conditions like this. Even when the water is really rough, a carp roll is very obvious. Because you are facing the wind you hear the evidence easily enough, and what you see is a calm patch appear as if by magic in the middle of the waves.

In the larger, hard-bottomed pits, location is much more difficult, especially if the stock density of carp is low. If there are few visual sightings to guide you, and little wind either, then you have to rely on common sense and watercraft. You have to try to work out where the fish are most likely to be. The first essential is to know your water and mapping, as described in the bream chapter, is invaluable. If you can do it by boat, preferably in the close season, so much the better. Like most fish, the gravel bars have a great attraction for carp, as do shallow plateaux, natural weed beds and silt beds. The shallow water around gravel islands and any foliage attached thereto are also very reliable holding areas. The gravel bars themselves are used by the carp as highways across the water, and the troughs between them act as food traps. Any silt present on the bars will accumulate in the troughs and will encourage the formation of bloodworm colonies, on which the carp feed avidly. Obviously, the same comments apply to the uniform silty areas, and the areas around weed beds.

On calm days, carp frequently bask and show little apparent inclination to feed. In such conditions, areas such as lily beds and beds of potamogeton are favoured holding areas, as is the shade afforded by bank-side foliage. Carp are by no means easy to tempt when they are basking but a strategically positioned bait may tempt the odd fish to pick it up.

The last and most obvious guide to location – especially on the more popular waters – is, of course, swims which receive a lot of attention from other anglers. Like it or not, an area which receives regular baiting will eventually become a natural feeding area. After a time, the fish may well become spooky and difficult to tempt but they will remain in the area, wise enough to take advantage of an abundant source of easily obtainable food.

METHODS AND TACTICS

On the smaller lakes in particular, the first approach to the fishing is a mobile one, stalking individual fish as they are located. This, of course, is largely dictated by angling pressure on the water. But if you have room, stalking is still one of the best ways of taking carp, and certainly the most exciting.

Bubblers

The first category of carp that respond to the stalking approach are the bubblers, or those fish responsible for clouds of mud rising from the bottom. These fish can be frustratingly difficult to tempt at times, particularly if they are preoccupied with bloodworm. On occasions, however, several carp can be taken quickly, the fish suddenly switching on for no apparent reason. It's as if they say, 'Right, the bloodworms are all gone, what else is there to eat?' I had a day like this at a small estate lake this summer. For four hours, great clouds of mud rose all around my bait as carp fed furiously in the margins, without a sign of a bite. And then I had three doubles in twenty minutes.

The traditional approach to bubblers and 'smoke screeners', as they used to be called, is a natural bait such as a lobworm, and, in truth, there is still a lot of merit in that. The humble lob has accounted for many big fish, as has a bunch of redworms or maggots under similar circumstances. If I am fishing lobs for bubblers, I like to put a little air in the tail to give it a slow-sinking natural look. Bubblers and smoke screeners are, however, feeding fish, and most baits will take them, provided the presentation is up to scratch. A substantial bait, such as a lob, ball of paste or boilie, could be free-lined for this fishing, and although that would appear to be the most natural presentation, it is not the one I favour. A group of big carp have a large body area and they will be feeding hard in one spot. Free-lining therefore carries the considerable risk of both foul hooking, and indeed deep hooking. I prefer to use either a small self-cocking float to indicate the immediate attention of a fish or, preferably, a bolt rig, with the line hard on the bottom to minimize the risk of the fish fouling it. When the bait is picked up, of course, the bolt rig will prevent the fish swallowing the bait on the spot. It will have felt the lead and bolted before then, giving both an obvious indication and one that ensures correct hooking.

When carp are seen disturbing weed beds, lilies or rushes, one of my favourite ploys is to fish for them with a floating bait hard against the foliage. Anchored bread crust is still a good bait, as are all the modern carp floaters and floating particle baits. On some small intimate waters, on a calm night, carp become very active around such features after dark. This is when the use of floating crust can produce several fish when boilies may well go untouched.

Having described stalking individual fish, it has to be said that most modern carp angling is static, a permanent swim being selected after giving due consideration to the prevailing conditions. Having said that, the swim should only be permanent for as long as the conditions remain unaltered, or you are convinced there are fish in the vicinity. If a change in conditions suggests that you ought to move to the other side of the lake, then move, no matter how inconvenient it is to shift that mountain of gear. It is all too easy to settle into a swim and then remain there no matter what, simply because you are too comfortable. Although much carp fishing is physically inactive, it is fatal to become mentally stagnant as well.

The Basic Set-Up

In common with most carp anglers, my basic set-up for static fishing revolves around the use of two rods, in conjunction with Optonic alarms and monkey climbers, which undoubtedly makes for more relaxing fishing during the long hours often required in this branch of specimen hunting. It is important to use monkey climbers that are heavy enough to register drop backs as well as runs. In one lake I fish, most of the takes involve carp running in to the bank, creating slack line. In my first season, I missed fish at night because the monkeys never registered the line slackening. At that water, I now actually load my monkeys with lead wire. A run shows up in the normal way but a slack liner gives a very dramatic drop back.

I also fish with open bale arms, using a butt clip to prevent slack line spillage from the open spool. As I play large fish off the clutch, my anti-reverses are on. Obviously, if you favour backwinding, then you can fish with bale arms closed. The only danger with this is an overrun if a fish stops suddenly after a fast run. One answer, of course, is the use of a modern baitrunner reel. These are excellent, but I must admit I still prefer the traditional tool. I have been used to fishing open bales for thirty years and am afraid that if I used a baitrunner now, I would forget which lever to pull or which button to press in the excitement of a carp run and end up making a mess of it. I also know of two friends who have nearly lost rods using them. Fast runs have shaken the rods in the rests so much that the reels have triggered from baitrunner mode to normal tension, with obvious results.

The normal set-up will also have one more addition, and that is line clips on the rod in front of the Optonics. Whenever possible, these are not used as they will obviously prevent slack line bites from registering. However, in very windy weather or where drifting weed is in evidence, the continual little bleeps from the alarms, caused by the line moving around, can drive you to distraction. In these circumstances, the line is inserted into the front clip to keep it still. Not an ideal solution, of course, but a good compromise to allow you to fish efficiently when conditions are rough.

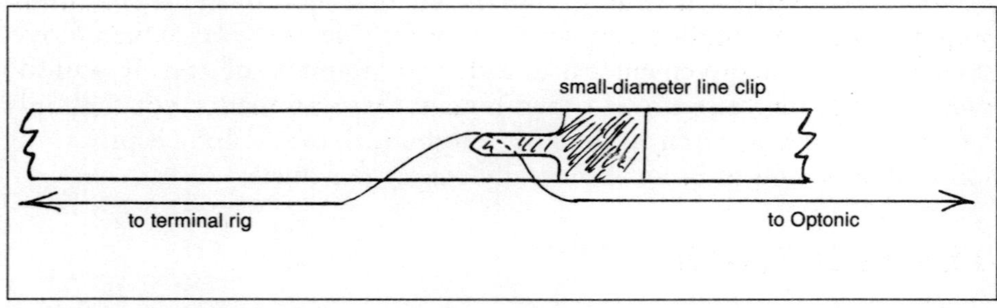

Use of a small line clip adjacent to a butt ring.

4 Carp

Having established what is the general set-up on the bank, let us now have a more detailed look at the various terminal rigs that can be used in different circumstances.

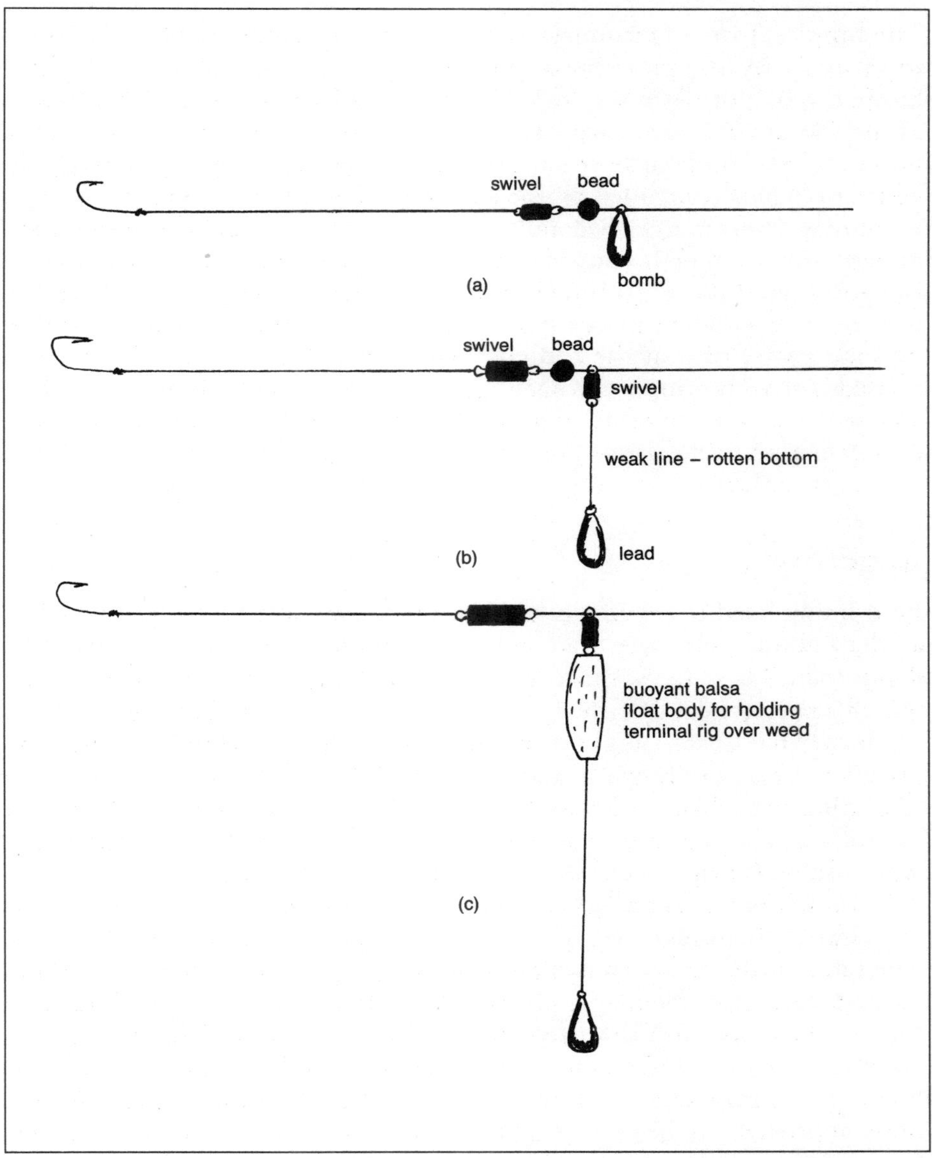

Standard legering rigs.

BAIT PRESENTATION AND TERMINAL RIGS

Free-Lining

The simplest form of terminal rig is, of course, free-lining, which was used extensively by the pioneers of modern carping in the forties and fifties. Simply, a ball of paste was moulded round a large hook, and cast out to await the arrival of a carp. The method does have severe limitations, however, and finds little application in the carping of today. Firstly, the casting range is controlled by the size of the bait, unless you are fishing at extremely short range. Secondly, loose lining gives an inefficient early registration of a bite. If you are fishing a heavy bait at longish range or there is a good wind putting a bow in the line, there will be plenty of slack line out, and this could mean a carp moving yards with the bait before you ever become aware of it at the rod end. That could lead to many bites being missed that were simply not seen or, conversely, deeply hooked fish. And any fish that ran towards you would give no bite indication whatever, other than a visible slackening of the line which would not of course be visible at night.

Legering

Free-lining used to be effective simply because there were very few carp anglers about, and carp had not been taught that anglers' baits were dangerous. These days, most of our carp fishing is carried out on waters which are very heavily fished every week of the season, and a great many of the carp have been caught many times over. Because of this, the fish have grown to be naturally wary, and the requirement now is for a much earlier indication that a bait has been picked up. The amount of slack line has to be minimized, and the way to achieve that is by legering. On a lightly fished water, standard rigs could be all that are required initially.

In a water where such rigs have been used for some time, problems begin to manifest themselves when the carp begin to wise up a little. The most frustrating is the one of twitch bites, as the fish pick up the baits and almost immediately drop them again because they have learned to be suspicious. One way to catch fish that are behaving like this is to attempt to hit these twitches. This involves fishing closed bale arms and hovering over the rod like a praying mantis, waiting to strike at the slightest movement. The other approach is to be patient, sit back and ignore all the twitches, and wait for a fish to gain enough confidence to trundle off with the bait. Both are extremely inefficient, the first because the success rate with twitcher hitting is very low, and the continual striking and recasting must make the carp even more spooky; the second because a number of potential bites will have been ignored.

Bolt Rigs

The answer is to adapt the rig into one that will encourage the carp to run with the bait. Obviously, if a carp feels the resistance of the lead immediately it twitches a bait, it is likely to bolt in alarm. The shorter the hooklink, the sooner this is going to happen. On feeling the resistance, the carp will also drop the bait as being something dangerous but, if the rig incorporates a hooklink so short that picking up the bait and feeling the lead happen at one and the same time, the carp will often bolt with the bait

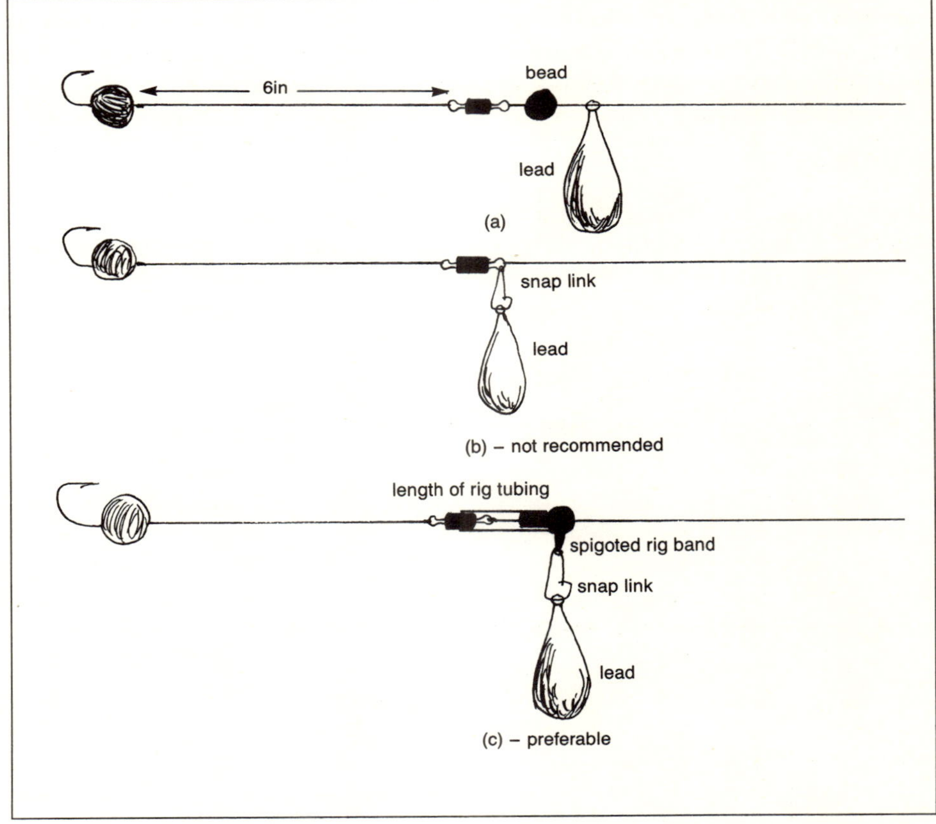

Bolt-rig variations.

still in its mouth. It will find it very difficult to eject the bait while swimming fast. From the above, it follows that if a bait is fished so that the hook point is exposed, the carp may tend to hook itself against the resistance of the lead when it bolts.

Occasionally, even bolt rigs result in twitchy bites, and fixed rigs no bites at all, as the carp wise up even to them. What appears to happen is that the fish move a bait very gently in their lips, for an inch or so at a time, as if expecting something to happen. If they feel the lead immediately, they have learned to drop it straight away without dashing off. If they feel nothing, however, they may continue twitching for a long time, and we are back with the problem we had with the standard legering rig. A way round this problem is to fish with the lead free-running for a short distance to a back stop. The theory is that the fish gradually gains more confidence as he twitches the bait without any nasty reaction. As the lead hits the back stop, however, there is a sudden large increase in resistance, and if the fish has the bait in its mouth this may be different enough to make him bolt. The length of line between the lead and the back stop can be varied, depending on how the carp are found to be behaving on the day.

Hair Rigs

The more often carp are fished for, caught and returned, the faster they wise up to terminal rigs, and on a great many of our more popular fisheries

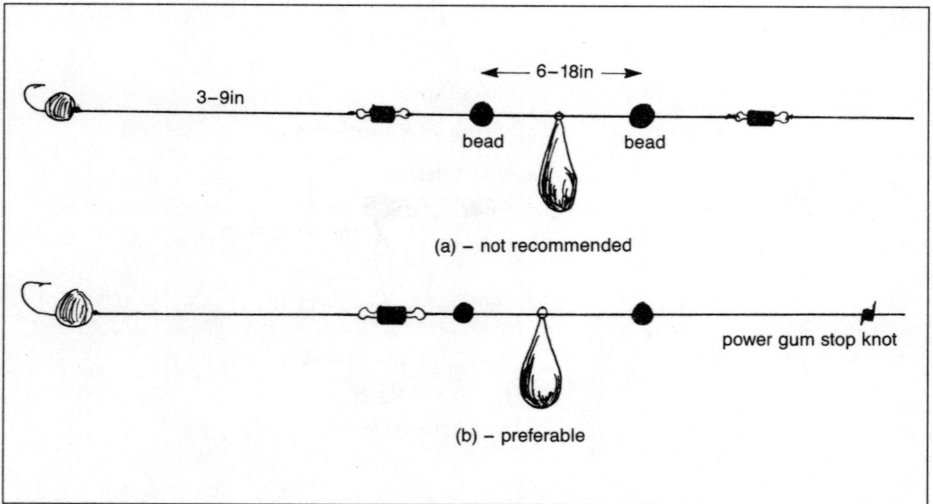

Shock-rig variations.

today even bolt and shock rigs have been sussed out by all but a small proportion of them. If they have learned to pick up the bait very gently in the edge of their lips without moving, the bait can be discarded if the fish feels the hook or the hooklink, without a bite being registered. Obviously, burying the hook in the bait would alleviate the first problem, but hooking would be rendered uncertain with any but the softest baits. The line would still be felt, however, and the answer to the problem lies with the hair rig, whereby the bait is not mounted on the hook at all. Instead, the bait is mounted on a hair attached to the hook.

The theory is simple enough: when the carp initially picks up the bait in its lips, provided the hair is long enough, the bait appears unfettered, and the fish will take it confidently. As the bait goes to the back of the mouth, the hook naturally follows. At this point, obviously, the carp feels the hook, realizes something is wrong and tries to eject the bait. The hook then pricks the mouth, resulting in the carp bolting in alarm, hitting the

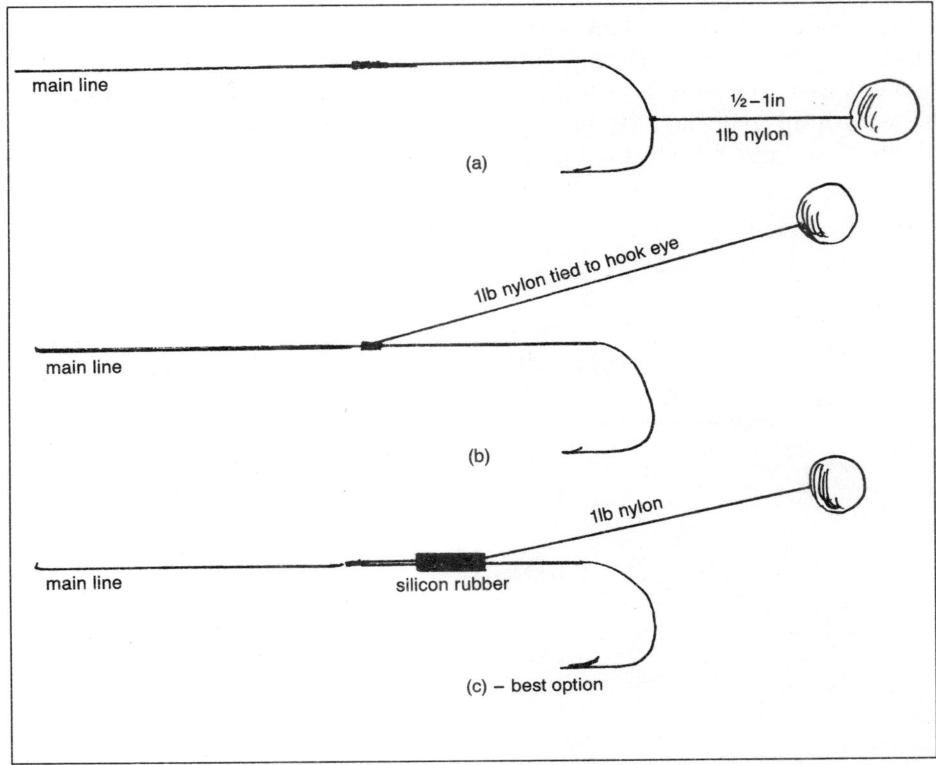

Hair-rig variations.

resistance of the lead and effectively hooking itself. This is an obvious natural progression from the cruder bolt rig.

When you consider that the hair rig is designed to encourage the carp to pick up the bait without suspicion, it follows that the hair itself should be as soft and supple as possible, like natural weed if you like. We need, therefore, to use materials such as very fine nylon or dental floss, fine Dacron or the new Kryston, which are all very limp.

The theory of the hair rig depends on a bait being taken confidently into the back of the mouth. If a bait could be crushed in the carp's lips, then it need never take in the hook. We need, therefore, a hard bait for the technique to be at its most effective, one that the fish can crush only with its throat teeth. This then ensures the hook is well in the mouth at some stage. When big carp are the quarry, the distance from the lips to the throat teeth can be several inches and, therefore, even with the hair rig, the fish will still feel the main line fairly early. If the line is stiff strong nylon, this in itself could cause the fish to bolt, possibly before the hook is far enough in the mouth. I am sure that the fish find a consistent long length of stiff nylon more alarming than a small hard object like a hook. Premature bolting would obviously see lots of fish on the bank, but also possibly many missed as well. So most carp anglers use hooklinks, as well as hair, of very limp materials. By far the most popular is black Dacron, although dental floss and Kryston are gaining ground rapidly.

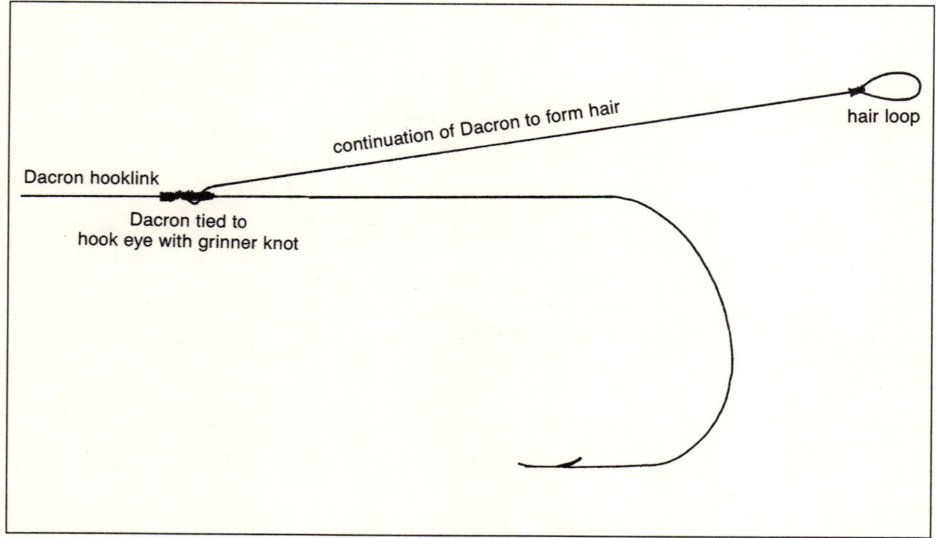

Dacron hair rig.

Another very common feeding trait amongst carp is fanning vigorously over the bottom with their powerful fins, creating underwater vortices which lift food items, including anglers' baits, off the bottom. Anyone who has not observed this behaviour would not believe how far a big carp can move a boilie by fin action alone. This habit allows the carp to select out naturally anglers' baits which are connected to leads or large heavy hooks, even on hair rigs. The anchoring effect of the terminal rig makes the hookbait act in a totally different manner from the free offerings. In fact, it is probably the lack of action that is the giveaway and, once again, the hookbait can be the only boilie left in the area after a feeding spell. The way to beat this problem is with the use of buoyant baits or baits of neutral buoyancy, by which I mean those that only just sink, and then very slowly. A buoyant bait will fish permanently off bottom, while one of neutral buoyancy will rest on the bottom and yet pop up with any turbulence in the same way that the free offerings do. These buoyant or semi-buoyant baits are popularly known as pop-ups.

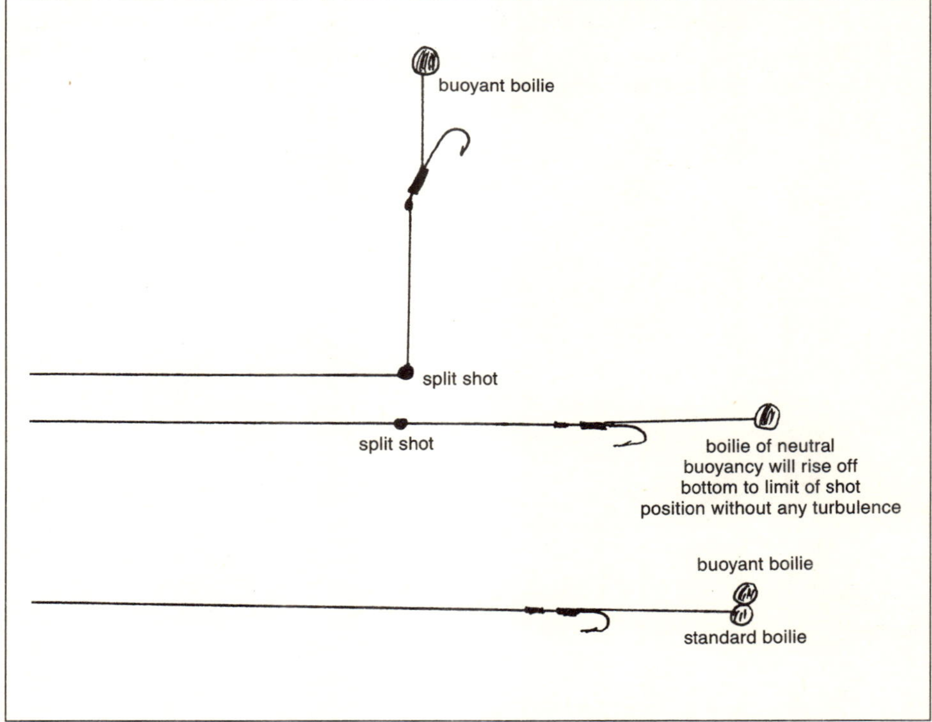

Pop-up rigs.

Paternosters

If you are faced with two feet or more of silt, then you are better off with a standard paternoster. The paternoster rig can be fished running or fixed, and as the bomb is buried in the surface of the silt, I don't really think that it makes any difference to the presentation or to bite indication. My own results certainly show no advantage for one or the other. Whichever I use, I always use a bomb link substantially weaker than the main line. The risk of snagging is obviously higher when the bomb is immersed in the bottom debris, and I would rather it break away than lose a big fish.

Small Surface Baits

The forementioned rigs are for fishing baits on or just off bottom. When we want to present a small surface bait, however, such as a single chum mixer, a different approach is called for. This will depend on whether we want to present a drifting bait or an anchored one, and at what range. For fishing a bait on the move, following free offerings down a wind lane for instance, we can use a simple self-cocking float rig. If more than a modest casting range is involved, the float can be replaced by one of those commercially available floating carp bombs.

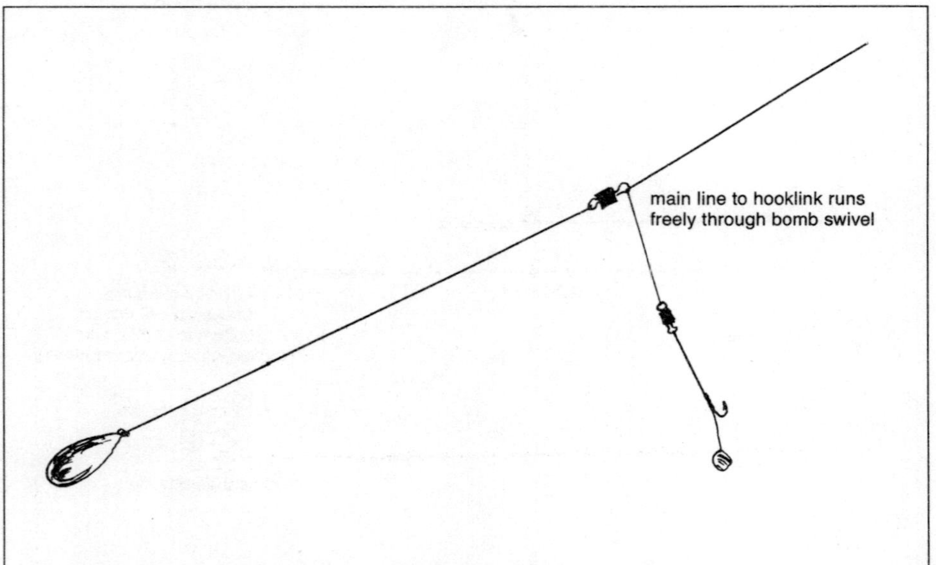

Paternoster rig.

4 CARP

BAITS

Standards, Pastes and Boilies

What a long way we have come from the humble ball of bread paste to the complex boiled baits of today. Of all the aspects of modern carp fishing, this is the one that throws the newcomers into the most confusion. One thing that ought to be realized from the outset is that carp will eat anything edible, unless they have been taught that it is dangerous to do so. If you have access to a little-fished pool, therefore, there is no need to buy expensive boiled baits initially as the fish are just as likely to respond to bread and worms. Even on our hard-fished waters, bread in its various forms is still an excellent bait. Floating bread crust, of course, has been a standard carp offering for forty years and, when fish have been caught on it a few times, it can be varied endlessly by the addition of both colourings and flavourings. Bread flake is a highly versatile bait with a unique consistency that is almost impossible to reproduce with synthetic carp baits. When you need to present a light buoyant bait delicately on top of soft silt or blanket weed, nothing fits the bill as well as a piece of fresh fluffy flake. Again, endless permutations can be achieved with modern carp flavourings, if required.

Earlier, when discussing bubblers, I mentioned how good lobs are as a carp bait. On my local syndicate water, which is bombarded with boilies every day of the season, several good fish have been caught lately on lobs

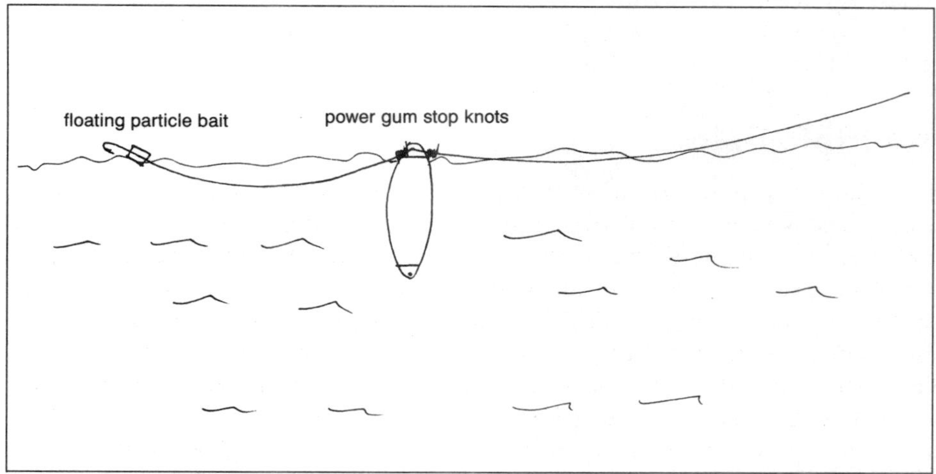

The drifting floating bomb.

when boilies were being ignored. As in all fishing, an open mind is a great asset. The same comments apply equally to maggots and sweetcorn which carp will eat by the bucketful if they aren't frightened.

The four baits mentioned so far can be classed as standards, with bread and lobs being fished as large individual baits, and maggots and corn as mass particles. The next step up from these basic offerings is more specialized baits of various kinds. In this category I would place luncheon meat, bacon grill, trout-pellet paste, cheese paste, sausage paste, pastes made by stiffening moist cat and dog foods and tinned fish of various kinds. Tinned cat meat, with fine breadcrumbs as a binder, has caught an enormous number of carp, and two of my favourite soft pastes are trout-fry crumb mixed with gluten, milk powder and eggs, and tinned pilchards, mashed and stiffened with wholemeal flour. Luncheon meat and bacon grill, straight from the tin, are excellent baits and will always catch their share of carp.

Specials

The class of baits known as 'specials' is one that has received a great deal of attention over recent years, and it can develop into a very complex subject indeed, especially when it is subdivided into those of high or low protein content, or into natural or 'synthetic' types. I do not propose to enter into an extended catalogue of all the possible permutations in the various categories because that would take too long and, I believe, become unnecessarily complicated in a book about all-round angling. Anyone who wishes to delve deeper into what is, admittedly, a fascinating subject can do no better than study what the experts like Kevin Maddocks and Rod Hutchinson have to say.

Multiple Baits

The theory of preoccupation, with large quantities of small food items, is one that has been proved time and time again, and with bubblers we have the classic example of a carp so intent on eating bloodworms that it will often ignore anything else. In most waters there are times when carp will not respond to boilies, and fishing for them with multiple or mass baits can be the answer. Quite simply, we are trying to achieve a localized pre-occupation effect, by introducing a sufficiently large number of baits into a small area. It is next to impossible to preoccupy the entire carp stock of a water with your selected bait unless it is an extremely small water, and therefore the technique is one of localized heavy baiting and then accurate casting. With boilies, you can scatter baits over quite a wide area and achieve good results, but not so with particles. You must be fishing among your bed of bait to stand any chance. For a given poundage of bait, the smaller each individual item is, the more there will be and therefore the greater will be the possibility of exclusive feeding. For this reason, five gallons of hemp are likely to preoccupy the carp more than five gallons of butter beans.

The best-known particle baits are sweetcorn, chick peas, peanuts, tiger nuts, maple peas and sultanas, and these are big enough to be used on their own as hookbaits. The same comments obviously apply to mini-boilies, on which I've had a great deal of success. When we come to the real mass baits, such as hemp, tares or red dari seeds, we have to use hookbaits consisting of many individual seeds. This can be achieved by coating a hook with superglue or mystic paste and smothering it with the seeds. Alternatively, a hair rig can be used, incorporating one or more hairs, which are coated with superglue and again dipped in the seeds.

Whichever multiple bait you decide to use, make sure that seeds and beans are well cooked before you introduce them or they may harm the fish. This is especially true of things like tiger nuts which require pressure cooking for some time before they become soft enough to be used as hookbaits.

Particle rigs.

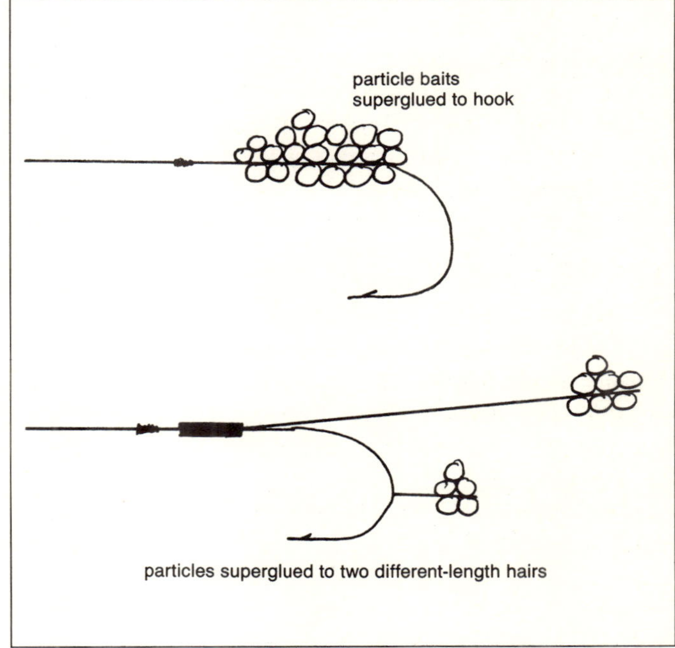

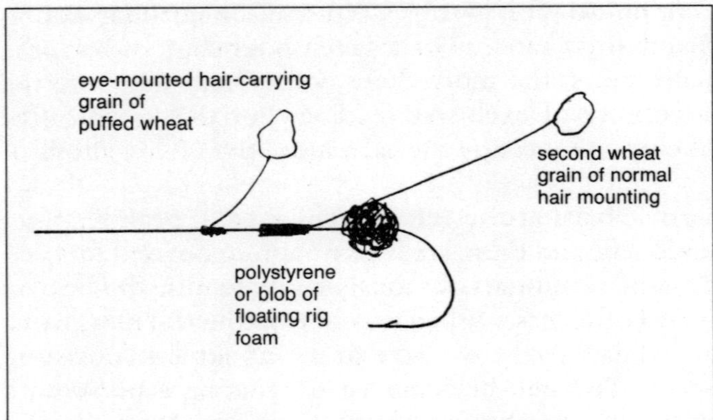

Use of two floating particles on a rig.

As in barbel fishing, a good ploy is to lay down a good bed of particles and fish over them with a larger bait. This works very well fishing boilies over hemp, peanuts or mini-boilies, and I have had some nice fish on large cubes of bacon grill over tiger nuts. Under certain circumstances, one isolated large bait will be taken preferentially, whereas you could wait a long time for the carp to find your particle hookbait among the mass of freebies. When I am baiting with hemp, I particularly like to fish a pop-up over it, to enhance this selectivity further.

Floating Multiples

Surface-feeding carp that have learned to avoid crust or large floaters could well be tempted by floating multiples, using the rigs mentioned in the previous section. The most popular baits for this fishing are dog and cat biscuits, as well as cereals such as Sugar Puffs and Puffed Wheat. Some of these are buoyant enough to be used with a large hook, but where the weight of the hook is a problem, it can be counterbalanced with a piece of polystyrene. Floating particles can be deadly when drifted down the wind with free offerings, and I like to use more than one on the terminal rig. They are also deadly when anchored alongside the marginal rushes on the downwind side of a water, where all the freebies will end up.

PRE-BAITING AND BAITING TECHNIQUES

When I talk about pre-baiting, I do not mean introducing free offerings just before a fishing session commences, but rather putting in your selected bait possibly days or even weeks before you contemplate fishing. On a little-fished water, with perhaps a small head of carp which may be well scattered through that water, then pre-baiting over a decent period of time can be a very effective way to concentrate the fish, and thereby increase your chances of success.

I know of quite a few waters where this has been done. On one, there were about a hundred good carp in some eighty acres, and those fish were caught very rarely indeed. The water was fished mainly for roach and bream, so there was little competition from other carp anglers. Two friends of mine, who had fished there for a couple of seasons with very little success, embarked upon a campaign of pre-baiting, with hard boilies because of the head of nuisance fish. To start with, they introduced boilies over the entire lake, from the margins to maximum catapulting range. Initially, no one area received a tremendous concentration of baits, the main idea being to make the bait available to any carp, wherever in the lake it happened to be. Every other day for two weeks the baiting took this pattern, and then they began to introduce more baits into two selected areas than anywhere else. Gradually, over the next two weeks, they cut down the number of boilies in other parts of the lake and stepped up the baiting in the selected swims. In the end, for the week before fishing, boilies were introduced only into those swims. The night before they commenced their first session, two hundred boilies went into each. Fishing commenced at midnight, and the results were incredible, with eleven carp coming to their rods the first day, when two or three fish a season had been the norm.

It is easy to see the principle behind this procedure. First, you get the carp used to eating the bait, and hopefully they like it sufficiently to look for more. Initially, they can pick up samples almost anywhere but, as time goes by, they learn that there is more to be found in certain areas. As those areas appear to have a constant abundance of food, there is little point in the fish moving, and so those areas attract a large proportion of the carp in the water. Pretty soon, they are regarded as natural feeding areas, and when that situation has been achieved, fish will be caught regularly, providing that the swim is kept baited. Eventually, obviously, the fish will become wary of the bait and the rig being used, and you will then have to start looking for alternatives.

Although the above technique most definitely does work, often dramatically, it is important to realize its restrictions. It is only at its most effective where the water is not fished for carp, or at best lightly fished. If it is hammered by carp anglers every week in every swim, then the carp are going to know what boilies are all about, without pre-baiting. They will certainly eat the baits you are introducing, but they will not be encouraged especially to remain in your selected areas, as there will be boilies always available to them all over the lake. You could, therefore, go to a lot of time and trouble, not to mention expense, and achieve nothing more than you could achieve without any pre-baiting whatever, and by just introducing free offerings on the day of fishing. Pre-baiting on a heavily fished carp water I thus consider of doubtful value.

The only exception to this would be if you were the only one allowed access to a water in the close season, and could pre-bait ready for 16 June. You would still have to make sure that you were there first to get the swim you wanted, of course, and this raises the other major drawback of pre-baiting popular waters. Even if it were proved to work, you could never be sure that the swim would not be occupied when you were able to fish. I can think of nothing more galling than to see another angler filling his boots on a water to which I had just devoted weeks of effort and money.

Having said all that, let me say that there is one circumstance when extensive pre-baiting, even on a hard-fished water, could pay handsome dividends. It would depend, though, on being able to introduce the bait in secrecy, which is not very easy, admittedly. A water that is being constantly hammered on boilies can respond very well to localized concentrations of particles, and if you are able to build up, say, a hemp hot spot, you may be surprised at the results. Only this summer, my local water, which receives many thousands of boilies every week, has yielded a spate of big carp from two swims, on hair-rigged tares presented over gallons of hemp. In heavily fished carp waters, it's not so much keeping one step ahead of the fish that is important, but keeping ahead of other anglers!

Quantities

One last point on pre-baiting. If it is going to be of any value, especially on lightly fished waters where it is most sensibly employed, you have to use sufficient bait so that there is always some available at all times. If you are going to use boilies, and really you have to ensure that mainly carp eat them, then you have to talk in thousands. The last time I undertook such a campaign, I introduced about ten thousand boilies over about four weeks. If that sounds a lot, be under no illusions as to how many boilies a carp can eat. Last summer, I watched a common of about twelve pounds devour forty Tutti Frutti in about ten minutes! Before you start such a campaign, therefore, weigh up the costs first, not just of the bait but also the petrol costs. If you cannot afford to do it properly, then the money you do spend will probably be wasted.

Free Offerings

These days, because I fish mainly syndicate waters containing big carp, I very rarely pre-bait, preferring to introduce free offerings during the session. If I know that I will be able to get a particular swim, I may go to the trouble of putting in some bait the day before I start. The general baiting up is done by catapult or throwing stick if I am using boilies, or by one of those excellent floating bait droppers for distributing particles. For boilies, I usually use about two hundred baits a day to start with, amending this baiting intensity depending on results. If the carp are active and runs are coming, I will step up the baiting frequency. After every run, whether it results in a carp on the bank or not, I always put a few more baits out. I work on the principle that it is statistically likely that my bait was not the first the carp had eaten. It is more likely to be one of the last available, since no rig exists which can give such a natural presentation as a totally unattached bait.

On the other hand, if the lake appears dead, with no action to anyone, I assume that the carp may well be in the mood to pick up one or two baits only, and therefore the fewer there are available, the higher the likelihood of the hookbait being one of the few taken. In this situation, a small cluster of baits in a small area could be more appropriate, and this is where introduction of the hookbait in conjunction with stringers is so efficient. A stringer is simply a length of PVA attached to the terminal rig, carrying free offerings. As the PVA dissolves, the freebies are deposited close to the hookbait.

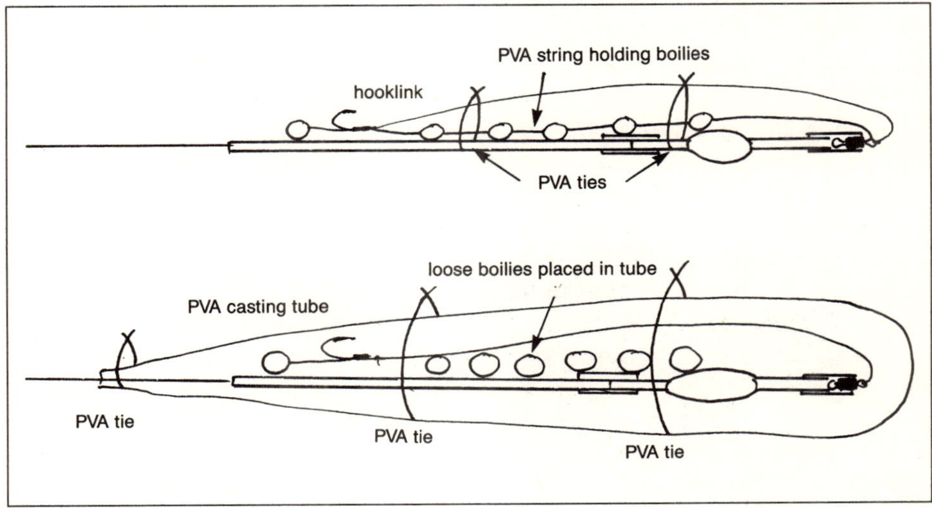

Use of stringers and PVA tubes.

5

Chub

SUMMER CHUBBING

Although it has to be said that chub are at their fighting best in the winter months, and that is when I prefer to fish for them, there is no denying that summer chubbing, especially in shallow clear and weedy rivers, is great fun. Moreover, it provides a marvellous training in the reaction of fish to baits, and the necessity for stealth and concealment in our fishing. To me, true summer chubbing is when I can see the fish I am after, and each specimen can be stalked individually.

Natural Baits

Without a doubt, perhaps the deadliest approach to the fishing is with large natural baits. In this category come crayfish, small fish of all kinds, slugs and lobworms, although I have to say that I hesitate to use crayfish these days as much as I did, since their numbers appear to be declining alarmingly in the rivers I fish. If your river has a thriving crayfish population, then there is no doubt that that is the bait *par excellence* for a big summer chub.

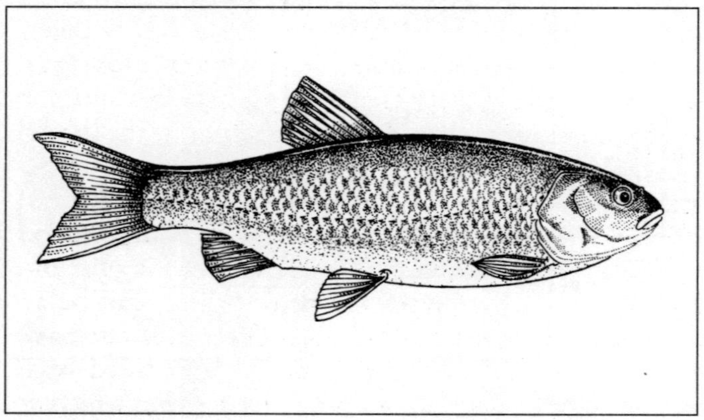

Chub.

There are several ways of catching crays, the easiest being the use of a drop net at dusk, in an area of reasonably steady water under the near bank, an area which preferably is not too far away from gravelly shallows. With a piece of fish tied to an old keep-net, tied flat and weighted so that it sinks, sufficient crayfish can be caught in a few drops of the net to provide enough bait for the next day. The technique is to lower the net to the river bed, leave it for ten minutes or so, and then quickly withdraw it. You should then have trapped two or three crays. I must make one plea: if you adopt this method of cray collecting, and your river has a decent population of these crustacea, please do not take more than you need for your fishing; and any that are unused at the end of the day please take home and freeze. They work just as well frozen.

The second method of gathering crayfish is more convenient for the odd day's fishing, and that is searching the gravel shallows at dawn. You want an area with a healthy supply of average-size stones for the crays to hide under. Two feet deep is ideal, otherwise the water becomes a little murky to see what you are doing, and it is also advisable to pick an area where there is a steady current flowing through. The current will quickly wash away the silt as you disturb it. The technique is simple. As you come to each stone, lift it up in an upstream direction, so that the silt washes downstream. You will then see a little depression where the stone lay and, if you are lucky, a crayfish lying in that depression. You have to be quick. Grasp him firmly behind the shoulders, between finger and thumb, and transfer him to a bait bucket containing a few stones, and only a few inches of water. Do not be afraid of the claws. Crayfish are not capable of nipping very hard, and if you hold them in the way I've advised they cannot get their claws at you anyway.

Stone loach and bullheads also inhabit similar places, and you can catch one or two of those at the same time. They are almost impossible to catch with bare hands, however, and you need to arm yourself with a short-handled triangular net if you are going to search for these. To obtain a supply of minnows, nothing beats the old minnow-trap principle, using an old wine bottle, with a small hole in the recessed bottom knocked out, the neck plugged and the bottle baited with bread and placed flat in the gravel shallows.

I said a little earlier that I am getting very miserly in the numbers of crayfish I take for chub baits these days, but I have no such compunction about slugs, which are among the deadliest of all chub baits, the bigger and blacker the better. Keeping a supply of slugs for chub fishing can be an absolute pain, and I have never been particularly successful at it. If you have a big wooden box that can be kept cool and moist, and kept filled with vegetable leaves, slugs can be kept for a short while, but I don't bother trying these days. If I want slugs for chubbing, I can generally collect plenty on the bank at dawn to last me the day. You find them at the waterline, under the roots of many marginal plants, burdocks being particular favourites.

I would never consider a summer chubbing foray without a few lobworms in my tackle box. They are particularly good when you need to present a static bait, and I have lost count of the big fish I have caught on the humble lob. Many years of summer chubbing have convinced me beyond doubt that crayfish, slugs and natural fish baits are at their most effective when fished on the move.

Presentation

Generally speaking, the only thing I have on the line for summer chubbing is the hook, unless I am using a small live or deadbait, when I'll pinch a swan shot about a foot from the hook. One exception is trotting minnows at the tail of weirs or down other fast runs, when sport can be hectic, especially early in the season. A small balsa will suffice for this fishing. I invariably use Au Lion d'Or hooks, in pattern number 1534, which have never let me down yet, in sizes 6 or 4, the 4 being selected for crayfish or black slugs, with a 6-pound Maxima line.

One item of tackle that I never overlook for this fishing is a tin of line grease. Summer chub chasing involves a lot of fishing among thick vegetation, with the corresponding risk of frequent snagging. By greasing all but the last few feet of line, most of the line between rod and bait can be kept floating, and therefore minimizes snagging. Also, the greased line makes a very effective bite indicator, shooting across the surface in very exciting fashion when you get a take. I'm thinking here principally of situations where you may be presenting a bait in shallow water, perhaps under a frond of streamer, or in a small gap amongst cabbages or rushes. In the event that you come to a large raft, and require more of the line to sink to enable a long drift under the rubbish without the line floating around everywhere, the requisite length of line can be degreased with washing-up liquid, and I always carry a small bottle for the purpose.

Natural-bait chubbing is short-range work for the most part, and you simply must learn how to move around without scaring every fish within miles. When you can actually see their reactions to your movement it can be quite a chastening experience. Another thing that will take you aback, if you have never tried naturals before, is the savagery with which chub attack them. For this reason, it is a great mistake to fish on too tight a line, or the chub will often smash the rod round and have the bait away before you can move. I have even been broken on the bite! More than once, I have had crayfish bitten clean in half in a fraction of a second. I would not have believed it possible unless I had experienced it. The procedure to adopt, having cast the bait into position, is to leave a nice slack loop of line as the bait sinks. Allow all the loose line to tighten before striking and you should have no trouble connecting with the bites. Do not give the chub all the time in the world, however, or you will be bitten off. It's a matter of common sense.

Crust

In some of our streamier, weedier and shallower chub rivers, one of the most entertaining ways of taking chub is with floating bread crust. Many swims, in fact, are only fishable using this technique; I will come to the reasons for this later. The ideal crust swim is one in which we have rapid gravel shallows, terminated by a slowing down of the flow and a deepening at the tail of the run. Chub that position themselves at the end of such runs are avid surface feeders, and it is possible to take large bags of fish if you can keep the disturbance to a minimum. The trick is to be as far away from the feeding area as possible, while maintaining correct tackle control.

When you arrive at a streamy stretch, the easiest way to establish whether the chub are in the mood is to drift some free offerings down the likely swims and watch what happens. Provided you keep out of sight, it should not be too long before the odd sample starts to be taken. Once a chub is taking crust confidently, he is as good as yours, so long as your bait presentation is good enough. There is no necessity for ultra-fine lines, in fact most summer chubbing situations on the rivers I fish make 6 pounds the minimum I would ever consider, but there is a necessity that the presentation be as natural as possible. This means that the crust should drift over the chub's head with no dragging, and no stopping and starting, causing a wake in the water. In particular, the crust should follow the current and should not be pulled across the flow by continually mending the line. If there is the slightest thing wrong with the behaviour of a surface bait, the chub will have none of it.

One of the biggest causes of poor floating-crust presentation is sinking line causing drag. This is a greater problem at longer ranges so you should always grease the line. The line must float and sufficient slack be left so that any wind loops that form do not hinder the bait's progress down the current. If the wind is very strong, floating-crust fishing can become very difficult to carry out efficiently, but the consolation is that the chub seem to tolerate a less than perfect presentation if the surface of the water is heavily rippled.

In much the same way as with natural bait fishing, once a couple of fish have been taken from a swim on floating crust, the rest of the shoal start to become very agitated. That is when they start coming short at the crust or swirling at it to knock bits off, which they can then eat at their leisure. A tackle modification that sometimes works is to fish a combination of crust and flake so that a small piece of flake is drifting down an inch or so under the surface, below a normal crust offering, which is about the size of a ten-pence piece. The simplest way to achieve this is with a double-hook rig, with a size 10 for the flake, tied an inch from the normal 6. That is a bit fiddly, however, and I normally content myself with sliding the crust bait an inch up the line, holding it there with a piece of grass tied round the line, and covering the 6 with a piece of squeezed flake.

Swims for Floating Baits

A floating bait is often the only option in certain swims, so let us have a look now at some of the areas I mean. First of all we have the bed of thick lilies where there are the tiniest gaps of clear water imaginable between the pads. Because lilies are extremely tough, bottom-bait fishing with naturals is not really viable, and the only way is to use strong tackle and crust. Once a chub takes the bait, hold it hard – there is no room for finesse. Another very similar circumstance is an area in the midst of fallen trees, the kind of place so beloved of big chub. If the river bed is littered with old timber, a floating bait is again the answer. Once again, though, do not compromise on tackle strength.

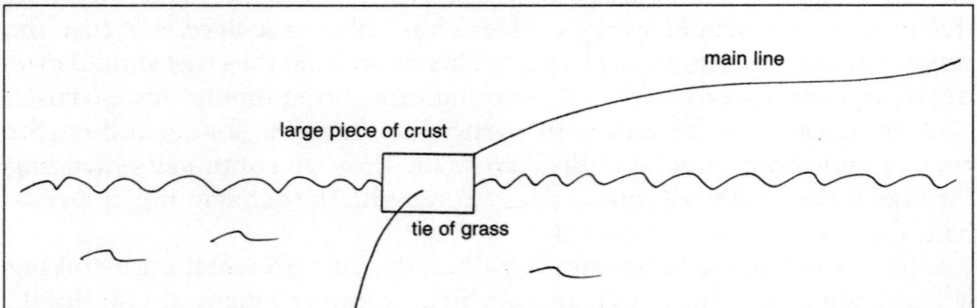

Subsurface drifting flake.

Another rather special circumstance, when the use of floating crust is a lot of fun, is where large thick mats of algae have accumulated. In swims of this type, I poke a small hole in the algae, and then manoeuvre a piece of bread crust into it. You usually find that the algae quickly closes round it again. Once again, the tackle can be as strong as you wish, since none of it is in the water. Swims like this can be fished with bottom baits as well, but the floating-crust approach I find much more fun. It is fascinating to see the algae suddenly bulge upwards, just before the crust is sucked out of sight.

What I have had to say so far in this summer section applies in the main to the smaller type of chub river. As natural-bait and floating-crust fishing are essentially short-range techniques, they are not quite so applicable to the bigger rivers or to those rivers of deeper, stronger flows. Here the more orthodox techniques, as outlined in the winter section, are more relevant, the only difference being that the weight on the terminal rig will be greatly less, often being non-existent for dense baits such as luncheon meat and cheese paste.

Free-Lining

This brings me quite naturally on to free-lining, a very neglected art. A ball of cheese paste or sausage-meat paste is particularly suitable for rolling round a lively swim and, being unfettered, gives a natural presentation. I especially like free-lining in streamer weed with big baits, placing the bait so that the current carries it under the tresses. The streamer fronds will then hold the tackle in position, with the result that the bait wavers about underneath very invitingly. On streamy rivers such as the Dorset Stour, it is often not possible to free-line, but you can usually get away with just the addition of a couple of shot to achieve the same presentation. When you first attempt this fishing, you have to get used to the constant undulations down the rod, caused by the continual wafting backwards and forwards of the streamer weed. These movements do not matter, and in fact the bait movements they create are the reason why the bites you get in streamer beds are usually so positive.

Static Fishing

Most of the summer chubbing I have covered so far is very active, and during a day I can cover a few miles of river. If you do not enjoy this type of fishing and prefer a static approach, then you will need to select a swim which has the potential to contain a reasonable head of chub, and hold them there. There is no doubt at all that the best approach is by the use of hemp, with a change bait fished over the top of it. The actual hookbait is often immaterial, although an obvious front runner is sweetcorn. Other hookbaits which have given me many summer chub when fished in conjunction with hemp are tares, casters, maggots, lobworms, meat, maple peas and mini-boilies. My approach is to introduce about six droppers of hemp into the swim, each dropper containing a small number of free offerings of the hookbait, if I am using corn, casters, or the like. For large baits such as meat or lobs, the only sample will be the one on the hook. Whatever the hookbait, I always include with the hemp some grains of corn, both as an attractor and as a visual aid. The corn is very visible, and when I can no longer see any, that is my cue to put in another couple of droppers of feed.

From the above, you will see that, for the technique to be at its most effective, it pays to fish a swim at short range, and one in which the depth allows you to see the river bed. The ideal arrangement is a patch of clean gravel, close to an amount of cover that would harbour several chub. My favourite type of swim is upstream of a raft. Patient baiting, and the ability to keep quiet and low at all other times, will attract many fish out of the cover and onto the hemp. I like to have two or three swims on the go, so that I can commute between them, after the fish in one have been spooked, either by my catching one or following a topping-up baiting. I realize, however, with angling pressure nowadays, that this is not always possible.

In exactly the same way as with floating crust, it only takes one or two fish to be taken from a swim, for the rest to become very wary. On both the Wensum and the Cherwell, I have seen chub take every single grain of corn except the one on the hook, after a couple of easy fish had been caught. This is when a change to a hair rig can produce another fish or two, and it is worth going to the trouble of making up a few hooks with thin strips of cork superglued to the shank, to make them only just sink when baited with a single grain of corn. I call these counterbalanced hooks, and I use them for summer fishing in sizes 6 to 10. I have actually watched suspicious chub fanning the gravel vigorously with their fins, and any grain of corn that remained anchored to the bottom was left well alone. The counterbalanced tackle will lift off the gravel with the undercurrent, just as the free offerings do, and is then taken with confidence.

For all of the above fishing, I like to keep the tackle as simple as possible, and the ideal presentation is free-lining, which is no problem with large baits at short range if the current is negligible. Where there is more flow, I will add a swan shot or two, particularly if I am fishing particles. One thing I do recommend is keeping the line from bait to rod fairly slack after casting. This helps to keep the line at the business end on the bottom, where it is less likely to scare the fish, and it also helps to minimize the major problem with this type of fishing, which is false bites, caused by the chub milling around and continually swimming into the line. For this reason, it is best to ignore all the small lifts and trembles on the line, and strike only when the bow in the line straightens completely.

The Swimfeeder

The other approach, of course, is with the swimfeeder, either feeding maggots in the traditional manner or still fishing hemp, in a feeder with the holes opened out sufficiently to allow the hemp to escape easily, either by the action of the current or on the retrieve. The only time I use the feeder for chubbing is where I want to fish hemp in a swim where perhaps the range does not allow accurate introduction by dropper. I never fish the swimfeeder with maggots as feed for chub as I much prefer all the other alternatives, although the large numbers of chub I have taken on the method while barbel fishing demonstrates its efficiency. The biggest drawback I find with heavy maggot feeding, is that the rivers where it would most be used, such as the Dorset Stour, are infested with bootlace eels in the summer months. There are not many things in angling that make me lose my cool, but catching bootlaces on chub and barbel baits is one of them!

WINTER CHUBBING

Streamy Rivers

Location of the Fish

To my mind, the most pleasurable chub fishing of all is fishing a relatively shallow, moderately paced river in the winter months. A winding stream of constantly changing character provides such an endless variety of swims that I can never tire of it.

The winter river is a very different proposition from that of the summer, and any angler who has not had the chance to study the water in the early part of the season, when the water is low and clear, is at an immediate disadvantage. I say that because it is certainly true that chub, like other river species, do not like to wander far from their normal summer haunts, unless forced to do so by prevailing water or weather conditions. It follows that, having found chub in the summer, those same areas are the starting points for a winter campaign.

The reality is, however, that most anglers who fish for chub only do so in the winter, when the fish are undoubtedly at their best. Location of the fish is then either from knowing a stretch very well, by trial and error or by assessing likely areas by reading the current variables. Most underwater features give a clue as to their nature and extent by creating recognizable surface features, and once we have learned to interpret these we are half-way towards consistent chub catching.

If the river you are fishing has many trees and bushes along its banks, then there are going to be a number of swims that are very obvious chub-holding areas. Overhanging foliage of any kind is an attraction, as are rubbish rafts created around trailing branches or fallen trees. Lines of bank-side brambles are reliable areas, as what often happens is that undercuts are created, the topsoil being held in place by the interlaced bramble roots. Provided that the current speed and depth of water is to the chubs' liking, these features will hold chub at all times, and will always be bankers for a few fish. It is a mistake, however, to fish such swims exclusively, because there will always be many more fish in the open swims than ever live under rafts. By ignoring these, or never making an attempt to find out more about them, you are passing up a lot of fun. Some rivers, of course, and the Wensum and Dorset Stour are obvious examples, have very few over-hanging foliage-type swims, and you either learn how to read the river or you catch very few chub.

So how do we go about it? The first thing you have to do is look at the water surface, perhaps a little more intently than you have in the past. Once you really start to study it, many features become apparent that are not so obvious on first impression. What looks a uniform stretch, at first glance apparently of constant flow from bank to bank, will soon be seen to be anything but that; it is the variation of surface characteristics that gives us the vital information we need about depth, bottom composition and contours, and flow rates. The most obvious initial information we glean is the strength and direction of the current, and the positions of any change in these. By studying a particular section for a while, it is easy to establish what the surface water is doing. Is it constantly smooth or constantly rippled? Is it boiling, or does it appear fragmented, with odd smooth bits and odd rippled bits? Or is there a constant or intermittent boil in one spot?

Creases

If we take the current direction to start with, the most obvious feature is a sudden change in the course of the main flow, which creates a division between fast and slower water, a division I know as a crease. Many things can cause a crease: a bend in the river, an underwater gravel bank or bank-side protrusion such as a weed bed, a tree stump or a clay bank. Whatever the reason, these crease swims are favoured chub-holding areas, providing the other features are to their liking. Under normal conditions, the chub like to hold on the edge of such a crease, and allow the main current to bring food down to them, which they can then intercept from the comparative comfort of a more gentle flow.

A similar effect is seen when the main flow passes small bays, or the mouths of small inlets of various kinds. On my local Warwickshire Leam, which is a marvellous chub river, the water-meadows on various sections consist of pools connected by narrow faster runs, and these pools feature many creases. The bait presentation you need to achieve normally is one in which the bait is cast to land in the faster flow, and then rolls round to hold right on the junction. The exception to this is often in higher water or colder conditions, when the chub are not feeding so avidly or they are seeking more shelter, and they will often be found more away from the main stream, further into the slacker water itself. By adjusting the weight of the leger link, the terminal rig can be made to roll as far into the slack as you think appropriate.

We can now take this a stage further. Having established areas where we feel the current strength to be suitable, it is time to study the characteristics of the water surface to give us a clue as to what is going on underneath. If the water is constantly smooth, we have almost certainly located a reliable winter chub swim, as this indicates a clean even bottom, free of large irregularities, and a reasonable depth of water. The same swim, of much less depth, or one in which the bottom consists of large stones, will have a constantly rippled surface.

While I am on the subject of swims with a rippled surface, many rivers have long stretches of extreme shallows, and these exhibit constantly broken water. If you walk the length of a section like this and study the surface very carefully, you will notice now and again small areas that appear much smoother than the rest. These are deeper holes in the bed. In winter conditions, such depressions in the midst of shallow water will often hold numbers of chub.

Weed Beds

Underwater weed beds provide many interesting features, and these are the ones that confuse anglers most when they first embark on a course of watercraft. If you come to a stretch where there are smooth areas of water, interspersed with either constantly or intermittently broken areas; or the current appears to keep changing direction, the main flow splits into two or more separate flows, or the water boils in places, you can be sure that weed beds are responsible. Rush beds usually betray their presence by occasional stems breaking surface, and the immediate downstream area of a dead rush bed is an extremely reliable chub-holding area. The rushes have the effect of holding back and splitting the flow, creating a lee of much slacker water behind.

When there are bottom cabbage patches, or beds of weed such as ranunculus, the effect on the surface is very distinctive, with smooth areas of flow dotted amongst the ripple. These stretches usually confuse the novice most, but in actual fact they are very easy to read. All you have to remember is that the smooth areas indicate a clean bottom between the weed, and these areas are obviously where the baits should be placed. If there is a stretch of this type, but one in which certain areas are intermittently boily, then streamer weed is probably responsible. Chub love to hide under the trailing fronds, so a bait positioned so that it lands on a clean bottom, and can then be persuaded to roll under the fronds, achieves a perfect and deadly presentation.

Techniques

For nearly all my chub fishing, I use a simple swan-shot link leger, using 6-pound line and a size 6 Au Lion d'Or hook. The tail length will vary from an inch to several feet, depending on the bait and the presentation I am trying to achieve. My favourite winter approach to chubbing is definitely with legered bread crust, except in coloured water, when I prefer meat,

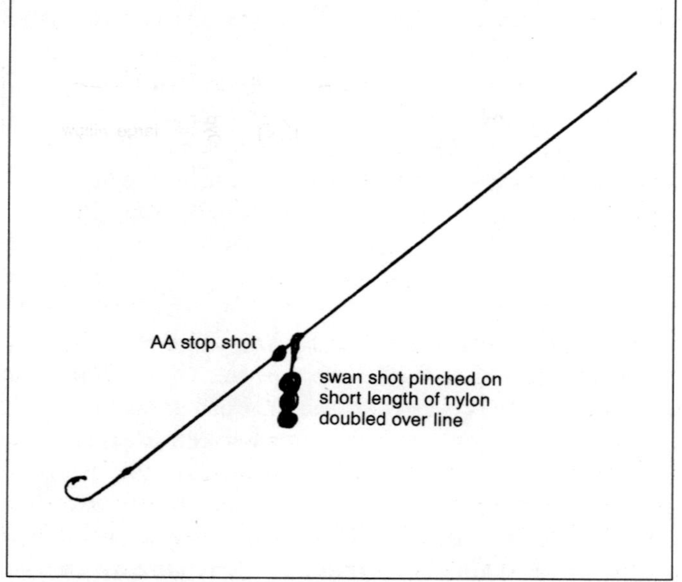

Swan-shot leger.

cheese or lobworms. Rarely will I use a hooklength of more than six inches when fishing crust.

Having stated that this simple terminal rig serves almost all my chub-fishing situations, it is clear that it is not the rig that is important for consistent catches, but the way in which it is adapted for use in varying circumstances. A winter chub swim may require several amendments in bait presentation to yield its maximum potential, and this is best explained by reference to real life situations. Because of that, I will go through part of a presentation I gave at the 1988 NASA conference, and I hope many of the simple but vitally important principles will become clear.

A Cherwell Swim

The drawing illustrates a Cherwell swim. This swim contains many interesting features over forty yards, and chub could be stationed in several areas. First of all, we have the clay bank protrusion creating a mid-

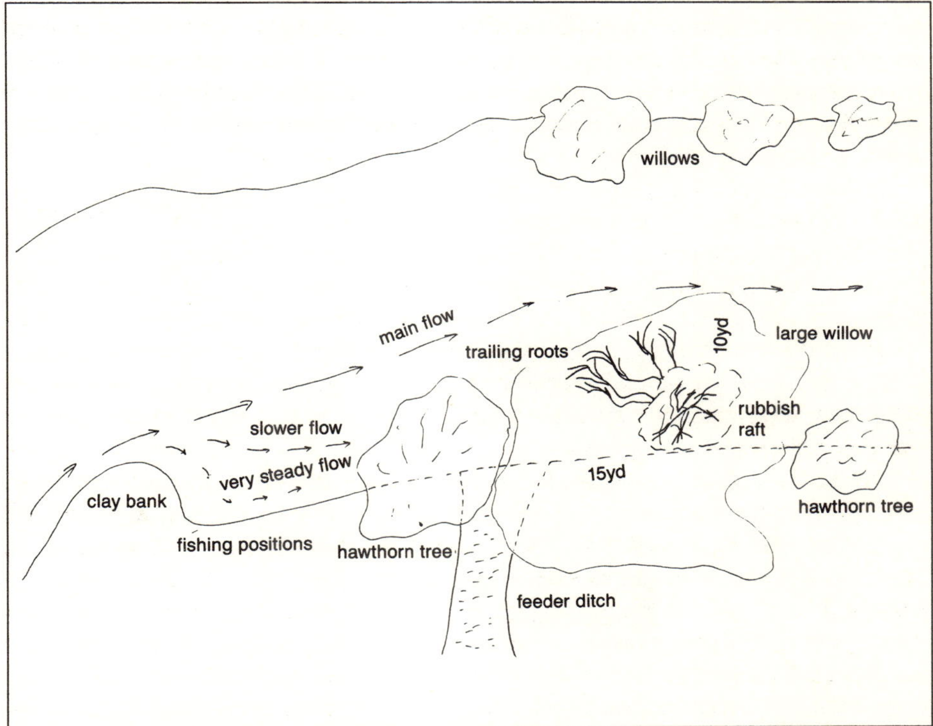

A Cherwell Swim.

stream junction of fast and slower water, or crease. Chub will be found along this crease, their exact position depending on weather and water conditions. Further downstream, we have a small hawthorn overhanging the very steady water, and this will be another reliable area, particularly when the river is higher or colder than normal, when the fish seek out the shelter from the main stream. Then we have the major feature of the swim: the big willows, whose branches span some twenty-five yards, and overhang the river to midstream. Under the willows, about fifteen yards down from the upstream extremity of the branches, is a large raft of rubbish, which has accumulated around trailing willow branches. Under this raft, on the river bed, is a tangle of fallen branches which extend, as shown, to nearly midstream, and this timber is an obvious attractant for big chub.

My first approach to this swim, in normal winter conditions, is to fish progressively down the crease with legered crust baits, introducing mashed bread feed along the line I judge the fish to be lying. With the water at normal height and flow, a three swan-shot link sees the terminal rig settle right at the junction of fast and slow water, after being cast out initially to land in the faster flow, and then rolled round naturally. The crease extends right to the outer extremity of the willow branches. The furthest downstream that can be fished along the crease is obviously determined by the sunken snags, and in fact a deadly presentation is to leger a bait hard against these snags.

Making the bait roll round to fish more into the steadier flow is accomplished by the simple expedient of taking one shot off the link, thereby making the rig more buoyant for a given size of bait. I can then fish down a different line, but the lighter the link becomes for increased bait movement, the more chance there is of the bait actually climbing over the snags under the willow and becoming hung up. When I am rolling a bait round from midstream, therefore, the very light link is reserved for searching the near bank areas only, as far down as the downstream edge of the hawthorn bush.

Obviously, an area that screams chub is that immediately under the raft. The simple, and normal, presentation of rolling a bait under the rubbish from midstream is not possible because of the snags; placing a bait in position under the trees is also impossible because the deep feeder ditch makes access impossible, and so a different approach is required. How I overcome the problem is to put on bigger than average crust bait, using a single AAA as weight. I then simply lower the bait adjacent to the upstream edge of the hawthorn, and pay out line as it drifts downstream, sinking very slowly as it goes. I want a sinking rate to make it just hit bottom as it arrives under the raft, when I then close the bail arm. When I am fishing this swim, or swims like it, I will go upstream and experiment with different-sized baits, to calculate how many yards of river it takes to sink. It really is ridiculously simple, and at the same time you would be hard pressed to imagine a more natural presentation.

Fishing Rafts

When you are fishing more orthodox rafts, which are more accessible, it can still pay to adopt a progressive approach to the fishing, rather than simply plonking a bait immediately under the rubbish and waiting. Most good raft swims contain numbers of chub and, if you are hoping to tempt a specimen, the approach just mentioned is very unselective. If all the chub are condensed in a tight area and you drop a bait among them, the chances are that a small fish will be most likely to take it first, thereby scaring every other chub in the swim. I try to split up the fish so that my chances of taking the biggest fish are maximized.

My first approach is to bait up well upstream of the raft so that the fish are encouraged to move out from the cover and swim upstream to investigate the source of the food. Being less cautious, the smaller fish will be the first to do this. I will sit perhaps twenty yards or so above the raft, fishing down to just above the rubbish, and in this way hopefully will take a chub or two, which I return well away from the swim. Each small fish removed will increase the chance of the biggest fish under the raft taking my bait, if in fact there is a big one there in the first place. A ploy I adopt while fishing the water above the raft, is to creep down occasionally and introduce some heavier feed under the raft itself. The idea is this: the loose feed I am introducing should be drawing the smaller fish away, but eventually it will also draw the bigger fish out as well, and I try to prevent this by putting the feed under the rubbish. I want to keep the bigger chub segregated, if possible.

Once I feel I have exhausted the possibilities above the raft, I will try one more little dodge to make my chances of a big chub as high as possible. If the geography of the swim allows, I will go below the raft and leger upstream under the downstream edge of the swim. The reasons are similar to those for starting well above the swim. When placing the heavier feed under the raft, some of it will obviously drift down, and fish may follow it. Again, the smaller fish present will be most likely to do this, and therefore fishing the tail of the swim first could well remove one or two of those. Having fished both above and below the swim to start with, I am now confident that any really big fish present will have little competition from his smaller brethren, when I eventually place a bait in the hot spot under the rubbish. The numbers of big chub both Trefor West and I have caught using this technique have been tremendous. What is more, where two fish from under a raft swim used to be the most we would get before spooking the others, it is now quite common for us to catch five or six. It is another simple but very effective idea.

Open Swims

For the more open swims, the fishing technique using the link leger, experimenting with different link weights to achieve varying bait presentation, has already been dealt with in the foregoing paragraphs, and requires little elaboration. What I would point out, however, is how important it is to be aware how chub react to changing water and weather conditions. If, for instance, a crease swim is always fished with a three-shot link so that the bait fishes the junction of the flows, that may not be effective if there has been a sudden cold snap. You may arrive to find the river the same height and flow, but fishing on the crease produces nothing. A change to a single swan may see you start catching again, as the chub may well have become much more lethargic with the lowering of the water temperature, and consequently moved into much slacker water. A similar situation can arise with high water conditions. Because of increased flow rates, the chub may have moved much closer in to the bank, and that is where a bait has to be presented.

Upstream Legering

Certain swims will demand an upstream presentation, and upstream legering allows us perhaps the most delicate bait presentation of all. One of my favourite swims for upstreaming is the vee of quiet water created immediately downstream of a midriver rush bed. In this type of swim, it is usual to be fishing over a faster current than that in which the bait is to settle, and so it pays to use slightly more weight on the link than normal, and also to hold the rod point high to keep as much line off the water as possible. The technique is to use a fairly soft quivertip, I use a Drennan 2-ounce version, and cast upstream so that the bait lands in the quiet water just below the dead rushes. The link weight should be such that you can put a respectable bend into the tip without dislodging the terminal rig. With the tackle balanced in that manner, the slightest pull on the bait will dislodge the link, and the line falls slack, resulting in an unmissable spring back on the tip. Because of the delicate balance, it is best to fish off a rest, rather than holding the rod, as I invariably do when fishing downstream. The major problem with upstream legering is the one of false bites. If there is any rubbish or cut weed coming down, upstream legering can become very trying, and even impossible if the problem is very bad. You can overcome it to a certain extent by overloading the terminal rig so that it requires a stronger pull to dislodge the tackle. If you go too far with this, however, you will get savage pulls on the rod top rather than slack line bites. This will result in missing many of the bites, and rather destroys the reason for fishing upstream in the first place.

Mentioning missed bites is a good cue to say that upstream legering is a very valuable technique to practise for those occasions when missed bites to a normal downstream presentation become a problem. On many heavily fished waters, even with quivertips, chub can give frustratingly snatchy pulls that are repeatedly missed. Throop is the best example I know of where this is a common problem. A switch to upstreaming is often the only alteration in approach required. Because the method depends on the creation of slack line by the pull of the fish, the chub is encouraged to hang on to the bait for that vital few extra moments. It never ceases to amaze me how I can miss bite after bite, simply move my chair a few yards downstream, and, still fishing the same spot, subsequently connect with every single indication.

Baits and Feeding Techniques

The list of things that chub will eat with relish is almost endless, and I do not believe that there is one single bait that is a more attractive food to the chub than any other. If there is a fish lying under a tree in the Cherwell it will just as happily take bread, meat, cheese or anything else you care to name, provided of course that he has not learned from bitter experience to be wary of a particular food item.

Because of this, my choice of winter chub bait is governed by a factor other than the actual bait itself. I believe it is far more important how the characteristics and texture of the chosen bait affect the bait presentation, rather than what the bait actually consists of. The more naturally a bait can be introduced into a chub's field of vision, the more effective is that bait likely to be.

The baits I use for my winter chubbing are bread flake, bread crust, luncheon meat, cheese paste and lobworms. In their fish catching properties, I believe that all those baits are the equal of one another. It is the bait presentation properties that have led me to the conclusion that bread crust is the best winter chub bait of them all. As the bait is naturally buoyant, adjustments in bait size and link weight can give us a floating bait or one that is well anchored, and fast- or slow-sinking variations to meet particular circumstances. I don't think I have ever come across a winter chub swim where link-legered bread crust could not be presented naturally, by relative adjustment to the buoyancy of the terminal rig.

Obviously, the clearer the water, the more vital it is that the bait presentation be natural, and I believe this is one of the main reasons why baits such as cheese, meat and lobs come more into their own in coloured water, or indeed at night. In coloured water especially, the chub rely more and more on their sense of smell to locate food, and these more static baits give the fish something to home in on. Delicate bait presentation is therefore less important in these conditions.

Under normal winter conditions in the day, however, the way you present your bait can make all the difference between success and failure. When I am using crust for chubbing, I do not usually allow it to lie still for long, and so it is important that the right kind of bread is bought. You want to avoid that prepacked plastic rubbish. The only bread I use is an unsliced home-baked loaf, the kind with the thick brown crust all round. When you buy these loaves fresh, the crust is often crisp and brittle, and as such it is obviously useless for fishing. What I do is wrap it tightly in a polythene bag to make it sweat a little, and leave it for at least twenty-four hours before fishing with it. You then find that the brittle crust has become nicely tough and pliable, allowing you to fish a moving bait with absolute confidence. As I have said earlier, it is not so much the crust itself but its natural buoyancy that makes it such an effective bait. Once we appreciate that, many interesting variations can be made on the basic method, which become more and more important as the chub become more wary of the orthodox baits.

For instance, crust can be smeared in all kinds of pastes to give variety, and in the last few seasons I have had some good catches on crust covered in soft cheese spread, potted meat pastes of various kinds, honey, yeast extract, golden syrup and condensed milk. Perhaps even better nowadays, because they are not so messy, are liquid carp-bait flavourings. There is no limit to how far we can go in this direction.

Loose Feeding

A vital component of successful winter chubbing is loose feeding, which can make all the difference between a big bag of fish or just an occasional bite. Obviously, the amount of feed to use depends upon the conditions. If it is very cold, for instance, you need to feed much more sparingly than if the water temperature is higher, and therefore the chub much more active. If I am fishing crust, then I will feed with mashed bread or squeezed dry breadcrumbs, supplemented by occasional flake samples. If I want the loose feed to sink rapidly, which could be dictated by the water conditions or by the swim fished, then I will plump for well-mashed bread. If the conditions are so good that I think the chub will be actively foraging around, then I will often use an occasional handful of dry breadcrumbs, tightly squeezed. On hitting the water, the crumb disperses almost instantly, the particles sinking very slowly. Obviously, you would not use this ploy if you were trying to keep chub in a small tight area, but if you are fishing a long steady glide for instance, then it is an excellent way of continually attracting new fish into the swim.

When I am using this method of feeding, I will often couple it with a much longer tail length than normal. My usual approach would be to use a tail of about two to three inches for legered crust, going down to perhaps an inch if the water is very cold. But when I am using dry breadcrumb feed, I will often use tails of between eight and twelve inches. The slow-sinking feed and the hookbait waving about well off bottom often prove an irresistible combination.

Pre-baiting

I consider one of the most important aspects of winter chubbing to be pre-baiting swims. Obviously, on some waters, particularly at the weekends, there will be a lot of anglers about, and pre-baiting will not really be viable. But if you have got the water to yourself, or you can find a stretch that doesn't get too much attention, you should try my method. When I arrive, the first thing I do is put two or three large handfuls of mashed bread into the first swim I intend fishing. Then, before I even set my tackle up, I will walk downstream and put bait into another five swims I fancy. The kind of swims I bait will be ones where the current is such that it will allow the bait to settle in an area. Obviously, this is the area where the hookbait will eventually be placed. When I have finished fishing the first swim and move down to the second, I will again walk down and put another handful of bread into the remaining four swims before my first cast. Also, I will then pre-bait one more new swim. In this way, I always have five swims waiting for me that have been primed.

On any day's fishing, there will be one or two swims that strike me as the ones most likely to produce a really big chub. During the course of the day, I will visit them periodically, perhaps taking the odd chub from them and keeping the bait topped up. What I try to do is have one or two bankers, swims that I will concentrate on in the evening and into the dark.

Trotting

The fact that most of my winter chubbing time is spent actively searching long stretches of the smaller rivers, means that I do not do as much float trotting as perhaps I should. That superb float angler, John Wilson, has shown how effective a method it can be for catching large numbers of chub. On any one day's chubbing, most of the swims I fish simply would not lend themselves to the float. The ideal way, of course, would be to take two rods with me, one rigged up for legering and one for trotting, but as I try to keep the gear to a minimum, that is something I do very rarely. As with any form of angling, the more tackle you have to lug around, the less inclined you are to keep on the move.

Having said all that, I have been doing more trotting for chub over the last couple of winters, taking the trouble to change over to the float when the right swim presents itself. It makes a pleasant change, and is great fun. The type of swim I am looking for is a nice steady glide, preferably adjacent to a near-bank slacker area, or alongside near-bank rushes. Also good are deep uniform glides under high banks or lines of bushes, or steady runs that suddenly shelve up to much shallower water.

Steady glides alongside slack areas or rushes are my favourites, as they allow periodic variation of approach from trotting to laying on – stret pegging as it used to be called. Quite simply, push the float up so that it is overdepth, and then place the rod on a rest after casting in. The float will swing round on the tight line to settle the bait in the steadier water under the near bank. By increasing the amount of line out, the entire run can obviously be covered in this way. The amount you have to push the float up from its trotting setting will depend on the current speed and the depth of water, and will usually need a little trial and error before you get it right. Set it too shallow and the action of the current will continually drag it under. During a trotting session, reverting to such laying on tactics periodically is useful for two reasons. Firstly, it gives your trotting arm a rest, and secondly, it often sorts out some of the bigger fish.

Near-bank glides under steep banks, and particularly where there are bank-side bushes overhanging slightly, frequently contain undercuts, and trotting tactics hard against the near bank, holding back occasionally to allow the float to search upwards and inwards in these undercuts, often produces a big fish. Obviously, holding back the float now and again in any trotting swim is a well-known ploy in chubbing, and one which is very effective. It's the old induced bite principle again. This approach is particularly appropriate when fishing a swim with shelving gravel at its downstream extremity.

For chub trotting, I usually revert to 4-pound main line, and the float is a balsa or large stick, taking up to three swan shot. I usually fish with the shots bunched about a foot from the hook, normally a size 6 or 8 baited with bread flake. As with progressively legering long glides, regular baiting with mashed bread or squeezed breadcrumbs is effective in keeping the fish foraging around. One important feature of trotting is that it pays to grease the line above the float, to prevent it sinking, thereby impeding the float's progress and adversely affecting the bait presentation. The chub do not take kindly to a large float dragging across the flow and creating a wake.

The float is set to just clear bottom in the shallowest part of the swim, and this is simply achieved by noting where the float drags on the first few trots down. Obviously, if there are large depth variations, the float will be fishing a long way off bottom in certain areas. Although this does not matter that much, as chub will rise a long way to intercept a bait, it has to be said that a swim with extreme depth variations is not an ideal trotting swim. If it contains any number of chub, they are better sought by leger tactics.

The Dragging Float

One method of float trotting that I have seen Trefor West use with devastating effect on the Stour, but which I must admit I am very unpractised at myself, is the use of the dragging float technique. This is

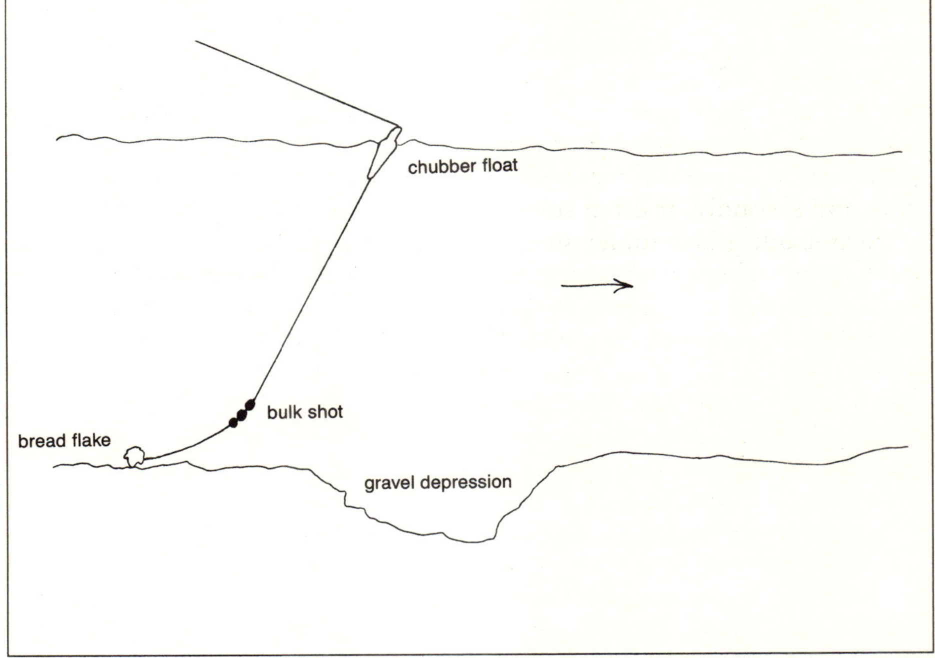

Trotting over depth.

only really viable where the bottom is clean, with no weed stalks to halt the bait's progress. Fine, clean gravel is the only bottom where I can achieve any kind of reasonable presentation. The method is deadly where there is a depression in an otherwise smooth and uniform gravelly run. With the float set overdepth, it is allowed to progress normally down the swim, towing the bait behind it. As it reaches the onset of the depression, the float is then held back hard until the bait catches up, and then drops into the hollow, searching it with a pendulum-type motion and swinging up again at the downstream end. It is very easy to explain in theory, but very difficult to get right in practice. If you can master the technique, however, bearing in mind that a clean river bed is essential, it can be deadly.

6

Perch

BIG PERCH FROM SMALL STREAMS

Location

Let us first look at some of the basic fundamentals of big perch location in small rivers and streams. As with any river fish, preliminary swim location is best carried out in midsummer when the river is low and clear. A day at this time of the year spent walking the banks making notes, and even getting in the river with swimming trunks, is invaluable. It does not take too long to establish where the deeper, steadier stretches are, what type of bottom exists, where there are any bank undercuts, and so on. You may come to a lily bed that looks uniform from bank to bank, but by getting in

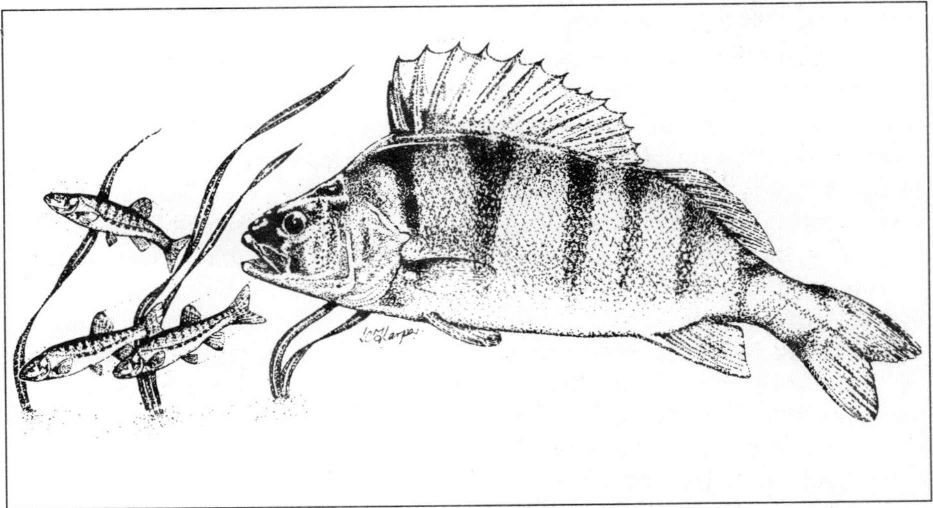

Perch chasing minnows.

the river and wading through the lilies, you may discover a depression. Such depressions under lilies should be graphed, as they have produced very good fish for me over the years.

The same comments apply to bulrush beds, which are without doubt my favourite swims for summer perching. For this type of swim, the ideal set-up is a fairly extensive bed of bulrushes over gravel, where the depth of water is slightly greater than the average for the river, and the current speed steady. While long, uniformly deep and steady stretches do produce big perch, I much prefer a smaller rushy area located at the edge of the main flow, and hopefully fairly close to gravel shallows. The reasons for this will become obvious later. Bulrush beds are not to be confused with beds of giant reedmace, the plants with those brown sausage-like heads. Reedmace thrives in silty mud, but I am looking for clean gravel, in which proper bulrushes grow. When you think about a bed of rushes, and the colouration of a perch, you can well imagine how a perch lying amongst the stems will be well nigh invisible to its prey. I am convinced that this is a frequently used tactic by big perch, borne out by the fact that the closer to the rush stems you fish a bait, the more bites you get.

The best summer perch swim I ever fished contained many of the features I now look for when searching new areas. It was on the Claydon Brook before the last dredging in the early seventies which, together with the perch disease, devastated the river as a perch fishery. The swim lay downstream of a very shallow gravelly area, which the cattle used for drinking. Under the near bank, the river deepened quite rapidly to about five feet maximum, and the main current was concentrated under this bank. Because of the sudden depth increase, the current speed was quite steady. At about a third of the way across the stream, the bottom started to shelve up at the commencement of a thick bed of bulrushes and, beyond the rushes, the water was about three feet deep, nearly slack and heavily overgrown with surface lily pads. About ten yards downstream of the end of the gravelly shallows, the near bank was quite steeply undercut for a further ten yards, before the commencement of an impenetrable blackthorn thicket some fifteen yards long along the near bank. The undercut continued under the blackthorns, the depth remaining fairly constant until the downstream extremity of the bushes, where the river again shallowed and was heavily overgrown with cabbages. From the commencement of the swim at the shallows to the downstream end of the blackthorns was one long perch swim, the perch being located at different points along its length, depending on conditions. The lessons I learned in many happy hours fishing that swim have stood me in good stead ever since.

Let us have a look at the various features of this swim in more detail and examine how I go about fishing them, taking first of all those midriver rushes, which would be my first choice under normal summer conditions. I normally start off at first light, laying on a large lobworm under a simple porcupine quill, fishing as close to the rushes as possible. Generally speaking, if a perch is there at first light it will take the bait almost immediately. If, therefore, no bite is forth coming in about ten minutes, I wind in and place the bait further down the rushes. Depending on events, I will work my way down the rush bed this way. If a perch is landed, the next cast will go back into exactly the same spot. I have had up to four good perch in quick succession from one small area.

Baits and Presentation

Generally speaking, a big perch from such a swim on an early summer morning will take a large lobworm without hesitation, and I've found few occasions when this is not the case. Occasionally, however, a lob will be continually tweaked without being taken properly, and this is when a twitched lobworm will induce a bold bite. Failing that, a change to lob tail only or to a redworm on a size 12 will do the trick. If perch are about, it is very rarely that a layed-on lobworm or redworm will not produce sport but, now and again, the fish will not touch a bottom bait. In these circumstances, I may find that I need to move the float down a few inches so that the bait is trotting alongside the rushes just off bottom, or I may have to fish the bait midwater.

If the fish are being particularly difficult, fishing the float self-cocking and baiting with air-injected lob will tempt the occasional big fish. If a lob is injected with sufficient air so that it floats, and then fished under a self-cocking float, using a small counterbalance shot so that it sinks very slowly, you have achieved a perfectly natural presentation that can be deadly. Of course, on those occasions when the perch prefer an off-bottom bait, float-fished minnows are an obvious and very effective alternative. Strangely, I have found minnows fished on the bottom, either alive or dead, to be not as effective as lobworms for big perch. I once spent two whole summers exclusively fishing for small-stream perch, and in that time fished minnows and lobs on alternate weeks. At the end of that period, the average size of fish taken on lobs was considerably higher than that on minnows.

After the first three hours or so of daylight in the summer, the chances of a big perch in the more open water adjacent to the rushes recede rapidly, and it is now time to search for them in more shaded areas. This is especially true on bright mornings, as perch show a marked dislike of strong light. An overcast morning can see the active feeding spell prolonged, and I have known big perch feed steadily until lunchtime if the day is particularly dark and dismal. This, however, is rare in open swims, and you have usually had the best of it after two or three hours of daylight. In very hot and settled conditions, with the water-level very low and clear, and the sky blue, I have known plenty of occasions when perch sport was finished for the day an hour after daybreak.

In shaded areas, however, there is still the chance of an occasional big fish, and good places to try now are under extensive beds of lily pads, under rubbish rafts, around tree roots, where overhanging foliage abounds, and right amongst dense rushes. To go back to the swim I am discussing, many years of fishing it convinced me that the perch slowly retreated into the rush bed as the light intensity increased, to come out eventually on the other side into the shade of the lily pads. The lower the water level, and the sunnier and brighter the morning, the faster this process occurred. I proved this theory sound on many occasions. What I would do was fish the rush bed as described, and when sport had tailed off I would cross the river shallows and fish under the lily pads from the opposite bank. It was vital that the bait was right under the pads, and I used to either free-line a lobworm, dropping the bait on top of a pad and then inching it off the edge or, better still, fish a lob under a small self-cocking float attached both ends by valve rubber to prevent snagging. By greasing the line above the float, I ensured that the only sunken line in the water was the three feet between float and bait. Allowing line from float to rod top to sink between a myriad of lily pads is inviting lost fish. Obviously, you can do the same thing when free-lining, greasing all but the last few feet of line.

However, there is a more important reason why I go to more trouble to position a float tackle in such a situation, and that is the timing of the strike at a bite from a big perch is critical. Very commonly, the bite on a bait such as a lobworm or minnow can be a protracted affair, with the float dipping and bobbing for several minutes, before finally tilting and sliding away. With free-lining, there is a strong temptation to strike prematurely at all the preliminary lifts and twitches, resulting in either the fish being missed completely or, far worse, the fish being pricked and lost. In this respect, I am in accord with writers on river perch from previous generations. Pulling out of a big perch in a confined swim is guaranteed to reduce drastically your chances of further sport in the vicinity.

Having searched perhaps three or four areas under the pads, it would now be time to spend the last couple of hours of the morning fishing the dark water under the overhanging blackthorns at the tail end of the swim. In normal or below normal summer levels, the swim is best fished from the opposite bank, casting a bait across right under the trailing branches. If the current was particularly sluggish, I would lay on, but usually I fished a simple free-lined lob, with the addition of one or two swan shot, depending on current speed. Fishing in this style, for the reasons stated earlier, I leave a large slack loop of line and sit a little back from the rod to avoid the temptation of striking too early. Only when the slack has been taken do I hit it. Strangely, perhaps, it is very rare in my experience for a big perch to be deeply hooked, although as we all know it is a common problem with their more suicidal junior colleagues.

Autumn and Winter Fishing

As the season progresses, and summer merges into autumn, the chances of good fish throughout the day are improved. Having said that, I have never had any success with big perch in late afternoon, at dusk or at night, although I have often tried. This seems to be true of all waters. Through all the thousands of hours I've sat on gravel pits fishing lobs for tench and bream, I have never once taken a perch in the dark hours. I do not doubt that it happens, but I would lay odds on its being a very rare occurrence.

Without a doubt, the rise in water-level, increased colour and current speed, during late autumn and winter, provide the conditions necessary for a large bag of good perch, if they can be found. As the season progresses, the perch form tighter shoals, and it is often a case of all or nothing. During the summer, I am always confident of a fish or two, but the autumn to winter period is a very different proposition. Blanks are much more common, but if you do find the fish, a red letter day can result.

I have always found the transition period from autumn to winter perhaps the most difficult time of all for catching big perch consistently. With the river bed often fouled by decaying vegetation, bottom fishing is often a waste of time, and the perch tend to be more than usually nomadic. Under these conditions, I am sure that the bigger fish are better sought with small trotted livebaits presented well off bottom. This is also the time of the year when spinning can come into its own, not only as a method of catching perch, but also as a very effective way of locating them. While by no stretch of the imagination could I be described as an authority on spinning, I have done enough spinning for small river perch to know that it is usually the first cast to a new area that produces a take, indicating to me that, if perch are present, one of them will attack the lure as soon as it sees it. Conversely, two or three retrieves along the same path without a take is a good indication that no perch are there, and it's time to move on.

In autumn perch fishing then, spinning can be a method of locating the shoals quickly. You can then, depending on your temperament, either continue spinning for them or revert to bait fishing methods. Almost always, I would opt for the latter, not because I consider spinning an inferior method in any way, but simply because I enjoy bait fishing more.

After the first floods have shifted most of the rubbish, and the river settles down into its winter trim, I have found the perch more or less in the areas in which they were resident in the summer. The critical factor, however, is current speed. Big perch do not like strong flows, and once they begin to feel uncomfortable in their normal haunts, they search out the quieter water. Like chub, however, they seem to move only as far as they have to, and so in conditions of higher water and sharper current, it pays to look for them first in the nearest available gentle flow to the normal swim. This could be a bay off the main current, a slack caused by a protruding bank-side obstruction, creating a crease-type swim, an undercut vertical bank, a river-bed depression, the mouth of a feeder stream or backwater, and so on.

Fishing Undercuts

For winter fishing, one of my favourite types of swim is the undercut vertical bank. Where the undercut is at all pronounced, you have an area which will be particularly favoured in high water or even semi-flood conditions, when the perch often pack tightly in such places. It follows that the right combination of conditions can often lead to red letter days in swims of this type. In the winter, such swims will always hold one or two resident perch under all conditions, but the higher the water becomes, the more perch will pack under there. A stage is reached, however, when increasing flow and volume of water begins to create substantial back eddies in the undercut, and turbulence results. At this stage, the perch move out.

There are several very effective methods of fishing undercuts, the one used on any particular day depending upon prevailing conditions and the mood of the fish. At, or slightly above, normal winter level, my favourite method is float fishing, with stick or light Avon, using lobs fished a couple of feet overdepth. Depending on the flow, I may fish the float self-cocking, but I always want at least two feet from the bottom shot to the bait. The float is then allowed to trot along the near bank, being held back hard periodically so that the bait swings upwards and inwards, and searches under the undercut. If you haven't tried this method of fishing, you are missing a treat, for it can be deadly.

The Rolling Leger

As I prefer to float fish for perch whenever possible, because of their dislike of resistance, and the frequent difficulty of timing the strike correctly. In these undercut swims, however, increasing height and flow render trotting tactics less and less viable, until the float becomes a positive handicap. Then is the time to use a light rolling leger, preferably in conjunction with a very flexible quivertip to minimize the amount of resistance to a biting perch. It is very important with swims of this type that the terminal rig is light enough to be washed right into the undercut, rather than holding in the faster current. A soft quivertip is a good indicator of when the weight is about right. When the bait is dropped into the main current, the force of the water will put a large deflection in the tip. If the rig is too heavy to roll under the undercut, this deflection will stay constant. If, however, the tackle fishes as intended and settles in the quieter, more sheltered water, the tip will ease back so that you are fishing very sensitively. Until you have

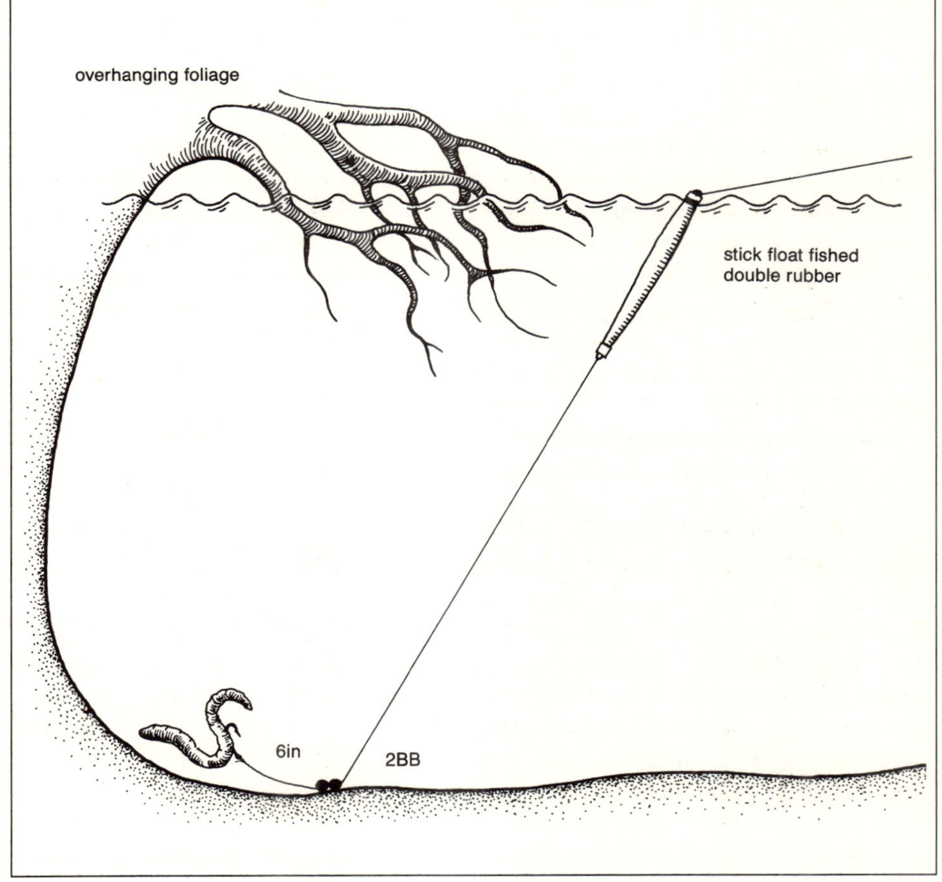

Simple laying-on rig.

fished in this manner a few times, you'll be surprised how little lead is required, even when the current appears far too fierce.

The Paternoster

Under certain conditions, the best method of approach is the good old paternoster. This would be my choice if I wished to present a bait mid-water in a situation where the use of a moving trotted bait was not viable for whatever reason. There may be just that bit too much flow for an efficient presentation, or the general geography of the swim may dictate that the only way of presenting a bait under a float is by static means, which the paternoster provides. It is also a useful alternative to try when, despite fishing as sensitively as possible, you continually miss bites on legered baits.

Backwaters

When water-levels are high with strong currents, this is the time when backwaters, offshoots, and feeder streams really come into their own as far as specimen perch are concerned. This is especially true of quiet back-waters, which may have a sluggish flow even when the main river is raging through. A backwater on my favourite stretch of the Claydon Brook, which under normal conditions was stagnant and contained little of note, was ideal under high water conditions. As it then had a steady current, as opposed to the heavy flow on the main river, big fish of all species moved into the sanctuary it provided. Big perch in particular found it to their liking, and many of my biggest fish came from it in the winter months.

BIG PERCH FROM POOLS, RESERVOIRS AND GRAVEL PITS

A still unfulfilled ambition is a perch of over four pounds. If ever I decide upon a determined campaign to put that right, there is no doubt whatever about the type of water I would choose. It would be a deep clay pit of fairly small acreage, surrounded either by cliffs or trees to keep it sheltered from extreme winds. Unquestionably, big perch have an affinity for such waters, and if you study the angling reports carefully, you will be able to verify for yourself the truth of that statement. How often have you read of the young lad taking the four pounder from a deep farm pond or flooded quarry? What is also very common is that these captures are out-of-the-blue occurrences, very rarely repeated, tending to indicate a very low stock density of big fish. Now and again, of course, a water comes along that for some unknown reason produces big perch consistently. An example of this is the water from where the present record came, but this has to be seen as an exception.

A couple of waters I am fishing at the moment are much more typical, and there are dozens of such examples up and down the country. The first water is a very deep flooded quarry, sixty feet at the deepest point. It is perhaps four acres in surface area, being surrounded on three sides by sheer cliffs, the only shallows being a narrow strip at the remaining end. At least eighty per cent of the periphery of the water is very steeply shelving, being eighteen to twenty feet deep only a couple of rod lengths out.

The other water is a clay pit of no more than two acres, but it is remarkably deep for such a small water, being over forty feet deep in the middle. This is one of those waters that could well produce a monstrous perch. It is infested with stunted rudd and gudgeon, and equally stunted

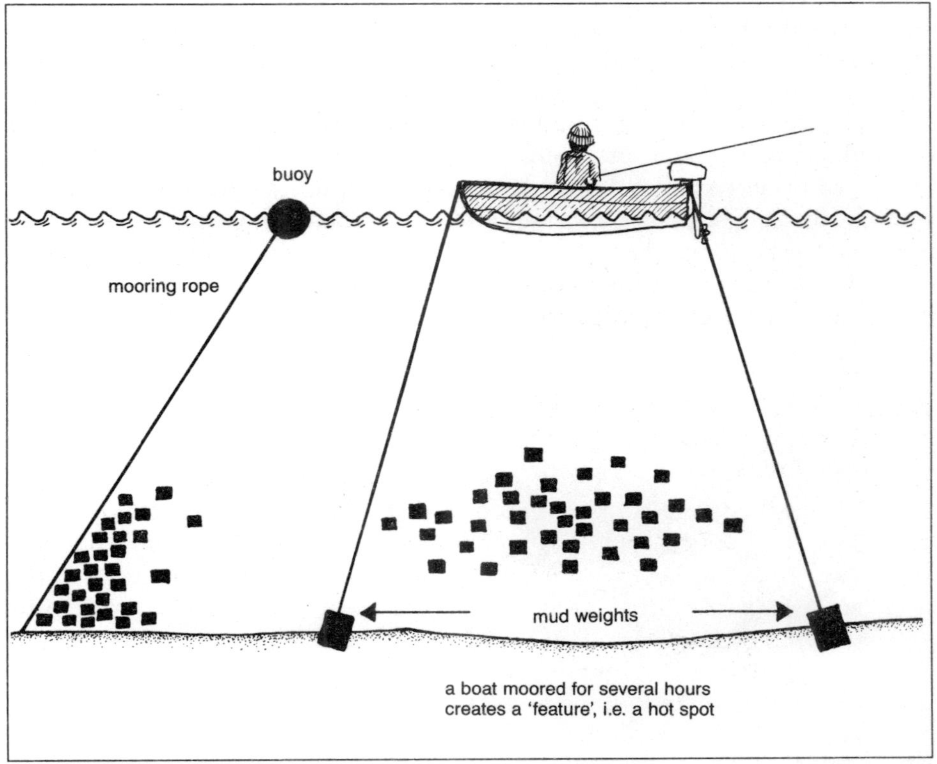

Reservoir hot spots for perch as shown by fish recorders.

pike. But just occasionally a big perch puts in an appearance. In the two years I have had my ticket, only five perch have been caught as far as I know. The smallest of those five was three pounds eight ounces – exciting prospects indeed.

Location

In waters of the types mentioned above, the main problem is the one of location. If there are areas of sunken snags, or overhanging trees giving underwater root formations, then these are worth thorough investigation. Like our small-stream rush bed, such features provide cover for perch to lie in ambush. However, many deep quarries and pits are essentially featureless, and in these circumstances the perch become very nomadic, continually following the fry shoals.

Techniques

Let us examine first of all the techniques that can be used for fishing an underwater snag. Depending on the water you are fishing, this could be a sunken tree, old quarry workings, flooded hedgerows and fences, and so on. Many of the comments in this section will also apply to deep reservoirs, including trout reservoirs such as Ardleigh, and in these waters there all kinds of bizarre sunken snags that could harbour big perch.

Snag fishing, of necessity, calls for static bait presentation, the alternatives being straightforward legering and paternostering. Straightforward bottom fishing with worms or deadbait is a method which

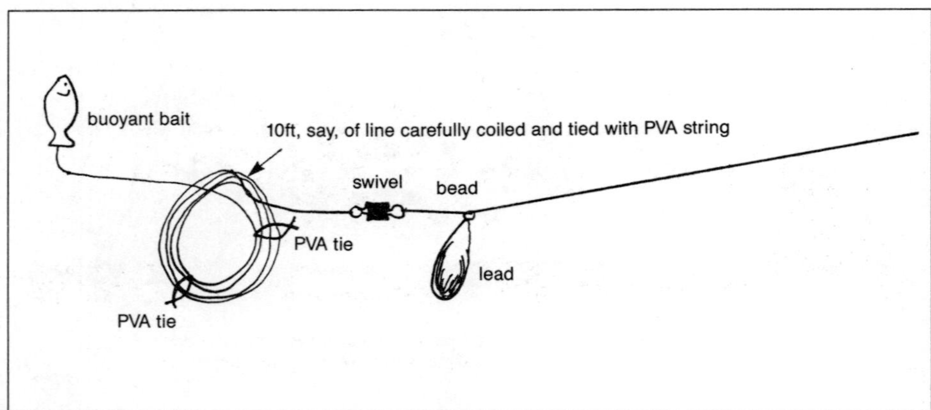

A rig for fishing buoyant bait well off the bottom in deep water.

6 Perch

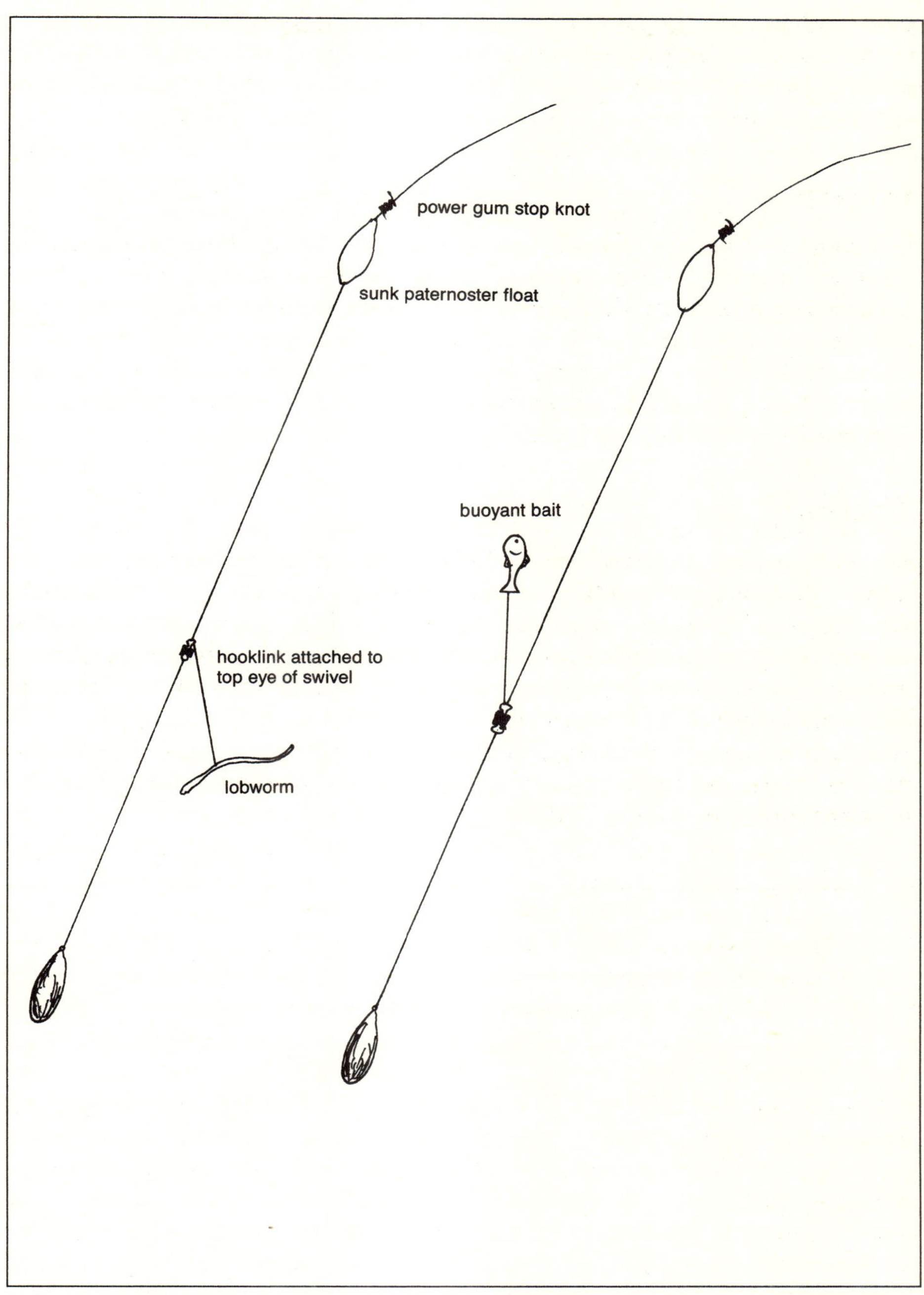

Sunk-float paternoster variations.

decreases in effectiveness as the water depth increases. Up to perhaps twenty-five feet deep, there is no doubt that big perch often feed on the bottom, specially in the winter, and legering is a well-proven method of taking extra-big fish. It is a slow old game, however. When you start talking of substantially greater depth, I am not at all confident in bottom fishing as an effective method, and this is when I prefer to fish with buoyant baits, if I have to leger. These can be arranged to fish a few inches to several feet off the bottom, and alternatives are small deadbaits stuffed with polystyrene, free-swimming legered livebaits, and air-injected lobs.

If you are casting any distance, of course, a tail length of more than a few feet becomes cumbersome. In these circumstances, if you wanted to present a bait, say, ten feet off the bottom, then you could make use of thin PVA string. Having decided upon the hooklength, fold it carefully into a neat coil, being careful not to tangle the line, and then nip the coils together at two points with PVA. A few minutes after casting, the PVA dissolves and the buoyancy of the bait allows it to rise to the required position.

For fishing static baits off bottom, however, a better and less fiddling approach is to use a paternoster rig. Depending on personal preference, a surface or sunken float may be used, although the deeper the water fished the more the sunken float paternoster is the more effective method.

Whether you are fishing straight leger technique with buoyant baits, or the paternoster rig, the difficulty is knowing at what distance to fish from the bottom. With two rods, and varying either the tail length or the positioning of the float stop knot, you will be able to cover a great variation in depth. As an extra refinement, a double-hook rig presents other possibilities.

The use of two rods – each with a double-hook rig, and one hook offering a buoyant bait on each tackle – allows baits to be presented simultaneously at four different levels. Obviously, this will facilitate the location process. I would add at this point that before you use either two rods or double-hook rigs you should ascertain that the dub rules actually permit it. By working to a logical plan, and altering the depth settings of the various baits, it should not take long to pin-point the perch if any are there and willing to feed.

For this kind of fishing, I much prefer a small livebait or small buoyant deadbait to worms. Large lobs will always be an effective perch bait of course, but in the kind of waters I am discussing here they are not as effective as fish baits. Where worms do come into their own is where you decide upon a truly bottom bait. A very appealing way of presenting a legered worm is to air-inject a short portion of the tail. The worm should be lying on the bottom with just that injected portion wavering above it. This is often irresistible.

6 PERCH

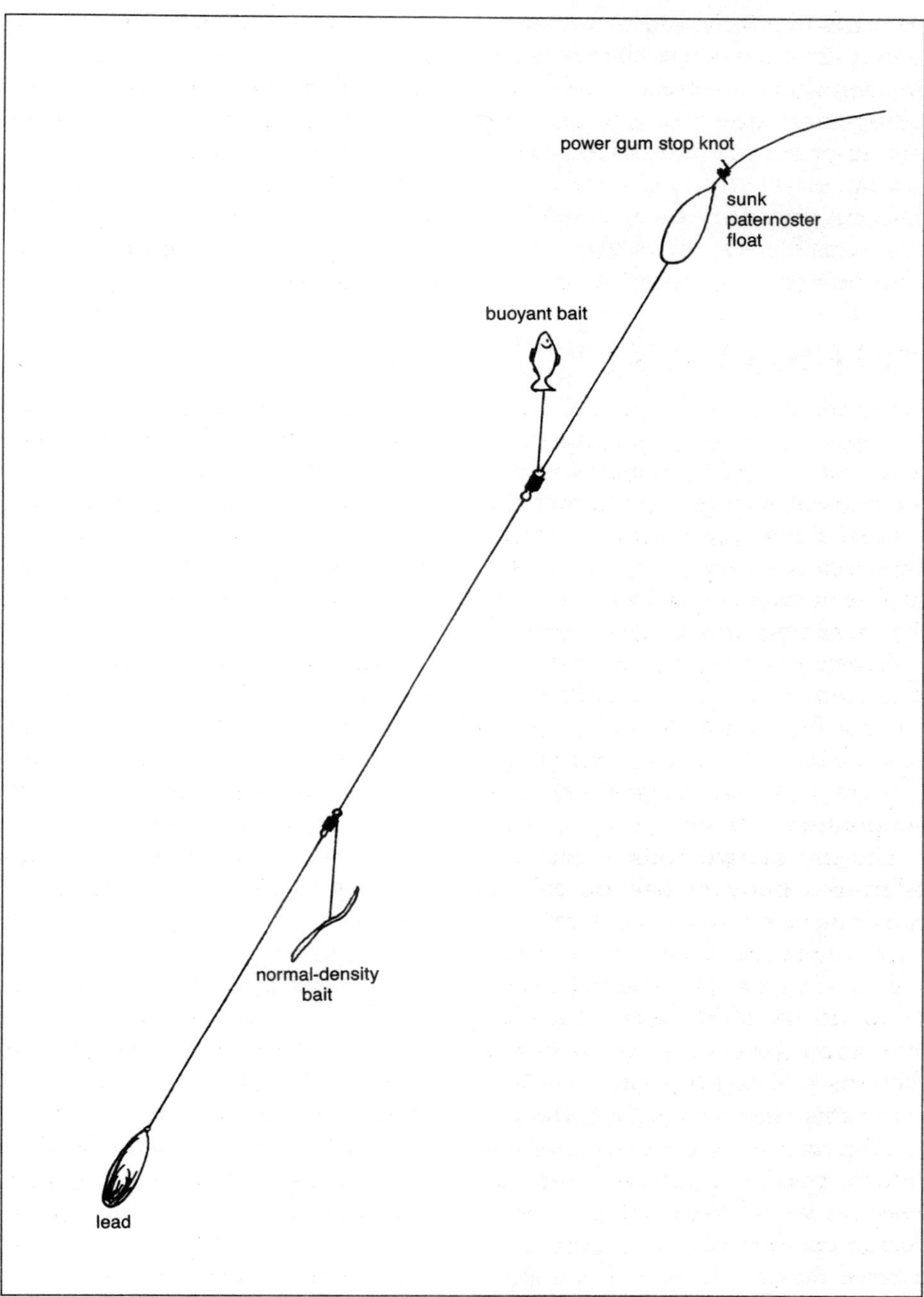

Double-hook paternoster.

With the exception of the special circumstance of definite features or snags in which the perch may permanently reside, pit or reservoir perch are frequently very nomadic, and could be found literally anywhere. Location now comes down to a painstaking procedure of trial and error. If this is undertaken in a totally haphazard manner, and the particular water is of any substantial size, you are really relying on luck. It is impossible to form any meaningful conclusions from the results of such an approach. There is only one sensible way to go about the fishing, and that is to work to a logical fixed pattern, in much the same way as we did with the static approach.

Drift-Bait Fishing

The most effective ways of locating nomadic specimen perch, and the ways in which the information is gathered in the fastest possible time, are drift-bait fishing and spinning. Let us look at drift-bait fishing first, with an example from my own fishing to illustrate the technique. There is a small water I fish occasionally of some three acres or so, which is totally featureless under the surface as far as I can ascertain, and which is a fairly uniform twenty-six feet deep, with the exception of a narrow marginal shelf. I do not think that the water holds any monster perch, although it has produced a couple just over three pounds, but it does contain a respectable number of two pounders. These perch are never found in the same spot twice. The way I tackle this fishing usually is to set up two sliding float tackles, with stop knots set at twenty-four and twenty feet respectively, and drift them downwind across the lake, using a greased line so as not to impede the floats' progress. It goes without saying that this is not particularly effective in a flat calm. On my particular water, a normal westerly wind allows me to drift across the entire lake from several positions on the upwind bank.

If I have a moderate breeze, the float may have covered forty or fifty yards of water in ten minutes or so, at which point I generally close the bail arm and allow the bait to fish one area for a few more minutes. If there are no takes, then I wind about five yards of line towards me and then allow the bait to search that new area for a few more minutes. In this way I cover the whole line of the drift, the outward journey being continually on the move, and the inward one presenting a static bait at various points along the way. Having retrieved the baits, and assuming that there had been no takes, I would then adjust the stop knots and repeat the whole procedure using depth settings of sixteen feet and twelve feet. Obviously, if at any time a perch is landed, I will generally maintain the depth setting at that which produced the take. On any particular day, it is very common to have all the perch swimming at one level, and once one has been taken, there is every chance that more will follow. I think that you will be able to see the simple principles behind this approach. Covering one line of drift thoroughly in this way, and then progressively moving along the bank covering other lines in the same manner, gives me a very good chance of arriving at the combination of position and depth at which the perch are to be found on any one day. It is easy, very effective, and also very active fishing.

As far as baits are concerned, there is nothing to beat a small livebait for this style of fishing, and my favourite is a gudgeon, although small roach, rudd and perch are also good. Drifted deadbaits are also worth trying, although I do not think that drifted deadbait is as effective a bait for perch as it is for pike.

Spinning

Without a doubt, an extremely efficient method of locating perch in pits is spinning, and many would argue that it is the most effective way. As I said in the small-stream section, perch seem to attack a spinner as soon as it is in their field of vision, and it therefore follows that a systematic searching of a water will eventually locate the fish if they are in a feeding mood. Again work to a logical pattern. From the first spot you intend fishing, you could perhaps make casts along four or five different lines, making perhaps six casts along each line, with two retrieves along each of three different depths. Once again, this very efficiently covers a great deal of water. Having covered one spot in this way, move along the bank a few yards and repeat the procedure.

I am the wrong person to advise on the most effective lures to use for perch spinning, since I do not do enough of it to be considered any kind of expert on the subject. But I have had a fair amount of success with three Mepps varieties, which are the Aglia, both in silver and gold, and the Comet Black Fury. My favourite, however, from recent fishing is a Rublex Ondex. This lure has a black and silver striped spoon, with a red central spine, and sports a red wool tassel. In the smallish waters where I have done much of my perch spinning, these lures are perfectly adequate, but if you are fishing bigger waters, you will find that more casting weight may be required, and in these circumstances the heavier lures come into their own.

While we are discussing perch fishing with either livebait, deadbait or artificial lure, a point of angling ethics has to be made. The methods mentioned are, obviously, ones that attract pike, and for me that is their biggest drawback. However, if they are to be used, and the water in question does contain pike, then care should be taken that hooks or lures will not be left in them. Depending upon the quality of the pike fishing, we have to consider whether it is advisable to use light wire traces. On the water I am fishing which has the best potential for a very big perch, the only pike ever caught are stunted, and on this water I am happy to use a monofilament trace and accept an occasional bite off. If however, the water contains a good head of big pike, it is totally irresponsible to use fish baits or artificials for perch without wire. Although the use of wire undoubtedly adversely affects bait presentation, running the deliberate risk of leaving hooks in big pike simply cannot be condoned. Big pike are under enough pressure from some incompetent pike anglers as it is.

Cycles

As with most other species, gravel pits have the conditions to produce monster perch, but it is more common in pits to find a large head of small ones, and only the occasional specimen. For some reason, perch seem to be one of the most successful species in gravel pits as far as fry survival goes, and the margins at every pit I know can at times be black with them. Most of the fish, however, seem to have a very short life span, before succumbing to the perch disease. I believe this to be far more prevalent in gravel pits than other stillwaters. The small percentage of survivors are the ones, possibly immune to the disease, that are our potential monsters. An identical pattern has been noticed on the two pits I have fished in recent years for bream.

For two years at TC, it was very rare to catch a perch of any size, and then, all of a sudden, we were all plagued with four-ounce ones. Within two more seasons, the numbers of perch had decreased, but they averaged about a pound. Two seasons later, perch were caught only occasionally, but they were all good fish, many well over two pounds, and including my three pounder. The following season, they had all gone again, and it was rare to catch one at all. It remained that way for two years, when small perch began to show again. Exactly the same pattern has been repeated at Queenford. The first year of the syndicate, the only bites we had, other than the first handful of bream, were from jack pike. No perch were in evidence. Within two years we were all catching pounders, and in 1987/88, all of the syndicate members had several two-pound-plus specimens. It had become quite a trial using lobs at dawn because of the perch interest. And yet in 1988/89, I did not catch a single perch from Queenford, and I fished a great many hours. As far as I can tell, only a handful of perch were taken the whole season.

From the above evidence, it would seem to me that planning a big perch campaign on a gravel pit depends on finding a water at the peak of its cycle.

If big perch are showing regularly, take advantage of the situation there and then, because next season it could be too late.

Without a doubt, the best time to locate pit perch is at dawn, in the summer and autumn months, when they are at their most active. They will harass the fry shoals on the gravel bars at first light, and for about two hours thereafter, at which time the bites begin to tail off. As with small-stream fish, these bigger perch are very light sensitive, and I believe they retire to the deeper areas when the sun gets high in the sky. Just before dawn, then, is the time to be in position, presenting a bait, either small livebait or legered lobworm, on a shallow bar, or the drop off from the bar. From about midmorning onwards, I would tackle the fishing exactly as described previously, locating the fish with drifting livebaits or by spinning. If there exists deep water around the pit margins, overhung by foliage, that would be a favoured holding area, as would any uniformly deep area. Small bays are also worth investigating, as big perch use them to their advantage to herd shoals of fry into.

During the cold winter months, gravel-pit perch are difficult to locate, but it is worth concentrating your efforts on the deeper areas almost exclusively. The best method of location in the winter is undoubtedly spinning unless, of course, you have access to an echo sounder and can fish off a boat. A shoal of perch, once located, can be fished for either by jigging for them, spinning at the appropriate depth, or paternostering livebaits. Deep-water perch fishing tends to be all or nothing. Once you have found the fish, several can be caught quickly. The trick is, of course, finding them.

7

Pike

FISHING STILLWATERS

Reservoir Piking

Without a doubt, my favourite stillwater piking is in reservoirs, waters I believe to have a vast potential for specimen pike, as they do for big roach. I do not propose to discuss here the pike of trout reservoirs, as I have no experience of fishing for them, but there is ample evidence that they can grow to huge proportions in such an environment. Obviously, if you have the opportunity to fish a water like this, you should grasp it with both hands. One or two far-sighted owners of trout fisheries are now allowing piking out of the trout season, and the results have been generally very good.

The bulk of my reservoir piking experience has been on the Midlands reservoirs, most of which have been constructed by damming shallow valleys, and it is the fishing in these waters that I shall be discussing.

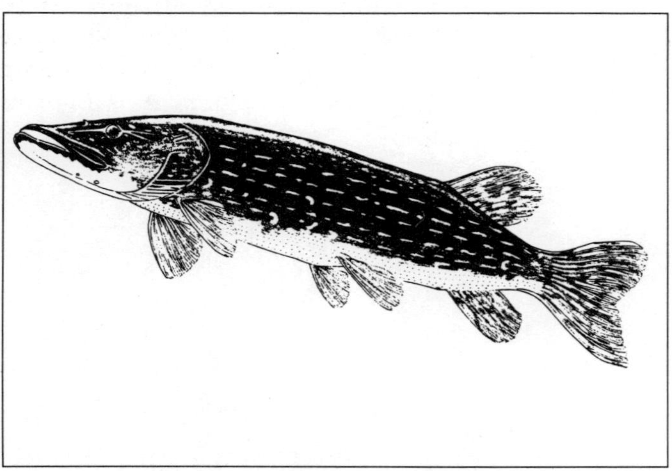

Pike body markings – full fish.

Having said that, the methods are standard, and can be adapted for any circumstances. Particular variations of approach to suit the conditions found in gravel pits and other stillwaters I shall be covering later.

Location

Very rarely in reservoirs do you get sudden depth changes, as you do in gravel pits. The usual situation is one in which shallow water exists where the original stream enters the valley, the deepest water obviously being found under the dam. However, each water will have its own particular variations, and these should always be located and noted, but generally we find a fairly extensive shallow area, gradually deepening as we approach the dam end. The contours of the surrounding land give us a clue as to how fast the bottom drops away.

There are really no hard and fast rules about pike location in these waters – the fish could be anywhere. Obviously, they will follow the food fish shoals around, so find those and the pike will not be far away. If there are areas that naturally attract fish, such as extensive weed beds, sunken trees or sudden depth changes, then these are likely to be hot spots. This particularly applies to the original bed of the stream that feeds the reservoir. In all the waters I fish, this watercourse, which is usually gravelly, and deeper than the surrounding flooded valley, is a very reliable pike-producing area. A large reservoir may well have several streams converging into one main watercourse, and each of these stream beds will be worth thorough investigation.

As I have very little summer piking experience, I am not qualified to offer any advice on the subject, but I understand from friends that this is the time of year when the use of spoons and plugs can offer spectacular sport. My piking starts in late autumn, from October onwards, and at this time of the year the fish are into fry feeding, mopping up the fingerling roach, bream, etc., that were bred earlier in the summer. This takes place all over the reservoir, but is more concentrated in the shallower areas. A very reliable short cut is to watch the activities of the grebes, since they will find the fry for you. At this time of the year, small livebaits, either free-roving or paternostered, are deadly, and I believe far superior to deadbaits.

As the season wears on, and the water temperature drops, the remainder of the fry shoals tend to have scattered, and migrated to slightly deeper water. From about mid-November to late January, I am always more confident concentrating my pike-fishing efforts at the dam end, and this is when some very big fish fall to both legered deadbait and large livebaits. By about February, another factor enters the equation. Pike are one of the earliest fish to spawn, and this spawning urge begins to make the big females restless; they start a progressive migration back to the shallows, in readiness for the procreation ritual, sometime in March or April. My piking is concentrated entirely on the shallows at the back end of the season, and during the last few winters I have had some tremendous bags of fish. An easy mistake to make is to assume that, because the weather is still very cold, the pike will remain in the deeps. I have taken big pike from three feet of water in the bitterest of weather, even when there had been substantial ice margins.

Weather and Times

Weather and water conditions do have a part to play, however. In the chapter on roach I discuss the best conditions for winter reservoir roach. Chief among those are coloured water and a good undertow, if one exists. I believe that one of the reasons why these conditions are reliable for producing roach is that they are poor for piking. For all my pike fishing, whether in stillwaters or rivers, coloured water in particular is bad news. If, though, the water is clear and an undertow exists, the roach will still seek it out, and pike fishing in the vicinity is obviously taking sensible advantage of the conditions.

The effect of the wind is not quite so clear-cut, and it only affects the pike location in so far as it affects the location of the prey fish. I believe the effect of the wind itself to be minimal on bait fish movement, apart from changes it creates in the water, such as undertow. And each species of fish is affected differently, roach responding far faster to wind changes than bream, for instance. The net result is that I believe it virtually impossible to base pike location purely on wind direction alone as there are far too many other variable factors. These days, when I am faced with a good wind, I will use it to search as much of the water as possible with drifting techniques (discussed later). Although I haven't done this myself, a whole winter spent piking on a water, using drifting methods when there is any wind, and recording the positions of all pike takes as well as detailed notes of the conditions, could provide invaluable information on the relationship between pike location and wind strength and direction. It would certainly be a very interesting experiment.

This back-end fishing is when the original stream bed really becomes a super hot spot, especially during a cold snap. Big pike really pack together around this feature, and you can really bag up if you have done your homework properly. Over three weekends in late February and early March I have had no fewer than twenty-one doubles and two twenties, from an area of such a stream bed only about thirty yards long. There was only one recapture, which is a good indication of the concentration of big fish I had in front of me. The interesting thing is that, during the same period, several very competent pike anglers put some time in on the dam, and were rewarded with only the occasional jack.

From my experience, big deadbaits heavily outscore livebaits at this time of the year for the big fish. I believe the big females become extremely lazy, and spend much of their day leisurely drifting along close to the bottom. More often than I care to remember, I have fished a big deadbait and a good livebait close together, and on most occasions the deadbait was the one that scored. Bear in mind, though, that I am talking about fish from mid-doubles upwards. The smaller males, which will be in attendance in large numbers, will provide hectic sport on small- to medium-sized livebaits. It depends what you want. My preference is one or two good fish, as opposed to a lot of action from jacks.

After a great deal of time spent in the pursuit of reservoir pike, I am in no doubt that the most productive time is the few hours either side of dawn. If you are keen enough to be on the water a couple of hours before daybreak, even when it is very cold, the results will make the effort very worthwhile. My records show that the period from about 1 p.m. to 2.30 p.m. is also good, as is the dusk period and the first two or three hours of darkness.

Fishing Methods

Free-Roving Livebait

I have differentiated between free-roving livebait and drifted livebait quite deliberately, as by free roving I am discussing only livebaits that are big enough, and strong enough to cover a large area of water under their own volition. No casting is involved, the fish being placed in the margins and then persuaded to search around by manipulation of the line. As such, it is a method that can be successfully used in a complete flat calm, which is where drift float fishing falls down, of course. To me, fishing a drift float, which is a method of presenting a bait at a longer range than is normally possible, is reserved for smaller livebaits or suspended deadbaits. There is nothing to prevent you drifting a large livebait, of course, but they do present substantial hooking problems at range. As we shall see shortly, it is imperative that you strike a take instantly on drift tackle, and large baits make this uncertain of success.

For efficient presentation with a free rover, it is essential that the bait has as much freedom of movement as possible, as the name implies. The three factors that will tire the bait, and therefore inhibit movement, are excessively large hooks and floats, incorrect bait attachment, and a large length of sunken line creating drag. My normal terminal rig is illustrated. Rarely these days do I use trebles larger than size 8, and they will be semi-barbless, apart from the point attached to the bait. By semi-barbless, I mean trebles that have had two of the barbs partially flattened. I use Ryobi eagle claw, which is a super strong and sharp hook. After some considerable trial, I have stopped using totally barbless trebles. The proportion of pike that I pulled out of while using them was far too high for my liking. If you are fishing a free rover, avoid using one treble to lip hook the fish. Without a doubt, that discourages all but the largest baits from swimming freely.

Correct choice of float is important. It should be just large enough so that the bait cannot comfortably hold it underwater for long periods, but not so big that it is like dragging an anchor around. It's a matter of common sense, and a little trial and error. Also, the more streamlined the float, the less resistance it creates.

One of the most important features of efficient free roving is the line between float and rod top. If any or all of that line is sunken, then it will create a tremendous drag on the bait. Thus it is imperative that the line

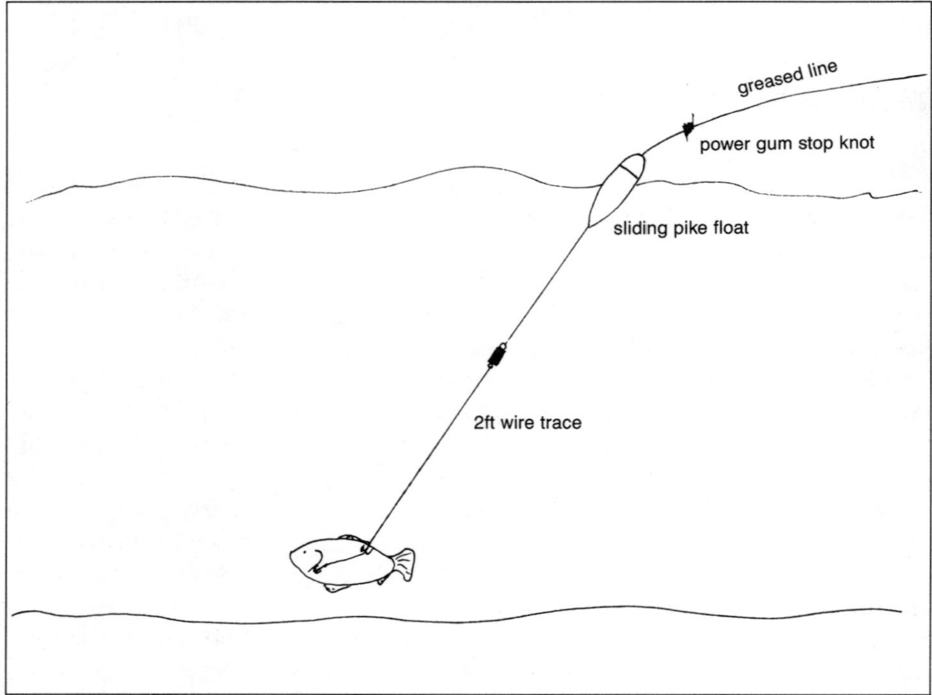

Free-roving livebait.

should float; I always grease it heavily before fishing and regrease it periodically throughout the day. If there is a good breeze, it is also important not to have too much greased line out either, as this will form a large belly in the wind, and create almost as much drag as the sunken line would. For this reason, and to get the best out of free roving, I always hold the rod, only keeping a moderate amount of slack between rod top and float. Also, by holding the rod, you learn how to control the direction of the bait's movement, by bending the greased line into the wind. Keeping the line slightly taut all the time encourages the bait to keep moving, rather than leaving it to its own devices, with slack line everywhere. Controlling the bait's direction by rod and line movements is an impossible thing to describe on paper, and has to be learnt by trial and error. Once learnt, however, a bait can be made to swim wherever you want it to.

I find that it's best to fish a free rover no nearer than about eighteen inches to the bottom or bottom weed, whichever is appropriate. Any closer than that, and the bait will continually dive into the bottom debris and sulk there, unless you are using an excessively heavy float. Also, for ease of tackle control, I normally fish the float as a slider, using a power gum stop knot. Takes to this presentation are normally spectacular. My personal best pike of thirty-two pounds one ounce was taken from the Thurne on a free-roving crucian. That afternoon, the bait had covered some hundred yards of river, swimming just above the bottom weed, when it was taken. A huge whirlpool just appeared in the surface, and the float disappeared. I'll never forget that take!

One of the greatest dilemmas when free roving with a biggish livebait is timing the strike. As will become obvious throughout this chapter, I am a firm advocate of striking pike runs early, but I am the first to admit that it is much more difficult when big baits are involved. If the float bobs up and down, this will generally indicate the interest of a small pike which cannot take the bait properly. When the float disappears and remains out of sight a big pike is indicated. I have to say, however, that I am these days quite paranoid about delaying the strike on any pike run, as I detest deep hooking fish, and for this season rarely use baits much above about eight ounces.

Paternostering

Where you want to fish a static livebait, or even a suspended deadbait, then you can revert to the paternoster, using either a surface float, or a sunken float. I tend to reserve the surface float for fairly close-range work where the depth is fairly uniform, and can be gauged accurately enough so that the line from float to lead is taut. If the float has been set overdepth, so that the

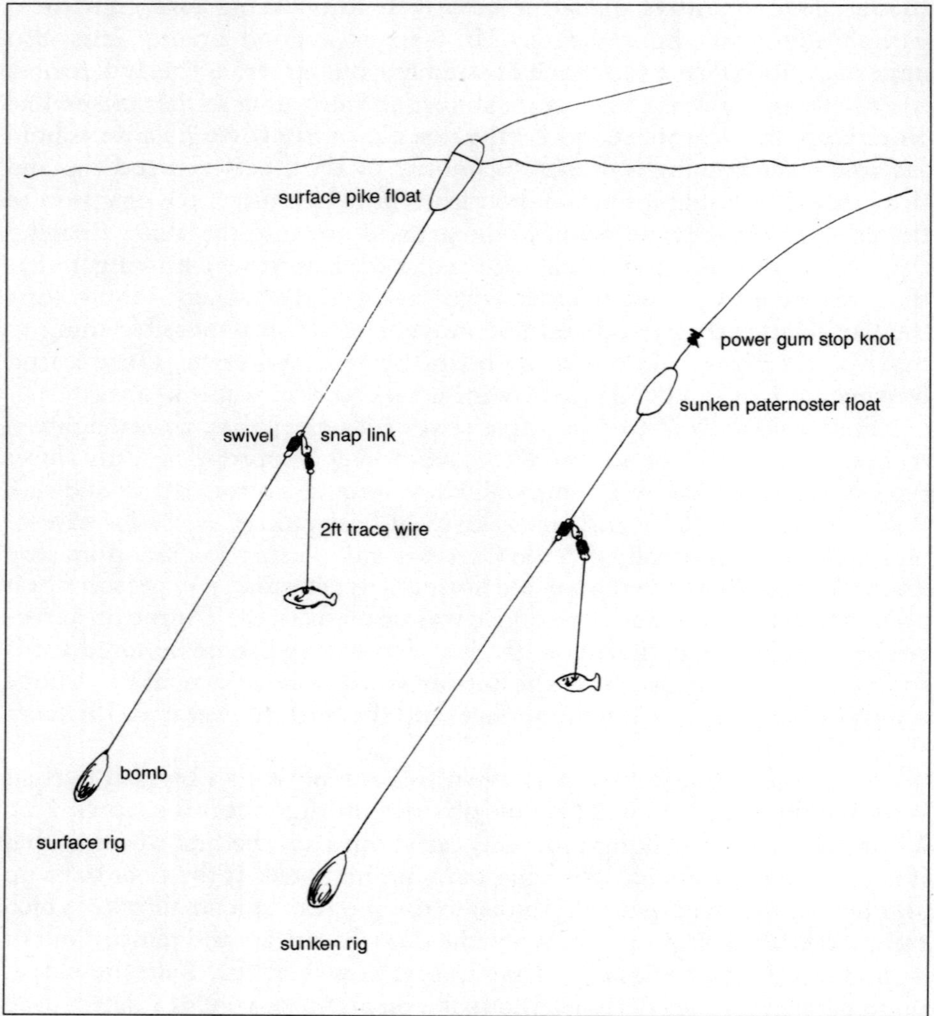

Standard paternoster rigs.

line is slack, the terminal rig will not fish properly and you end up with one tangle after another.

For anything but short-range work, the sunk float rig is a far superior presentation, and is especially useful where you have depth variations. It ensures that the bait fishes the required distance from the bottom, whatever the depth of the water. I usually use a sunk float paternoster in conjunction with a drop-off pike indicator, and it is important that this is set correctly, for maximum efficiency and to minimize tangling. After casting, I tighten the line as much as I can, without dislodging the lead, to set it at a shallow angle. By letting out line slowly through my fingers it is easy, after a little practice, to feel the point at which the tension goes out of it. This is when the float has reached the vertical. The bigger the sunken float you are using, the easier it is to tell, as there is greater natural buoyancy. At that point, place the rod on the rests, and take in a few turns of the reel handle to pull the float down slightly, and attach the indicator. That is now as perfect as you will be able to get it.

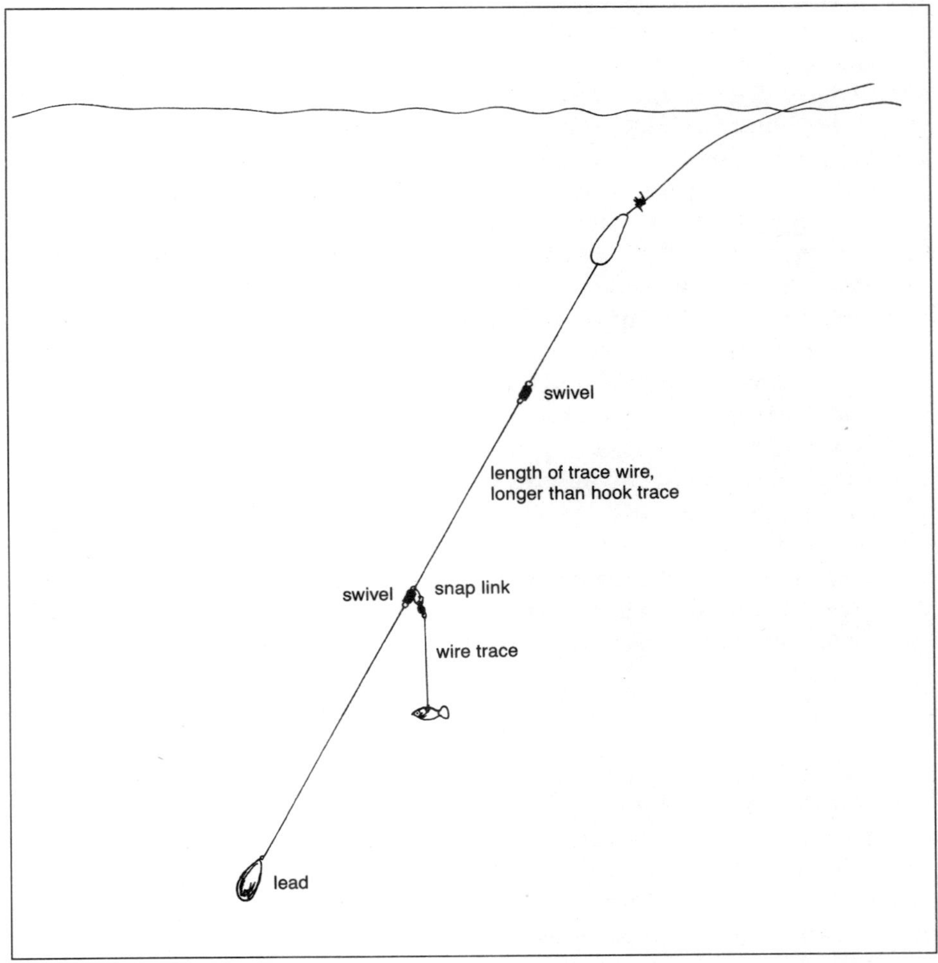

Use of the up-trace trace.

One of the great problems with the paternoster is the pike biting through the main line when it takes the bait. I have seen this happen numerous times and it arises because the bait, in its panic to escape, rises in the water, often taking the trace round the line as it does so. This must be avoided at all costs, as it results in pike swimming around with trebles in them. So I strongly recommend the use of an up-trace trace, which is quite simply a length of wire between swivels. This must be longer than the hook trace being used, and it is then impossible for the pike to take bait and main line together.

While on the subject of avoiding leaving trebles in pike at all costs, there is no justification whatever in using main lines of less than about 12 pounds for piking, and 15 pounds is safer. Use good quality trace wire, such as that marketed by Pete Drennan, of at least 15 pounds, and please use traces of at least two feet in length. The number of experienced pike men I have seen using ridiculous traces of as short as nine inches really makes me shudder. Think about it; even a modest pike is quite capable of taking a bait more than nine inches into its mouth and the result is one potentially dead pike. Also test your line and traces regularly and thoroughly. At the slightest sign of any weakness, discard them and replace. Personally, I renew my traces after every session. We all have a collective responsibility to do everything possible to ensure that every pike we catch is returned unharmed. It takes many years to grow a twenty-pound pike, and one that dies through incompetent or irresponsible angling is not easily replaced. There are fewer big pike about than is generally realized, so let's take care of them.

When you have a run on a paternostered bait, which will be indicated by the line pulling out of the indicator clip, or by the indicator falling slowly if the line slackens because a pike is running towards the bank, you should always strike immediately. It is completely irresponsible to wait for minutes before striking, as this will result in big fish being deeply hooked. I always work on the principle that any fish I have missed on an early strike was probably a small jack anyway.

Unhooking

After a pike has been successfully landed, it has to be unhooked, and this is where more damage is done to our pike stocks than at any other time. Inexperienced or inadequately equipped anglers are chiefly responsible, often because they are simply afraid of the fish. Many pike have been released by biting through the line and leaving the trace in the fish, because it was easier to do that than do the job properly.

The correct way to unhook a pike is to place a tough glove on one hand, and with that hand insert your fingers into the vee under the pike's chin.

Your fingers enter the mouth at the rear, where the teeth cannot bite you. Gently lift the head, and nine times out of ten the fish's mouth will drop open. It is best if the pike is lying on its back initially, on one of those soft unhooking mats. With the mouth open, it is a simple matter to reach in and extract the hooks with long-handled forceps. If the hooks are at the back of the throat, go in through the gill opening, being careful not to damage the delicate membranes. Even with the quickest striking, you will get the occasional deeply hooked fish, one that has gulped the bait straight down. You should still extract the hooks to give the fish a chance for survival. If you cannot see a hook, very gently draw on the line until it is in sight. Then disengage each point of the treble in turn until it comes free. One of those commercially available long-handled pike disgorgers is useful in these circumstances.

It is helpful if there are two of you with a deeply hooked fish, as one can keep the line tight and the fish still while the other removes the trebles. Deeply hooked pike are, however, rare if you strike immediately a run commences. One last point on unhooking: I always carry a pair of long-handled wire cutters (although I cannot remember the last time I used them), and in the event of a point of a treble taking a hold in tissue so that it cannot be safely extracted, it is advisable to cut the offending point as close to the point of entry as possible. The pike will recover from that, whereas it would not from having the entire treble left in it. I'll finish this little diversion on unhooking with a plea. Under no circumstances should you contemplate using a pike gaff. They are totally unnecessary as well as being barbaric and belong more to the Middle Ages than to modern pike angling.

Drift Float Fishing

On the larger reservoirs, normal methods restrict the angler to about eighty yards of the bank if there are no boats available. Certainly, on a great many fisheries the use of boats is not permitted, and there are therefore large areas of water that may well hold monster pike that have never before seen an angler's bait. The only way to tackle these pike is with the use of the drift float technique, an extension of the old ballooning method. It goes without saying that the only days when drifting is impossible is when there is a complete flat calm.

There is an excellent range of drifting floats on the market nowadays, from several well-respected manufacturers. Most of them are very good, and the ones I use are made by my old mate Andy Barker, from his Ideas in Action range. There are two basic designs, each one with interchangeable bodies of various sizes, and the floats are therefore suitable for all size ranges of baits, from very small livebaits up to large deadbaits.

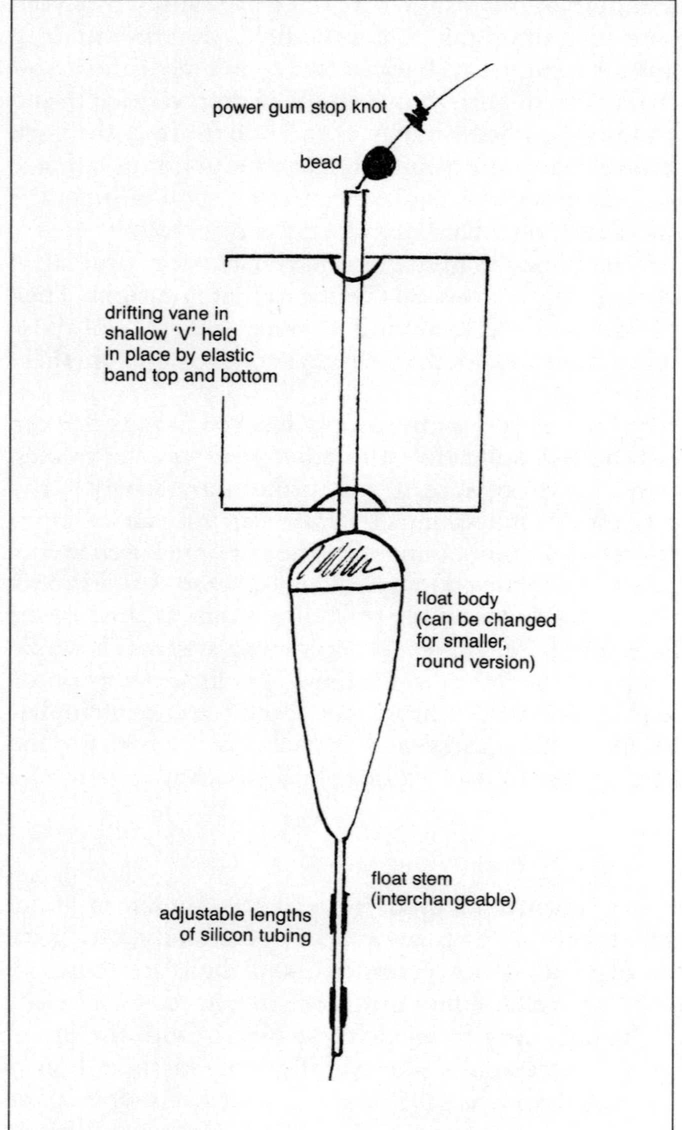

Drifting floats.

Each float consists of a hollow central stem, through which the line goes, and at the top of the stem is fitted the drifting vane, which has been preformed into a shallow vee. This V-shaped vane automatically adjusts to catch the prevailing wind and is far superior to the flat version. On the central stem, under the vane, the body of the float is locked in position by two pieces of adjustable silicon tubing. This is an interesting feature, as it allows the body of the float to be moved nearer to the stem if required. In extremely rough conditions, for example, you could have the float body near the base of the stem, and load it so that the entire body is underwater, with just the vane showing. This would mean that the float would be much more stable, and therefore more controllable. For the same reason, the base of the stem is equipped with two pieces of spare silicon tube. If necessary, the stem can be loaded with lead wire between this tubing and this also promotes stability. Loading the stem in this way is useful when using very small livebaits. Do not add weight to the trace itself, as that would impede the bait's movement, but load the float instead. In this way, the float fishes properly, no matter at what level the bait is swimming. Normally, however, I would want the bait working at about two feet off the bottom.

Drifting is a very effective method for both live and dead baits. Livebaits are fished head up the trace, as in river piking. The reason is that retrieving a livebait from perhaps a two-hundred-yard drift, with the bait attached as in paternostering, exerts tremendous pressure on the flanks, which does it no favours at all. Obviously, this is not a hard and fast rule, and baits can be attached conventionally if required. Also, as already explained, the size of float body employed would depend on bait size and weather conditions. Whether or not lead wire is used on the float stem would depend on the same variables.

Before you start fishing, it is vital that your reel spools are well loaded. By using these drifting floats, it is quite feasible to fish at over two hundred yards, and my spools contain at least two hundred and fifty yards of

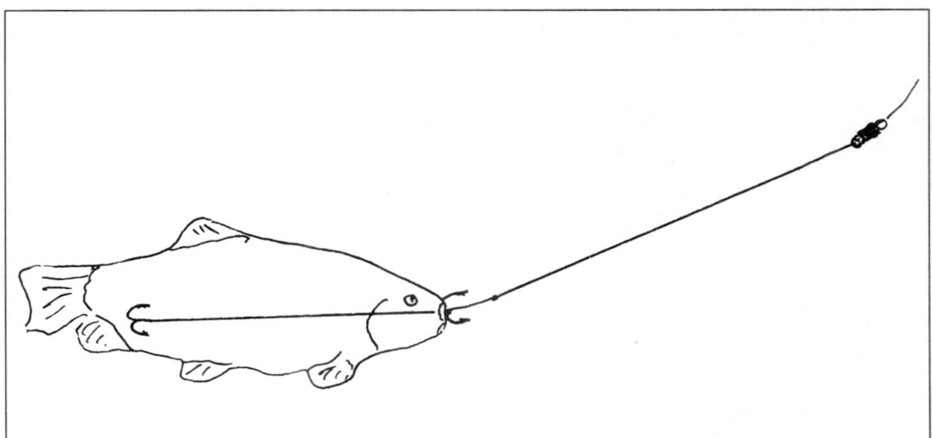

Bait attachment for long-range drifting.

12-pound Maxima. The line must also be well greased, and kept that way, for exactly the same reasons mentioned in the free-roving section, but magnified many times over. The simplest way to keep the line greased is to use one of those little autogreasers, which is simply a rubber ring that fits tightly into the butt ring. This rubber ring is packed with grease so that, as the drift pulls line off the open reel spool, it automatically greases at the same time. Do not get the impression, however, that drifting is a method of fishing where you can set up your autogreaser and then let the fishing take care of itself. It is a method that must be used responsibly, and you must keep your eye on the float at all times, even if you have to use binoculars. Also, do not allow any more line out than necessary. Yards of slack line are to be avoided at all costs. The reason why these two factors are so important is that, if a big pike takes at extreme range, and you have either not been concentrating on the float, or there is so much slack out that it takes a while to tighten right down, many fish can be deeply hooked. Please, if you are going to drift fish, fish the method properly and concentrate on your float.

Striking

Immediately you get a take, wind down and tighten into the pike, walking backwards if you can. There is no way you can effectively strike as such at

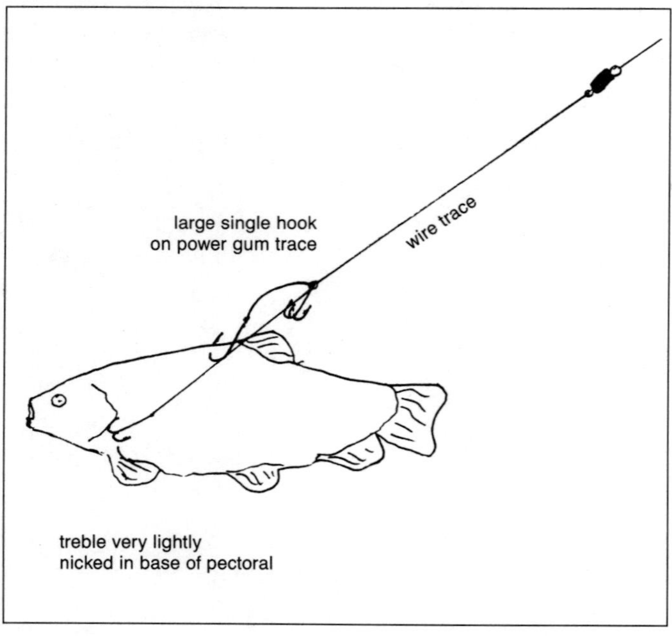

Good hooking rig at a long range.

extreme range, and this creates the other problem with the method, the one of setting the hooks. There is no foolproof way of ensuring that no pike hooked at range comes adrift, but using a modified trace as illustrated will be found beneficial. With the trebles being fished completely free, there is no impediment to them taking a firm hold in the pike's jaw.

One of the biggest problems with long-range stillwater drift fishing is knowing at which depth to fish. The problem in reservoirs, where depth changes are generally more gradual, is not so acute as in gravel pits. One good ploy is to start a drift from the dam, if the wind direction is right of course, and drift and bait into the shallows. By starting off with the maximum depth setting, and then reducing it slightly after each drift, it can easily be seen that you can cover a line from deeps to shallows very efficiently, at all levels in the water. Obviously, the shallower the setting, the further the float will go before fouling the bottom.

For perfect drift float presentation, you want a steady moderate breeze. If the wind is too light, the technique still works well enough, but if you do locate fish well offshore, it can be frustratingly slow drifting another bait out to them! If the wind is very strong, there are two problems. Firstly, the chop may be such that it renders float visibility difficult, and secondly the bait may be moving much too rapidly. Ideally, we do not want a bait to be whistling through the pike's field of vision, since this is a very poor presentation.

The simple answer to the first problem is to use a much bigger float than usual, fished higher in the water to improve visibility. The problem here is

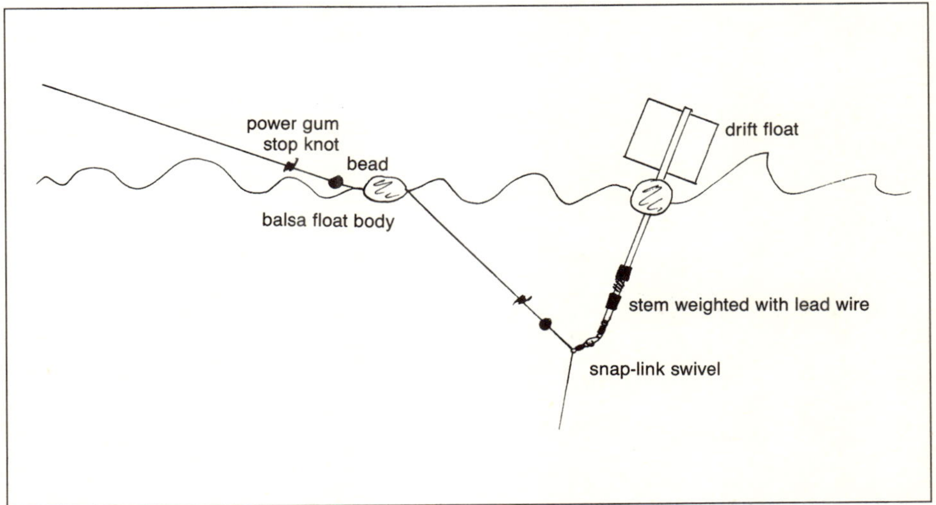

Drift-float adaptation by Dave Batten.

that this makes the speed of the drift even faster, and therefore the attachment of the float has to be modified to allow a bottom only one. We can then hold back the float during its drift to a controlled speed, without it being pulled flat. I am indebted to a modification attributed to Dave Batten of Norwich, which I first saw described in that excellent book, *Pike – The Predator becomes the Prey*.

Static Deadbaiting

The importance of static deadbaiting for the man after specimen pike cannot be overstated, since the method produces a very high proportion of the big pike caught each season.

The simplest version of the method is free-lining, using a bait heavy enough to cast without the addition of lead. In this category would come dead naturals of about six ounces, or sea fish such as herrings, mackerel, sardines or large smelt. In the case of herrings and mackerel, large fish are better used as half baits, and in fact the tail end of a medium-sized mackerel is my favourite deadbait. Sardines are a superb bait, but they have to be cast out at least partially frozen. They are so delicate that, unfrozen, they will simply break up on the cast. In fact, most deadbaits are more convenient to use when they are partially frozen, for all but very close-range work. An efficient cool box is therefore a very important part of my pike gear. What I always do is pack each bait in its own foil, making sure the bait is perfectly straight, before freezing. This ensures that I do not end up with a frozen block of fish when I arrive on the bank at dawn, which I then have to untangle somehow – no fun on a bitter cold winter's morning, I can assure you!

The terminal rig I use for my deadbaiting is standard enough. As I have stated previously, the trebles will usually be size 8, semi-barbless, and my

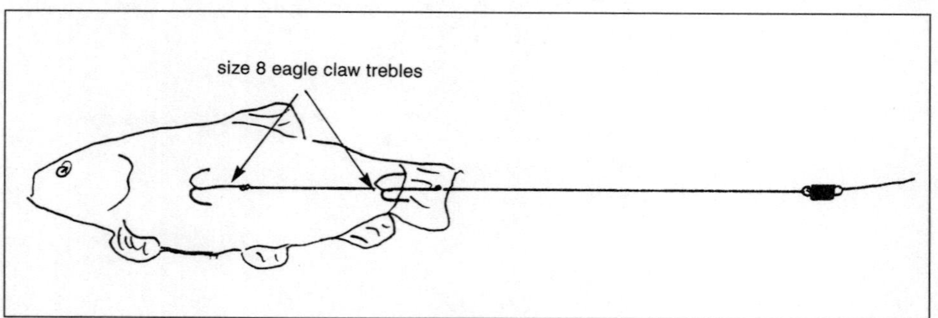

Standard dead-bait rig.

traces are always two feet long at least. Generally speaking, after casting out I will clip the line into a drop-off pike indicator, but if I am fishing close range or from a boat, I will add a float. For the bank fishing, the use of a float is purely because it is pleasant to have something to watch, but if I am fishing from a boat the float is more important. It is difficult to use a butt indicator efficiently from a boat, and therefore we have to resort to putting the line in a clip at the butt, and wait for a pike to pull the line out of the clip. That is fine as far as it goes, but it will not show up runs when the pike is coming towards you. A float obviously solves this problem. Again, it's all about taking the trouble to minimize deep hooking.

For long casting, the use of frozen baits is almost essential, and the denser, tougher-skinned fish are the ones to use. For very long-range work, the half mackerel reigns supreme, and the head or tail is equally effective, using a portion of about six ounces. I always trim off the tail fin, and this helps to cut down wind resistance. It is also a good idea to secure the upper treble with a loop of PVA, which prevents the bait flying off on a strenuous cast.

Smaller baits such as small smelt and sprats will require the addition of lead, and I normally add a casting boom to my standard rig. For small baits, I dispense with two trebles, contenting myself with a single hook through the bait's tail, and a treble nicked in at the gill cover. When using small baits, it is more important than ever to hit runs immediately.

There are days when pike are picking up deadbaits and will take whatever fish they come across, and these days will often produce bumper catches. I had one incredible day at one of my reservoirs, when no fewer than twelve pike from eight pounds to nineteen pounds were landed on deads. I had taken a box of mixed baits, and took pike on mackerel heads and tails, herrings, smelts, sprats, a sardine, and two on the same frozen roach! At the end of the day I ran out of bait – I think I could have offered them anything that day and they would have taken it.

On other days, however, pike show a distinct preference for one type of fish. I do not pretend to understand why, but nevertheless it is a fact. In one three-week period the only bait that would take pike was half mackerel.

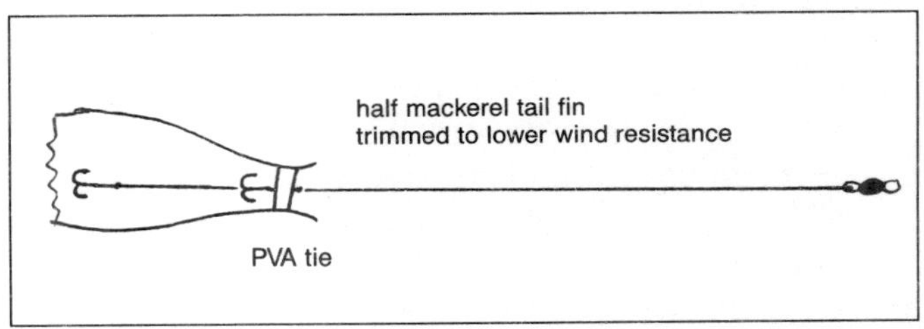

Long-casting rig for half baits.

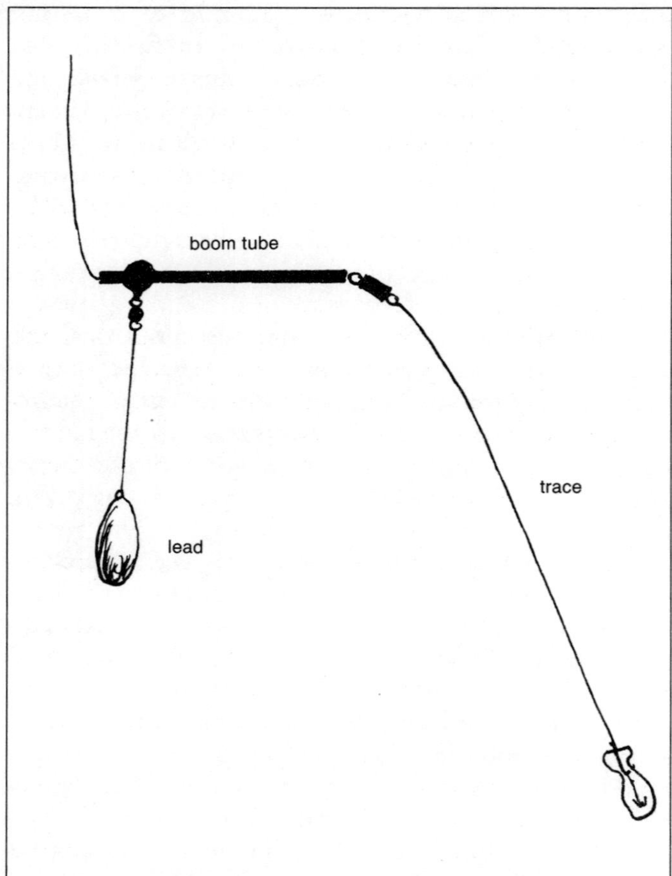

Long-casting rig for small baits.

This didn't just happen to me, but to several other anglers fishing the water at the same time. We were all fishing a variety of deadbaits, and in my case at least I was swapping the rods about, but still every single pike took mackerel while everything else was ignored.

Size preference is well known, particularly when the pike are preoccupied with fry. But even at the back end of the season, there can be days when large baits are ignored but when smelts and sprats will score. And there have been numerous occasions when I have replaced a sprat with a larger bait, and been rewarded with a run almost immediately.

It is certainly difficult to understand why the above variations should occur, but by recognizing that they do, we can approach the fishing in such a way that we can identify quickly what the fish want on the day. Two or three anglers using two or three rods each and fishing a variety of baits, can cover all the variables. If a pattern starts to emerge, each angler can then adjust his approach accordingly.

As I fish largely on my own, my normal starting line up is one rod on half mackerel, one on a small whole sardine or herring, and one on smelt. This assumes, of course, that I am fishing a water where the use of three rods is allowed! Depending on events, I will switch during the day, perhaps replacing the smelt with a sprat, the herring with a roach, and so on. If the pike are showing any preference, this process of elimination will identify it.

Although most of my deadbait-caught pike are taken on baits presented hard on the bottom, there are occasions, if the pike are in a particularly dour mood, when a switch to a buoyant bait will produce a fish. Undoubtedly, the best bait to use for this fishing is a smallish whole natural, with the swim bladder intact, and a roach of about four ounces is ideal. I generally arrange my terminal rig so that the bait fishes between six and nine inches off the bottom, by addition of a couple of shot at the appropriate point on the trace. If you have to use deadbaits, or even half baits, you can still fish efficiently in this way by inserting cork, balsa or polystyrene into the bait. The amount you will have to use depends obviously on the bait size, and has to be found by trial and error.

I will also use buoyant baits if there is a layer of bottom weed, purely to ensure that they are visible. However, if the bottom weed or debris is deeper than an inch or two then it is simpler to revert to the sunk float paternoster, with the trace positioned according to the weed depth.

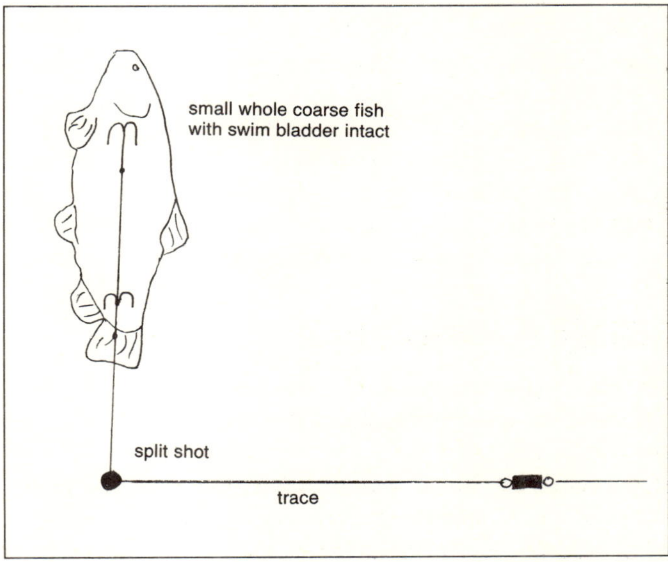

Buoyant deadbaits.

In recent years, many anglers have been experimenting with coloured and flavoured baits. Personally, I have noticed no significant difference in my catch rate when fishing a coloured bait alongside an identical uncoloured version, although others have reported an immediate improvement in sport when using them. I have to say, though, that I have put in insufficient time with coloured baits for my results to have any real statistical worth. In spite of that, it is certainly a lot of fun, and that is sufficient reason for me to continue persevering with them.

Any deadbait can be quite easily coloured on the bank, using fast bait dyes such as Rayners colouring dyes, simply painting it on the bait with a small brush. Alternatively, commercially produced coloured baits are now available through Lucebaits.

If I have not yet seen any advantage in coloured baits, the same certainly cannot be said about flavoured ones. By flavoured I am referring to deadbaits that have been injected with various oils and essences. The most obvious will be natural oils such as cod liver, herring and pilchard, and I have used all three extensively with very good results. Pilchard oil I particularly like, and over the last two winters, I have had many catches where my injected baits have outcaught plain ones by as much as four to one. I like to make my baits really reek, and usually inject with as much oil as the bait will take; then I paint more oil over the surface as well to give an immediate area of attraction when the bait settles.

There is one thing that I find tremendously exciting about using baits that have been saturated with oil, particularly in a flat calm. If you watch the spot where the bait landed, or the float if you are using one, you will often see a large oil slick rise to the surface before you see any evidence of a bite, which occurs when the pike initially picks up the bait and clamps his teeth in it. One day in March, I was casually looking out over a mirror-smooth reservoir, on a sunny and cold afternoon. Nothing had happened for quite a while, and then several large bubbles burst on the surface, and a circular slick formed. Sure enough, within thirty seconds, line was pouring from the spool, resulting eventually in a twenty pounder. That was another of those little incidents that make fishing so fascinating.

Piking in Gravel Pits

All the standard methods outlined in the previous section are equally effective in gravel pits, the differences in the fishing being concerned with pike location.

It can easily be seen that all the depressions, bars, gullies and drop offs that are found in most gravel pits will be used by the resident pike as natural ambush points. As most pits contain a multitude of such features, the food fish spend much of their time commuting from one to another. Gravel pit fish of most species are nomadic, and the pike are no exception. Obviously, they will follow their food supply.

Certain features may provide more permanent residence, both for the prey fish and the pike. Large weed beds will attract fish at all times of course, while I particularly like areas where there are sunken trees. Big pike often take up permanent residence in such an area, only venturing out to feed.

One of the most reliable areas to find numbers of gravel-pit pike is around a narrow channel connecting two larger areas of water. This channel could be a deep trench between two very much shallower areas or, even better, a trench between two dry areas, in other words, islands. I love to see islands in a gravel pit, particularly for piking. Any prey fish moving in that area will naturally be concentrated in a narrow waterway, and the pike will know it, lying in wait for an easy meal both in the trench itself, or just at its extremities. Several gravel-pit complexes actually have two separate pits connected by a small canalized causeway, and in every pit I know of this type such an area has invariably proved to be a pike hot spot.

In the absence of any of the features mentioned, and assuming that you are fishing a pit for the first time, without the benefits of having charted it, a reliable rule of thumb is to fish in the vicinity of any promontory extending into the pit. This will give easily visible evidence of a gravel bar running out into the water, and pike will be located along the sloping drop offs either side of it, as well as at the point where the bottom eventually levels off. A promontory causes a similar effect to a channel, in that prey fish patrolling around the pit margins will invariably pack closer together as they pass the headland. On all the pits I pike fish, promontories are consistent areas.

A very interesting location method on gravel pits is with the use of the drifting technique outlined earlier, which is deadly in these waters. The reason is that it naturally searches out the bars. What I normally do is start with a comparatively shallow float setting, gradually deepening the float with each subsequent drift. Eventually, the float will stop in mid-drift, and then I have located a gravel bar or plateau. Having found such a feature, it is not a bad idea to leave the bait there for a few minutes, as they are superb pike-holding areas. Having found a bar in this manner, I will walk along the bank a few yards between each drift, and in this way search the whole length of the bar. By going back over the same ground, gradually increasing the depth setting, I progressively present the bait further and further down the drop off from the bar to the pit bottom.

Once such a feature has been thoroughly investigated, it can be quite tricky to drift past the bar at a greater depth setting than the bar itself, and if there is weed on the top of the bar it is almost impossible. However, if we have clean gravel, it can be achieved by concentrating all the lead under the float, and using a bigger float, riding much higher in the water than would normally be appropriate. With a decent wind, the pressure on the float vane will eventually drag the terminal rig over the bar.

Piking in Large Lakes

It is in very large, deep lakes, Scottish lochs and Irish loughs, where my pike fishing experience is sketchy in the extreme, and I am therefore simply not qualified to offer any advice on the subject. What I would say is that the writings of people like Gord Burton and George Higgins should be studied by anyone contemplating piking on these large and very daunting waters. Gord has very many years experience of waters like Loch Lomond, and I would recommend the reader to his chapter on Loch Lomond piking in *Pike – The Predator becomes the Prey* (The Crowood Press). Similarly, no one has a more in-depth knowledge of the Irish loughs than has George Higgins.

For fishing in large deep waters for pike, an echo sounder is an invaluable location aid. Opinions differ as to the ethics of such devices, but my stance is that they are part of progress and, in the case of large waters that could take a lifetime to get to know by conventional means, I can see no objection to their use. The favoured method of using them seems to be the one of slow float trolling, keeping an eye on the screen both for establishing the underwater features likely to attract the pike and for the pike themselves. If a pike is seen swimming at thirty feet, the bait is adjusted to fish at thirty feet, thereby giving the angler a chance at a fish that would probably never see an angler's bait in its lifetime. For such fishing, the set-up is standard free-roving livebait or float-trolled deadbaits, fishing the floats as sliders for rapid depth adjustment. For fishing at extreme depths, the use of special downriggers is recommended.

It will be obvious to the reader that I have no experience at the time of writing of fishing these waters with a coupled echo sounder, but it certainly sounds exciting. Friends of mine who have used the method with great success tell me that it is fascinating fishing, and I am looking forward to my first trips this coming winter.

RIVER PIKING

In this section, I shall be dealing with the fishing on rivers with a good flow of water, such as the Hampshire Avon, Dorset Stour and Wensum, as opposed to much more sluggish waterways. Fishing slow, uniform waters is much more akin to stillwater fishing, and all the tactics discussed so far will apply.

True river piking to me is to be found in the same kind of waters where I am happiest barbel and chub fishing, rivers with plenty of character in the shape of fast glides, deep pools, slow sections, slacks, eddies and creases. Chub fishing, in fact, gives a clue to river pike location, since all the most reliable chub-holding areas will be found to contain good pike as well. This is especially true of rubbish rafts, lines of overhanging bushes, smooth glides alongside the marginal rushes, and crease-type swims in particular. These steady glides alongside a faster flow, or created by the main current swinging away at a bend in the river, are the most productive pike swims, which is hardly surprising as they are good roach and chub swims also.

The biggest enigmas are dead slacks and slow eddies. Most people who pike fish the faster rivers seem to concentrate solely on the slacks simply, I believe, because they are easy to fish. Although these swims do obviously produce pike, I do not believe that they are particularly good areas, as indeed they are not good for other species. I have found that the productivity of a true slack decreases, the further it is located from the main flow and the greater the amount of bottom debris. For this latter reason, I do not rate slow eddies at all. The current circulation has the effect of creating a rubbish vortex at its centre, and this is not conducive to consistent sport with any species. It is probably important here to differentiate between stagnant slacks off the main flow and actual cuttings or offshoots, which may well be still, but contain a large resident fish population. These little backwaters can be pike hot spots.

Methods and Tactics

Undoubtedly, my favourite approach to river piking is trotting livebaits down a steady glide alongside the main flow. There is nothing revolutionary about the terminal rig for this, and the set-up described for free-roving earlier is the one I adopt, with one modification in that the bait is mounted head up the trace, instead of the usual attachment. The reason for this is simple. Retrieving a livebait after a long trot down against a good current, will do a it no good at all unless it is facing upstream during the retrieve. As with stillwater roving, it is important to fish with a greased line, and to control the amount of slack billowing around. If you want to trot a bait down a sharper current than normal, you can attach a dragging paternoster link. Using this arrangement, the speed of the trot can be controlled by the weight of the bomb used, and of course, if a heavy enough bomb is employed, you end up with a static paternostered bait in streamy water which in itself can be deadly. Don't be tempted to ignore the faster glides in river piking. River pike are tough brutes, well adapted to combat the heaviest currents, and they will be found out there in the middle with the best of them.

If you cannot obtain livebaits or you do not use them for your own reasons, then these streamy glides can be fished nearly as efficiently with trotted deads, although livebaits are definitely superior here. The best deadbaits to use for this fishing are small naturals, say five-inch roach or chub, although sprats and smelt will take fish. Such things as herrings, sardines or mackerel I prefer for the more static methods.

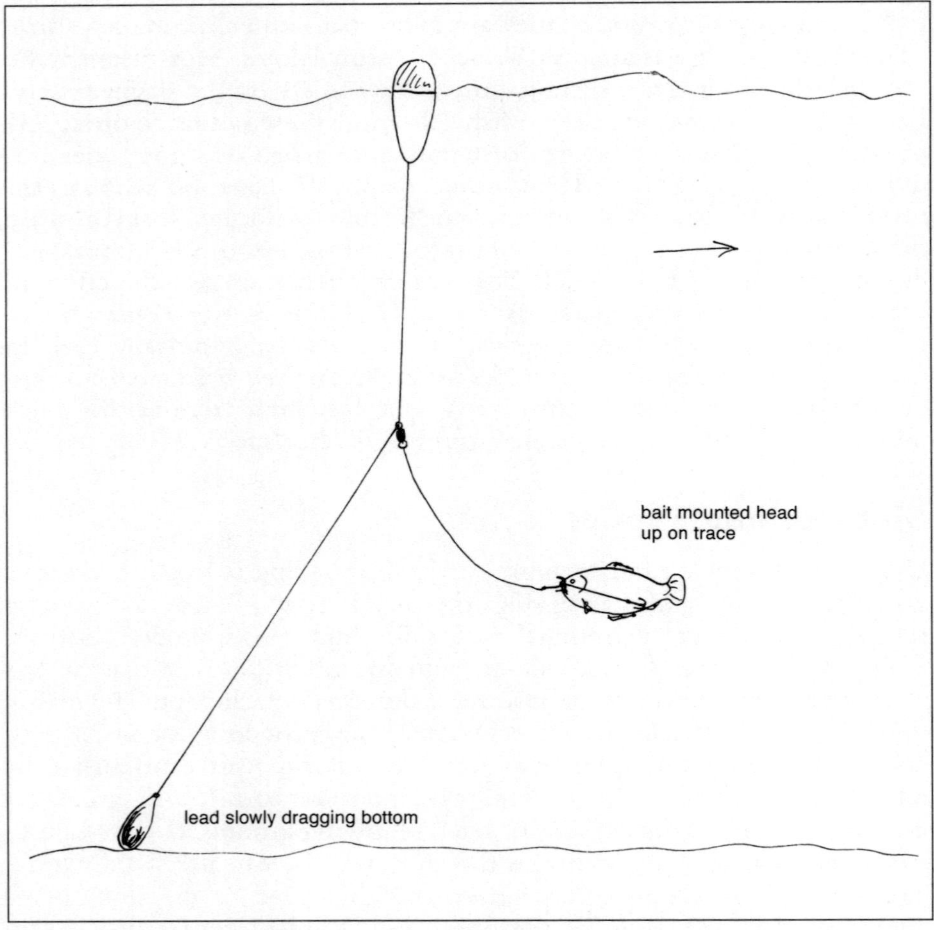

Dragging paternoster for rivers.

7 Pike

Wobbled Deadbaits

Where small to medium deadbaits really come into their own is for deadbait wobbling, which is a super method in streamy water and can at times drive the pike crazy. The bait is mounted on a conventional trace, but set with a kink in the tail to impart a wobbling action when it is retrieved through the water. A fair-sized deadbait, with the swim bladder punctured, will require no additional weight, but I generally prefer a rig used by Bob Mousley on the Wessex rivers, which incorporates a couple of inches of steel bar in the bait. When wobbling a deadbait, the current can be used to enable the bait to cover a large area of water in a most enticing fashion. By casting slightly upstream and across the main flow, the bait can be allowed to sink as it flutters downstream. As the line tightens, it will bump across the flow and into the slacker area, when you can then impart the additional movement by commencing a slow erratic retrieve. By lengthening the cast each time, a section of river can be very thoroughly investigated in this manner. You must, however, keep alert as under the right conditions, this presentation drives pike into a frenzy and they can hit the bait with breathtaking ferocity.

Static Baits

For presenting a bait alongside a rubbish raft, around tree roots and under marginal foliage, there is nothing to beat the static paternostered livebait. Deepish near-bank runs of steady water, with overgrown vertical banks, will often be found to harbour large numbers of pike, and sport can be fast and furious when conditions are favourable.

As far as large static legered deadbaits are concerned, there is little to say that has not been said previously. I prefer to use the static dead in the slower

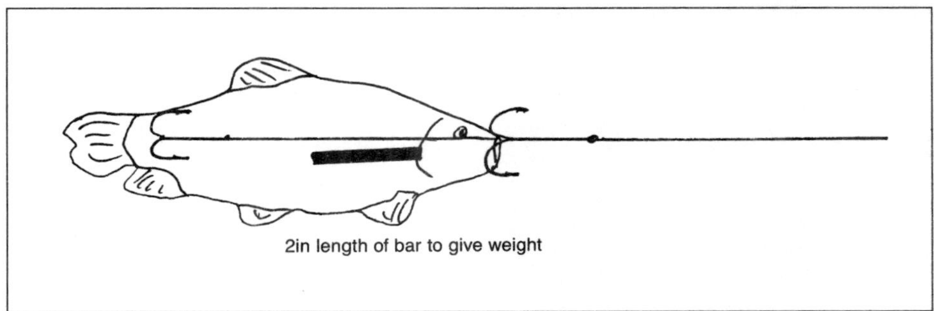

Weighted wobbling rig.

flows or the slacks and I will normally adopt this approach when I am using a second rod during a chub, roach or barbel session. For river deadbaiting, though, I always add a surface float so that there is an immediate indication of a take. There is no doubt that the static deadbait is a far slower method of taking river pike but, as in stillwaters, it does occasionally throw up a much bigger than average specimen. In a recent winter on the Dorset Stour, two thirty-pound pike were taken on successive weekends, and each accepted a legered herring. Interestingly, each pike was the only run of the day.

Water Height and Colour

For river piking, there is no doubt at all that the best conditions are those of clear water and a river at normal height. Low water temperatures do not seem to have any adverse effect, in fact a clear river after a frost will often provide some of the best pike sport. High, coloured water, however, is the kiss of death, and pike are particularly unresponsive in these conditions. The bulk of my fast-river piking is carried out on the Hampshire Avon and Dorset Stour, and whenever I am embarking on a trip to Hampshire, I always hedge my bets by taking roach and barbel gear as well as pike equipment. If the water is coloured, then I will switch to these species, which both feed well in murky conditions.

8
Roach

RESERVOIR ROACH FISHING

For very many years now, reservoirs have been particularly identified with extra-large roach. The most famous brace of roach in history, Bill Penney's fish of three pounds fourteen ounces and three pounds one ounce, were taken from London's Lambeth reservoir, but it was the writings of Peter Butler in the sixties that largely focused the attention of modern specialist roach anglers on these waters. Nowadays, reservoir roach potential is well known, and literally hundreds of such venues regularly produce very big roach indeed.

Location

Very broadly speaking, reservoirs fall into two categories: those created by damming a stream so that a shallow valley becomes flooded naturally, or those more artificially formed by constructing large bowls supported by massive earthworks, so that there is a steep bank to climb to reach the water surface, which is often considerably elevated above the level of the surrounding countryside.

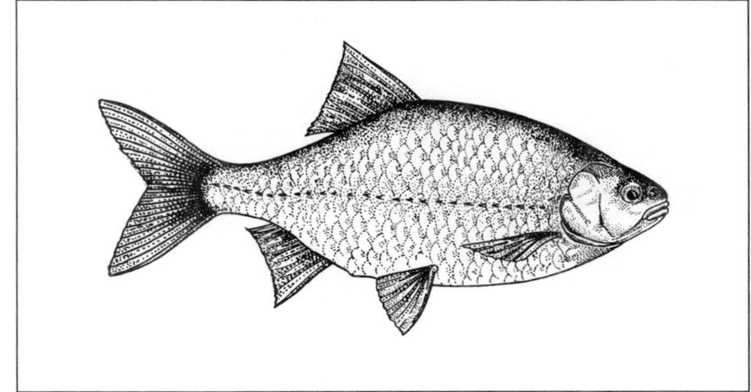

Roach.

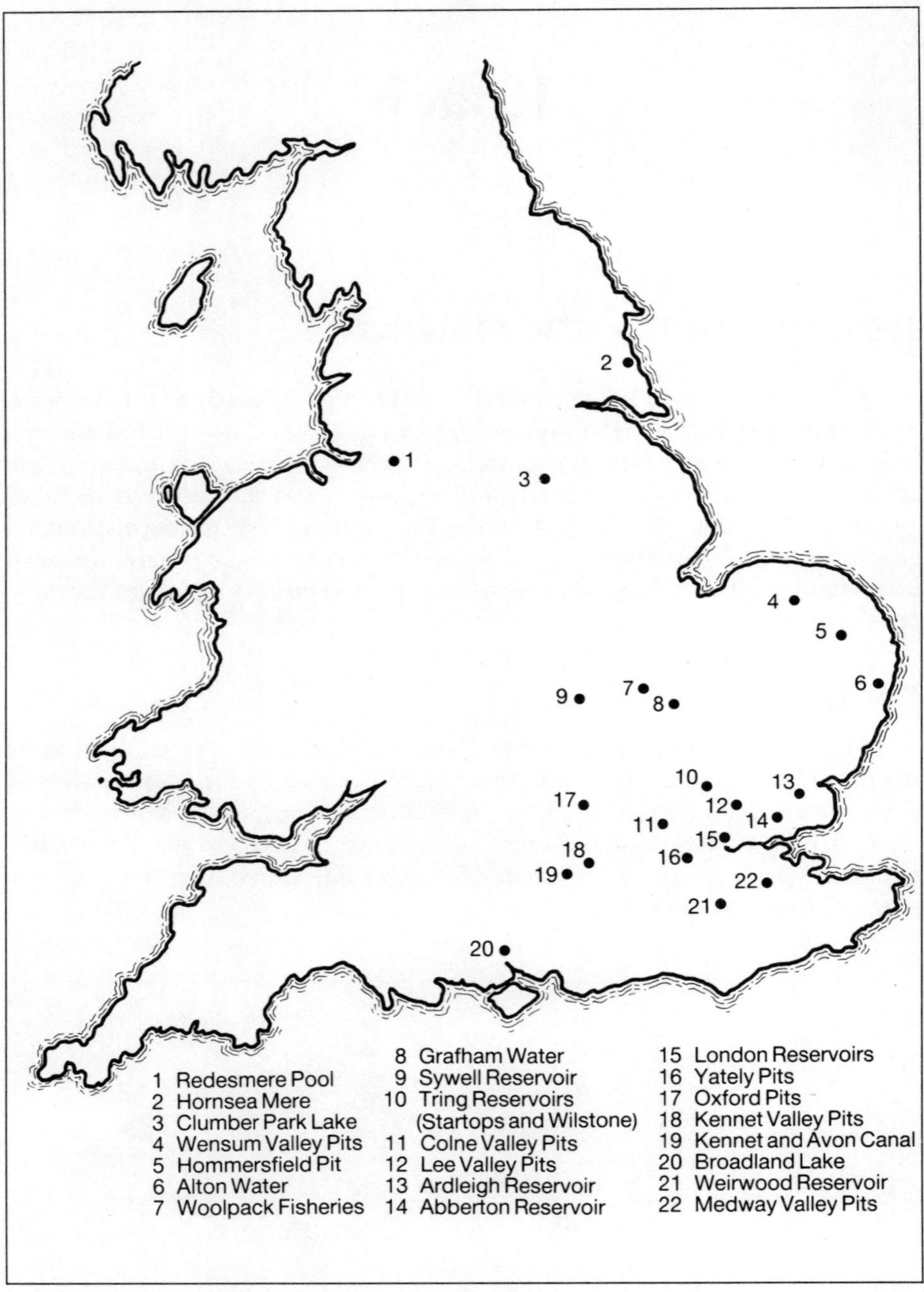

Past and present big roach stillwater fisheries.

Because the first type mentioned are often large sprawling waters, and the second type are raised structures, affording little protection from the elements, all reservoirs appear to share one characteristic, and that is that they are very quickly affected by any wind. This is a vitally important consideration in the location of reservoir roach since, after carp, they are the fish most likely to move round a water in response to a change in wind strength or direction.

Most of my experience with reservoir roach has been confined to the shallow, stream-fed type of water, in the autumn and winter months, and it is on these waters at this time of the year that I feel most qualified to offer advice. Having said that, I have fished Startops quite frequently, and most of the comments I have to make on the stream-fed reservoirs apply equally to the artificial waters. The deeper the water, however, the more difficult I have found it to predict the exact effect of prevailing conditions on the location of the fish. With the shallower waters, the roach will react almost instantly to condition changes, and once the basic governing factors controlling their movements on any particular water have been established, location of the fish in a given set of circumstances becomes fairly straightforward. It is not quite so easy on the deeper waters, where the fish can often take several days to respond to a change in wind direction, for instance.

Shallow Reservoirs

On the shallower waters, then, what are these governing factors? I have already mentioned the wind direction, and I cannot stress too strongly how important this is. Although there are other contributory factors, as we shall see later, I generally fish where the effect of the prevailing wind is greatest, even when there is a howling gale. Fishing into a strong wind, with breakers crashing at your feet, may be uncomfortable, and tackle control may be difficult but, believe me, roach feed well under such conditions. Important though wind strength and direction are, however, they are not the only factors. There are other considerations to take into account, before a decision is taken where to fish on any particular day.

Undertows

The first of these is the presence of any undertow. Most stream-fed reservoirs exhibit these subsurface currents to a greater or lesser extent, and pin-pointing them can be critical in the location of the roach.

After countless hours' reservoir roach fishing, I am no nearer to understanding what controls undertows. Obviously, the combination of current speed of the feeder stream, extraction rate for canal feeding, drinking supplies or irrigation, and wind strength and direction, will give endless permutations of water conditions, determining the presence or not of any undertow and, if one exists, its direction and strength. I used to be under the impression that undertow was entirely wind-related, but having now experienced several days' fishing in a flat calm where there has been an undertow present, I know this not to be true. It is clear from my observations that winds accentuate the currents, but they are certainly not the entire cause. I have laboured that point a little quite purposely, since a flat calm need not be the daunting prospect it first appears. If an undertow can be located in these conditions, roach will certainly not be far away. The way I locate any undertow is to cast out at points along the bank with an empty swimfeeder, using an unweighted swingtip. If, after the feeder has settled, you see the tip continually creeping upwards, you have found an undertow.

If we now examine the combination of wind and undertow on the roach movement, it is not good enough in my experience simply to select the area where the effect of the wind is greatest, without first establishing whether there is any undertow, and if so, where its effect is most marked. While it is generally true that any tow will be more obvious where the effect of any wind is greatest, it is not always so. On those occasions where there is a stronger undertow in an area only moderately affected by the wind, I would fish there in preference to another area of greater wind disturbance, but one in which there was little or no underwater current. From this you will obviously deduce, quite correctly, that I consider the undertow to be the more reliable guide to roach location. As I said earlier, the area of greatest wind effect is a generally reliable guide to the whereabouts of any undertow, but if you bear in mind that this is not always the case, then you will not go far wrong. It's a matter of keeping an open mind, and weighing up all the available evidence, before deciding where to fish.

Feeder Streams

Another factor to take into account is the feeder-stream flow rate, height and colour. Following heavy rain, the feeder stream can colour up, obviously carrying the coloured water into the reservoir itself. It may take several days for the colouration to become a general condition affecting the whole water, and initially the colouring may be a localized condition roughly approximating to the original stream bed. Unless it is extremely cold, coloured water can promote uninhibited feeding in roach, both in rivers and stillwaters, and reservoirs are no exception. I particularly like localized colouring, before there has been sufficient time for it to become an overall condition, and if an area could be found like this, which also happened to be affected by both a good wind and a steady undertow, then I would guarantee the presence of roach. Conversely, the most difficult conditions in which to locate fish are flat calms with no wind whatever, no undertow, and clear cold water. Undoubtedly, these are very poor conditions for roach.

Bait Presentation and Bite Detection Methods

One of the most fascinating aspects of reservoir roaching in the autumn and winter months is how the prevailing weather and water conditions, which have such a bearing on location, also give rise to wide variations in feeding behaviour. I find it utterly absorbing how, at times, really subtle condition changes can demand often radical alterations in terminal rig arrangements. This first became apparent in my early days of reservoir roaching when I experienced tremendous frustration with missed bites, obviously attributable to incorrect bait presentation. It was only when I made a study of feeding characteristics in relation to weather and water condition variations that I was able to prove to my own satisfaction that terminal rig adjustments would often dramatically improve the successful hooking ratio.

I well remember the circumstances which led up to my being forced to rethink totally my approach to reservoir roach fishing. For two seasons I had been fishing one particular water, and during that time, although I caught many nice fish, I experienced an alarmingly high proportion of missed bites. Looking back on it now, I was obviously foolish to tolerate the problem for so long. It was, however, happening to everyone who fished the water and I felt it was something I just had to live with. One particular two-day session, however, resulted in my becoming so frustrated that I just had to work out where I was going wrong.

On the first day, conditions were certainly not ideal for roach, with clear water and only a very gentle ripple. I used my standard approach of two matched feeder rods, butt-mounted bobbins and free-running inverted Drennan feeders, coupled with eighteen-inch hooklinks to size 16 hooks, baited with two white maggots. The fishing was very slow, and I had only four bites all day. But they were good confident indications, with the bobbin smoothly rising to the butt ring on each occasion, and each bite resulted in a good roach successfully landed. I was very pleased, and could not wait to get back the following morning.

I was back in the swim at dawn, and was delighted to see that the wind had picked up considerably in the night. It was still pleasantly mild, but there was now a substantial chop on the water, and I knew that the roach would feed well in these conditions. I turned out to be perfectly correct in my assessment, because that day I had twenty bites identical to those I had experienced the day before. The trouble was that I missed nineteen of them. The one roach I did manage to land almost contrived to escape, the hook dropping out just as it came over the net rim. I remember the mood I was in as I drove home that night, but I now know that I needed a session like that to shake me out of my obvious complacency.

Solving the Problem of Missed Bites

Once I had analysed the situation rationally, the reasons for the missed bite problem became obvious to me. Hindsight really can be a wonderful thing; I had become far too set in my ways, idle if you like. The matched rod approach, using the standard set-up mentioned which had served me so well in the past, was being used automatically in all conditions. It was now painfully apparent that there were occasions when the rig was nearly useless. A lot more thought was needed, and I determined that on my next session I would respond to a missed bite by trying to figure out why I had missed it, and alter my terminal rig accordingly. The next few sessions were to prove fascinating, and they revolutionized my reservoir roaching to such an extent that missed bites are now an extremely minor irritation. What is more important, the lessons I learned in those days now mean that I can fairly accurately predict the terminal arrangement required under any particular conditions. What follows is a summary of the events of those early days, and I think that the description is the clearest way of outlining the general principles involved.

At first light, I settled in the swim in which I had missed all the bites, and initially set up with my normal arrangement, using the terminal rig as outlined earlier. The swim was one in which I'd had success in the past, and as it was located on the eastern bank of the reservoir it generally received the maximum effect from the prevailing westerly or north-westerly wind. On the morning in question, there was a fairly gentle wind blowing directly into the pitch, creating a very moderate ripple. It was unusually mild and, apart from the water being a little clearer than I would have liked, conditions really could have been a lot worse. On one of the eighteen-inch, 2-pound hook-links was a size 18 hook baited with a single pinkie, while on the other I had kept faith with two white maggots on a size 16. Bite indication was by means of my usual butt-mounted bobbins, with an eighteen-inch drop.

I had not been fishing long when there was a half-inch lift on one bobbin, followed in the next few minutes by two similar indications. After the third, I tried a strike. I was not at all surprised when I connected with nothing, as the indication had been very slight, but I certainly was surprised to discover that the maggots were completely smashed. Obviously, the bait must have been well inside a fish's mouth for this to have happened, and it was therefore apparent that the rig was hopelessly inefficient. I needed to see the bite earlier, and therefore my first decision was to reduce the tail length from eighteen inches to six inches.

This first change appeared to have made little difference, for in the next hour or so I was to strike at two similar indications, again missing both and again finding the maggots sucked dry. This time, I decided to stick with the six-inch tail, but to introduce more resistance into the arrangement by converting from a totally free-running feeder into one that would lock after two or three inches of line had been taken. This was achieved by the simple expedient of putting a swan shot about three inches above the feeder. Using a lock shot in this manner had proved a very effective ploy in both tench and bream fishing, so why not roach? My reasoning was to prove sound, and I had two bites in quick succession after the change. Both bites consisted of a couple of initial twitches: the bobbin then shot to the butt and the reel started to backwind, caused by the roach feeling the feeder drag and bolting. Well-hooked roach of one pound six ounces and one pound eleven ounces were landed and I was highly delighted. I was getting somewhere.

Almost imperceptibly, the wind strength had been steadily increasing as the morning wore on, and by about 11 a.m. I was fishing into the teeth of a fairly strong blow. At about this time an undertow started, and I began to experience trouble with the bobbins creeping up. This got more and more annoying as the strength of the undertow increased, and eventually I resorted to line clips at the butt ring. As I was now expecting definite bites on the bolt-rig variation I was using, I expected that I would miss seeing the initial twitch, but that the run itself would be very obvious. I sat back and relaxed.

At about mid-afternoon, it was time to put the thinking-cap on again. As I wound in one of the rods to rebait, I unexpectedly found myself playing a fish, a roach of one pound nine ounces well hooked in the mouth. I had seen no indication. Mistakenly, I thought this was an isolated occurrence not warranting a further tackle modification, and I fished on in the same manner. I was soon to discover my mistake: the next time I wound in to refill the feeders, the baits on both rods were smashed, although I had had no noticeable indication at all. Obviously, I had to dispense with the line clips, and I minimized the bobbin creep by loading them with swan shot.

The next time I retrieved the tackles, I again had sucked maggots on one rod, so it was apparent that the roach were no longer bolting against the resistance. In fact, the resistance was now definitely detrimental. What appeared to be happening was that the roach were mouthing the bait, slowly moving off with it until they encountered the drag of the feeder, and then, instead of running, were simply dropping the maggots. Accordingly, I removed the stop shot behind the feeder, reverting to the free-running arrangement. Almost immediately, this resulted in a very positive bite, with the bobbin running smoothly to the butt. Surprisingly, I missed it, and this time the maggots were apparently untouched. It was now head-scratching time!

Eventually, I worked it all out. The fish were not prepared to tolerate resistance, but they were moving off leisurely with the bait. The fact that the bait appeared untouched after the previous bite indicated that I had struck too early which, in turn, suggested that the tail length of six inches was now too short. The fish needed to be given longer on the bait with no resistance whatever, and therefore I increased the tail length to eighteen inches. It struck me as comical that I was now back with exactly the same rig as the one which I had started with. When my next bite was also missed in the same way, I again increased the link, this time to three feet. This proved to be the correct combination for the rest of that day, for the remaining six bites all resulted in fish landed – five nice roach and a seven-pound bream.

That day was interesting in that the end-rig modifications I made had enabled me to see quite clearly how the frequency of roach bites increased both with increasing wind velocity and more significantly, with the onset and steadily increasing influence of undertow. The more turbulent the conditions had become the more leisurely and confidently the roach appeared to feed.

On the next day, the wind had increased to gale force, with steady cold rain most of the day. In view of the conditions, and the previous day's events, I started off with the same terminal rig with which I had finished the night before. There was a significant change in my approach, however: I had decided to fish with one rod only, and use a tip indicator in place of the bobbin. There was nothing inherently wrong with a bobbin as indicator, but while I was experimenting with end rigs, I decided to use an indicator that allowed me to hold the rod all day, and thus be in a position to respond much faster to bite indications. It is almost impossible to react to small movements as quickly with bobbins as it is with tip indicators. Also, the continual creeping even of loaded bobbins due to the undertow was extremely distracting and therefore inefficient.

I started off that day using a swingtip indicator, which I had to load with lead wire quite significantly to balance it against the steady subsurface current. Eventually, the swingtip was not creeping upwards, but it was flapping about uncontrollably in the strong wind, so I changed over to a fairly heavy Drennan quivertip quite early on in the day. With this arrangement I found that the tip would pull round slowly after the cast for a few minutes, until it found a level where the tension in the tip and the pressure on the line from the undertow were balanced, when it then held a constant curvature. It occurred to me that this was not unlike upstreaming for chub, with balanced tackle. Although the tackle set-up looked crude, it was in fact anything but that. The slightest touch on the bait would pull the tip round further or, more probably, result in a momentary relaxation of tension, allowing the tip to spring back straight.

Once I had the tackle arranged to my satisfaction, it was not too long before I had my first bite, a solid pull on the tip followed by a slack line. When that bite was missed and the maggots came back as good as new, I immediately increased the hooklink length to five feet, a simple decision following the pattern of the previous day. With the weather conditions remaining constant, there was no need for any other modification that day. When I packed up at dusk, I had had a further seven bites, all slack liners which had produced seven roach up to one pound fifteen ounces.

A week later, I was back in the original swim. Conditions could hardly have been more different, as I was now faced with a warm breathless morning, with not a trace of a ripple. I fished for two days under those conditions, and bites were few and far between. But there was some action, and more valuable lessons were learned. I started off using a three-foot hooklink, again fishing with one rod only using a swingtip indicator, which required no loading as there was no undertow. During the morning, I had occasional tiny lifts of the tip, and several times found my bait crushed. I had progressively reduced the tail length without significantly affecting the bites, and it was not until I arrived at a tail length of three inches, using a fixed feeder, that I had my first positive indication. A fair roach was hooked, but unfortunately fell off after a few minutes. When I missed another lift a few minutes later, I decided that perhaps I had now overdone it and gone to too short a tail. A twelve-inch tail with the fixed feeder proved to be the answer. That combination gave me two unmistakable drop-back bites which yielded roach of two pounds two ounces and one pound fourteen ounces.

After those two weekends, I remember thinking that I had cracked it. All the evidence suggested that the more ideal the conditions, the more resistance-free the tackle had to be. Under the perfect combination of a mild westerly air stream, steady undertow and a tinge of colour in the water, a long hooklink of anything up to six feet was the order of the day. I could not see that it made too much difference whether the feeder was fixed or free with long tails. However, the opposite situation, with perhaps clear cold conditions and the water flat calm with no undertow, demanded the total contrast of a fixed bolt-rig type of arrangement, with a short hooklength. On the whole, that précis is really not far from the truth, and I always work on that basis when I am trying to assess the conditions at the start of any new session. It is not an inflexible rule of thumb, however, and you should always keep an open mind. This was brought home to me only a couple of weeks after the session mentioned above.

Keeping an Open Mind

I had apparently perfect conditions: good chop, good colour and a steady current. From previous experience, I knew, or thought I did, that the rig to use was a longtail variety. Smugly, I expected to bag up, but I reckoned without the roach, which that day decided to make me eat humble pie. All day, they nearly drove me crazy and, apart from a fish I wound in deeply hooked after seeing no bite whatever, all I had were a succession of twitches and trembles which resulted in crushed maggots only, but no fish.

I had tried several permutations of terminal rig by late afternoon, when all of a sudden I realized what was wrong. A frost was starting to form, as it had the previous two nights. Perhaps the conditions were not as good as they actually appeared, as it was possible a low water temperature was having a negative effect. If that was the case, the roach would probably not be moving around so much, and therefore the bolt-rig set-up might be more appropriate. Immediately, I switched to a fixed feeder, coupled with a three-inch tail only. The result of that change was almost magical: within minutes, the swingtip shot out and the rod lurched in my hand, as a one-pound seven-ounce roach bolted against the resistance. Three more fish quickly followed before I had to pack up, very much wiser than I had been several hours before.

Holding the Rod

In the foregoing description, which I purposely made very detailed to convey the full importance of the principles, I have made many references to the use of one rod only, hand held, with either swingtip or quivertip. It is important that I stress that I used this approach almost exclusively in my learning days, simply because I felt that it would enable me to appreciate the idiosyncrasies of roach feeding behaviour that much faster. In no way am I suggesting that this approach is always the superior one, because I now know that there are many occasions when it is not. In most average-to-good conditions, provided the roach can be found, they will give positive bites to a correctly presented bait, and it does not really matter which approach you adopt. In my own fishing nowadays, it depends on my mood. If the correct terminal rig is being employed, bites will be just as positive on a bobbin, a butt indicator or a tip indicator. If I am feeling particularly lazy, then I will use two rods with bobbins and Optonics, especially if I am fishing a long session into the dark, for I know I will get just as many bites as if I sat hovering over the rod all day. On occasions, this more laid-back approach is preferable. The roach bites may be particularly slow and deliberate, and in these circumstances it can pay to sit a little back from the rods to allow the bites time to develop. Holding the rod on these days could result in premature striking.

Having made the point that on most days it is a question of personal choice which approach you adopt, there is no doubt in my mind that, on occasions, the use of one delicately balanced hand-held rod will produce roach when other methods fail through lack of sensitivity. These occasions are when the conditions are extreme or when I know from experience that I can expect finicky bites, whatever terminal rig I adopt.

Firstly, there is the total flat calm, without a breath of wind. The sky is blue, the water gin clear, and there was perhaps a frost in the night. These are terrible conditions for reservoir roach, but I have picked up a lot of fish by fishing the swingtip, in conjunction with fixed feeders and tail lengths of as little as two inches. After casting, the line is tightened so that the tip is virtually straight to the feeder. I fish with the rod supported on a rest and the butt on my knee, and the balance in the tackle is so fine that even the most circumspect roach bite will register, usually by a one- or two-inch drop back of the tip. I have caught dozens of roach in this manner, when I am absolutely convinced that I would not have seen the bite on a more orthodox method of bite indication.

The second set of conditions is the exact opposite of the first. I am thinking here of the howling gale, with the wind so strong that you can hardly erect an umbrella in safety, and an undertow so fierce that the heaviest bobbin rises to the butt in seconds. Here we are faced with a situation where we know that the roach will be feeding if only we can see the bites. This is where I personally favour the quivertip approach. What I do is use a fairly stiff tip, say a 2-ounce Drennan, and then load the feeder with lead until it holds against the undertow. It does not matter if it takes 2 ounces, as long as the feeder does not roll. Then tighten the tip into the lead, until it has taken on an obvious curve, without dislodging the terminal rig. The curvature should be such that either a pull or a spring back is unmissable. I generally settle for about a four-inch deflection, and if this cannot be achieved without disturbing the feeder, then I will either use more lead on the feeder or a more flexible tip.

The whole point about this set-up is that it is very wind resistant, once the correct balance has been achieved. As with fishing the flat calm, the rod must be supported on a rest to eliminate false bites, with the rod butt resting on your knee to avoid the rod being blown around. When I am fishing the quivertip in this way, I always fish side on to the swim, and then I have a direct pull in response to a bite. With the tackle set up in this way, bites can be incredible. Indications that would hardly register on slack-line indication methods can really make the rod lurch back in your hand. As before, the slightest movement of the bait removes all the tension from the tackle, resulting in an unmissable spring back of the quivertip. A comparable effect can be achieved by using a heavily loaded rigid butt indicator in place of the quivertip. In this case, instead of the tip spring back, the bite is indicated by the indicator dropping like a stone.

Baits and Feeding

So far, we have looked at the vital areas of location, bait presentation and bite detection methods, relevant to varying weather and water conditions. Once we have got these right, there is no doubt at all that the actual choice of hookbait is not quite so critical. Most of my reservoir fish have come on

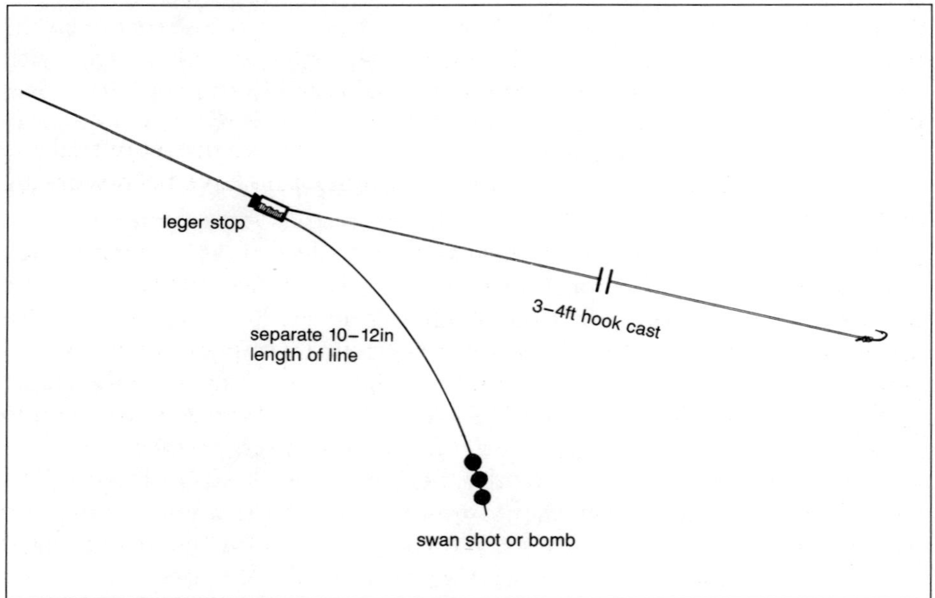

Link leger rig.

maggots, flake or maggot/flake cocktail. Flake in particular is a superb big-roach bait, being more selective than maggots if you are fishing a water with a roach population consisting of a few big fish and hordes of little ones. I have also had nice fish on crust, link legered a few inches off the bottom, redworms, lobs, sweetcorn and trout-pellet paste, but for most situations maggots and flake fit the bill.

Flavouring

One particularly fascinating aspect of feeder fishing for reservoir roach, using maggot or flake hookbaits, is flavouring the bait. This is something I have been involved with for quite some years now, and there is absolutely no doubt in my mind that on occasions the addition of a flavour makes a dramatic difference to the number of bites. Many times now, I have conducted the experiment of fishing two identical feeder rigs adjacent to each other, the only difference between them being that one bait was flavoured and the other plain. To keep the experiment totally fair, I have been careful to alternate the rods periodically, so that each bait fished an equal amount of time on the left- and right-hand sides of the swim. Not once has the plain bait outfished the flavoured one, and on those days when I have had sufficient indications for a statistical analysis to be at all meaningful, the flavoured baits have produced at least four times as many bites as the plain ones. If that had happened once or twice, I may have been tempted to dismiss it as coincidence, but it has occurred so consistently that I can now state categorically that flavouring maggot and flake hookbaits is beneficial.

As far as the actual flavours are concerned, it really is a matter of trial and error, for each particular water. Friends of mine who have been working along similar lines to myself have had very poor results using flavours I have done well with, and vice versa, so there can be no hard and fast rules. For what it's worth, the flavours that have worked best for me are strawberry and vanilla, as well as the commercially available 'Roach Attractor'. I have had isolated good results using pineapple and Catchum's Scopex, but these appear more inconsistent.

Whichever flavour you decide to try, it is important that you do not overdo the quantity, or you will make the bait bitter. This is particularly true with maggots, which take a surprisingly small amount of flavour to become totally impregnated. I generally use about 10 millilitres of concentrated flavour for every pint of maggots. What I do is pour the flavour into the maggots and then give the bait a vigorous shake for a few minutes to disperse it thoroughly. For flake, I will either put a large piece in the maggot box or, alternatively, put it in a polythene bag and then tip in the required amount of concentrated flavour. I will use about 5 millilitres for the amount of flake from a tin loaf. Once the bag has been sealed for a few minutes, which makes the bread sweat, you will find that the flake retains the flavour all day.

Loose Feed

A very important consideration with reservoir roaching is the amount of loose feed you introduce and, more importantly, the accuracy of its introduction. There seems to have been a wide difference of experience among my angling friends, some of whom say that the more feed introduced, both on the day and by way of pre-baiting, the more big roach result. Others have found it very easy to overdo the groundbaiting, discovering over and over again that heavy feeding had a detrimental effect on sport. On the reservoirs where I have done most of my roach fishing, my experience puts me firmly in the second category. I think it boils down to a simple matter of big roach density in the water in question. In my case, the waters contain hordes of small fish, plus bream and hybrids, and these in turn attract the large numbers of pike present. Only rarely have I caught a good roach when the swim has been full of these nuisance fish, and heavy feeding, especially pre-baiting, brings them in in droves.

The baiting needs to be accurate. There is no doubt at all that the swimfeeder technique is a very effective one for introducing controlled amounts of feed, but only if you are casting into the same tight area each time. To get the best out of reservoir roaching, you really must go to the trouble of hitting the same spot every time, otherwise you are going to scatter bait all over the place. The simplest method I know is to cast out to the required spot initially, and then put a turn of insulating tape around the spool. Taking up the slack line then leaves a few turns of line on top of the tape. On every subsequent cast, assuming you can cast in a straight line, the feeder will drop in the same place. If you prefer a visual target, then you can use a detachable marker buoy. I am indebted to Jim Gibbinson for this idea, which first appeared in his excellent book, *Modern Specimen Hunting*.

Like all good ideas, it is so simple. Once you have found the exact depth by orthodox plumbing, set a sliding float on the correct length of line, the end of which is tied in a loop. Tie a loop in the reel line, and then simply tie the two loops with PVA tape. Brilliant, isn't it? I wish I'd thought of it! After you have cast out, of course, the tape dissolves, leaving the marker in place. At the end of the session, it's a simple matter to retrieve the marker by casting over it and snagging the line.

While we are on the subject of accurate casting, here is a little tip that I have found useful when fishing in a big wind, and using long hooklinks. I

Detachable marker buoy.

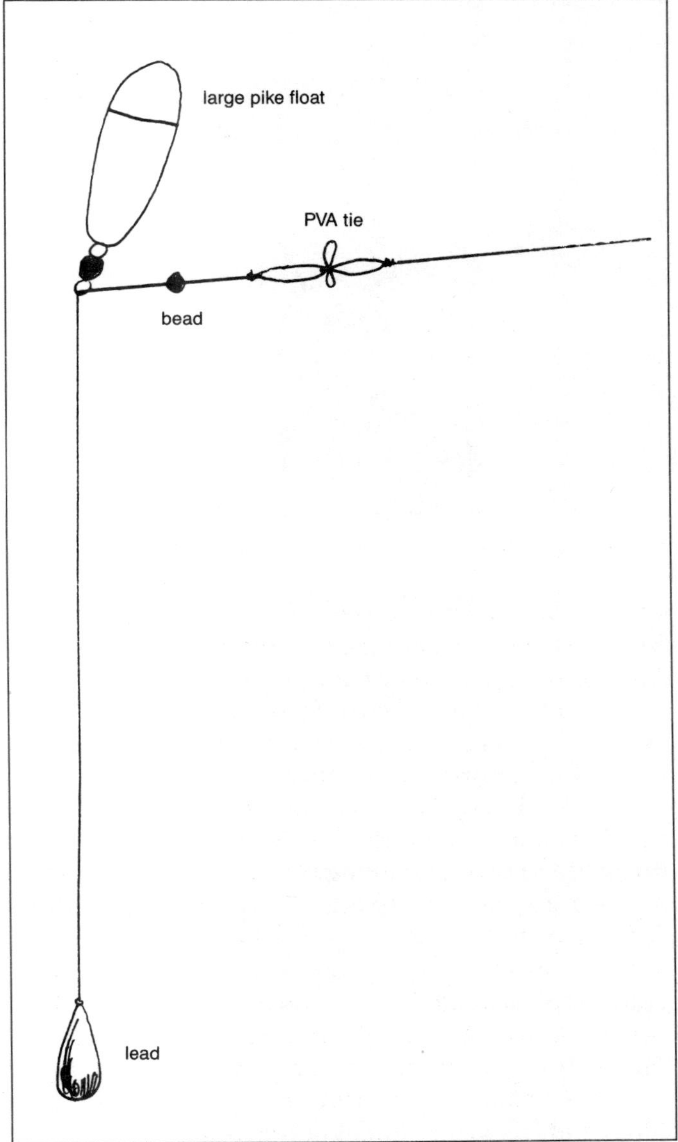

loop the hooklink so that it is tied, close to the bait, to the feeder by PVA tape. This is useful in preventing tangles, and it does of course have another advantage. The point behind using a long tail in the first place is to give the roach time to move off at their leisure with the bait before encountering any resistance. By tying the link to the feeder in this way, you are ensuring

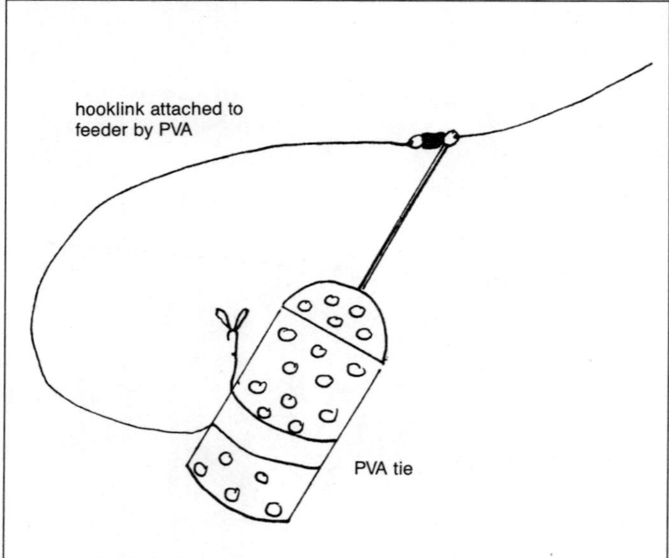

Anti-tangle feeder rig.

the maximum free travel. Also, of course, you are presenting your hookbait right among the free offerings. So effective is this approach that I am now using it more and more often.

As I said earlier, the swimfeeder I use for my reservoir roach fishing is the largest Drennan, fished inverted, with the bottom open-ended to receive a plug of groundbait. My normal approach will be to put out between six and ten feeder loads of bait into each area, before commencing fishing, and then top up periodically every half-hour or so throughout the day by recasting. If fish are coming or there is lots of activity, this feed rate may be stepped up. As with hookbaits, there is great scope for experiment with flavoured and coloured groundbaits, and I have had some interesting sessions using various combinations. Flavourings certainly work, but colourings are much more indefinable. I did fish for quite a long period using exclusively yellow coloured feed, and though I caught fish I was unable to draw any firm conclusions.

I have caught roach using many weird concoctions in the groundbait plug, and it really is fun experimenting. My favourite combination is fine breadcrumb, mixed with a small amount of finely ground rusk to make the bait explode from the feeder quickly, and an equal amount of trout-fry or salmon-fry crumb. I have had equally good results by dispensing with the crumb, but by flavouring the breadcrumb with flavours such as Maple, Maple Cream and Ultra Spice. One trap to avoid is the introduction of too many variables on any one day. If you are experimenting with a flavoured groundbait, do not use a different flavour for the hookbait. Either use the same one or none at all; otherwise, if you do catch fish, you will have no way of knowing the cause of your success. One thing which I would certainly agree with is that hemp is a superb attractant, although its use in large quantities is more relevant where there is a big head of large roach. Startops is the classic example of where the introduction of hemp has worked well.

ROACH FISHING IN SMALL STREAMS

Summer Fishing

Location of the roach shoals on a small, shallow and weedy stream in high summer is simplicity itself. Unlike perch, the roach show themselves readily. However, if we are looking for the bigger roach, the number of specimens I have caught accidentally while chub or perch fishing tells me, obviously, that the features that are attractive to those species have a similar appeal to large roach. This is important in that it allows us to be selective to a large extent in the size of the fish we are after.

The first areas that are worthy of attention are the classic chub swims of a raft over steady water and long lines of overhanging bushes over uniform glides. My own fishing has shown a high average weight here for the occasional roach I catch from such places. Almost all my summer roach from swims of this type have been accidental captures while chubbing, especially with lobworms and large pieces of flake, either free-lined or using a very light leger.

Obviously, if I am deliberately fishing for large roach, I will scale down the gear from that used for chub fishing, usually opting for a 3- or 4-pound line, depending on how snaggy the swim is, with hook sizes from 8 to 12. For this fishing I use a very flexible quivertip, a Drennan 1½ pound is about right, and I also leave a nice bow in the line for the roach to take up. As with perch, it pays not to be in too much of a hurry to strike a roach bite on leger tackle, if you are not to suffer the frustration of continual missed bites. Also in a similar way to perch, roach respond to diminishing light intensity, and the dawn and dusk periods are excellent, as are the first couple of hours of darkness. The gathering gloom of the dusk period undoubtedly increases the roaches' confidence, and at this time of the day a big roach will give you a solid thump the equal of any chub bite.

Without a doubt, my favourite summer roach swims are the cabbage patch, and the uniform, evenly paced glide alongside rushes. Cabbage patches – those beds of lilies where the depth and current are such that many of the pads are permanently submerged – are very reliable harbouring areas for large roach. In the halcyon days when I fished Dick Walker's Ouse stretch quite frequently, one of my favourite swims was one known as the small cabbage patch, and it is typical of dozens of such swims on many small streams. Under normal summer conditions, there was about four feet of steady current in that area, and the way I fish a swim of that type is to find out where the small areas of clean gravel exist in the middle of all the foliage, and then lay on. A simple peacock quill, fixed bottom-end only, and cocked by one shot resting on the bottom, will suffice. Because of the nature of the swim, it is important that the bait be presented dead still on the bottom, if you are not to become repeatedly snagged, For this reason, I favour the more compact baits such as sweetcorn, tares, and flake. I purposely avoid maggots to minimize interference from small fry, which can be an absolute pain in the summer, especially in the more weedy swims.

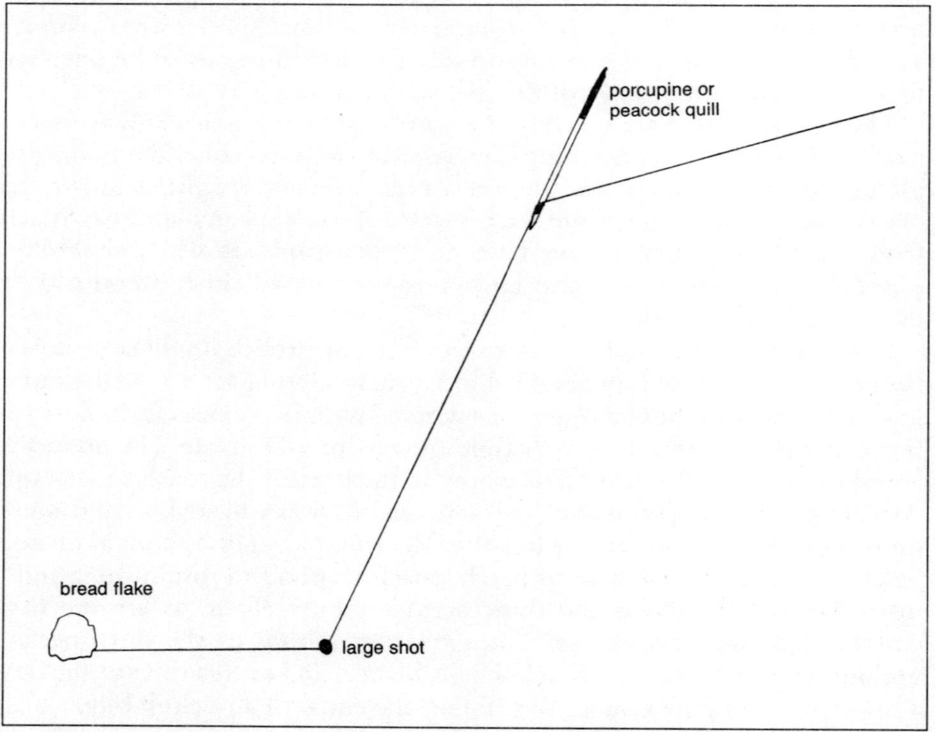

Laying on.

8 Roach

Stewed Wheat

As each cabbage patch is unlikely to hold a colossal head of roach, it is well to be careful about the quantity of free offerings you introduce. I usually content myself with a bait-dropper load of bait samples in each hole I intend fishing or, better still, a few baits in a dropper load of hemp. One bait that I really rate for summer roach is stewed wheat, and I caught most of my Great Ouse roach on this. Believe me, this bait can be deadly, and although it appears to have gone out of fashion lately, I advise you to give it a try. A word of warning though: stewed wheat is a heavy bait and extremely filling; although the roach love the stuff, it does not take much to satisfy them, so it pays to be extra sparing about the amount you introduce. Again, the best way to feed is to put in a dropper of hemp occasionally, containing just a few wheat grains. In that way you are able to keep a summer roach swim on the boil all day. For those readers who have never used stewed wheat, you prepare it in the same way as you do hemp, simmering it as slowly as possible until the grains split. One of the beauties of cabbage patch swim, of course, is that because it contains a large amount of shade in the form of lily pads, under which the roach can hide, the fish can feed avidly on and off all day, even in the hottest and sunniest weather. My most memorable session in the small cabbage patch on Dick Walker's stretch was in July 1972, when I took fourteen fish on wheat on a blazing hot afternoon, of between one pound six ounces and one pound fifteen ounces.

Other swims which are great favourites of mine for roach, summer and winter, are steady glides alongside bank-side rushes. The current should not be too sluggish, however, and I always look for a clean gravel or fine silk-weed bottom, rather than one covered in that horrible greenish-black blanket weed. I like to fish these swims with the float, and although my trotting ability generally hovers between poor and mediocre, even I can cope with swims of this type. The set-up is simple enough: a light stick float, or waggler if the wind is troublesome, combined with a 2- or 3-pound hooklength and a size 10 to size 16 hook. For trotting, I generally confine myself to maggots or flake, introducing either a few maggots before each trot down or, if I am fishing flake, an occasional small ball of mashed bread feed. The bait is fished tripping bottom, occasionally being held back to make it swing upwards. At intervals during such a session, I will push up the float, and fish it laying on at the tail of the swim, with a tight line and the rod on a rest. This serves the dual purpose of giving my arm a rest, and is also a well-proven ploy for picking up the extra-big roach that is hanging back at the rear of the shoal. As the light begins to fade in the evening, I dispense with trotting altogether, and concentrate on laying on in this way, swapping the float tackle at dusk for a light link leger and quivertip. Flake now becomes the big-roach bait *par excellence*.

Stalking

In some heavily overgrown rivers and streams, there will be a small head of large roach and it is in waters of this type that you can pick up the occasional specimen by stalking. I am thinking here of the tiny gaps of clear gravel in the midst of thick rush beds or lily beds, small inaccessible areas under trees and bushes and narrow gravelly channels between streamer beds. Big roach in waters of this type can be solitary creatures, and catching them is very much a scaled-down version of summer chub chasing. Because of the light weightless tackle needed to make a delicate bait presentation possible, the fishing has to be short-range work, and therefore it is essential to keep all movements as stealthy as possible. For this fishing, I will normally use 3-pound line straight through to a size 12, and because there is nothing more exciting than watching a fish take your bait at close quarters, I generally opt for an easily seen offering such as bread flake or sweetcorn.

It pays to take the trouble to make the bait behave as naturally as possible. For bread flake, I squeeze it flat so that it sinks slowly, whereas for denser baits such as sweetcorn or tares, it can make all the difference if you counterbalance the weight of the hook with a tiny sliver of cork glued to the hook shank. Use sufficient cork for the hook so that it only just sinks. When this has been achieved, the hookbait will behave similarly to the free samples, rising and falling as fish fan over them. Any bait that remains anchored to the bottom is immediately treated with suspicion.

Winter Fishing

Having located the big roach under the low clear conditions of summer gives us a reliable starting point in our winter fishing, when the level is higher and the water more coloured. Like all fish, roach do not tend to wander far from their summer haunts, and they will move only as far as they need to, in response to any change in water or weather conditions. If you are preoccupied with other things in the summer months you can, with practice, learn to read the river in winter, to establish the likely roach-holding areas. It is true, though, that you can waste a lot of time on trial and error, when just an occasional spotting trip in the early part of the season could prevent it. This is particularly important in the case of submerged cabbages, which are just as reliable roach-producing areas in the winter as they are in the warmer months. The problem in the winter is that all that remains of the cabbages are the dead root systems, with little or no visual evidence to indicate their presence, and without prior knowledge many excellent swims can be totally overlooked.

High, Coloured Water

Most of the basic techniques outlined in the summer section still hold good for the winter, and really there is little to add for fishing in what might be termed normal winter conditions. Therefore, I want to devote the rest of this particular section to talking about fishing high, coloured water, conditions that are the peak of perfection for small-river roaching, providing that the increased height and colour have not been caused by melting snow.

The first thing we have to determine is how the change in conditions will affect the location of the roach. Once again, we should start from the area where they are normally to be found, and then try to deduce where they would move with least effort. A good rule of thumb is that they will probably move to an area of similar flow rate to that to which they are accustomed. Let's have a look at how this works in practical application.

The drawing overleaf illustrates are some of the most important areas to look for, in my experience. You will not, of course, normally come across so many good swims in such a short section of river, but if you do, I suggest you keep the stretch to yourself! Let us have a look first of all at the swims lettered A, from which we would fish from 1. Under summer or normal winter conditions, the areas indicated by broken lines are very shallow gravelly sections, which may be dry or at most only inches deep, with the main flow being concentrated through the narrow central channel. With three feet of water on, these areas become cracking roach swims. Because they are still away from the main current, they will now have a gentle steady flow over clean gravel, in an area which is otherwise quite turbulent. Such swims will often attract a large concentration of roach, and an excellent way of tackling the fishing is with the use of a small swimfeeder. They are also perfect for laying on tactics with a tight line. By fishing the float overdepth, casting on to the edge of the fast flow, and allowing the float to swing round and settle in the slack, you achieve a superb presentation. On my local river Leam, which contains a good head of excellent roach, there are many swims of this type in the water-meadows, and I have had many memorable days fishing in the manner described, using redworms, flake or best of all, large lobworms. Using a full-size lob on a size 8 for roach fishing may sound crude, but in coloured water it is a deadly approach.

Moving downstream, we come to swim B, which we would fish from 2. What we have here is a glide alongside bank-side rushes, normally with a

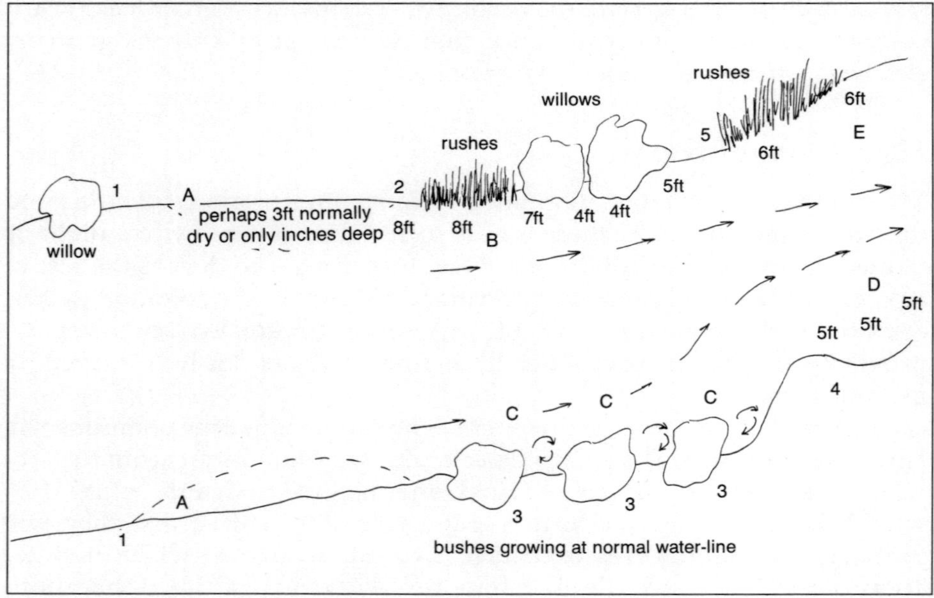

Fishing in high water.

maximum depth of about five feet, but now nearer eight. This will be a good bet under normal summer and winter conditions, as we have already seen, and it is possible of course that it still will be with three feet of extra water on. It depends on the speed of the current, and if it has become too fast, or possibly boily, the roach will move out. The question is, where are they likely to go? They could, of course, move up to A, and it is possible that some would do this. It is, however, much more likely that the fish normally resident at B would drop downstream to E. If we study the diagram, we can see why this should be. Because of the bend in the river by the trees at 5, the main current swings out into midstream at this point. This normally means that the water adjacent to the rushes at E is slack or, at best, very sluggish. With considerably increased flow rates, however, this area has now become a beautiful, evenly paced smooth glide, closely mirroring the characteristics normally associated with B. Our fishing position would be from 5, and the swim would be an ideal one for trotting tactics or fishing with a light link leger. As I mentioned in the summer section, a few maggots every trot down, or alternatively a handful of mashed bread periodically for flake hookbaits, should keep the swim active all day.

Without a doubt, swims of this type are the most reliable of all, and under the right conditions, large bags of fish may be taken. Because of the nature of the swim, in that the main flow is going away from it, it is an excellent area for pre-baiting, as the bait will settle at the tail of the swim, close in to the near bank, without being washed downstream. We can make use of this fact at dusk: after a day spent trotting or quivertipping, a large piece of flake, legered right at the extreme downstream end of the glide, could produce that extra-big specimen.

We find a similar situation at D. Just upstream of fishing position 4 there is a protrusion in the river bank, and D is normally two feet deep and dead slack. Increased height and flow again has the effect of creating a steady current at D, and fish will move into the bay thus created to escape the full force of the current in their normal holding area in midstream.

In very high water conditions, very interesting swims are created at C, close in to the near bank between the bushes. The kind of situation I have in mind here is where bank-side bushes have their roots just above the water-line in conditions of normal winter level. In these conditions, the swims I am about to describe do not exist, as the flow of the river goes straight under the bushes. As the water-level rises, however, the bush gradually becomes partially submerged, and this has the effect of creating an obstruction to the flow. This in turn diverts the flow a little towards midriver, thereby forming little back eddies and areas of slack immediately behind each bush. There is one particular stretch of the Leam that springs immediately to mind. In normal conditions it is simply a long straight of uniform flow from bank to bank, the only feature giving the stretch any interest being the frequent blackthorns dotted along its length. As the water rises during a flood, however, a transformation occurs, and it is then one of the most productive roach stretches on the river.

For this kind of fishing, there is no finer bait than lobworms or lob tails. I prefer to fish them upstream, sitting downstream of each bush as I come to it and legering the bait under the downstream branches. You can easily fish in the traditional downstream manner of course, but as roach on leger tackle at short range are notoriously difficult to connect with, the upstream presentation allows more time for the strike to be made, as the roach moving off with the bait creates a little slack in the line, thereby causing very little resistance. As I have explained in the chub chapter, use a quivertip soft enough to be able to put a decent curvature in without dislodging the bait from the river bed. The bite is then easily seen as the tip will straighten suddenly.

Having caught hundreds of good roach to over two pounds accidentally while chubbing under rafts, I know that winter roach share with chub a love of taking up residence in these areas, and in fact one of the major difficulties on occasions when I am fishing for a big chub is avoiding the roach bites. The more extensive rafts are usually associated with large areas of slack or slowly moving water, and I think it is for this reason that such places are often where the largest roach are to be found. The bigger and lazier they become, the more they want a quiet life, away from the youngsters dashing around in the main stream. They also tend to become more solitary, and fishing for them is then just like scaled-down chubbing. Rarely do I go below 4-pound line and a size 10 for this fishing, bait usually being a large fluffy piece of fresh bread flake. In very high or coloured water I might switch to worm, as in some of the conditions covered earlier, but generally there is no finer bait for big roach than bread flake.

Talking about high, coloured water brings to mind the last point I want to make about the location of big roach in small rivers and streams. In the section on small-stream perch, I discussed fishing undercuts, and how often big perch would pack in such places under flood conditions. Exactly the same comments apply to roach, and if your stream contains undercuts, there is a good chance they will produce the odd bigger-than-average roach.

THE BIG ROACH OF THE WESSEX RIVERS

In recent years some quite remarkable roach have been taken from Wessex rivers, notably the Avon and the Stour, and the number of three-pounders reported has been amazing. For the time being, at least, the roaching to be had there is unique. In the Hampshire Avon, for example, it appears that there are very few small roach to be caught; every one that puts in an appearance is likely to be two pounds plus. This present spate of enormous fish is all very well while it lasts, but when they die off what will there be to replace them? In the meantime, there is some outstanding sport to be had with outsize roach and there is nothing wrong in taking advantage of it while it lasts.

The situation does not appear to be the same on the Dorset Stour, which has a fairly healthy head of smaller roach as well as many very big ones. People who know the river a lot better than I do tell me that the numbers of fish are far reduced from levels of a few years previously, but admit that the situation is not as worrying as on the Avon, and that the fish are growing much bigger. The Stour has produced its own crop of three-pound roach in recent seasons.

After the first floods, with a nice colour in the water and all the accumulated rubbish washed away, is when the roaching starts in earnest. Within reason, the deeper the colour and the higher the river, the better the fish like it. As far as location is concerned, much of what I had to say about

8 ROACH

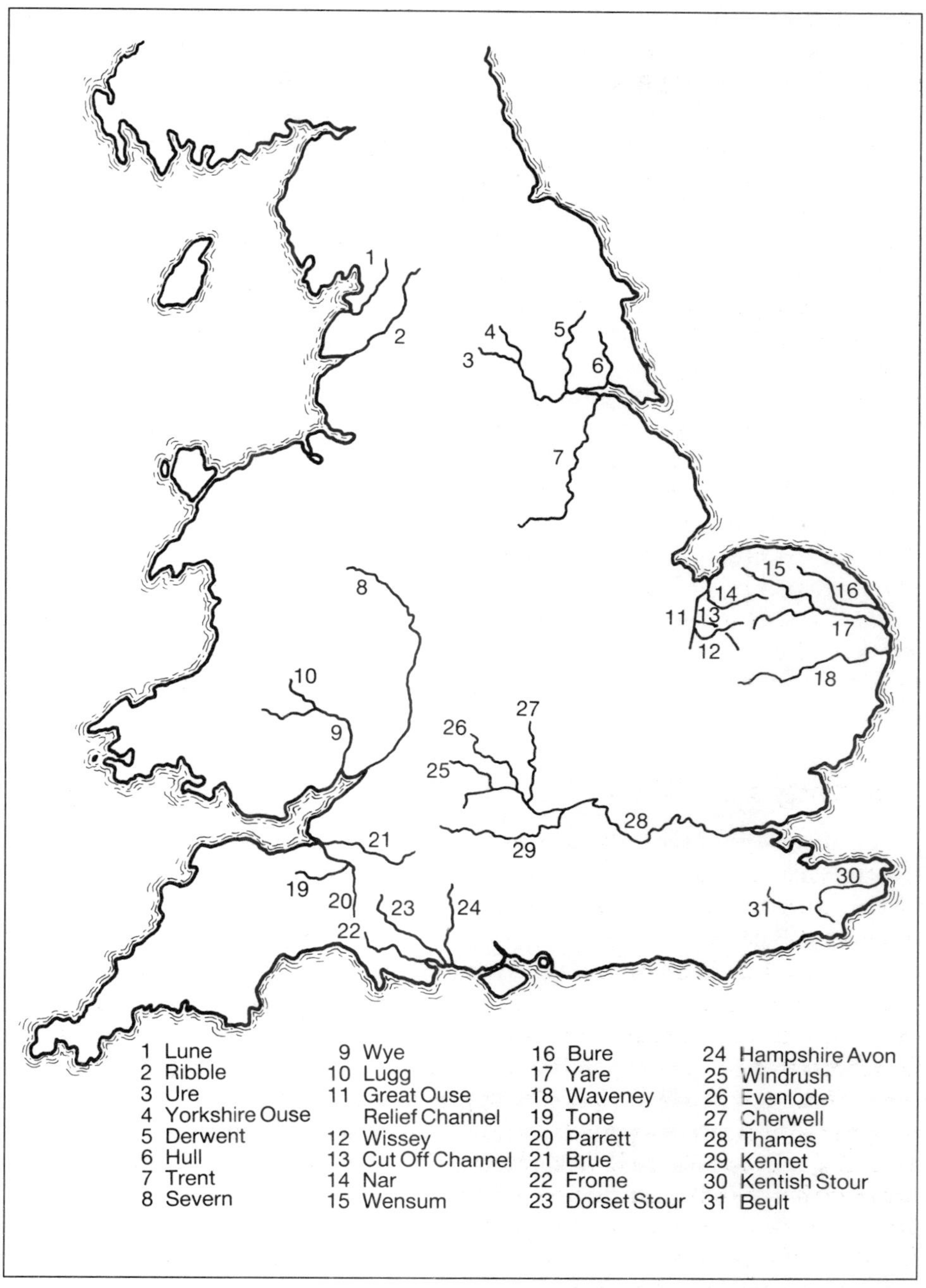

Big roach river fisheries.

winter location in small streams applies to these southern waters. Particularly good areas are the slowly moving water adjacent to slack areas, or the slacks themselves if the water-level is very high, and smooth steady glides alongside rushes. Lovely swims are where a steady glide runs alongside a bank-side slack. These can be fished by trotting the edge of the crease, periodically putting the rod in the rest, and allowing the float to swing round and lay on in the slack itself. Bread flake again is without doubt the best bait, and it pays to introduce mashed bread along the line of the trot every now and again to keep the fish interested. As you are feeding in this fashion, some of the feed inevitably settles in the slack, and laying on will often produce a fish that has discovered this source of easily obtained food.

Although there is no doubting the efficiency of trotting as a pleasant means of taking quality roach on these rivers, and the legendary catches of men like Gerry Swanton and Owen Wentworth is evidence enough, I have to admit that I am happier presenting a static bait, either by laying on or, more normally, by legering. My trips to the southern rivers are somewhat limited by where I live, and I rarely seem to find conditions ideal for trotting tactics. Also, as I have admitted earlier, my skill with trotting tackle is at best modest, and I know that I fish far more efficiently with static bottom baits. I realize that my trotting skills would improve with practice, but as I love legering it is always something that I promise myself I will do tomorrow.

Feeding and Baits

Whichever approach you adopt, there is one common requirement, and that is that the feeding must be accurate. With the strong currents of the Avon and Stour, haphazard feeding will see everywhere on the river receiving bait other than where you are presenting your hookbait, if you are not careful. It is fairly easy to control the free feed with trotting simply by introducing the feed on the same line as the float. With the static bait, however, it is vital that the free feed is on the bottom at the same place as the hookbait, and the obvious method of presentation is via the swim-feeder. The end rig is basic enough, a blockend feeder if I am using maggots, or a small open-ended one for mashed bread. A 4-pound main line and a 3-pound hooklink is my usual choice in normal winter conditions, but I will step this up to 4 pounds straight through in heavier flows with more colour. Depending on the bait, I will use hook sizes in the range 8 to 14, the larger sizes obviously for bread baits. Again, bread is the first choice of hookbait, either in the form of flake or crust, unless the water is very clear, in which case I have more confidence in maggots. The only problem with maggots is that they can sometimes promote snatchy bites, and the way to cure this problem is to wrap a small piece of flake around the hook shank. As a general-purpose roach bait in less than ideal conditions, a flake maggot-cocktail on a size 12 takes some beating.

For this roaching, I usually use the feeder fixed in conjunction with an eighteen-inch hooklength and a softish quivertip, and in this way the big roach give a good, solid, and unmissable bite. If I decide to try a piece of crust off the bottom, it is a simple matter to pinch on a small shot an inch or so from the hook.

The amount of feed to use in this roaching is debatable, and opinions vary so widely among the most successful southern roach anglers that it is difficult to make sense of it all. Personally, I err on the side of caution, obviously being more liberal with the feed if conditions are perfect. As a general rule of thumb, if I am fishing flake using a medium feeder, I will refill the feeder with mashed bread every half-hour or so, this being stepped up of course if bites are coming regularly. If maggots are in use, it means that conditions are not that good anyway, and I would rarely require more than about three pints for a day's roaching.

Wessex river roaching is really little different from the roach fishing of other rivers as far as technique is concerned. What obviously sets them apart at the moment is the fantastic average size of the fish. Long may this continue, but personally I would be far happier if I were plagued by smaller roach while I was waiting for the odd bite from a specimen.

9

Rudd

The main reason why big rudd are not a popular quarry is the severe shortage of waters known to hold them. Many waters, of course, teem with stunted rudd, but there is no doubt that really big rudd are rare. There is a further problem when it comes to specimen rudd, and that is the question of hybridization. In recent seasons, it has been established that the very big rudd from several waters are in fact hybrids, or should I say that some of the captures are definitely hybrids. This is, of course, the real problem. When one big fish from a water is identified as a hybrid, especially with a fish like a rudd where a hybrid can be very difficult to distinguish from the real thing, it throws into doubt all the other specimens, some of which could be true rudd.

The best examples I know are several of the Midlands reservoirs, principally Hollowell, Ravensthorpe and Pitsford. At Hollowell, a catch of fish will see some that are definitely hybrids, some that are roach-shaped but highly coloured, some that look like true roach, and a few that apparently meet all the criteria of true rudd. It is only when you see a few fish together that the subtle differences become obvious. The same situation existed in the water in Norfolk where Dave Plummer and others caught what at first appeared to be colossal rudd. The fish from Hollowell

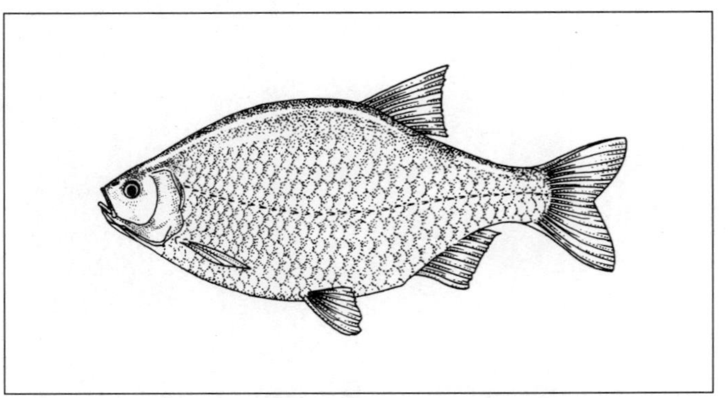

The rudd, Scardinius erythrophthalmus.

are all simply classed as hybrids, but my own view is that this is too sweeping a classification. For many years, the water produced good roach and the occasional good rudd, and the fish were very different. It is only in the last ten years or so that all the intermediate varieties have appeared. In my own fishing at Hollowell, therefore, I adopt this simple method for recording my catches: if the fish meets all the external features of a true roach or rudd, that is what I call it; if it fails on any one count, then I call it a hybrid. I know that that is extremely arbitrary, but it satisfies me. Obviously, if I were to catch a potential record, then the fish would have to be subjected to all the known tests. Even this, however, is fallible. The present record 'rudd' from Ravensthorpe was almost certainly a roach-rudd hybrid. The water has been producing them for years, and the same stock fish went into Hollowell!

There is thus no doubt that waters holding rudd of impeccable pedigree are few and far between. If you know of such a water, you have found a goldmine, and you should take advantage while it is available.

Big rudd are found both in very shallow waters and deep pits, and the fishing methods will vary correspondingly. Let us look first of all at the more traditional rudd fishing to be found in shallow lakes.

FISHING IN SHALLOW WATERS

Where good rudd inhabit a shallow water, they will betray their presence eventually by rolling noisily at the surface, and location of the fish is therefore largely visual. The rolling can be especially hectic in the evening, and time spent with binoculars will be found to be invaluable. Rudd are very pronounced surface and midwater feeders, and on very shallow waters their progress through the water can be observed simply by watching the dorsals continually breaking surface. In these circumstances, the fish can be caught by stalking them, casting in front of the shoal as it moves around the water. In a large water, such as the shallow reedy bays off the southern Irish loughs, the shoals can be followed quietly by boat, keeping a sufficient distance away to avoid unduly alarming the fish. Many years ago, Merv Wilkinson and I had some fascinating fishing at Lake Killinure, off Lough Ree. The water was rarely more than two feet deep, and we would row gently around until rudd were seen priming. Then we anchored at a decent distance, and fired out a few loose crusts to occupy the fish for a while. We fished with floating crust, using a simple bubble float to give casting weight, and generally two or three fish would come in quick succession, before the shoal became agitated and drifted away. They could be followed for hours in this way, and good catches were accumulated.

These days, I do not use a bubble float, as it is too clumsy, preferring a small self-cocking quill float, or, if greater distance is required and there is no boat available, the floating leger comes into its own. Obviously, for very short-range work, even a weightless tackle can be employed, using a greased line and a buoyant bait. This is a method of extremely limited use, however, since the casting range is restricted, and the slightest breeze makes it impractical. One exception to this is where a wind has blown crusts alongside reeds. A crust drifted down on the wind can prove deadly. Drift is also the drawback with the float or floating leger arrangements, and a static surface bait can be presented with the use of long-tail paternoster. A very good alternative to this is to replace the paternoster lead with a small open-ended feeder. The feeder is packed with small crust fragments, and sealed in with groundbait plugs containing rusk. When these plugs disintegrate, the crusts float to the surface all around the hookbait, which will generally be crust also.

So far, I have been discussing surface-feeding fish, in calm conditions or conditions of gentle ripple at worst. The only bite indication needed at times is simply to watch the bait itself. The British weather being what it is, however, the conditions will often be such as to inhibit surface feeding. Either it is cold and overcast, or a strong wind is in evidence. In these circumstances, the fish will usually be found feeding anywhere from the bottom to just under the surface. The paternoster rig previously mentioned is my favourite for this fishing, using slow-sinking baits rather than truly buoyant ones, and using a swingtip as bite indicator. The baits could be

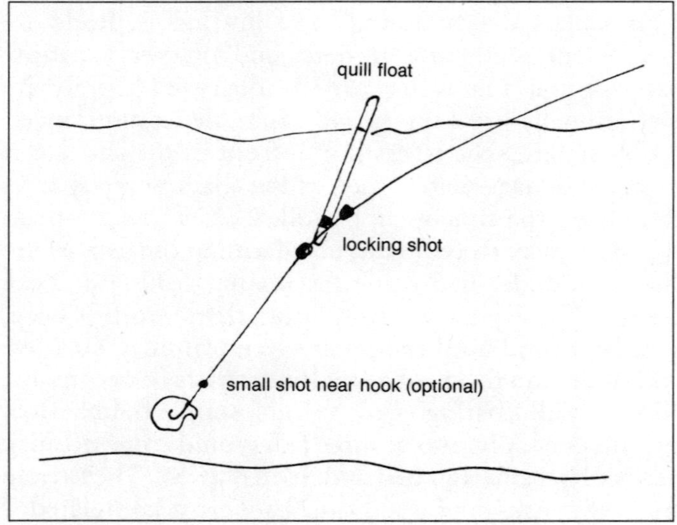

Self-cocking float rig.

squeezed flake, maggots, casters, counterbalanced corn or air-injected worms, all fished on a long weightless tail. After casting, the bait may take several minutes to rest gently on the bottom, and at any time during that slow descent, the tip could indicate a bite. This is a method of fishing that requires frequent casting to attain the maximum benefit. If the rudd are concentrated in midwater, the bait may be ignored once it has touched bottom.

Big rudd are, however, good bottom feeders, especially at night or in colder conditions. Even at the height of summer, the very biggest fish may prefer to feed on the bottom, rather than compete with all the youngsters splashing around on top. It is, therefore, a good ploy when fishing in the above style to allow one cast occasionally to remain on the bottom for ten minutes or so, to see whether a bigger fish than normal is lying there. There may well be one on the bottom quietly mopping up all the sunken food items.

If you have at your disposal a water containing a small head of exceptional rudd, they will often be found to behave more like tench, in that they become predominantly midwater or bottom feeders. In these circumstances, the best approach is with the swimfeeder, still using a longish tail to give a slow-sinking hookbait. Bread flake, or bread flake/maggot cocktail are my favourite baits, and I prefer an open-ended feeder filled with maggots, and sealed with a mixture of pure breadcrumbs and sausage rusk. A good alternative to this is one of the Sensas range of cloud groundbaits, which keeps fish foraging around among the drifting particles. If you intend a long campaign for some big rudd, involving pre-baiting swims tench or bream style, there is nothing better than plain mashed bread.

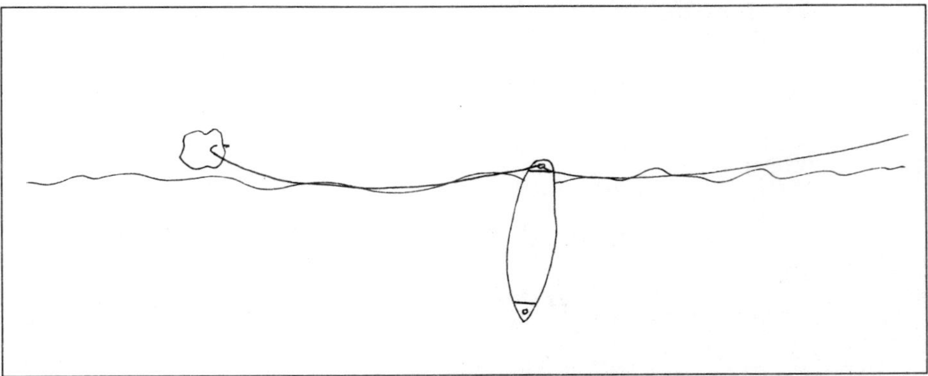

Use of a carp floating leger.

FISHING IN DEEP WATERS

Establishing the presence of specimen rudd in a deep water is the first problem, since they are not as prone to showing themselves as their shallow-water counterparts. If the water concerned is a gravel pit, there will often be only a small head of big fish, making their location even more of a hit and miss affair. Initial captures are usually flukes, and if a water does suddenly turn up a big fish out of the blue, it is then worth deliberately fishing for them. TC pit is a good example of what I mean. That water was first fished for its big tench and bream, but now and again big roach and rudd put in an appearance. Anglers have since deliberately fished for roach and rudd, and more have been caught as a result.

As far as fishing methods are concerned, the basic legering techniques are obviously the same as for the shallow-water fishing. Also, if fish are found feeding at the surface, the same methods will apply here also. The difficulty arises when the fish are thought to be feeding somewhere around mid-

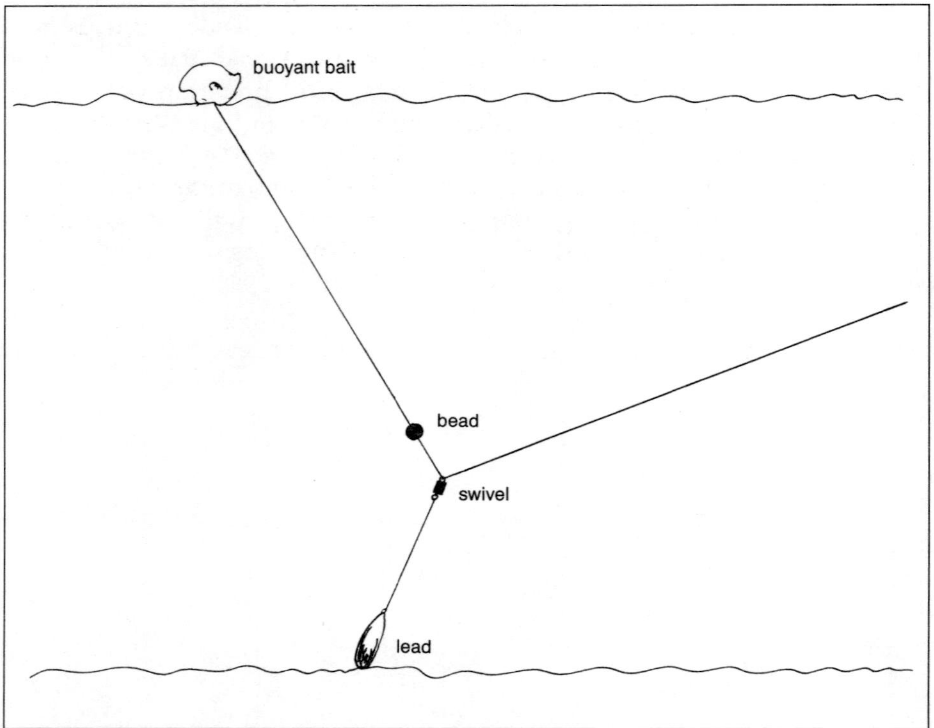

Long-tail paternoster.

water. If the depth is twenty feet or so, it is obviously impractical to use a paternoster rig with a twenty-foot hooklink! There are two answers to this problem: either float fishing, continually adjusting the depth setting until fish are contacted, or the use of a slow-sinking leger. An Arlesey bomb glued to the requisite amount of balsa will suffice, and this is fished in conjunction with a normal two- or three-foot tail and a swingtip. After casting, you must watch the tip constantly. Normal slow sinking of the terminal rig will see the tip adopting a forty-five degree angle, as line is drawn through it. If the tip suddenly shoots out straight, or drops really slack, you know that a fish has intercepted the bait on the way down.

Many years ago, the Coventry Specimen Group used to fish a deep brick pit which contained big rudd, and that water went down to twenty-five feet in places. After a few casts, by counting how long it took for the bait to hit bottom, it was possible to tell roughly at what depth the bait was being intercepted. Armed with that information, the alternative was there to switch to the float, with the depth setting having been established using the slow-sinking leger. We had some good rudd using this approach.

The other method that is useful for deep-water rudd is the use of a sliding driftbeater float, set to fish lift style. When the fish are hard on the bottom, a nice piece of flake, or small piece of crust fished an inch or so from the bottom shot, is as good an approach as any.

10

Tench

GRAVEL-PIT TECHNIQUES

Location

Suffice it to say that all features that attract bream will be equally attractive to tench. Gravel bars and gentle drop offs are particularly reliable. There is one factor to bear in mind with tench location, however, that is very different from that of bream. Weed is no deterrent to tench; in fact, it is beneficial to have weed close at hand to the area in which you propose to fish. A very good ploy is to find a feature to fish at in a weedy area, and then make a clearing in it by dragging. If that area is then kept clear and regularly baited, it will contain tench through the season. Running the drag through the swim every day you fish often proves beneficial in maintaining the tenches' interest, both by disturbing the gravel itself, and by scattering any uneaten bait items that may have become lodged under stones. For gravel-pit tenching, then, I consider a weed rake and weed drag to be essential items of equipment.

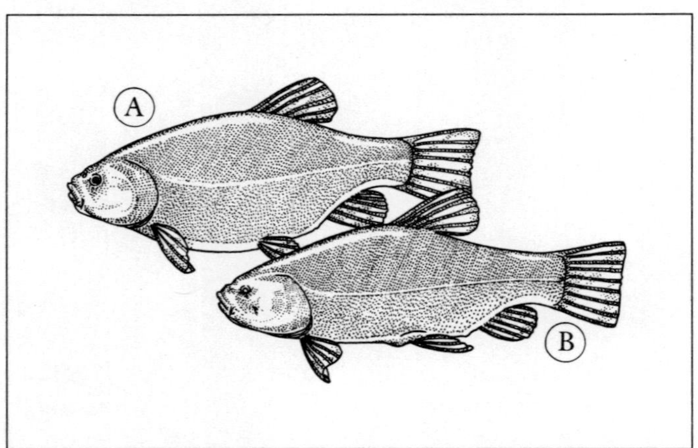

The tench, Tinca tinca *(B is female, A is male).*

If it is allowed, a boat makes life so much easier. A word of warning, however, especially to younger anglers: if you are going to use an inflatable boat, under no circumstances should you do so without a life jacket if you are a non-swimmer. It is also the height of folly to paddle out on one wearing waders and heavy waterproofs. I have seen this done on many occasions, and am ashamed to admit that I have done it myself for quickness, but it really is stupidly irresponsible. Inflatables can burst apart without warning, and if you go in deep water, well away from the bank, wearing heavy clothes and waders, you are in trouble. I know of two friends who came close to drowning like this. So if you are going to use an inflatable, do so wearing a T-shirt and shorts only, and perhaps a pair of light beach shoes that you could easily kick off if necessary. You may get cold or wet, but that's better than risking your life. You can soon get warm and dry when you return to shore.

Most gravel pits of my acquaintance have a marginal weed fringe, before the water drops away a few yards out from the bank. If you only fished just over these margins, you would catch a great many tench. Margin fishing for gravel-pit tench is one of the most reliable methods, and yet most anglers seem to want to fish as far out as they can cast. I will never forget an angler at TC pit, who had fished for four days without a single tench. He was putting his feeders out over fifty yards, and yet, in front of him only a rod-length out, tench were constantly patrolling backwards and forwards. He even complained that they were giving him line bites! It had never occurred to him actually to fish for them, and I'm sure that's a common situation on many pits.

Do not be stereotyped by what other anglers are doing, and think that, because they are fishing a long way out, you have to do so as well. Thoroughly map out the water for yourself, and let that information, together with visual evidence such as rolling and bubbling, dictate where you fish. Make your choice by common sense, not by imitating others.

Groundbaiting Techniques

Having decided where you are going to fish, the next consideration is the one of groundbait. This topic deserves special thought because it has an absolutely vital role to play in determining how successful you are with pit tench. There are limitless permutations as to what ingredients you use in your groundbait, and all manner of meals can be successfully incorporated. To the base mix can be added whatever takes your fancy, and it will normally be dictated by your hookbaits, although not necessarily. There is a lot of merit in the argument that a good groundbait should be strongly attractive in its own right initially, and then should contain enough particles of food to keep the fish in the area, foraging around for them. These particles could be casters, maggots of various kinds, sweetcorn, hempseed, stewed wheat, grains of rice, and so on. In its simplest form, the bait could consist of good quality, pure breadcrumbs containing chopped worms. This simple feed was all Trefor and I used in our first three seasons on TC pit, and we had some fabulous catches of tench. Don't think that if you are using particles in your feed you have to use the same particles on the hook. You can, of course, but a big bait such as flake or a whole lobworm is usually equally effective. If a tench is feeding furiously on, say, a carpet of hemp and casters, and comes across a large piece of bread flake, it will take it quite readily as an unexpected bonus.

The groundbait should be of such a consistency that it forms an appealing carpet on the gravel, and obviously the technical problems of its introduction are eased considerably if you have a boat available. If this is the case, the bait can be made as sloppy as you like. If, however, you are forced to introduce your feed either by catapult, by hand, or by throwing stick, then you have to make the bait stiff enough to resist breaking up in flight. The problem with this is the danger of the feed lying around the bottom as a series of unappealing lumps. One way round this is to poke a hole in each ball of bait as you roll it, and then introduce a small amount of dry sausage rusk, before sealing the hole. Rusk has such a rapid absorption rate of water that it literally blows the ball of bait apart after a few minutes on the bottom.

The only particles that cannot be incorporated in the feed successfully, when you have to bait from the bank, are maggots. Their wriggling constantly breaks the balls of bait open, and I feed them separately, with a few casts over the feed with a large and lightly plugged open-ended feeder. Those commercially available inverting bait droppers are also very good. Alternatively, you can scald the maggots, which solves the wriggling problem, and also ensures that they stay in your swim for the tench to find.

Whatever groundbait you use, it is common to find that its effectiveness wears off after a time, the tench having learned to associate it with danger. How the bait is varied depends upon trial and error, but I would normally start off by changing the particle content. Sweetcorn in particular is a bait that seems to have a short life with tench, if it is used in any quantity. The odd few grains appear to do no harm, but mass baiting with it only works for a short while before the tench become terrified of it. Substituting casters for the corn may be all that is required to start catching again.

A dramatic improvement in catches can often follow a small change in the base mix, and one of the most startling examples of this from my own fishing was colouring the bait yellow. One of the best tench anglers I know is Alan Smith of Northampton, and one day on the bank at TC he told me that yellow bait had led to some good catches for him at Sywell. Over the next few weeks, I was to have some fabulous tench sport by adopting this idea.

Flavourings

The modern range of bait flavourings now gives us a limitless amount of variation in our baits, and I have had a lot of fun in this area. The two most successful I have used are Maple Cream and Almond, and I have had several good catches on each. When I fished Deans Farm in 1984 for the very big tench it contained, the major problem was in getting fish into the swim, for various reasons. It was a very big water, containing literally hundreds of gravel bars which all looked equally good, with a low stock of big fish. Many good anglers blanked at the water, and fish that did come out usually did so by stalking or as isolated captures. On both the sessions I fished there, the first twenty-four hours were blank, and then I had several fish. On each occasion the number of rolls told me I had quite a few fish in the swim, and I attribute this to the high concentration of Maple Cream I used in the feed. I am sure that the aroma attracted the tench in to investigate, and then a few of them found the hookbaits. This, after all, is the whole idea behind groundbaiting.

Particle Baits

For tench that are very intensively fished for, the groundbait mix itself may become the factor that has the effect of alarming the fish rather than attracting them, and this is when the change to a loose feed of particles only may pay dividends. We are now into scaled-down particle carp-fishing tactics, and among the best are casters and maple peas. I have already outlined the potential danger of extending this principle to sweetcorn. Although it is stretching the point slightly to call lobworms particles, one of the deadliest methods that can be employed for taking tench is to fish for them over loose feed consisting solely of hundreds of chopped lobworms.

Of course, the ultimate expression of the particle-only loose-feed principle is fishing maggots in the swimfeeder, and this is without doubt one of the most effective ways of fishing for tench. Flavouring the maggots is a very effective ploy, and I have proved to my own satisfaction many times that it can make all the difference between success and failure. Every flavour I have ever used on maggots has caught fish, but the most successful by far has been Pineapple, closely followed by Vanilla, Strawberry, and Maple.

Larger Baits

When we arrive at a situation where even mass baiting with particles becomes ineffective, which eventually happens on our most heavily fished tench waters, we are forced to switch to using isolated and selective larger food items, fishing to pick up the odd tench that happens along. We can do this by fishing in a small concentration of flake samples, or by scattering balls of paste around in an area, but the obvious answer is by using carp boiled baits. When we arrive at the situation where we are tench fishing by mass baiting with boilies, we have in some respects come to the end of the road in groundbaiting alternatives. So where do we go next, when boilies start to lose their appeal? I suspect that this is then the time when a switch back to really basic principles could pay handsome dividends. A water that has been hammered on boilies for several years, may contain tench that would be suckers for a piece of fluffy flake fished over a carpet of pure, uncorrupted breadcrumbs. Strangely, as I write this, I have just heard of some nice tench coming from Johnsons on lobworms and sweetcorn. For years, all those fish would look at were boilies.

An important consideration in loose feeding, whatever bait you are using, is when, and how often, to introduce it. As in my bream fishing, I always bait up in the evening, ready for the expected dawn feeding period. The amount of feed to use can only be determined by experience and would depend on the stock of tench. Having carried out a substantial baiting in the evening, I would then introduce a little bait at regular intervals the following morning. A couple of balls of bait can be catapulted or thrown out every hour or so, or more regularly if I am taking fish. Unlike gravel-pit bream, tench seem to respond to bait being introduced over their heads. This principle could be extended to the dark hours of course, if fish have started coming at night.

The problem with throwing or catapulting feed, especially at distance, is the one of accuracy. I therefore prefer to introduce feed on each cast. The way this is done depends on the loose feed involved, obviously. The swimfeeder takes care of maggots, casters and smaller particles, fishing an open-ended variety with the ends lightly plugged with cereal feed. For larger particle baits and boilies, I go to the trouble of attaching stringers on each cast, exactly as described in the carp chapter. Cereal groundbaits pose the biggest problem, and I now use a special bait-holding rig, the original idea for which was again Alan Smith's. On a paternoster link, I use a combination of beads and small washers, which very effectively holds an oval of bait together during a cast. As for catapulting, the bait has to be slightly stiffer than would be ideal, so I invariably include a small percentage of rusk, to make the bait blow apart a short while after settling.

Using this method, I have successfully fished at over fifty yards. Even when the use of a boat is allowed, I would not top up the bait from a boat, as I believe it creates undue disturbance and is unfair to other anglers. There is nothing wrong with swim preparation and the initial baiting by boat, but regular sorties backwards and forwards is a completely different matter.

Special Tench Baits

In the previous section, most of the orthodox tench baits have been mentioned, and in reality the bulk of my tench are still caught on lobs, flake or maggots. As has been mentioned, however, hard-fished waters often require a little more thought to keep one step ahead of the fish, and this is where I like to use special paste baits in combination with appropriate loose feed. Any of the recipes using commercially available ingredients for carp baits will work equally well for tench, but use the bait as a soft paste rather than boiling it. When using these soft pastes, I normally groundbait with ordinary breadcrumb, flavoured with whatever I am using, with the addition of bait samples.

The base mix I have used for my tench pastes has been the simple one of three parts fine white breadcrumb, two parts baby-milk powder, and one

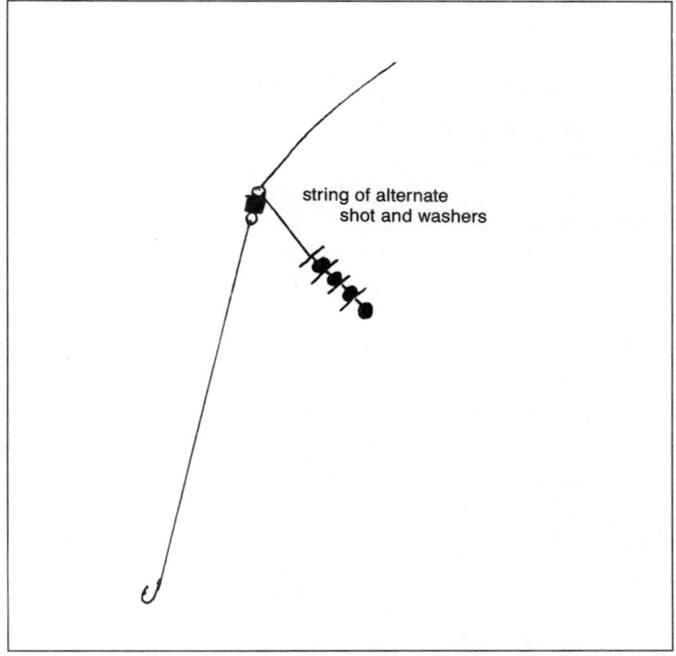

Baitholder rig.

part gluten, appropriately flavoured and coloured. For fishing as a paste, it can be mixed with eggs or water, the eggs giving a more waxy feel to the bait that I think the fish find appealing. A very effective bait indeed can be made by substituting in the above recipe salmon- or trout-fry crumb for the breadcrumbs, and using the paste without additional flavouring or colouring. I have had a lot of tench on this version.

The two most devastating pastes I have used were Almond- and Maple-cream-flavoured versions of the above, both coloured bright yellow. The Almond one in particular gave me some incredible tench sport one summer at TC, the last summer I seriously fished the water. I will never forget the first day I used it. I was at the water for a three-day session in July. The previous two weeks, quite a few tench had come my way on lobs, and I naturally had started this session on them also. After an initial 24-hour blank, I switched to Almond paste on one rod. During that afternoon, I had the most hectic action I ever had at that water. I had bite after bite on the paste, several times having takes before I had time to adjust the bobbins. I honestly don't know exactly how many tench I caught that afternoon, but it must have been about twenty, as well as losing some in the weed, and missing several bites. I reckon I must have had about three dozen positive bites in five hours. The following day, the pace of the action had slowed down, but I still managed another thirteen fish. During all that time, I had only one fish on lobworm, and anglers either side of me, fishing maggots in the feeder, both blanked.

When you discover a bait like that, one that achieves tremendous early results, the drawback is that it often blows just as quickly, and you have to start thinking all over again. One way to extend its useful life is to make the bait slowly dissolving, another idea I must credit to Alan Smith. Keeping the bait mix exactly the same, I add a small amount of very finely ground sausage rusk. The effect this has is to make the outer skin of a ball of paste appear to fizz gently, as the rusk slowly expands and breaks away. The best way I can describe it is that a narrow halo is created around the hookbait, and of course this halo will be carrying whatever flavour you are using. Obviously, this will distribute it over a much wider area. The dissolution rate can be closely controlled by carefully measuring the rusk content. If too much is used, the bait will disintegrate far too quickly to be effective. Also, if the rusk is too coarse it tends to split the bait and it needs to be ground as finely as possible. What I like to achieve is a bait that takes about four hours to dissolve totally, leaving a pile of powder with a hook in the middle. The tench will still take it, sucking up bait and hook together, but really it is a bait for renewal before total dissolution, as a number of tench fanning the bottom will disturb the bait, leaving a bare hook. Believe me, these fizzing baits can be deadly, and are worth the time and trouble to prepare properly.

A superb barbel from the River Wensum, displayed by Trefor West, perhaps the top barbel angler in the country.

The bait had not been in the water very long, when Tim Paisley caught this common carp.

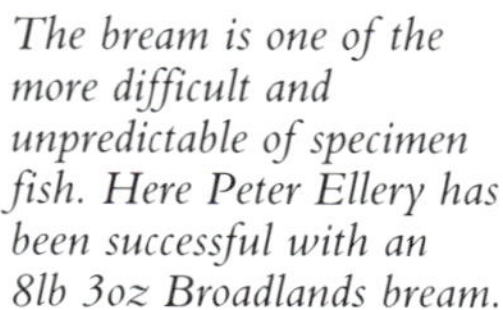

The bream is one of the more difficult and unpredictable of specimen fish. Here Peter Ellery has been successful with an 8lb 3oz Broadlands bream.

A beautiful example of a perch, with its tall dorsal fin and bold black markings on an almost gold background making it very distinctive.

The success that all anglers dream of: a fine pike caught on a perch.

Right: *Two tench of 5lb 9oz and 5lb 4oz. This species can be easily identified by the thick mucus which covers its small scales.*

Far right: *Shore fishing for cod.*

Below: *A wonderfully marked double-figure pit pike.*

A bass caught on wire line.

Plaice prefer very shallow water. Worm is the best catcher of this elusive and highly prized fish.

Champion fly fisher, Bob Church, displays an impressive rainbow trout.

The natural trout of Britain, a 3lb 12oz brown trout from the River Test.

The king of game fish: an Atlantic salmon caught on prawn.

The next step up from these pastes is, of course, boilies. Most of the home-made pastes can be skinned by mixing with eggs instead of water and boiling, but I must admit that these days I don't go to the trouble. There are so many excellent boiled baits available commercially, most of which are super tench baits. I have always used the Richworth range of boilies made by Streamselect Ltd, and shall continue to do so as they are top quality. I have caught a fair few fish on both Tutti Frutti and Salmon Supreme flavours, but I generally use the neutral boilies, atomized with a flavour of my choice. That way, I can be reasonably confident that I am using a different bait from most other anglers. Once again, Almond is a reliable flavour, and I have had instant success with Sweet Peanut and Blue Cheese.

Terrific tench baits are to be found in the Richworth mini-boilie range, using the baits as in particle fishing. Again, the Tutti Frutti variety takes some beating, and what I like to do is fish a normal-sized boilie over a bed of minis. When the tench get shy of this presentation, one or two mini-baits on a fine hair or on the bristle rig as used by Len Arbery will produce results.

Rigs and Tactics

Float Fishing

Under this heading come traditional laying on, and variations on lift float fishing. On a water where the tench have not been hammered, and where

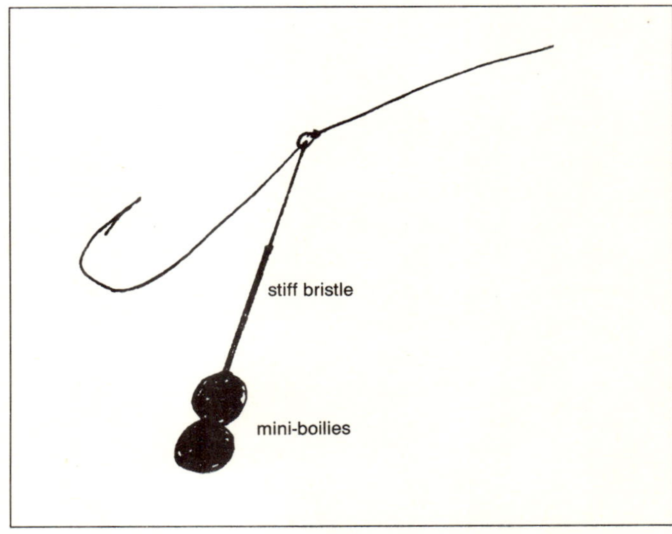

Bristle rig.

they will still accept large baits confidently, there is nothing more aesthetically pleasing than laying on for tench, close in to the bank. This method is at its best when fished with a simple quill float cocked by one large shot, the shot resting on the bottom so that the float is fishing at half cock. When tench are feeding confidently, bites are signified by either the float falling flat and moving across the surface, or by the float shooting under. This method is designed to give the tench some time on a large bait before the strike is made, and the distance between the shot and the hook would usually be at least eighteen inches. For fishing at a range where one single shot gives insufficient casting weight, obviously use a bigger, more heavily loaded float, still with at least one shot fished on the bottom for stability of the bait.

When the tench become finicky, the float will dance and dither for ages before going away properly, if indeed it ever does. This is the time when a switch to fishing the lift float is indicated. The basic principle behind this method is of using a float which is overshotted. The bottom shot, which is fished on the bottom, is of such a weight that, without it, the float rides much too high in the water, and with it, the float sinks. The float is set overdepth, and having been cast out will obviously be too high, as the bottom shot will be hard on the bottom, with slack line above it. By now drawing in line carefully, the float is submerged to its correct fishing position, and the rod should now be placed on rests. The lift method is normally utilized with a very short hooklink, often as short as one inch, and as such it is highly sensitive. As soon as a tench lifts the bait, it also partially or wholly lifts the anchor shot, with the result that the float rises very dramatically in the water. At short range, the bottom shot could be the only shot used, and this is where an even more dramatic effect can be gained. When the shot is completely lifted, the float will shoot up in the water and lay flat.

The beauty of lift float fishing is that it can be used for close-range fishing with a small quill, or for long-range work with the heaviest antenna or windbeater. For windswept gravel pits, the driftbeater float, with a sight bob, allows very sensitive tench fishing at long range.

The lift method really comes into its own when fishing particles, my favourite being casters. For short-range work, I dispense with any cereal feed, simply catapulting a few free hookbaits around the float every so often. Again, the more action I am getting, the more often the bait is topped up. For fishing out of particle catapulting range, another alternative has to be found. The obvious one is to use normal groundbait, mixed with a high particle content, so that a small ball will break up soon after hitting the water. Alternatively, for inert particles such as corn, tares, wheat, etc., some can be dried and attached to the tackle by stringers, or – you can use a PVA casting tube for distributing maggots or casters around the hookbait. If you decide to use PVA string or tubes in these rigs, bear in mind that the more bait you introduce with each cast, the more your casting range will be cut down, especially with the tubes, which offer considerable wind resistance.

Legering

All of the standard legering rigs described in the bream chapter, and the boiled-bait rigs in the carp chapter, the latter appropriately scaled down, are equally effective for tench and to avoid undue repetition, I would refer you to those.

There are two circumstances where special rigs are used specifically for tench, one being for the use of mini-boilies on a hair rig, and the other for those occasions when the tench are giving finicky bites.

One man who has had as much experience as anyone with mini-boilies for gravel-pit tench fishing is Len Arbery. My own experience is sketchy in comparison. The major problem with hair-rigged minis is the one of splitting the small baits with the conventional loop and stop arrangement, and Len and his friends have overcome this by the use of the bristle rig, as devised originally by Bill Quinlan. The hair is tied to a short length of

Mini-boilie rig.

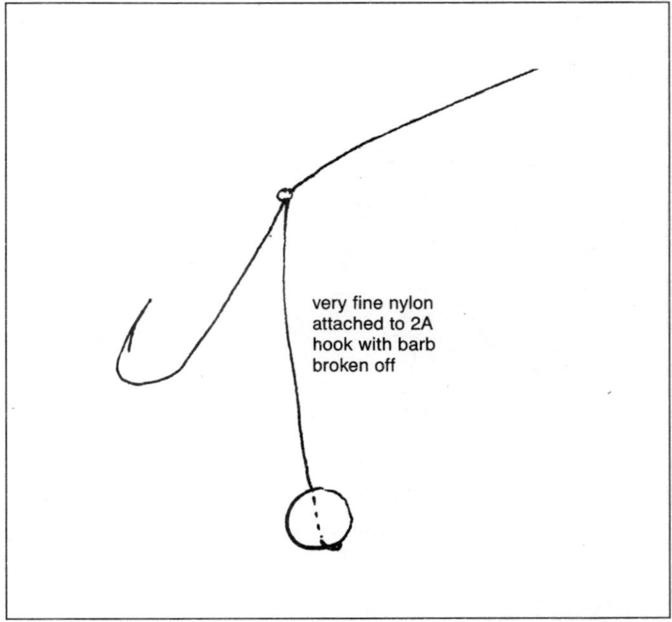

nylon bristle, as found on nylon brooms, the bristle being pointed at one end for insertion into the bait. I like to give the knot connecting the bristle a smear of superglue for added security. The hair itself can be main line passed through the hook eye, as in Dacron carp rigs, or, alternatively, you can use finer line trapped under the main line knot at the eye, or tied to the hook bend. The bristle rig undoubtedly works very well, the only reservations I have being with long-range fishing, when I feel there is a chance of the bait or baits flying off the bristle with the force of the cast. I admit that I have had no problems with this, but for fishing at range, I am still happier when using a method where the bait is actually firmly held on to the hair. There are two methods I use, and in both cases it is best to mount baits on the hair before tying the hair to the hooklink.

In the first, I tie up a tiny hook, say a 22 or 24, on a length of fine line, the hook being broken off at the barb. Using the finest darning needle possible, I then pass the free end of line through the bait or baits, until the tiny hook bend lodges in the boilie. The hair is then tied to the terminal tackle, usually from the hook eye in my case. The main problem with this rig is that it is undoubtedly more fiddly, and it is a good idea to have several baits mounted in your tackle box, to enable quick rebaiting.

A slight deviation from this arrangement, and one that I have a lot of faith in, is tying baits to a hair comprising of a single strand of Kryston. This material is exceptionally limp, and gives the bait a totally natural presentation. The drawback again is that this method is even more fiddly

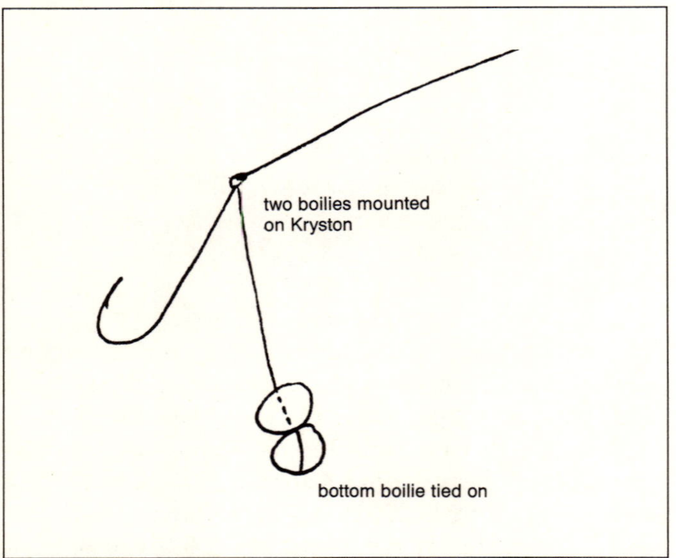

Mini-boilie Kryston rig.

than the last! Each Kryston strand is very fine, and you would be well advised to tie a supply of baits at home before going fishing. Believe me, trying to work with a single strand of the stuff with wet hands, or in the slightest breeze, can drive you to distraction! The above two methods are useful for fishing multiple baits, at different points on the terminal rig, which often tempts difficult tench.

The Fixed Paternoster

Most of my gravel-pit legering is carried out using the fixed paternoster rig, with a hooklink of two feet or so, and nine times out often this results in very positive bites that are rarely missed. On those occasions when good bites are missed, indicating premature striking, I will increase the hook-length, to as much as five feet if I think it warrants it, and that will usually solve the problem. In the case of small twitchy bites, which I have to admit are less of a problem to me than they seem to be to other anglers, there are several modifications of terminal rig or bite detection that will help. Firstly, a simple reduction in the hooklength may be the only alteration required, and I will go down to an inch if necessary.

On several occasions in my fishing, the problem has been solved simply by reverting from a fixed paternoster rig, to one incorporating a sliding bomb link. This is easily accomplished by disconnecting the short length or rig tube joining the casting boom to the hooklength swivel. This is an example of how reducing the amount of resistance to a biting fish will produce the goods, but often the small-bite problem is solved by doing the exact opposite! If the above solution gives no improvement, we can try reverting to the fixed lead arrangement with a very short hooklink, and also reduce the length of the bomb tail. If we increase the weight of the bomb at the same time, we move closer and closer to a full bolt-rig variation. I remember once, at TC, having a spate of two-inch lifts on the bobbin only when I was fishing my normal fixed tackle with two-foot hooklinks. I eventually arrived at a six-inch paternoster tail, ending in a two-ounce bomb, and a two-inch hooklength, and the bites for the rest of that session were real churners.

I've found that one of the most reliable answers to the small-bite problem is to use a system half-way between a sliding and fully fixed paternoster. I have had excellent results from using a sliding paternoster, but incorporating a power gum stop knot a few inches up the line to act as a back stop. With this set-up, it pays to ignore the initial twitches, and wait for the good bite which usually follows. What happens is that, as the fish twitches the bait, it slowly takes a little line, gaining in confidence as it does so. Eventually, it suddenly hits the heavy resistance, and bolts. Result: one

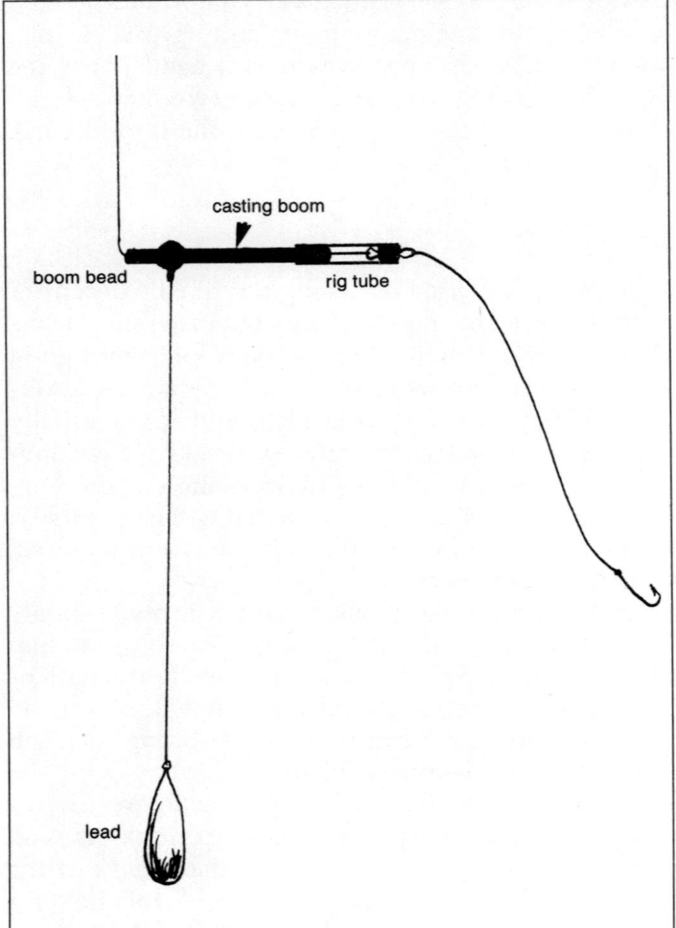

Fixed paternoster.

churner! To suit the conditions on any particular day, you may have to alter the position of the back stop. It depends how spooky the fish have become.

Much of the above advice sounds, and indeed is, contradictory, and it really is a case of trial and error to see which tackle modification is required on the day. The major problem is that, on most gravel pits, there are not that many tench bites about in a day. You simply have to go fishing to your particular water as often as you can, and learn what is a generally acceptable presentation to produce reasonable bites. During the course of a couple of seasons, you will have experienced most of the variations in tench feeding behaviour, and by experimenting with various tackle permutations, should have learned how to cope with most of them. Like many things in angling

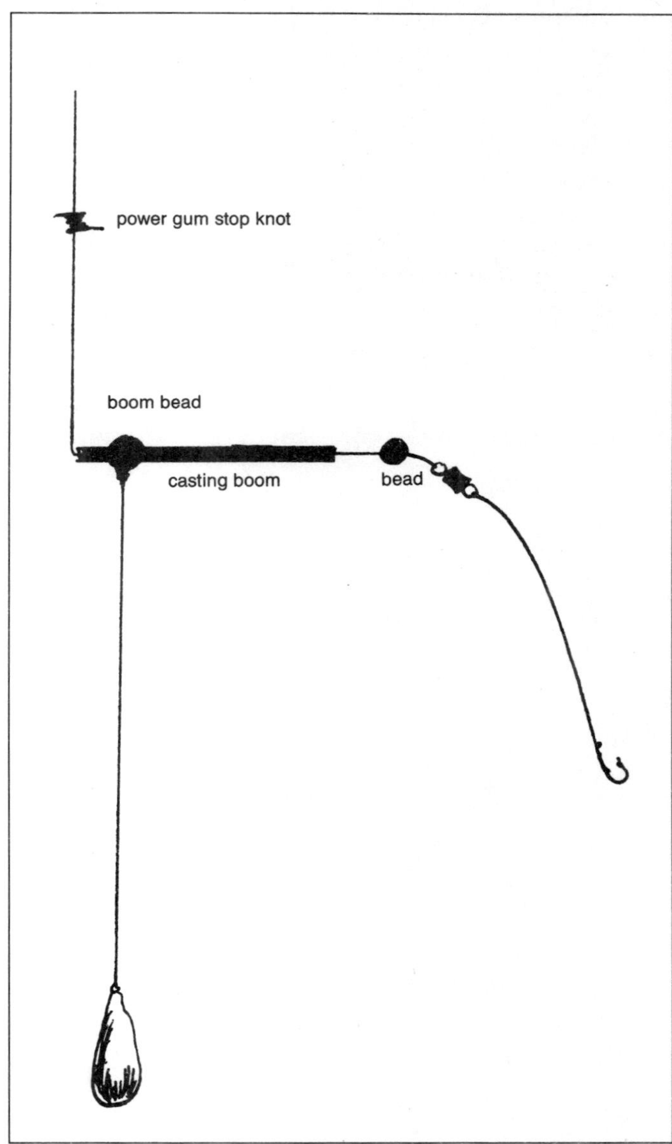

Paternoster shock rig.

that are basically concerned with reading situations, assessment of the terminal rig on any particular day is something that cannot be taught on paper. That skill only comes with experience, there are no short cuts.

In many tench legering situations, you will be fishing over weed, and this presents other problems. The paternoster rigs mentioned so far are at their best when used on clean gravel. In bottom weed, however, they are not so efficient, resulting in the baits becoming covered in weed, and impeding a biting fish from taking the bait cleanly. Twitchy bites can result simply because the line is fouled in the weed, and you can draw the mistaken conclusion that finicky tench are responsible. For fishing in bottom weed, I prefer a sliding hooklink, that will allow the bait to settle gently on the weed and allow a tench to move away with the bait freely, even though the bomb is weeded up. For fishing over bottom weed, a buoyant bait is a help, and flake fished on a longish tail takes some beating.

Bite Detection Methods

On every gravel pit I have ever fished for tench, one factor is a constant: gravel-pit tench do not conform to the traditional rules of feeding at dawn.

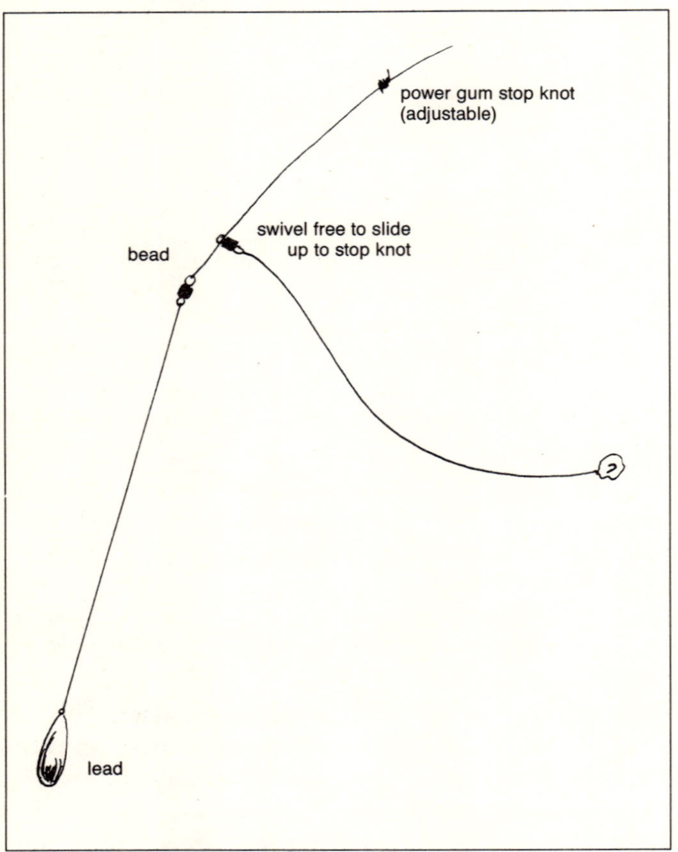

Sliding hooklink paternoster to beat bottom weed.

Bites can come at any time, although I have found late afternoon to be the least productive. There can be long spells of inactivity, followed by sudden spates of bites, and when these bites are likely to occur is totally unpredictable. More than once, I have had a few days on a pit when the fish fed at first light one day, early afternoon on the next day, and in the night on the third day. Because of this, my legering for tench incorporates the use of Optonic alarms, and bobbins fitted with Betalights. There are many excellent glow bobbins on the market, but I make my own, using adjustable Gardner clips, with the Betalight inserted into a length of transparent tubing and glued to the side of the clip. The adjustable tension feature I find useful in windy conditions. During the long unproductive hours the Optonics allow more relaxing fishing and they also allow you to watch the water for signs of fish movement, rather than having your eyes glued to the indicators for hour after hour. If I am fishing for only a short session, I like to use swingtips, but bobbins are my normal choice.

The swingtip has another use, in the small-bite situation. There will be occasions when, despite end-rig variations, bites are still circumspect. Striking at small bites on bobbins is always unreliable, and it pays to switch to swingtips, tightening the line so that the tip is only a short way from the horizontal. By holding the rod, any small movement in the tip can be responded to immediately. As with reservoir roaching, for very finicky bites, you can even revert to the quivertip, and fish side on. By bending the tip into the terminal rig to its maximum curvature before the lead moves, a state of delicate equilibrium is attained. No matter how small a movement there is on the bait, immediately it is disturbed the balance is destroyed and the tip springs back. The bomb and tip need to be matched for this method to be at its most effective. The lighter the lead you are using in your terminal arrangement, the more flexible a tip will be required. The greater the deflection can be achieved in the quivertip, the more obvious the bites become.

TRADITIONAL TENCH FISHING

What I mean by traditional tench fishing is that to be had in reservoirs, estate lakes, small pools, canals and even slow rivers. It is the tenching of still misty dawns, masses of bubbles on oily-looking water, and a redtipped float at half cock alongside the lilies. This is the tench fishing of my boyhood, and I often feel I ought to do a lot more of it, instead of spending so much time on the banks of windswept pits.

All the methods that have been outlined in the gravel-pit section will work equally well on every type of water, the differences in the fishing being mainly in the location of the tench. The waters that are the most similar to pits are the large reservoirs, which can be just as inhospitable and unpredictable. This is particularly true of the Tring group. Apart from individual features that most waters contain, such as the famous pier swim at Wilstone, the reservoirs are always of much more uniform contour than gravel pits, and the tench are more evenly distributed. If there are any weed beds, such as lilies or potamogeton, they will be concentrated around those, and that would always be a good starting point. If the weed is confined solely to bottom weed such as silkweed, then the tench could be almost anywhere, and you will have to create a hot spot by clearing an area and baiting it regularly. In these circumstances, the well-proven approach of dragging and regular pre-baiting will certainly pay dividends.

Shallow, weedy estate lakes, park pools and the small farm-pond-type of water, are the waters where the most enjoyable tench fishing is to be had, although the average fish rarely compare in size with their gravel-pit counterparts. That is the reason why I spend most of my available tenching time on pits. When I do fish one of these waters, therefore, it is purely for the sheer pleasure of it, rather than a serious specimen hunt, and for that reason I invariably float fish. Tench have a strong affinity for bulrushes and water-lilies, and if these plants inhabit the water tench will not be far away from them.

In muddy and silty bottomed pools, tench will betray their presence in a number of ways which are similar to carp. Feeding tench colour the water rapidly, and shake the weed stems as they brush against them. The most distinctive sign, however, is those masses of tiny bubbles that rise in a froth when tench are grubbing around. After all my years fishing, I still get excited at that sight. I have lost count of the good tench I have caught, by simply free-lining a lobworm into every patch of bubbles that appeared.

It is on these waters that the chances of good tench are highest at first light, and that is when they give good bites to large baits. Laying on with a quill float, using lobworms, redworms or flake, is as reliable a method as it ever was. As the morning wears on, the bites gradually tail off, and it is then that you will often get much more twitchy indications. That is the signal to switch to the lift method, decreasing the bait size.

PART TWO

SHORE FISHING

John Holden

Introduction

Beaches, estuaries and rocks are the last stronghold of real fishing. These fringes of the sea offer dazzling opportunities for the fisherman who accepts the challenge of seasons and tides. No sport for the faint hearted or those who demand guaranteed catches, beach fishing is ruled by natural forces, not man's whims. There are no artificial stocking programmes to boost the fish population, but neither are there catch limits, close seasons and restricted hours. Beaches are wild, as are the creatures that live on them and in the lapping waves. A bass, cod or even a whiting hooked from swirling breakers is worth more than the biggest carp or trout that ever swam; or so beach fishermen claim. Of course they are biased, but who can blame them?

There are fishermen, old-timers mostly, who say that the quality of beach fishing has fallen. Perhaps they are right: commercial fishing and pollution have reduced the number of fish that swim within casting range of beaches and piers. In the most important sense they are wrong: the pleasure of casting for cod, whiting, bass, tope, flat-fish and the many other species found in our waters is as great as it ever was. Indeed, many of us enjoy fishing more because of the greater demands on time, patience and skill.

The rapid development of new tackle and techniques has brought a technological revolution and a radical change in tactics. Rods, reels, terminal rigs and casting styles are important in their own right; and indeed there are thousands of dedicated fishermen for whom owning the latest rod or adding an extra twenty-five yards to the cast is just as satisfying as hooking fish. Fishing from estuaries, beaches, piers, harbours, rocks and jetties is a blend of Space Age technology and traditional hunting skills. Balanced against that is the fact that today's fisherman is content to land perhaps three or four fish in a day instead of the heavy catches that were common twenty years ago. Dedicated anglers consider this a small price to pay for the tremendous enjoyment of casting baits into salt-water.

OPPORTUNITIES

Wading into the surf to cast for bass is the only fishing that appeals to a few anglers. Others prefer to enter competitions rather than to fish purely for pleasure. Some would rather fish from a pier than learn to cast the long distances usually necessary for success on an open beach. Which option should the beginner choose? Most definitely he must resist any urge to specialize. First, it is essential to gain a balanced, overall insight into the world of shore fishing. Later he may discover, as the majority of fishermen do, that a general approach is better anyway. While there are benefits in becoming expert in just one small section of the sport, on the whole it is more rewarding to learn something about everything.

Good fishing depends on seasons, weather and the breeding/migratory patterns of fish as well as on baits, tackle and techniques. There are many weeks in every year when bass are unlikely to feed, or they are nowhere within casting range because the water is too cold. Similarly, it is almost impossible to catch cod and whiting south of the Straits of Dover between May and October unless you go far out to sea where the water remains cold throughout the summer. Even then, catches will be poor because the big shoals have migrated north. The man who fishes from the beach for cod during August is unlikely to catch even one fish. But the same spot will produce excellent sport in December.

These examples are very easy to understand even if you have never fished before. But there are patterns that even experienced fishermen tend to forget which also must be considered, or you may fish for hours or even days without getting a bite. Imagine a surf beach in autumn, calm and hot. Good fishing is available for bass, rays and flat-fish, perhaps even a turbot or a tope. Which species should you fish for today? Bass are a bad choice: unless the water is rough they usually stay well beyond casting range. To hook them, wait until the wind blows onshore and produces a steady surf. The swells wash sand-eels out of the sand; bass move close inshore to attack them. Therefore, by casting sand-eel baits into the white water you can be fairly confident of success. It is a logical process of cause and effect.

Today the water is so calm that you are unlikely to catch anything except a flat-fish. The knowledgeable angler stays at home until after dark, then he will fish the calm water using mackerel, sand-eel, crab or squid baits. He knows that big rays and tope – and yes, perhaps even a big solitary bass – cruise inshore at night to feed on small creatures that emerge from their sandy burrows under cover of darkness. As before, success is based on an understanding of natural history.

PRIORITIES

When and where are just as important as how to fish; often they are a more valuable part of the equation. The priority in learning to become an expert shore fisherman is to think about your sport in terms of wind, weather, seasons and how fish move and feed. There are broad trends and patterns to discover, such as how sea conditions vary from summer to winter, the annual migration of cod, bass and other major species. There is a local aspect as well.

Do you know where sand-eels, worms and crabs live on your favourite beach? How does a south-west wind affect the fishing? Where do the bass feed? Which is the best time and tide for cod and whiting? These and a thousand more questions you must identify and answer for yourself. Explore, look, listen and ask questions. Other fishermen are usually quite willing to assist; there is far less secrecy in shore fishing than you might imagine.

Nothing is difficult to learn, but it does take time. Two years is about the minimum period in which a shore fisherman can develop his basic skills, and ever afterwards the sport demands continuous attention to detail. I say this not to deter you from becoming a shore fisherman but rather to point out the reality of the situation: modern beach fishing calls for expertise and dedication.

PRACTICAL SKILLS

In contrast to the natural history aspect, tackle making, casting, bait collection and other practical skills are quite easy to learn. Modern rods and reels offer high performance and reliability at moderate expense. Terminal rigs and accessories are available in all good tackle shops and can be made at home if you prefer, as most experienced sea anglers do. Perhaps the single most important practical skill to learn is casting. Of course it is not necessary to cast huge distances every time you go fishing, but on balance most beaches produce a lot more fish if you can throw a bait 100 yards at least. If that seems a long, long way at the moment, do not worry. Today's tackle plus a basic but efficient style like the off-ground technique make it easy for anybody to cast that far at least. Many fishermen cast over 150 yards, and tournament champions have already achieved 275 yards with specialized equipment.

11

Rods and Reels

RODS

Rod selection is a hazardous proposition for any beginner because the majority are wrong for him personally, which is a different matter from being good or bad in their own right. Some are too long, too stiff, too slow or too fast in action; they either cast too powerfully or lack the strength to throw even eighty yards. Handles are too long or too short to be comfortable.

But you have to start somewhere, and common sense dictates caution at this stage. Do not buy an expensive or specialist rod until you know exactly which length, power and action suits you best. Opt instead for a semi-carbon or fibreglass rod 11½–12 feet long, strong enough to cast 5–6oz and of medium-fast action with a flexible tip and a stiff handle. If the rod is constructed as a long tip and detachable butt, the best handle material is either high tensile aluminium alloy or economy carbon. Well made but unsophisticated, such a rod is the perfect choice for learning how to catch fish from the seashore. Daiwa's Moonraker and Paul Kerry glass fibre models are excellent examples of off-the-peg rods that combine performance with modest price.

Second-hand rods are a welcome alternative for beginners on a tight budget. However, no matter how cheap the rod, no matter how good an investment it seems to be, do make sure that it conforms to the basic design requirements. Be wary of long, super-powerful tournament rods and blanks at this stage. Many are up for sale because their owners cannot cast them; some are unsuitable for fishing anyway, no matter how well you cast.

Before you can assess the various rods and blanks on sale, you must learn to cast reasonably well. But before you start practising you must have a suitable rod, otherwise all your efforts result in nothing but backlashes, frustration and poor distances. It seems an impossible situation. However, there are basic rules on rod selection which are guaranteed to lead even the rawest beginner through the minefield.

11 Rods and Reels

Rod length and handle spacing affect the amount of leverage you can exert during a cast. Too long a rod strains your muscles; an unnecessarily short rod wastes power. The same logic applies to the handle: if your hands are set too far apart, they cannot produce a fast enough whip at the end of the casting action. Hands set too close together seriously reduce your casting power.

Length

Ideal rod length for most beach fishermen regardless of their casting skill is between 11½ and 12 feet with a corresponding handle of 27 to 33 inches measured from butt cap to reel. Actually, 29 to 30 inches is the perfect spacing for most beach fishermen who standardize on the popular 5¼oz sinker. However, rough water and onshore winds sometimes demand sinkers up to 8oz. The more weight you cast the more leverage you need, so it pays to choose a rod with a slightly over-long butt. Shift your left hand up or down the handle to produce exactly the right amount of leverage for the sinker in use.

Action

Good casters seem effortless but they channel quite a bit of muscle power into the rod and through to the sinker. A stiff, powerful rod is difficult to master but produces exceptional distances. A soft, over-flexible rod butt simply sponges up power although it will compensate for mistakes. To get the best of both worlds, choose a rod with a stiffish lower half and a flexible tip. Support the middle of the rod with your left hand, rest the butt cap on the ground then push firmly with your right hand half-way along the butt section. A firm push (60–80lb) should flex the butt between one and three inches. Reject a rod that simply folds up with no resistance, or is so stiff that you cannot make an impression on it.

A flexible tip permits easy casting of a wide range of sinkers, cushions mistakes and smooths out the release phase of the cast. There are no easy tests for tip flexibility, but blank diameter is a reasonably good guide: the best modern blanks measure 3–4mm. Beware of any beach rod with a diameter over 4mm (measured just below the tip ring) – it will be dull and/or rigid.

Choose a rod with two equal length sections joined by a factory-fitted, well-whipped spigot, or buy a long tip plugged into or spigoted to a short handle. ABU-style lightweight metal ferrules with a locking screw are acceptable, but the majority of cheap ferrules and flimsy oriental overlapping joints (half of the rod pushes directly into the other) are too weak to withstand hard casting.

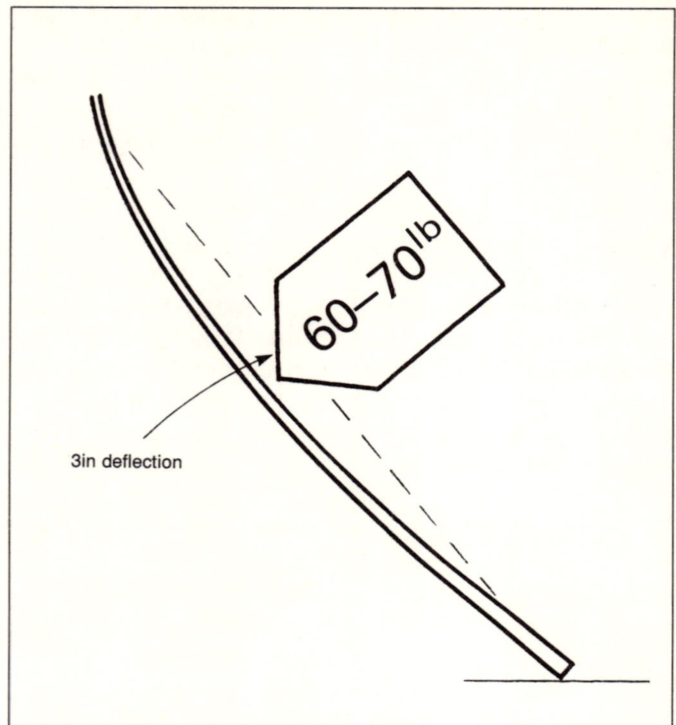

Butt section pressure test.

BEACH REELS

The choice is between multiplier and fixed spool. Backlash has virtually disappeared with the introduction of magnetic and centrifugal brakes, so do not be deterred from buying a multiplier on the basis that it is difficult to control. As long as you buy a casting model not a boat reel, there should be no difficulty in making it cast long distances. Of course there are significant differences between stationary and revolving spools. The fixed spool is less prone to backlash, less sensitive to tuning and quicker on the retrieve. Multipliers are smoother, better balanced and more precise. Some anglers prefer a fixed spool, others a multiplier, many use both. The important questions are which is better for distance work, and which reel is easier to master.

Distance

There is very little to choose between fixed spool and multiplier reels in pure distance terms. Both hold their own on the beach, and even in tournaments they run fairly close. Current records are 250 yards for the fixed spool with the multiplier some 30 yards ahead. In the 125–175 yard band, which is a realistic target for the beach, there is absolutely no difference in cast length. Given a good casting style, multipliers are docile and backlash-free; in fact they are no more difficult or demanding than a fixed spool.

The sticking point is not so much whether the fixed spool or the multiplier suits you better. Far more important, is the individual model you choose compatible with long range techniques? Most salt-water fixed spool reels guarantee excellent results, but with multipliers you have to be more careful. Some are incapable of delivering the goods no matter how hard you try. The finest big-game boat fishing multiplier costing hundreds of pounds will not cast as far as the cheapest reel designed for beach work. Such differences ought to be self-evident, but every year beginners make the same old mistakes.

Multipliers

Most beaches can be safely fished with 250 yards of 12–18lb nylon; a small reel holding that casts much further and more controllably than one that swallows 500 yards of 25lb line. Next comes basic design: there are boat reels, beach reels and some that do both. An all-round reel might well suit you, but make sure you avoid boat multipliers with heavy brass spools, mammoth line capacity and no cast controls. Insist on a reel with a built-in casting controller, either magnetic or centrifugal. Plain old-fashioned reels with lightweight plastic and alloy spools are capable of excellent results, but life is much easier if you can literally dial in some casting control or smooth line flow with interchangeable brake blocks. Braking systems boost confidence, and confidence is a key factor when you are learning to cast.

Choose a lightweight, one-piece spool running on ballraces or bronze bushes. High-speed gearing makes it easier to retrieve your terminal rig across rough ground. Higher-priced reels are a fine investment because they last longer, perform better and are backed by the manufacturer's after sales service.

Multiplier tuning

Tuning is the technique of producing maximum spool speed without creating too much risk of backlash. The more free-running a spool becomes, the less room exists for error. A fast spool generally casts further, therefore one side-effect of tuning for safe control is some loss of yardage.

Initial casting exercises hardly exceed 140 yards anyway, so by deliberately restricting speed for now you build in a fair amount of insurance. When a slow-running multiplier still backlashes every cast, you can be pretty sure there is a major fault somewhere in your style. Correct that rather than blame the reel.

Open the reel, wipe the ends of the spool spindle and clean out the ballraces. Squirt a little SAE20/50 or SAE90 motor oil into the races, smear a drop on each end of the spindle then reassemble the reel. Adjust the bearing cap until the spindle develops a slight end-float. Now load on your line, starting with a uni-knot to the spool core. Wind on line evenly until the reel is comfortably full. Attach a shock leader. Finally tape down the leader end, flip the reel out of gear and spin the spool by hand. It should run smoothly and not too quickly.

Start by tuning the spool for maximum control. If your reel has magnetic brakes, dial in the highest control number or wind the sideplate adjuster fully clockwise. Centrifugal braking is determined by the size and number of blocks inside the reel. Make your initial adjustment while the reel is stripped down for lubrication. Slide one large block on to each support bar. As your casting skill develops, gradually back off the magnet dial or change to smaller brake blocks.

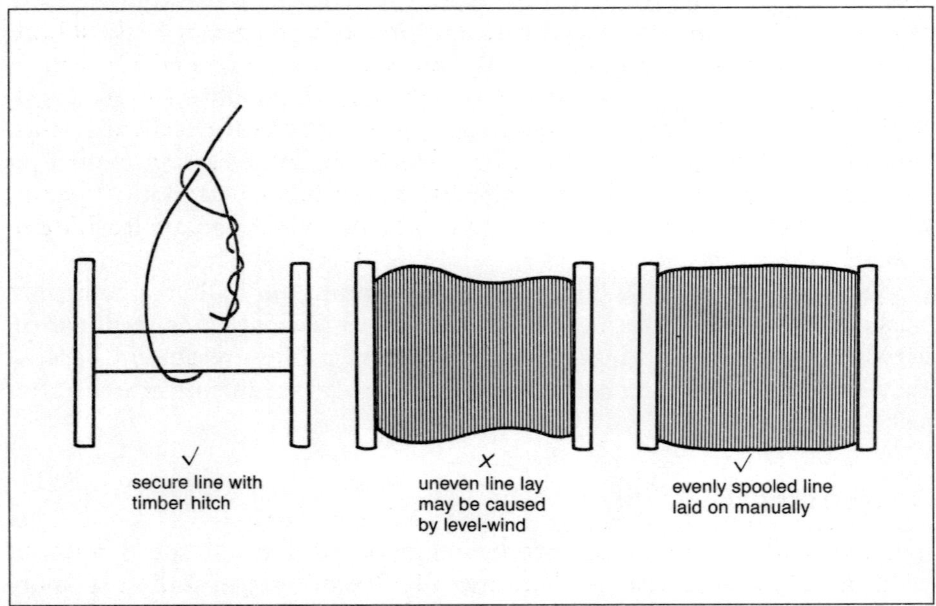

Multiplier loading.

Line tension

Even line tension and level spooling are essential for multiplier control. Level-wind reels automatically spread line across the spool but they do not control tension. Whichever kind of reel you use, learn to run the incoming nylon between finger and thumb. Apply steady, modest pressure so that line packs down reasonably tightly. Manual line-lay feels awkward at first but soon becomes second nature. Loose, uneven line guarantees backlash no matter how well you tune a multiplier.

Fixed Spools

Engineering quality and service back-up are important points to consider. They alone might well justify spending £30–40 on your first reel instead of £15–20 on a cheap and cheerful model that falls apart in six months. Fixed spool gears are always under severe stress due to the mechanical principles of the reel. You cannot expect long, reliable life from cheap metal and ill-cut gear teeth.

Choose a spool of at least 2½in diameter. Small spools strangle a potentially big cast by imposing too much rim friction on flowing line. Experts choose the largest salt-water models and cram them with line. Special tuning techniques ensure maximum line speed and minimum spool rim friction. Such steps are unnecessary while you learn to cast, but bring dividends when your casts exceed 150 yards.

Reduced casting power and cut fingers are a direct result of a spool that skids against its drag plates in mid-cast. Either the reel's drag should lock the spool for powerful casting, or you should modify the reel with an external locking gadget. Bale arms have a nasty habit of snapping shut in mid-cast. To prevent broken lines and lost tackle, fixed spool anglers either cut off the Bale arm wire or choose a reel like the Mitchell 498/499 with a manual pick-up roller. Penn now offer a manual bale arm conversion for the Spinfisher 850SS reel.

Setting up

A well-set-up fixed spool casts further, throws fewer spider's webs (clumps of loose line that catch in the butt ring) and reduces line twist. The golden rule of fixed spool casting is to choose a line as light as you can safely use, bearing in mind the beach, tidal force and size of fish, then cram on as much as the reel can handle without sloughing off loose coils.

Salt-water fixed spool reels swallow such huge amounts of thin nylon that it is essential to pack out the bottom of the spool before you wind on

250 to 300 yards of main line. Use old nylon, Dacron or even thin string. Make sure the backing is tight, even and concentric with the spool core.

Finger protection

Line release is second only to poor loading as a cause of lost control. A bare index finger cannot safely withstand a big cast. Even a 100-yard lob with a 5oz sinker builds up enough pressure to raise a blister. Angle of line grip is also important; the leader should form an angle of less than 90 degrees as it lies around your finger. Hold the reel with its stand clamped between your first and second, or second and third fingers. The leader forms an acute angle across your index finger which is fully protected by a leather guard – a cut-down glove or a finger stall.

Line twist

All fixed spool reels twist line, some worse than others. You cannot eliminate twist but you can reduce it to acceptable limits. The best trick is to wind on line under modest tension. Run incoming line between finger and thumb so that it packs down quite hard on the spool. Finger pressure also combs the majority of twists into the last few yards of main line. Cut them off after each fishing session.

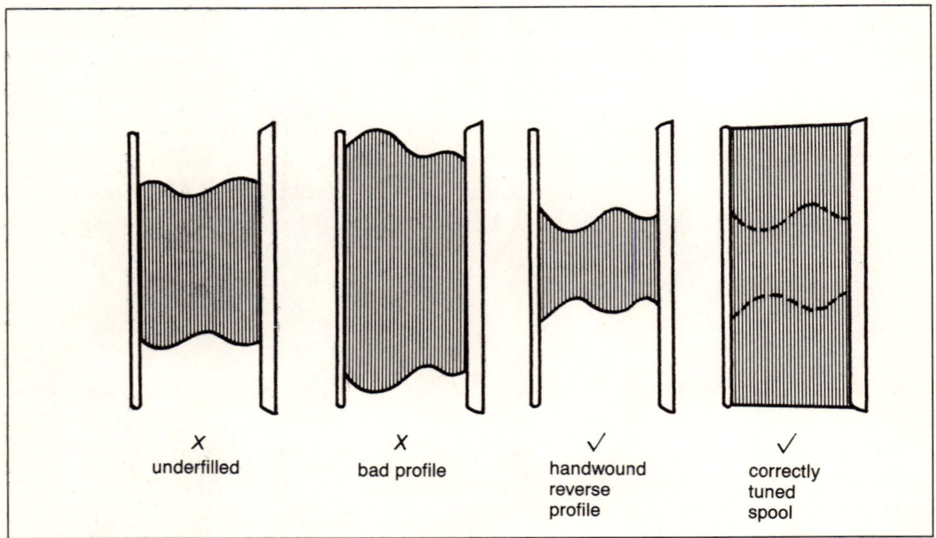

Fixed-spool line patterns.

12
Essential Tackle

LINE

Apart from its obvious function of connecting terminal rig to reel, line is enormously important in casting. A minor shift in line diameter adds or takes tens of yards from the cast. By matching line diameter to the beaches you fish and to your rod and reel, you could gain extra yardage without really trying. Monofilament is the only line seriously worth considering for use from the shore.

An effortless cast with 5oz of lead running on 18lb line (about 0.40mm diameter) should produce steady 150 yard casts without baits. With exactly the same rod, reel and casting weight, a much thicker 30lb line would reduce casting range by anything up to 60 yards. Conversely, thin 10lb monofilament would add about 30 yards to the original 150 yard maximum.

Line specification is a compromise between long casting performance and the demands of the sea. Everyone could add 50 yards to his present distances by changing down to 4–6lb line. But how many fish would he lose? How many sets of terminal tackle would be trapped by minor snags on the sea-bed? On the other hand, there is no need for 25–35lb line to haul dabs, whiting or even heavy cod across clean sand, mud and shingle; and you would lose a lot of distance by fishing so heavy. In all, it makes sense to pick a line whose safe breaking strain balances nicely against casting performance; 0.30–0.40mm (12–18lb breaking strain) almost always fits the bill.

Shock leader

Even 18lb line poses a problem in long range casting: as soon as you build any real power into the cast, the line snaps. Counter this by relieving the main line of direct casting stress. Instead of tying thin line directly to sinker or trace, insert a heavy shock leader between the terminal tackle and spool. Make the cast on heavy line then let the sinker fly out on lighter nylon.

Shock leaders add a significant measure of casting safety. Left to its own devices in free flight, a cracked-off sinker carries 300 yards with ease and you can never control its direction. Without a leader, a powerful caster would machine-gun the beach or practice field with lethal chunks of lead. Always use a shock leader with thin running lines. Attach the leader with a uni-knot, which is tough, easy to tie and streamlined for smooth running through the rod rings. For absolute security, insist on at least six full turns of heavy line around the spool when the tackle is set up ready to cast.

Safe breaking strain is reckoned by multiplying sinker weight by ten, and calling the result pounds. Thus, a safe leader for 5oz is 50lb monofilament nylon. Sometimes you do not need to cast really hard, so lighter leaders might be safe on an uncrowded beach. As a rule though, err on the pessimistic side. On the other hand, very few casters need more than 50lb line regardless of how much sinker weight they use.

SINKERS

Tournament casters find that just ¼oz makes ten yards difference to their maximum distances. Some choose 5oz, some 5¼oz; others hit peak performance with a full 6oz. There is no need to carry sinker selection to

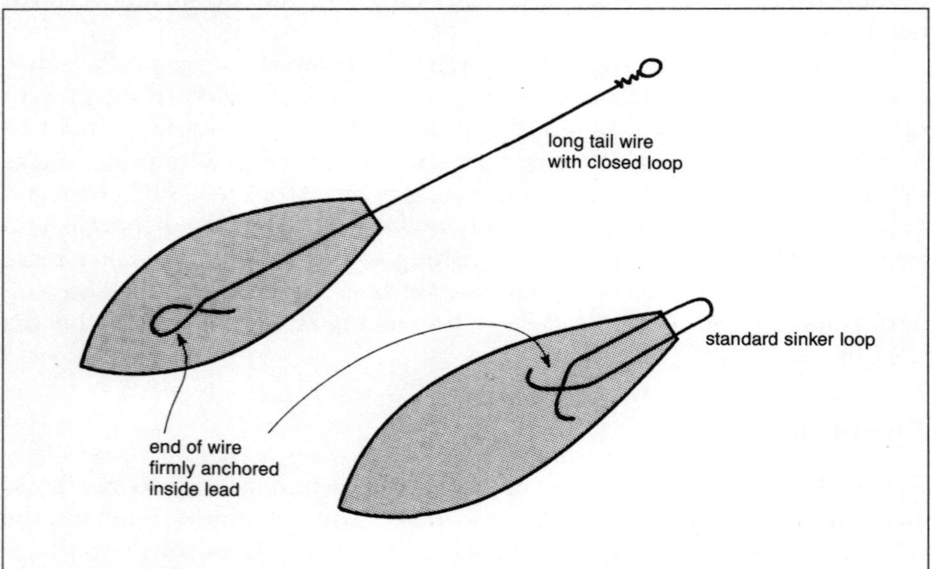

Standard and long-tailed sinkers.

such extremes while you learn to cast or for everyday beach work, but it still pays to choose your practice weight with some care.

A sinker must be light enough to cast without straining your muscles, but heavy enough to make the rod 'work' under moderate casting power. It is easier to time your cast with a reasonably heavy chunk of lead than with a lightweight sinker. In the early days you need all the help you can get, and the right sinker is a tremendous ally.

Five-ounce sinkers are ideal for casting practice and general beach work. A rod balanced to cast that much lead gives excellent, easy distance coupled with the bite sensitivity and fighting power to handle big fish while retaining enough action and delicacy to make catching small fish a pleasure. In addition, it has enough backbone in reserve to throw 7–8oz when rough weather and heavy water overwhelm standard sinkers.

Throwing a bait far enough is only half the battle. Making it stay put in fast tides and rough water is another matter. Also, most fish hook themselves against the inertia of the terminal rig. Here too a sinker in the 5–6oz band offers the ideal balance between mechanical efficiency and sport. However, grip wires moulded into the sinker are necessary to counteract tidal pressure and wave force.

If you are new to beach fishing, start fishing with 5–5½oz streamlined bombs: plain for casting practice and slow-water fishing, grip-wired for general fishing. Beachbomb, Aquazoom, Breakaway and Aquapedo are all excellent and should be fitted with swivelling wires rather than fixed spikes for easier retrieve.

Sinker Attachment

In allowing a sinker to escape from even a modest cast you turn loose enough energy to smash roof tiles, bury the lead a foot in soft ground or kill someone. It is your personal responsibility to be safe. That means picking the right place to practise, using a leader and inserting a strong metal link between leader and sinker tail loop. A leader alone does not guarantee safety; its strength and reliability are destroyed by the wrong knot or by subjecting the knot to abrasion.

Field practice hardly abrades a knot. Most of the time you walk up to the lead rather than drag it back through the grass. Beach fishing is another matter because the knot is chafed by sand, grit and rocks every time you reel in. Three or four 100-yard retrieves across rough ground reduce knot strength by 75 per cent. Cast number five snaps and the sinker whirrs out of control down the beach.

Always use a split ring or strong clip between sinker and leader. Check for quality – not all clips are as good as they look. The same goes for link

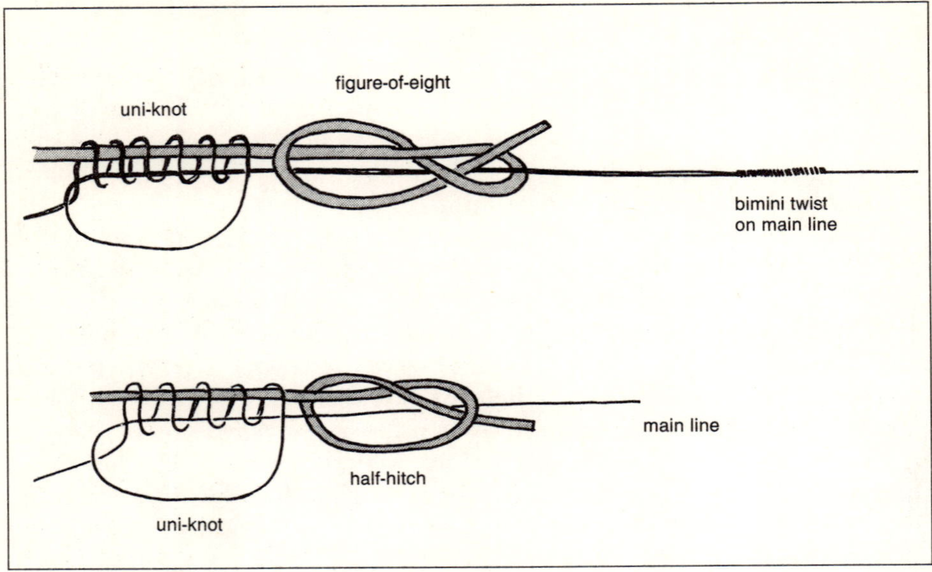

High-test leader knot (above); standard leader knot (below).

swivels, which are notoriously vulnerable to corrosion and sudden failure. Tie good knots and check them frequently. Palomar and uni-knot are an excellent choice, strong, easy to tie and reliable.

HOOKS

Eyed hooks offer the widest selection of bends, wire thicknesses, sizes and steel finishes. As a group, hooks with a direct attachment ring cannot be beaten. Spade ends and whipped hooks do have specific advantages for matchmen and light line anglers but they are nowhere near so versatile, nor are they as easy to use. Ordinary Aberdeens, Vikings, O'Shaughnessy, Kirbys, Baitholders . . . all the world's favourite hooks are made with eyes. Anglers like them that way. Certainly they are easy to tie, quick to change and best suited to beginners. Preferred knots are the old stalwarts used for tackle assembly in general: uni-knot, tucked half-blood and Palomar.

The eye itself can be a serious disadvantage in worm fishing. Other soft baits suffer as well, but lugworms, harbour rag and silvers are acutely sensitive to the size of that metal ring. Old-style hooks like the O'Shaughnessy, Model Perfect and Baitholder are almost sure to pop even a giant lugworm threaded around the bend, up the full length of the shank and on to the snood. Hooks of this type are impossible to use with small silver ragworm because wire thickness exceeds the diameter of the worm.

Eyed hooks most suitable for beach fishing include Breakaway's Spearpoint Mustad Viking 79515, Partridge MW and various brands of Aberdeen. It matters little whether an eye lies straight or angled. Wire thickness and ring diameter are what count, and all these hooks are adequate no matter which baits you use. There is little to be gained by resorting to whipped, plain shank hooks for average ragworms and lugworms, sand-eels and crabs. The slight deterioration in bait presentation as compared to a whipping is minimal and more than offset by an eyed hook's greater strength.

ROD RESTS

Today's beach rods are light and easy to handle but you still need a solid rod rest. Your sense of touch is far more sensitive than any indicator system, so why not dispense with the rest? Unfortunately, it is a classic case of theory being light years away from everyday practicality. It makes no difference whether your rod and reel weigh 12oz or 12lb. When the sinker is anchored in the sea-bed and water pressure builds up over 80, 100 even 150 yards of line, rod-tip leverage becomes enormously powerful. Ten minutes of bracing the rod against a fierce ebb current is enough to beat the toughest of fishermen. Invest in a solid rest or spend time in the garden shed and make your own. Get a robust rod holder now, and save losing your temper later.

ESSENTIAL ACCESSORIES

Beach fishing tackle can be as simple or as complex as you care to choose. Advanced-design rods, highly tuned reels, bass rods, specialist float and spinning tackle are yours for the asking. Basically though, very little is essential apart from the standard rod, reel, line and terminal tackle already described. But there are a few accessories and gadgets that make life more comfortable on the beach and certainly do help you catch more fish.

Successful fishing is often a matter of playing a waiting game. Sometimes beach fishermen stay out for days at a stretch, and 12- to 18-hour sessions are about average for cod and winter species in general. A big umbrella is highly desirable not only to shelter you and your tackle from the rain but even more importantly to ward off wind and cold. It is the wind-chill factor that threatens a beach fisherman's comfort, not necessarily low temperature itself. Buy the biggest, strongest umbrella you can find, preferably one fitted with a nylon skirt that stops wind creeping inside.

On balance, beaches fish better at night so a powerful lamp is essential. Paraffin pressure lamps are standard issue among anglers, the most popular models being Optimus, Tilley and Hipolito. Their 350–500 candlepower output provides more than enough light for baiting, casting and landing fish. Heat output is also substantial – a major bonus for winter fishing.

To complete your creature comforts, buy a good pair of knee-length rubber boots or waders. Fitted with insulated inserts, they keep your feet warm and dry and are much healthier than heavily insulated moon boots which, warm as they are, tend to make feet swell if worn for too long. A one-piece waterproof nylon suit or two-piece outfit of the same material wards off wind and rain without being so stiff and bulky that casting becomes impossible. Underneath in cold weather go fleecy insulated jacket and trousers such as Helly Hansen Polar Wear. And don't forget the hat: sixty per cent of body heat escapes through the top of your head.

Tools of the trade include a sharp filleting knife, pliers with sidecutters and a pair of long-handled forceps for unhooking, oilstone for hook sharpening, a kit of reel and lamp spares, screwdriver and reel oil. These along with spare tackle should be stored in plastic boxes with watertight lids. Spares, tackle in general, food drink and bait are stored and carried in either a rigid tackle box that doubles as a seat or better still in a tough rucksack which is much easier to carry long distances.

13

Casting

Nobody fishes for long without realizing that casting is one of the most important skills of the beach game. Of course there are times when fish feed within spitting distance. Unfortunately, many anglers think that they always behave this way and as a result they cannot be persuaded to learn a style more advanced than the traditional overhead thump. Good casters have the option of casting short, medium or to extreme range as conditions dictate. They can choose exactly where to drop the bait: behind the backwash, in a gully at 90 yards or on the far slope of a sandbank at extreme range. The sheer versatility of long distance casting more than justifies the effort of learning modern techniques.

THE ESSENCE OF CASTING

A rod is a mixture of lever and spring, characteristics that operate together but always with a see-saw effect. When a rod works at peak performance in its spring mode, it is a poor lever; and when it is a solid, powerful lever, a blank shows hardly any springiness. The art of good casting lies in balancing the two so that they work for rather than against you.

Until a blank is flexed to the point where its fibres lock, power input is wasted. Hit into the cast earlier and most of your effort is wasted because the springy side of the blank's character mops it up and wastes it. All good casters learn to feel for that locking sensation before they turn on the power. A good casting style should be a one-two action of bending the blank then adding the main power stroke. Get it even half right and you cannot fail to throw a respectable distance. Bend, lock and accelerate an ordinary glass fibre beach rod even moderately well and it will automatically cast at least 120 yards.

Long-range casting is simply the means of making a rod work along those lines. No secrets are involved; there are no complicated scientific formulae to learn. Make the rod bend before you dial in the main power, and the sinker has no option but to fly a long, long way. If you approach it from that angle, the arms-and-legs aspect of technique is so much easier to understand and put into practice.

I do not recommend any particular casting style to you. You must decide which best suits your physique and where you fish. Besides, there is no such thing as *the* pendulum cast, *the* South African and so on. You develop your personal variation along those themes. However, you cannot do so until you learn the mechanics involved in making the rod work. Concentrate on this very easy exercise, and do not write it off as too silly and obvious to bother about. It is the foundation of every powerful casting style including the most advanced of tournament techniques. Even in its simplest form it whips a 5oz beach rig well over 150 yards.

THE BASIC OFF-GROUND CAST

Step 1

Reach back as far as you can and lower the rod tip to the ground opposite the direction of the sea. Toss the sinker away from the tip at the same time so that it lies straight behind the tip on a three- to four-foot drop. The left elbow should be high, with the left hand parallel with your face, and the right arm straight but not strained.

Step 2

Without looking at the rod, pull the handle forward with your right hand as though you were throwing a spear. Your left hand will extend away from your shoulder and the right arm will bend ready to punch. During this pull forward you will feel the rod begin to lock. Concentrate on that sensation. When your arms reach the overhead thumping position the rod seems to be alive and eager. This is because the blank's fibres are locked.

Step 3

Punch with your right hand, pull with your left, and follow through. The tackle flies out smoothly and without effort because the rod has worked properly.

Practise this basic technique, gradually extending the power arc by swivelling round further before you drop the sinker on the ground. Only when this sensation of bending and locking is second nature should you investigate the more specialist casting styles.

BODY POWER

Good casters are totally relaxed. Certainly they flick the rod in a powerful arc that drives the tackle skyward, but they do not strain themselves nor do their reels backlash every cast. Their secret – and probably it is the secret of good casting – is that they use their bodies rather than their arms alone.

Body weight alone can add 30 to 40 yards to a cast. Go back to the Step 2, but this time on the layout make a conscious effort to extend your body and tackle away from the sea. Feel your weight come on to the right leg. Your left heel rises and the right knee bends a little.

Pull through and cast exactly as before, and concentrate on transferring body weight from right leg to left. Feel yourself literally adding weight to the casting action. The rod whips through faster even though your arms work no harder. Be particularly careful about head action and left elbow height. Without a definite aiming point and a full power stroke from the left hand you cannot achieve full rod efficiency, smoothness or power.

Consider the action of the left hand. Most important, it greatly improves the efficiency of the rod blank by forcing it to operate over the longest possible arc, which automatically boosts power and makes timing far less critical. By pulling the rod forward in spear-throwing fashion to full left arm stretch you delay that final whiplike arm action which flicks the blank over and rockets the sinker away.

All good casts drive the sinker high into the air. Head angle and the aerial aiming mark contribute greatly towards that, and the left hand should then naturally make its own contribution. If you get your head around early in the cast and look up, the left hand works better.

BODY ROTATION

Instead of laying out the cast as before, force your upper body round further so that your shoulders lie parallel with the water's edge. Bend your right knee and dip at the waist. Almost force your body into a semi-crouch so that you feel coiled up like a strong spring ready to unwind itself behind the cast. Toss the sinker away into its new position, further 'round the corner' than in the basic cast. The precise angle does not matter too much; similarly, the exact degree of body rotation also depends on physique and personal preference.

The cast itself is an anticlimax. Copy what you did in the previous exercises, this time over a longer arc and with the additional boost of body power. Unwind your body, transfer weight from right leg to left then flick the rod handle over with that same powerful, smooth punch and pull. A

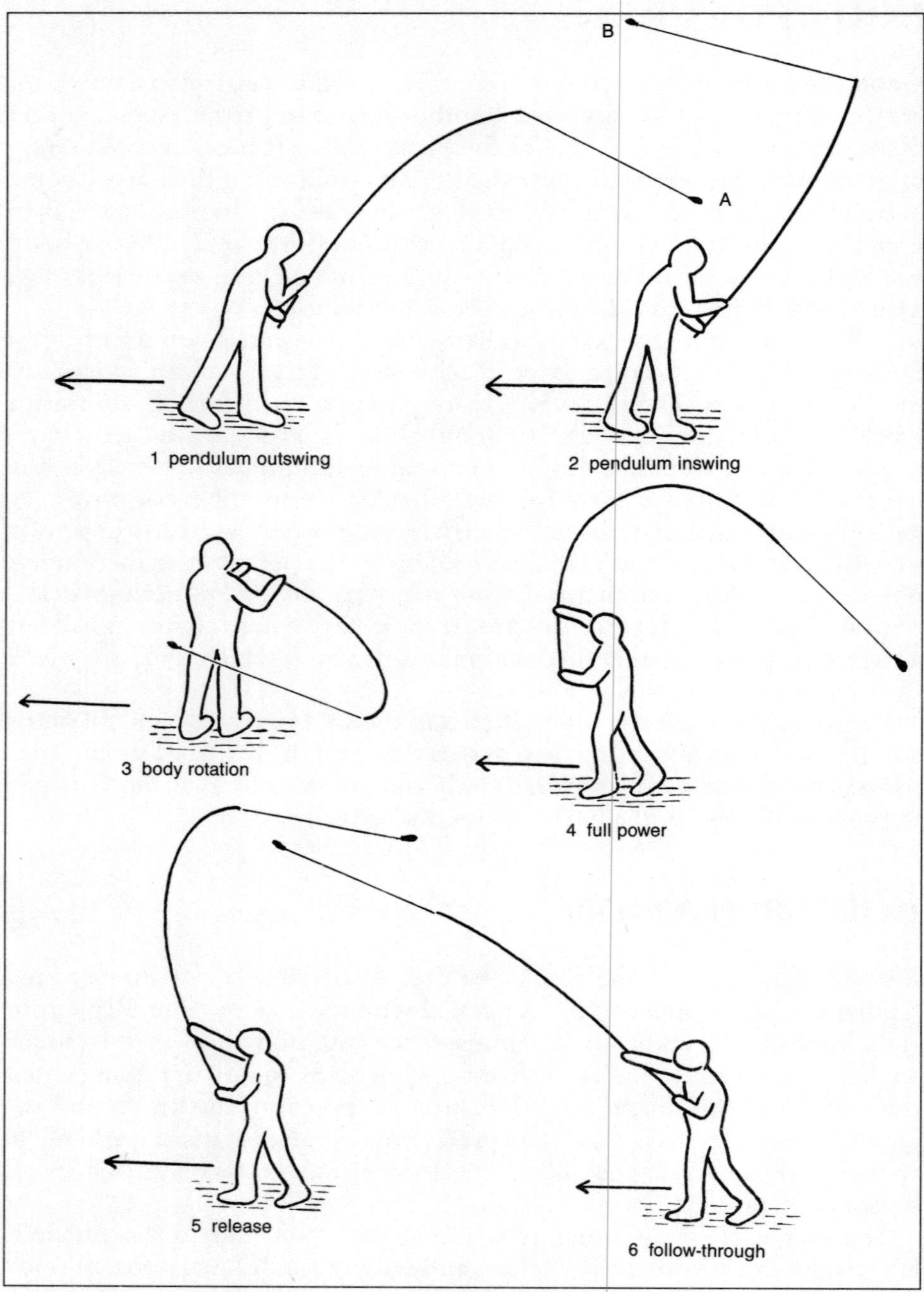

How the zones operate during a pendulum cast.

powerful cast will put you on your toes, and you may even have to take a half step forward to preserve balance. The right arm is high, punched at roughly 45 degrees. The left pulls down to the bottom left-hand corner of your rib cage. The rod tip points to that imaginary aiming mark in the sky and the sinker flies high and straight. If you finish the cast in roughly this position every time, there is a 90 per cent chance that your style is developing nicely. With practice, distances should creep into the 130s within a few weeks. Given more practice and a longer rod, this style which is known as the South African cast is easily capable of breaking the 200-yard mark and is surprisingly good for all-round fishing even though the sinker and baits are laid on the beach.

THE PENDULUM CAST

Pendulum casting is a group of styles which feature a preliminary swing of the sinker. Some casters use a huge arc, others cast big distances with a more abbreviated swing. Everyone's style must he built on fundamental rules that have little to do with personal preferences. From the mechanical point of view there are some things you can do with a pendulum cast, and some that will not work however much you practise.

Success depends on proper alignment of rod with sinker and leader. Unless they follow each other along the correct path the rod will not react properly and the cast will fly out of control.

Study the illustrations and in your mind's eye trace the line of the rod's tip ring as it powers through a big cast. The sinker swings out to position A, back in a pendulum arc to Position B, then follows the rod tip through its main power stroke. As the rod accelerates the leader and sinker must be properly aligned along the aerial pathway.

14

Rigs and Tactics

BASIC TACTICS

Everyone's first attempts at shore fishing are rather clumsy. Casts fly left and right, tackle refuses to anchor in the tide, baits tear from the hook in mid-cast. You do not even know exactly when to strike the bite. Go to an open, uncrowded stretch of seashore and take life as it comes. If you have an experienced angler to point you in the right direction, so much the better. But you can avoid the major pitfalls just by reading about rigs, baits and tackle assembly. Those and casting probably account for most early headaches. Legering catches more fish than all other methods combined because most fish hooked from open beaches, surf, estuaries and rocks are bottom feeders that prefer natural baits like worms, crabs and fish. Make learning to use a leger your priority, then you can fish 99 per cent of the British coastline with confidence. By reading about legering tactics and techniques on the following pages, you will be able to teach yourself the basics. However, being taught by an expert is always preferable, and as with anything, practice makes perfect.

Open Beaches

Competent anglers can easily fish close together but it takes just one who does not cast straight to ruin the day for everyone else. It is a nightmare to fish next to someone who casts over your line or whose tackle drifts in the current and tangles with a dozen others. Find yourself a spot at least fifty yards away from the next man and avoid the problem of casts that escape a little too late or early and fly astray. As long as you use a grip wired lead, your tackle will not drift too far out of control.

A reasonably flat beach with no offshore obstructions to trap the terminal rig and line is much easier to fish than rocks and rough ground. Even if your local coastline is predominantly rocky, choose a clean beach for your first attempts. At least you will not fall down the cliff while you struggle to master the rod and reel.

Terminal Rig Principles

Terminal rigs are systems of presenting baits so that fish find them easily and are encouraged to attack. Location and attraction are the overriding considerations. The object is to present the bait in the right place at the right time. Provided that bait is well chosen, the chances of a bite are excellent. Water conditions and the way fish feed dictate the design of terminal rigs. Sometimes baits must lie in place long enough for fish to find them. Static rigs cast from the beach catch a broad cross-section of fish, from dabs to conger eels. If you can locate the ideal spot on the sea-bed, legering is the

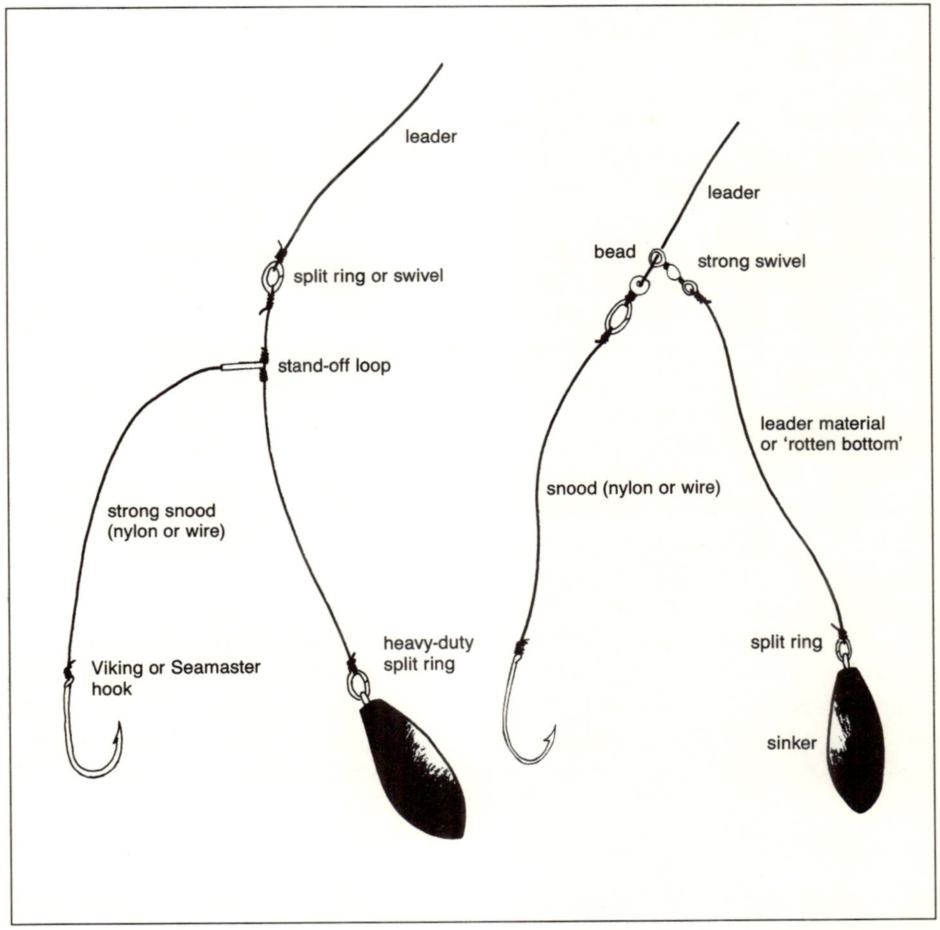

Single-hook paternoster (left); running paternoster (right).

perfect answer to bottom fishing because it is easy to control, highly effective and economical in tackle.

Sometimes an anchored bait is attacked and swallowed without hesitation, in which case fixed traces work adequately. Now and again the fish creeps up and plays with the bait. Unless the rig is constructed to give the fish plenty of leeway in the form of slack line, a bite never develops. Paternosters are inferior to a running leger in that respect. Learn to design and handle both rigs; they cover so many aspects of beach fishing and catch so many species of fish that you cannot afford to overlook either.

Paternosters

Paternoster construction is very simple. The sinker is attached to the very end of your line with the sinker knot protected from sea-bed abrasion by a split ring or a swivel. One, two or three hooks on short traces called snoods are spaced along the central rib of the paternoster. You can buy outriggers to support snoods and hooks but most anglers opt for stand-off loops tied directly into the main rib, or better still a tough, swivelling nylon boom like the Avis device.

Paternosters can be tied directly in the main reel line or casting leader but are better made detachable. Join the rig to the shock leader with a split ring, swivel or quick-fastening clip. You can store dozens of spare rigs in a plastic bag, so there is no need to waste time tying a new one should the original snap off in casting or foul on the sea-bed. *Important*: the central rib of a detachable paternoster must be of a breaking strain equal to or higher than that of the casting leader. Otherwise it snaps first cast.

The exact dimensions of a paternoster are seldom critical. As a rule, use a number of hooks appropriate to the size of fish and strength of rod and reel. It is no good hooking three conger eels at once; on the other hand why waste time catching whiting on a one-hook rig when you could just as easily haul them out two or three a cast?

Paternosters are useful for catching mackerel and other species attracted to artificial lures. A string of feathered snoods or bright strands of silver foil catch mackerel by the score. Four to six hooks are a neat balance between easy control and rapid results. Feathers backed up by natural baits, usually strips of mackerel, and jigged close to the bottom lure most species of fish.

Running Legers

One hook mounted below a sinker sliding freely on the shock leader is the preferred rig for shy species and a better means of fishing big single baits. Construction is very easy, and you can choose the length of trace best

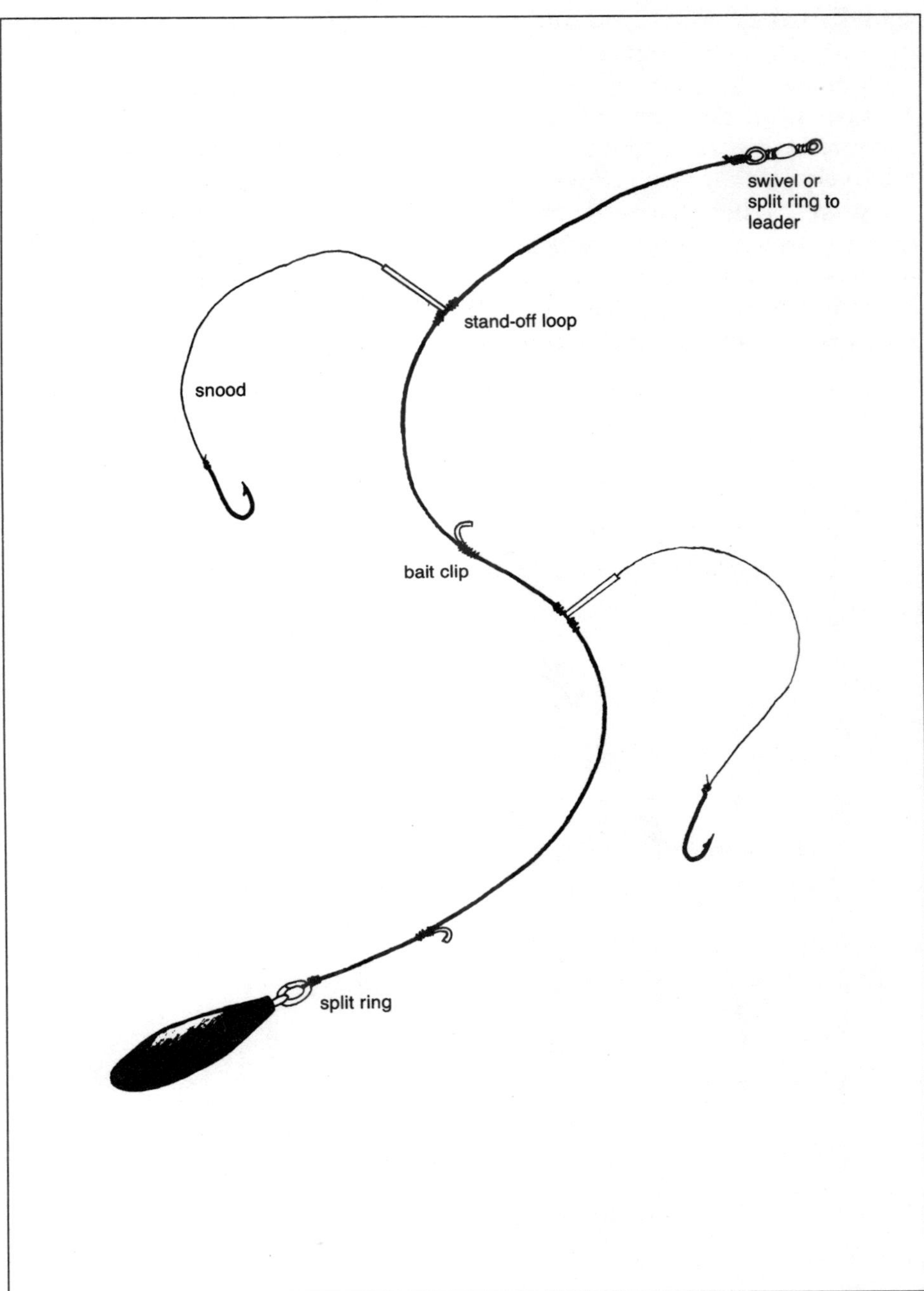

Two-hook paternoster.

suited to the species you aim to catch. Wire and monofilament traces between six inches and six feet long are equally well accommodated.

Running legers are fished static or slowly rolling across the sea-bed. Movement of the rig itself or pressure of tide against the main line of an anchored rig reduces the free-running properties. Unless the main line is relatively slack, a fish cannot move off with the trace without disturbing the sinker. When that is the case you may as well use a single-hook paternoster. However, on the whole the running leger works well enough to merit serious attention. Like the paternoster it is useful for all-round bottom fishing for the majority of fish. It excels for tope, conger eels, and rays that live in deep water close to rocks, piers and harbour walls.

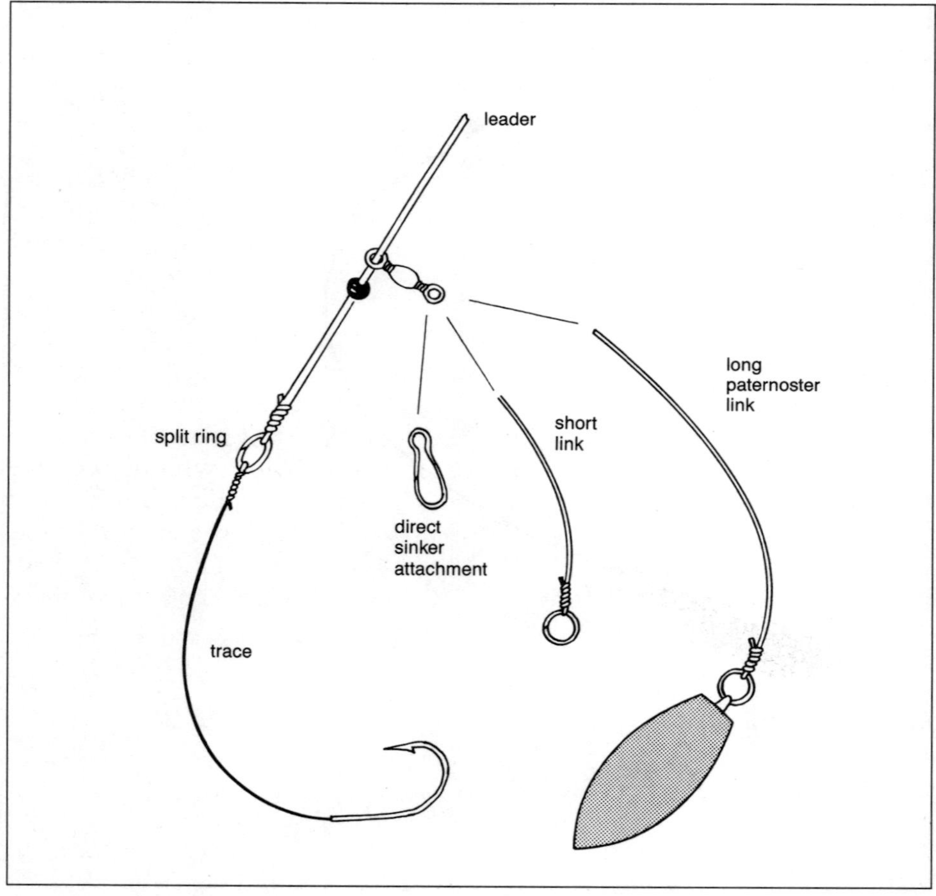

Running leger and variations.

14 Rigs and Tactics

Setting Up

As far as possible set up your tackle at home. Make up two or three double-hook paternosters and carry them to the beach in individual plastic bags. You could tie on the snooded hooks when you make up the rest of the rig, but it is neater to carry them separately. Tying them on the beach leaves you free to choose the right size hook for the day's conditions and baits.

Two sizes of hooks should accommodate most of your early fishing: size 2–1/0 for general fishing, and size 4/0–6/0 for cod and the other bigger species. Aberdeen eyed hooks are excellent in both cases. Use 15lb snoods on the smaller hooks, 20–25lb on the larger. Snoods of 18in are a handy length; you can soon cut them down if necessary.

Find your place on the beach, park your tackle well back from the water's edge and set up your rod rest. Push the two sections of rod tightly together with the rings lined up from tip to butt. Attach the reel and make sure the winch fitting is screwed down comfortably secure.

Clip a 5oz sinker on the paternoster's lower swivel or split ring. Make sure it is absolutely secure to withstand hard casting. Wired bombs of all types are satisfactory, but the Breakaway sinker available at most tackle shops is a favourite for routine beach fishing. Check that the swivelling wires are trapped by beads which slot into grooves in the lead. If the beads spring out prematurely, tackle drifts out of control.

Tie on two snooded hooks. Flat-fish, whiting, school bass, codling and silver eels – common species to catch from the beach – are easily hooked on small Aberdeens. Small hooks are usually more productive when you are fishing for anything that comes along. Save the bigger hooks until you know there are winter cod or specimen bass hunting the shallows.

Local preferences dictate your choice of baits. Most whiting, codling, bass and flat-fish are hooked on worms of some description. But do ask at the tackle shop and see what other anglers on the beach use for bait. It may be that sand-eels, fish strips or crabs are essential. Check first, then you will know exactly what to put on the trace. If in doubt stick to worms: lug in winter, ragworms in summer.

Tackle Control

Most beaches are swept by tidal currents powerful enough to drag sinker and line downstream. Sometimes it pays to drift the bait but on the whole a static rig hooks more fish. Grip wires on the sinker boost anchorage only if the angle of the line is correct in relation to the current. The worst mistake is to recover slack line immediately after the cast lands in the water. Instead, let go another 10–25 yards of line. The extra bow of nylon improves the sinker's efficiency and makes it dig hard into the sea-bed. Now prop your rod in the rest and wait for a bite.

Bites

Hungry fish bite hard enough to signal a clear reaction at the rod tip. Even dabs 150 yards away in rough water are easily detected . Most sea fish take the bait so eagerly they hook themselves. The trace snaps tight against the inertia of the grip sinker and drives the barb home. Striking in the accepted sense is unnecessary. Watch for a distinct and continuing reaction on the rod tip, pick up the rod and wind in until you feel resistance. Then raise the rod tip as high as you can reach and *hold the tension*. The worst mistake is to let the line go slack.

Sometimes a bite is so fierce that the sinker loses its grip. Line falls slack before you pick up the rod. Wind as fast as you can until you feel the weight of the fish, then lift the rod to maintain pressure. Reel the fish gently ashore; there is no need to rush: well-hooked fish seldom escape. Pump the line if necessary: lift the rod then drop the tip while winding back the slack line that results. Again lift the tip to haul back more line – drop the rod and turn the reel – lift the rod again. Pumping is the smooth, efficient way to pull in a heavy fish without straining the tackle or your winding arm.

Guide the fish towards the shore, wait until a wave picks it up then make a final, smooth lift which hauls it clear of the water and dumps it on the sand. Grab the fish by the tail and carry it high and dry. Small species like whiting and flatties are simply cranked out of the water and swung ashore on the rod. Unhook your fish, rebait the tackle and cast again. When a shoal is within casting range you cannot afford to waste time admiring the catch.

15

Whiting

The first whiting of the year bring summer fishing to a close and set the pace for long winter months of shore fishing. Whiting are an essential part of our sport, though in reality they have little enough to offer. Small, ravenous fish which invade every inch of the British coastline, they are amazingly easy to catch and therefore perfect for the newcomer. For all the commercial fishing, amateur netting and coastal pollution, whiting thrive where other fish suffer. Since cod fishing declined from the early 1960s glut, whiting have expanded to fill the vacuum.

Many species of fish prefer specific habitats and water depths. Whiting are happy in deep water over reefs and rocks, along open beaches of sand and shingle, in calm water and roaring surf. Though not particularly tolerant of low salinty they still infiltrate the upper reaches of estuaries.

Identification

The whiting is a member of the family that includes cod and pollack. It is a silvery fish, white bellied and greenish on the back with pearly scales which brush off at a touch. Like the cod it has a relatively large mouth with tiny, sharp teeth. At first glance you may confuse a small cod with a whiting but there are two tell-tale signs that separate the species. Whiting have no barbule under the chin; codling, no matter how small, possess a single barbule. There is a black spot at the base of the whiting's pectoral fin. Notice too that the whiting's eye is relatively much bigger. It is a less robust fish whose colours are really very different. Though exact shades and patterns vary in cod, whiting are uniformly immaculate, silvery fish which glow coral-pink in the autumn sunlight. Cod are drab by comparison, dirty on the belly, marbled back and flank.

Habits

The whiting's annual cycle steers massive shoals into casting range sometime during the middle weeks of September. Sometimes they move in earlier; other years the earliest fish show in October. But you can depend on their arriving at some stage. Then shore fishing changes into top gear. Anglers who never bother to cast a line all summer head for the beach. Tackle shops do a roaring trade with lugworms, tackle and mackerel baits.

Most whiting hooked are migrants; there are also a few small shoals that hang around deep water all year and which, like pouting and the occasional out-of-season codling, may show at any time. The whiting that interest us are the annual visitors which outnumber the rest a million to one. When the main shoals arrive you should be hauling them out by the dozens. Thirty or forty fish is good going but unlikely to set the world alight. Even a moderately successful trip in October–November should produce fifteen or twenty fish a rod.

Early season whiting bite better after dark. In mid-September, expect to hook little or nothing during the day and only a few fish at night. Daylight catches may be respectable by the middle of October, but the bulk of whiting are still hooked after dusk. The ratio of night to day whiting holds steady at five or more to one and may be far higher in the calm, bright days of late autumn when the sea lies glass-smooth. The basic rule is to fish at night whenever you can. Failing that, concentrate on late afternoon tides.

Tides

Whiting arrive inshore on some of the biggest tides of the year, the autumn equinox springs. The rush of water, its associated rough weather and a tailing off in water temperature flush summer away and encourage the seabed to close down for the coming winter. Falling air temperatures and shorter days accelerate the process. Big tides are the turning point of the year, a brief period between the easy living of summer and harsh reality of winter and they herald the beginning of the whiting season proper.

Tides are perhaps less a factor in fishing for whiting than for cod or bass. Whereas the bigger species tend to swim and feed to a tidal pattern, whiting are less fussy. Bass and cod switch on and off; whiting merely vary their feeding rate. The two hours each side of high water are universally successful and high water itself produces plenty of bites; far from the case with many other species, which tend to slow down or stop feeding during that brief spell of static water.

Tide, then, influences the number of whiting willing to feed at any given time but is seldom a make or break factor. The classic whiting tide is midway between neaps and springs with high water around 8 p.m. in late October. Sheer numbers of whiting override any criticism of their sporting merit. On very light tackle they fight hard enough, but any fish that weighs less than two pounds is hardly in the 'Jaws' class. It is the certainty and ease of whiting fishing that counts. No fish provides a beginner with such a mighty boost in confidence. On your first trip to sea or beach you could easily land a dozen prime fish. There cannot be a better introduction to the sport. It certainly beats waiting six months for your first bass.

Baits and Rigs

Whiting feed on or close to the sea-bed. Not a fussy creature by any means, it eats crabs, worms and small fish including smaller whiting. Shrimps are snapped up in vast numbers; early winter fish hooked from open beaches are sometimes full to overflowing. Lugworms and fresh fish baits account for the majority of whiting. Ragworms, sand-eels and peeler crab work well but prove too expensive when shoals are biting fast and furious. Two pounds of fresh herring or mackerel cost less than a quarter pound of ragworms and usually outfish them anyway, so why waste money?

To some extent lugworms are therefore unnecessary; indeed if anything. whiting attack fish more readily. Yet there is always the chance of cod turning up, and they certainly do take lugworms in preference to fish. Thus with all-round prospects in mind, you might choose a cocktail bait of lugworm tipped with fish strip. It covers the options and spins out those expensive worms.

Buy your mackerel (herrings if you can find a supply) in deep-frozen blocks. Order several pounds at a time because the price is more competitive and you are sure of adequate freshness. Order a box from your local fishmonger, visit the fish market or wait on the quayside for a commercial boat to come in with the day's catch. An even better plan is to feather a freezer-load of mackerel in summer and keep them specifically for the autumn whiting.

Though not as discriminating as, say, thornback rays, whiting are not enthralled by a chunk of greasy, soft mackerel which has been lurking on the slab for a week. Firm, bloody bait encourages more bites. Lay the whole fish on a board and cut it in back-to-belly chunks each half an inch wide. Work along the fish from head to tail. Flip each tiny cutlet face up, then slice it from top to bottom. The result is a comma-shaped chunk of flesh full of blood and oil, supported by a tough rind of skin. Each piece is the ideal size for whiting, and you waste none of the mackerel – even the head cuts down into attractive baits. Treat herrings the same way.

Hook size is less important than with most species but it pays to keep to a minimum. Size 4–2/0 fine wire Aberdeens, well sharpened, penetrate easily whatever the casting distance. You may find that too small a bend slides far into the whiting's throat, in which case step up a couple of sizes in the interests of conservation. The millions of whiting are still no excuse for killing fish unnecessarily.

Cocktails of mackerel and lugworm are economical and effective. Sometimes the bait appeals more if the lugworm goes on second and hangs down from the bend. The disadvantage is that during a hard cast the weight of the fish chunk pushes the worm off the hook. Mounted the other way around, the fish acts as a soft bed for the worm. By nicking the point and bend of the hook through the skin rather than directly into the flesh, you can be sure that the bait casts reliably and better withstands crab attack.

Shrimps score top marks with whiting fishermen. A live shrimp is all but impossible to cast on conventional terminal tackle because it rips from the hook under the lightest acceleration. Frozen shrimps cast better but are messy. Some fishermen bait the hook, then freeze it solid. Every cast therefore requires its own trace, and each baited hook must be stored in a vacuum flask of ice. Overall it is hardly worth the effort even if shrimp are freely available.

The Baitsafe capsule is the solution. Catch live shrimps and store them in a bucket of water or in damp weed in a cooler box. Use a small, fine wire hook like the Aberdeen Blue inserted once through the shrimp's back. Pack the trace in the Baitsafe and cast as hard as you like: safe inside its plastic box a shrimp stays intact over the longest distances.

The disadvantages of Baitsafes – one reason why matchmen shy away – is the restriction to one hook. You can cram two baits into the capsule, but it never works too well. Whiting fishing is traditionally the realm of the two- and three-hook paternoster. When the fish are biting well, expect to land a full house.

Cut a four-foot piece of leader, tie a split ring top and bottom for line and sinker attachment then tie in two or three stand-off loops or Avis booms. Add bait clips for long-distance work. Six to twelve inch snoods are plenty long enough, and within reason the breaking strain is immaterial. Even stiff snoods do not deter a whiting. On the other hand, avoid snoods under 10lb test unless you check for nylon abrasion after every fish. Whiting have small but sharp teeth which scour the line next to the hook.

Tactics

The whiting invasion triggers an annual renewal of interest in beach fishing. But the magic soon dulls. Two or three good sessions on the beach, up to your neck in whiting, fingers skinned from their rough teeth, and you would rather call it a day. As sporting fish whiting are a non-event. All right, they win matches and are so easy to catch that newcomers score on their first ever trip to the seashore. Is that all the species has to offer? It is if you stick to conventional beach tackle. Ordinary tackle is important of course. Sometimes you need the momentum of a 4–6oz sinker to drive baits far enough and to anchor them in a fast flood current. Beach-casting rods, fixed spool reels and multipliers are an essential feature of autumn beach fishing.

Later in the year and through until next spring, cod figure higher and higher in your list of priorities. Winter winds, powerful tides and rough water impose their own restrictions on tackle selection, so there is no point buying a lightweight rod as the mainstream weapon in your armoury. From the all-round shore fishing viewpoint, as opposed to specialized angling for whiting, a standard 5–6oz outfit is the better investment.

Now suppose you are several years into the sport. Although you look forward to the whiting if only as an excuse to remind yourself what it is like to hook fish cast after cast, the exercise soon pales. Six weeks into the new season you are fed up with the wretched things.

There are at least two avenues to explore. Lighter, more sporting tackle allows whiting enough breathing space to put up a bit of fight. Artificial lures really are a viable alternative to natural baits. You catch fewer fish perhaps, but they are fun – no comparison to the sluggish creature hauled out on normal casting tackle.

Variations

Autumn brings its share of still days when the sea cannot raise a tickle of surf. Onward of the last hour of daylight, whiting shoals creep within 30 yards of steep shingle beaches and rock marks. Carp/pike tackle is more than adequate. With 6lb line, fixed spool reel and an ounce of lead these rods toss baits plenty far enough. Such light tackle is restricted by waves and weather but it is far tougher than most sea anglers realize. When tidal current dies at low and high water an ordinary drilled bullet or swivelled ¾–1½oz bomb either holds its ground or drifts slowly. Often you can trigger an attack by inching the bait along the sea-bed. Dabs and flounders too are suckers for this treatment. At the highest flow of ebb and flood, switch to a miniature grip lead or Breakaway bomb weighing 1–3oz. Two ounces makes a handy combination with the six-pound line: tackle holds steady at 100 yards or can be drifted by pumping the rod every minute or two.

The terminal rig for light line whiting is either a running leger with the hook on a 12–18 inch trace of 10lb line or a single-hook paternoster with snoods under nine inches. Exact dimensions are not important and it does not matter if the paternoster has one or more hooks. The aim is to wring the last ounce of fight from an individual fish, not to fill the freezer.

Spinning

Whiting are ferocious little predators that spend less time scavenging than cod do. The shoals do chase their prey along the ground and in the layers of water just above the bottom, hunting by taste and smell, but they are equally geared to locating midwater meals by sight and vibration. Artificial lures are therefore potentially as good as legered natural baits.

Deep, fairly clean water at short range, falling light and actively feeding fish in tight shoals are the scenario for spinning and jigging. Toby, German sprat, spoons and Vibro lures catch whiting; feathers are excellent and slowly spun live sand-eel is devastating. Use light tackle and a selection of lures worked erratically. Even a 12oz fish hits very hard indeed. Hooked on sub-10lb class tackle, it is a very different animal from the same size whiting dragged ashore on the usual beach equipment.

16

Flounders and Dabs

FLOUNDERS

Flounders save the day for matchmen and pleasure anglers. Along with whiting these flat-fish form the backbone of shore fishing in Britain. An undemanding fish to catch, always hungry, living in estuaries and along the open coast, the flounder is a lot of fun even if it is one of the muddiest-tasting creatures in the sea.

Identification

Flounders are broadly similar to dabs. If you were to lay the species side by side the differences would be obvious, whereas an isolated fish hooked from the beach may create problems. The flounder is a burly fish compared to the dab. Dabs smell sweet but flounders usually stink. The shape of the lateral line is an instant clue: the flounder's is fairly straight, the dab's arches behind the gill cover. Brush your finger over the fish's back from tail to head. Scales on a flounder feel smooth whereas the dab's are distinctly rougher. Look on the head as well: flounders grow a patch of very rough, raised scales. The dab is featureless. Flounders weigh 8oz to 2lb on average. Any dab over 8oz is worth having: a one pounder is huge for most beaches and the rare 2lb fish is a prizewinner.

Flounders and plaice are closely related and may even cross-breed. That does create identification problems. The spots on a plaice are a vivid red which remain long after the fish is taken from the sea. A flounder's spots are duller red and fade rapidly. Some flounders do not have spots anyway. On the whole though, spots are a fairly reliable guide to species.

The back of a plaice's head shows a row of distinct raised lumps called tubercles. The overall shape of the fish is broader and slightly more circular-looking than a flounder's. A flounder's fins seem angular compared to the softly contoured fins of a plaice. Just in front of the flounder's anal fin protrudes a sharp spike which although not unique to the species is very well developed. It is an offshoot of the vertebral column, not a fin ray.

Habits

Flounders spend much of their time close inshore feeding on crustaceans, small fish and whatever else can be rooted from the sea-bed. They certainly are not fussy eaters. The annual breeding cycle takes them seaward between Christmas and April. Exact seasons seem to vary with location and water temperature but in all cases the aim is the same: flounder eggs require precise salinity concentrations which are found well offshore. The annual trek of millions of flounders from estuaries and beaches is directed at providing the right start in life for their offspring. Otherwise they prefer to be close to land.

Flounders are an all-weather species which you can hook at the height of summer and in the coldest frost except when very rough seas modify their behaviour to some extent. Wildly churning waves deter them from swimming within easy casting range and kill their appetite. Above all they try to avoid water clouded with swirling sand and silt, although much depends on the clarity of the normal environment. Flounders brought up on clean Atlantic beaches are much fussier than those resident in permanently grubby estuary tides.

Casting Distances

Water clarity, wave action and depth are important aspects of open-beach flounder fishing. Casting distance is linked to the flounder's pattern of feeding, so for best results learn to work in step with the fish. Sometimes you need to reverse the operation to avoid them, for they are a nuisance if your target is bass. As the tide rises from dead low water, bass move quickly on to the shallows and into the breaking surf. Flounders are far slower to swim in. If you aim to hook bass, cast short. For flounders, blast the bait beyond the lines of surf. Towards high tide, flounders move up to join the bass. Casts of 50–75 yards usually do the trick. Soon after the beginning of the main ebb run, flounders creep away while faster-moving bass, which rely on their speed to prevent being stranded, linger inshore. Go back to the original plan: cast short for bass, long for flounders.

Elsewhere the pattern is more obscure but as a basis for experiment it pays to cast long at low water and progressively shorten the range as the tide floods to maximum depth. Sometimes it is better to cast only 25 yards while flounders feed in the gully between the upper beach and the main foreshore slope. Avoid treading on a flounder as you wade to cast.

Surf beaches and shingle banks provide good flounder fishing throughout the year; expect to hook them on most baits and bottom-fished rigs. Elsewhere the odd flounder is likely to turn up any time whether you fish for them specifically or for codling, dabs, bass, dogfish and whiting. In most circumstances outside of match fishing it is probably not worth fishing for them exclusively anyway. Even so, they are an important species that no serious beach fisherman should ignore.

During the winter spawning migration, at its peak between December and March, flounders concentrate in the lower reaches of major river systems and in minor estuaries and saltwater inlets. Sheltered waters like the Thames, Blackwater and Humber, the Solent and Poole Harbour (indeed all natural and man-made harbours) support massive shoals of flatties. Catches of fifty fish a rod are not unknown.

Baits and Tackle

Flounders prefer meaty baits. Lugworms, ragworms, fish, sand-eels and crabs are snapped up. Peeler and soft crabs probably head the list of specialist flounder baits, closely followed by lively sand-eels and absolutely fresh herring strips. White and harbour ragworms are extremely good baits, and if all else fails lug and mackerel do well enough. Matchmen insist on the finest baits because a high percentage of beach matches are won or lost purely on flounders. The pressures are nowhere so great for pleasure fishing, so the secondary baits may well suffice for the occasional bash.

Two- and three-hook paternosters are excellent for general bottom fishing and permit hard casting when necessary. Flounders are often caught at short–medium range, but there are occasions when absolute distance pays off: you may want to stay in contact with a gully or creek as the tide forces you back up the beach. Short snoods tied direct to stand-off loops are spaced 18in apart along the centre rib of the paternoster. Nine-inch snoods of 15lb monofilament are adequate. No flounder can break even 6lb line on a direct pull, but you have to contend with its sharp teeth grinding the line just above the hook. A string of flatties caught on the same hook soon reduce the trace breaking strain.

Flounders are unpalatable so the majority of anglers throw them back, sizeable or not. Unhooking flounders is a real problem because they take the hook deep. Forceps sometimes wriggle the bend free but they do not work if the shank is right down to the base of the stomach. Small flatties are adept at gulping the hook completely beyond reach which causes problems with unhooking.

Small, fine wire hooks are one answer. Blue Aberdeens in the size 2–2/0 range are plenty big enough to hold the bait and strong enough to land big fish – even a cod if you hook one – but the wire is soft and pliable. Hold the fish across its back, pull on the trace until you feel the hook begin to straighten deep inside the fish's throat, then smoothly and quickly increase pressure until the barb pulls free. It sounds a brutal exercise but is far kinder than forceps. Afterwards, re-form the hook bend with pliers. You can straighten an Aberdeen at least half a dozen times before the metal is seriously weakened.

Sinker weight depends on the fishing ground. Calm water and modest tides allow 1–3oz rigs with appropriately light rods, lines and reels. Where distance is not important, as in harbour wall floundering, try a carp/pike outfit and 6lb line. Elsewhere, bass-grade tackle is excellent. Unfortunately many of the better flounder marks are swept by powerful tides. Big rivers push aside 5oz tackle and you may be forced to use 8oz of lead even at close range. However, as a rule you can fish 4–6oz with ease from most estuary banks and beaches except on springs.

Tactics

If the flounders are running and feeding hard, simply cast out and wait for a bite. At the height of the season you can afford to leave the first fish out there while other flounders attack. Three hook paternosters often produce a full house. The bite is both positive and powerful, and flounders hook themselves against the inertia of the sinker. Match anglers used to kill every flounder they landed. At the end of a big competition hundreds of dead fish were tossed into the sea for the gulls. Today's conservation-minded anglers protect the catch in a bucket of fresh sea water. Flounders lie quiet all day and provided you keep them out of direct sunlight and heat they survive to bite another day.

Atlantic surf beaches are excellent for flounders. Sometimes the entire beach is alive; more often shoals concentrate where freshwater flows over the sand. Small estuaries and streams are the hottest spots of all. Ordinary flounder techniques and baits work well though distance might pay off more than on other beaches. Cast your bait well behind the breaking surf where the water is deeper and mutes the effects of the churning waves. The advantage of surf beaches is their lack of strong cross currents. Replace your grip wired sinker with a plain bomb. Let it roll the bait along the sea-bed. If it stays put, pull the rod tip around every five minutes and take in the slack.

Work the bait across the sand in short jumps. Flounders home in on spurts of sand thrown up by the sinker, which they confuse with crab or sand-eel activity. Investigating the puff of sand, the hunting flounder pounces on your bait. It is a simple trick which pays off time after time. A couple of bright beads above the bait or a small spinner of silver foil mounted on the snood definitely does produce more bites than using a plain bait.

16 FLOUNDERS AND DABS

DABS

Hooked dabs do not exactly set the world alight. They bite hard but are incapable of testing even a spinning outfit. Why do so many beach anglers fish for them? Because they are dependable fish which taste at least as good as soles and plaice. Many anglers rate them the finest eating fish in the sea.

There is a rough parallel between the best times to fish for dabs and the peak months of the cod season. If cod are around in significant numbers, few anglers bother to chase dabs. Yet as soon as cod move away, even temporarily as they do around Christmas, dabs are suddenly a favourite target. During those codless weeks of the New Year, a bag of flatties brightens your day on the beach. There is another link between dabs and cod, especially along the east and south-east coasts. The dab population expands in poor cod seasons and the fish themselves grow heavier. Dabs probably figure high on an inshore cod's menu, which explains the see-saw balance between the two species.

Habits

Dabs are widely spread throughout the British Isles and like flounders they turn up all year. Almost everywhere the best fishing lies between October and April. Sometimes the peak time lasts for no more than six weeks, usually in the depths of winter. Unlike flounders they are intolerant of low salinity and prefer to live on an open coast unaffected by freshwater contamination. Much depends on the depth and area of an estuary: some deep, short inlets with little drainage capacity do attract lots of dabs. For most beach anglers though, it pays to fish the exposed open sea beaches and rocks.

Clean sea-beds with a scattering of sand, hardpacked mud and shingle are better dab marks than soft, oozing mud. Rocks and weed beds sometimes produce good hauls, but most heavier bags are caught on open beaches. Time and tide often make no difference. Daylight fishing continues to be excellent even in bright sunlight and a calm sea. Top and bottom water fish well, but sport usually slackens at the strongest flow of ebb and flood tide especially on big springs.

Dabs are essentially bottom-feeders but they are by no means slow moving. Most of their food – small fish, worms, crabs and shrimps – lives on or close to the sea-bed. Sometimes dabs lie in wait, half covered by sand, but more often they quarter the beach in search of a meal. Consequently, moving baits are sometimes far better than legered baits.

Even if they are not highly influenced by time and tide, dabs certainly do feed to a pattern which varies between beaches. Sometimes you pick up a steady stream of flatties throughout the day or night. More often they feed in spurts: you hook half a dozen fish in an hour then wait ages for the next shoal. Nor is an entire beach hunted by dabs. Some channels, gullies and sandbanks attract and hold masses of dabs; fifty yards away, there is not a fish from one week to the next. For some reason shoals of dabs feed between two or three groynes on a half-mile strip of apparently uniform beach but are seldom if ever hooked between any of the other breakwaters. Trial and error fishing is better than nothing: if you fish for half an hour without landing a dab, move 100 yards and try again.

Tactics

On average it pays to cast short. On beaches where an inshore gully is backed by a shallow sand-bar at, say, 100 yards range there might well be a case for long-distance casting if fish concentrate on the bank itself. Explore the near and far slopes of the bank plus the inshore gully. But remember that the strip of sand just beyond the breakers is equally attractive to these little fish. Many if not most fine dabs are hooked within 50 yards of the rod tip.

Small hooks rigged on a simple paternoster are a fine rig for all-round beach fishing for dabs, whiting and codling which often make up a mixed catch from a winter beach. The trick is to balance bait and hook size. Cod-size hooks are too big for dabs. Very fine wire flatty hooks tend to lose their grip on a cod's jaws. Size 4–1/0 blue Aberdeen hooks are excellent for dabs, handle whiting easily enough and give you a fair chance with cod. Size 2–1/0 Patridge MW are a neat balance between precision and power. Fine enough in the wire, razor sharp and small enough to handle dabs, they are still more than strong enough to land a 10lb cod. The neat eye does not burst small lugworms either.

Baits

Lugworms, white ragworms, harbour rag, slivers of fresh fish and small chunks of sand-eel are classic dab baits. Hermit and peeler crab are excellent as well. Of them all, lugworms take some beating and this is one case when second-rate baits sometimes hook more fish. When lugworms get old they either blow up and soften or shrivel into black strips as tough as liquorice. Either way they stink. Smell attracts dabs by the score. Thread a small bunch of shrivelled worms on the hook or pour on the runny kind. If necessary tip the bait with a small fresh lug or a sliver of fish to support the soft stuff for hard casting. If you do not need to throw a long way – and mostly with dabs you should limit your range – that buffer is not essential. Even semi-liquid lugworms should travel fifty yards without help.

It makes more sense to use light tackle than to heave out dabs on a standard beachcaster outfit. Sometimes you can fish just an ounce or two of lead on a spinning rod and 8lb line. In bad conditions you need the extra power and weight of a normal beach rod and reel matched to 5-6oz of lead. In extremes of winter, ultra-heavy tackle is necessary to beat tide and waves. Dabs keep right on feeding in the teeth of a gale. You may find they stick around when whiting and even cod move off.

17

Cod

Cod are powerful fish easily caught on sporting tackle, and in good seasons they shoal hundreds strong on almost every inch of the coastline. Without them sea fishing would nosedive into oblivion. Closely related to pollack, coalfish and haddock, cod are essentially a cold water species distributed from the North Polar region to well south of the English Channel. There are many races of cod, some resident, most migratory. The cod we catch are of the species *Gadus morrhua*, a fast-growing fish which moves into the waters around the British coast in late October and stays to feed until early April.

The cod season begins with an autumn run of well-conditioned fish of all sizes. October cod fall into the 3–7lb bracket along with enough double-figure fish to make life unpredictably pleasant. The cod season proper begins in November, peaks as the month runs into early December then settles down through the Christmas period.

Early January is disappointing because sprats and herrings preoccupy cod and draw them up from the sea-bed to feed in midwater. In theory, cod fishing develops a second peak between February and early April. Sometimes it happens according to plan; more often these days sport gradually dies off without a distinct recovery from the sprat invasion. The size of the spring cod varies considerably from that of the pre-Christmas peak. As well as producing occasional fish in the 20lb bracket plus a fair run of 5–10lb codling, the sea is crammed with tiny codling less than nine inches long.

Northern waters never used to hold as many big fish as those in the south and south-east, but sheer numbers of codling compensated for any lack of twenty pounders. Newcastle and Hull, for example, produced more codling per angler than East Anglia and the south-east. The north-west, Wales and western Scottish Borders are less consistent but annually deliver a string of heavyweight specimens. In recent years these Atlantic-influenced areas have begun to take over from the traditional North Sea and Channel marks as all-round cod fisheries as well. At the moment it is difficult to predict what the long-term trend may become.

17 Cod

Habits

A cod's aims in life are to breed and feed. Autumn/winter inshore migration triggers a feeding splurge which fattens the fish and boosts them into full breeding condition. Cod eat virtually anything that lives on the sea-bed, has died there or swims in midwater. Even so, a cod's appetite does vary. It is wrong to assume that every cod in the sea sets its sights on a full belly and will settle for nothing less.

High levels of sea-bed food decrease the success rate of big baits, as if the cod were sick of gorging. In those conditions a small bait catches fish when a hookload lies neglected. The emphasis also switches from the traditional lugworm to white ragworm, hermit crab and peeler shore crab.

Cod feed by sight, taste, feel and smell. In the dirty, fast-running tides that sweep the best cod marks, taste and smell are the major senses employed by hunting shoals. The scent trail exuded by a bait is vitally important. Too little scent washes away in the current and dilutes below the cod's sensory threshold. The key to bait selection lies more in scent content than in pure volume. Two or three small lugworms full of blood and juices cast into the water and changed before the sea destroys their scent trail always outfish half a dozen watery lugworms saturated by prolonged immersion.

Anglers who use tanked lugworms, which are notoriously low in natural scent, are forced to step up bait size to generate a sufficient trail. Six tanked worms are outgunned by two freshly dug lugworms. The traditional theory about big baits is a reflection of the balance between size and quality. Good baits for general codding do not need to be huge.

Stormy seas are an exception to the rule. When the sea swirls sand, foam and rubbish through the tide, bait scents are blocked to some extent. More precisely, the scent lane fractures and is overdiluted. The only answer – and at best even this is second rate – is to increase the bait until it does throw out enough scent to produce an acceptable zone of attraction. Big baits really do pay off in bad conditions: cod easily swallow half a dozen tough lugworms on an 8/0 long-shanked hook.

Smaller baits pay off in settled conditions. Cod are keen to take the easy pickings but, being well fed anyway, are less disposed to work hard for their dinner and seem reluctant to cover expanses of seabed to track down those elusive scents. A massive scent trail probably attracts more crabs, shrimps and flat-fish than it does cod. That alone wastes bait. You may as well stick to smaller baits which dabs and flounders find more manageable. Any cod that happens along will not pass up the opportunity for a snack, so either way you win.

In everyday fishing it comes down to this: if you must leave tackle out as long as possible in hard tides and rough weather, use big baits of the highest quality. Otherwise, thread on smaller baits and reload more often. Mixed species fishing – typically taking pot luck with whiting, dabs, flounders and cod – favours the latter technique. My own preference is smallish baits as routine unless the chances of a big cod are particularly high.

Baits

Lugworms merit star treatment because they are so widely used in cod fishing and, for the most part, produce the lion's share of the annual catch from the beach. Other baits are still valuable stand-bys and unbeatable when the going gets rough. Squid is the one bait which seems to discriminate between big and small fish of any species. Whole baby squid cast just behind the breakers of a steeply shelved beach – Chesil Beach is a favourite mark – take an annual toll of 20lb-plus fish.

The fussiest cod nose along east coast beaches in spring. Lugworms are completely ignored, as are squid, mackerel, herring and the other back-up baits. White ragworms and peeler crab are the only baits that stave off disaster. Both are expensive in cash or in the time and distance required to collect them, but the investment is more than justified if you are serious about the sport.

Cod Beaches

Shingle banks, estuary channels, mud and shell grit and clean sandy foreshores are included on the extensive list of winter cod beaches. Dungeness beach, a deep steeply shelved bank of sand and shingle swept by tide and winds, is worlds apart from the grubby banks of the Thames estuary at Gravesend and Tilbury. But both fish well for winter cod.

The essential features of an open-water cod beach lie beneath its surface. Sea-bed cover is negligible compared to the dense rock and weed kingdoms of North Yorkshire and Scottish cod. Open beaches rely more on fast tides and muddy water to encourage the cod to move inshore. Crabs, shrimps, worms and small bait fish lie behind boulders, beneath sand and mud, and in the shelter of gullies and sandbanks.

Cod gravitate towards rich feeding but their hunger is tempered by a healthy respect for their own skins. Calm water, good underwater visibility and slow currents discourage most bottom-feeding fish from swimming close inshore. Semi-darkness, vicious tidal currents and churning waves boost a cod's confidence. Rough water also rakes the sea-bed and swills food creatures from their hiding places.

Deep water is far from essential for shore codding. Some of the finest beach marks in Britain hold less than 10 feet of water on a spring high tide.

There are beaches that fish best on dead low tide with only 30 inches of dirty water. Generally though, modestly deep water (15–20 feet) produces more consistent sport and bigger fish. Shallow beaches normally fish badly in daylight but may transform after nightfall into the hottest spots on the coast.

Few beaches are truly featureless. Stones and weed patches speckle the foreshore; gullies and depressions intercut the sea-bed and provide cover and cross currents which attract and hold food. Make a point of surveying your local beaches at low water, preferably on big spring tides which strip the foreshore beyond casting range. Cod linger on weed beds and stony ground. They show a marked tendency to travel in gullies.

Tidal Effect

Tides motivate cod's movements and feeding patterns. Dead high and low waters, without the pressure of tidal current, offer dull sport at best and may switch off the fish altogether. Strength of tide is far more important than its direction. Anglers still hold to the theory that flood outfishes ebb but long-term statistics prove otherwise.

On the majority of open beaches swept by tides strong enough to attract cod within casting range, either flood or ebb proves better. Few beaches fish equally well on up and down tides. Even so, in peak season a beach that normally fishes better on the ebb may hold relatively more fish than normal on the flood. Flood-preferred beaches demonstrate a similar pattern.

Expect variations within each rise and fall cycle. Most beaches have a distinct and often narrow period which outfishes the rest. Depending on the beach gradient, tidal force and the location of the beach in relation to offshore migratory routes and holding ground, cod feed on the first of the flood or ebb, in the middle of the tide, throughout a rise or fall, or for a brief spell both sides of top and bottom dead water. It is important to know how your local mark is most likely to fish – beaches ten miles apart may well prove opposites. If so, fish one beach on the flood, then shift marks for the ebb.

There is evidence that cod move along the coast in a saw-tooth pattern rather than swim parallel to the tideline. This seems a particular feature of relatively shallow beaches protected by sandbanks. Cod move in and out through gullies cut into the sandy barrier. The habit reinforces the need to survey the beach at low tide. Frequent re-examination is necessary as well: a single winter storm generates enough power to shift sandbanks hundreds of yards and to rip out new channels.

Where a long, uniform beach shelves down on to hard-packed sand and mud, cod hunt along the base of the slope but are seldom evenly distributed along the entire length. At beach level the foreshore seems featureless, but from the air it is distinctly curved into a giant bay or a headland. Ordnance Survey maps and Admiralty charts provide the key to overall beach layout; although they are too imprecise to pin-point the best marks individually they do indicate areas that repay closer investigation. Look for deeper water and a swirl of tide, both of which concentrate and hold food.

Bites

Full-blooded cod bites are easily recognized – the rod bounces, dives out of the rest or flips backwards in response to a slack line. The important consideration is that the bite you see on the rod tip is a reaction which travels up the line from the terminal rig; it always arrives after the event. By the time you see the bite the fish is either hooked or gone. Beyond the 75 yard range, striking is ineffective no matter how hard you thrash the rod. Instead, force the cod to hook itself against the inertia of a well-anchored paternoster. If the hook is sharp, relatively fine in the wire and tethered close to the bottom by a grip lead, the momentum of the cod's attack drives home the barb.

The slack line bite is a result of the cod snatching the bait and trace so hard that the sinker wires lose their grip. It is the classic cod bite. Your only obligation is to reel in the slack line and tighten down on the fish before it has a chance to slip the hook. Cod are adept at spitting out a bait particularly if the hook skids on the tough skin around the jaw bones. Fine wire Aberdeen hooks are a step in the right direction though some are a little too soft in the wire for safety. Partridge Aberdeens and MW, Spearpoints and Vikings are excellent; Au Lion d'Or run them a close second with the Mustad standard Aberdeen ringed hooks only a little behind in strength.

Tactics

Cod fishing tactics depend on season and conditions. When cod are the prime target a single-hook paternoster well baited with lugworms is an all-round favourite. Distance casting is usually important and may be the key factor. Any suitable outfit cast tolerably well should produce consistent 130 yard fishing distances. Do not worry too much if you can not manage 200 yard casts – a middle of the road 100–140 yards is far enough for satisfactory codding. By all means practise to improve your distances but do remember that there is far more to successful beach angling than merely blasting a bait to the horizon.

Where really big fish are likely to turn up, a mound of worms on the hook sometimes tips the balance in your favour. These days though, most fish run in the one to five pound bracket with only an isolated fish above ten pounds Rather than stick with traditional cod hooks in the 4/0–8/0 range, try scaling down to 1/0–3/0 and never hesitate to cut down even more. Thread three or four medium lugworms along the hook and snood to produce a four to six inch column of bait. To reduce air resistance and bait damage during the cast, trap the hook against the leader with a casting clip and if necessary restrain the upper end of the bait with a nylon stop knot.

Cast as far into the tide as you can and make sure the grip wires on the sinker dig hard into the sea-bed. On the majority of open-beach cod marks you cannot afford to drift tackle around in the current: fishing distance drops; line tangles with other anglers' tackle. The secret of anchoring the weight is to let go an extra 15–25 yards of line after the sinker hits the water. A generous bow in the line sets the terminal rig at a more effective angle.

18

Surf Bass

After a continual pounding by commercial netsmen, the traditional surf beaches of the Atlantic coast are far less productive, but the opportunity to hook bass still exists if you are keen enough to travel. Surf-casting always was hit-and-miss, and never did produce many fish for even the skilled angler. Yet the rewards are great in other respects not least because the true surf beach environment is unique. A 5lb bass, tough and fast from seasons of life in the shifting tides and breakers, outfights a soft-muscled ten pounder hooked from some muddy creek.

'Surf ' merits some explanation, for though there are many kinds of rough water along our coastline, only one true surf exists. First, you need the right kind of beach. All surf beaches – also known as storm beaches or in Ireland as strands – are composed of hard-packed sand perhaps interspersed with low rocks. The beach itself slopes so gently that the rising tide pushes between 200 yards and half a mile from the low water mark of spring tides to just short of the high sand dunes which back the foreshore.

The classic surf beach is open and windswept, sandwiched between massive headlands that funnel wind and tide. There are vast bays of sand as well, such as Brandon Bay in Eire which is arguably the biggest beach in Europe. Closer to home, the major bays of Cornwall and Wales offer plenty of space for surf to generate. Two kinds of surf action are involved: local surf and swell surf.

Surf Action

Local winds and direct tidal action roughen the water from a ripple to a full-blooded sea with high rollers and tables of white surf. This local pattern is always accompanied by a stiff wind. The water is dirty, sometimes so filled with weed that within a minute of casting out you are fighting a mass of vegetation which threatens to break your line. Fishing can be excellent but usually tails off during the height of the storm and improves as it dies away.

18 Surf Bass

The keen bass man prefers real swell surf, perhaps with only a gentle breeze blowing onshore to maintain the action. Indeed, genuine swell surf roars on to the sand even when there is no wind. Sometimes a massive force of water drives ashore into the teeth of an offshore gale; you cast a mile, yet the waves literally push you back up the sand. The swells are created by storms far out in the ocean. The water is stirred violently and the swells radiate like ripples around a stone dropped into calm water. The humps of moving water drive over the continental shelf, slide towards the coast then dump their energy on to the shoreline as heavy surf.

The fetch of the waves – that is, the distance they travel over the open seas – is an important factor. It takes time and space to build a significant swell action which arrives on the beach as day or week-long pounding surf rather than a few hours of lightweight action. The sheer physics of the exercise rule out good swell surf fishing in Britain except on the Atlantic coast. You may find a short, sometimes vicious surf on east coast bass beaches, but never the high, lazy swells which roll in day after day from the westerly ocean.

Bare sand and rushing water disguise the teeming marine life which lives on a surf beach. Sand is a gentle medium with plenty of space, oxygen and water for small animals. At the lowest limits of the tideline live razor fish, clams and lugworms. Even in the wildest surf, sand-eels and crabs exist happily under the sand's protection. Small fish, plankton and fry inhabit the water itself. The surf beach throbs with life.

Calm water on rising or falling tides encourages the marine creatures to hide. They are keyed up to the dangers of clear water, bright sunlight and marauding predators – bigger fish, sea-birds and their own kind. During the day, species like bass, rays and tope tend to remain lingering far beyond casting range in deeper, darker water where they themselves feel safe. Surf action triggers a change in mood, especially with bass which are tolerant of swirling water and suspended sand. Swells rip up the sand, rake out food and wash it into the plateaux of water between the breakers. Then the bass move in.

Habits

Bass show a two-way movement according to conditions, time and tide. Calm, clear weather sends them offshore; surf encourages them in. While they are inshore they patrol sections of beach, feeding here, skipping several hundred yards of sand, settling elsewhere to feed again. If the surf remains constant – which it will do only in swell surf conditions on exposed beaches the cycle is repeated with each tide. Catch a bass one hour after low water, and you can be fairly confident of hooking another fish from the same shoal or group at the same stage of the next tide. This rhythm of fishing probably holds the secrets of catching surf bass.

The bigger tides and changeable weather of spring and autumn equinox tides are always a hot time for surf bass, as they are for all kinds of sea fish everywhere. There is a link between big tides and winds; you may have noticed that the wind blows harder in late April and early October. On the exposed western beaches the effects are especially pronounced. Sometimes beaches are hit by storms that make fishing impossible. Or the winds themselves remain at sea but fuel day after day of prime surf conditions. Keen to fatten for the lean winter ahead, autumn bass feed strongly and will hit your baits harder than at any other time of year.

Baits

Sheltered surf beaches and the backwaters and estuaries often associated with true storm beaches are a natural breeding ground for lugworms. For years, bass fishermen forked up boxes of big worms to bait their hooks. They work well: tough for casting, juicy and easily visible against a backdrop of sand. Of all the baits used to catch bass from the open surf, lugworms headed the list because of their availability and apparent superiority. Many surf anglers well versed in tides and the habits of their fish never bothered to look at alternatives.

Razor fish and clams are worth considering as well. Clams are the big. soft-shelled bivalves found when you dig lugworms in fairly clean sand or sand with a little mud. The long siphon that protrudes from the shell when the animal lies buried makes an extremely tough bass bait by itself, and combines with a bunch of lugworms to make a hookful no fish can resist.

To dig clams specifically, look for a neat hole drilled into the sand near a damp but not waterlogged section of the lower beach. The tell-tale sign is a jet of water squirted up to a foot into the air; it is more powerful and noticeable than the brief jet thrown up by big ragworms. Drive the fork tines full length into the sand so that the hole is neatly in the centre of the spit, and keep digging. Most anglers miss them because they give up the search too soon. Some anglers prefer to wash the shells and store the bivalve in a bucket of sea water. Others reckon bait lasts longer if the dirty shells are packed into a damp box. When you want to use them, crack the shell, tear out the entire siphon for bait, and save the innards in case you run out of siphons.

Once virtually a secret bait, sand-eels are now used for all kinds of beach fishing. Rock and beach fishermen in Cornwall are especially adept at sand-eel fishing; in their view it is the finest bait for virtually all their fishing. Certainly for bass there is nothing finer. Anglers elsewhere might not go all the way with the Cornish view, but at least they agree that the sand-eel has a great deal to offer if only as part of a more versatile bait armoury. Their role in surf bass fishing is immense though, and no keen bass man can afford to pass up any chance of at least trying them.

Sand-eels are easily caught by raking or netting. Netting is quicker and more productive, but an hour's raking along the tideline is worth a fortune if the bass are preoccupied with sand-eels, as they often are in autumn and spring. The bait has saved the day for anglers who found themselves beaten by shoals of bass that ignored the usual worms and clams. The best sand-eel is a live one, so consider investing in an aerated cooler box for your travels. If you are bassing nearer home, tank the sand-eels for long-term storage and take them fishing in an ice pack.

Squid and fish baits are normally thought of as an outside bet. Sometimes they work extremely well, but hardly ever in terms of numbers. The surf bass hooked on a side of mackerel or whole squid is likely to be a monster. But the odds are that you will never see a fish like that; on most surf beaches, squid and mackerel are baits for the dedicated big-fish man who is prepared to spend days or months chasing one specimen fish.

The beauty of mackerel – squid is borderline here – is its universal appeal to rays, tope, spurdogs, conger, pollack and the other species which may also be around. All of them, conger included, will move into the fringes of the surf at night. Very long casting sometimes picks up species which the old-time anglers never dreamt of hooking from the open surf. The value of a mackerel bait, and perhaps squid, is that you automatically cover another side of the sport at the same time as you fish for the bass. With bass stocks falling it makes sense to have an option. If necessary, fish with two rods: one with mackerel, the other hand-held and baited with a 'proper' bass bait like worms.

King ragworms are usually an excellent bait. On eastern bass grounds and along the south coasts, you can do no better than thread a chunk of bloody, lively ragworm on to your bass rig. The situation is different in the storm beach environment. Though one hesitates to lay down rules here, experience strongly points to one conclusion: on the majority of open surf beaches when the surf is running properly, ragworm makes a very poor bait for anything except flounders.

Some Welsh and Cornish beaches fall midway between true surf strands and ordinary sandbanks, and in estuaries particularly ragworm is a killer for bass and the general fish population. King ragworm works beautifully, closely followed by harbour ragworms and whites. Matchmen might prefer the smaller worms because they tend to excel with flatties and eels, the two major species essential for making up weights. Few matches are won with bass.

Tactics and Tackle

Presentation counts more in the surf than in average beach fishing. You may fish for a week with an ordinary paternoster and catch bass after bass, day and night. Then the fish stop biting. You know they are still there but whereas last night they hit your bait, tonight they ignore it. Change baits – no response; but switch to a running leger and you are back in action. Even an extended snood might do the trick.

Short snoods are better in rough water, longer ones in calm. The 9–12 inch snooded paternoster used in whiting and flatty fishing works well but you will probably prefer to cast one bait instead of the usual two or three. When the surf dies down extend the snood to 24 inches; if that tangles switch to the running paternoster, a most popular surf rig which offers tangle-free fishing, good presentation and yet still casts a long way. Use bait clips if you want those extra yards.

Just as important as the exact rig format – and I think perhaps more important in some ways – are the hooks. Bass in surf must surely be conditioned into picking up food that is washed around by the swells or is actively swimming around in the shallow, swirling water. A bait so heavily weighted down by sinker and hook that it sinks and just lies inert could be a turn-off. Test lightweight hooks like Aberdeens and Spearpoints if you cannot get good results on the normal brands; sometimes they make a vast difference.

Five to six ounce beach tackle fished from a rod rest planted on dry sand takes its toll of surf bass. When bass run the beaches, feeding hard on sand-eels and worms, there is no need to cast very far or to feel for the tiniest bite. A rested rod signals the bite and gives plenty of time to reel in hooked fish. Something is missing though: to fish that way is completely divorced, mentally and physically, from the inner world of the surf beach. Throw away your rod rest and tackle box, pull on a pair of long boots and wade out there with just rod and bait.

Half an hour fishing with a normal beachcaster strains your arms and your patience. Water pours ashore in rolling swells, but no sideways current tears line and sinker along the beach. Even a 2oz sinker holds nicely. What about a lighter rod? Fishermen who spend days and nights in the surf casting to bass running 25 to 150 yards from the shallows, insist on light, well-balanced rods. They do not compromise on reels either – it is multipliers only. Fixed spools never seem to blend with a surf rod, destroying smooth, fast handling of bites and hooked fish.

Sometimes you can afford to drop to one or two ounces, with a proportionate step down in line test from 12–15lb to 8–10lb. The snag is that you might well lose bass or hook them in the stomach because the inertia of smaller leads is insufficient to drive home the hook. At least 3oz rigged with grip wires, or 4–5oz of plain lead, are necessary to set a trap for feeding bass. In the long run anglers who fish slightly heavy catch more bass, especially when fish hit shy and short.

Modern glass fibre and semi-carbon rods about 11½ feet long, balanced to cast 4oz perfectly yet able to handle 5oz at a push, are light and easy to hold all day. The finest blanks weigh less than 10oz. Made up with lined rings, FPS seat and rubber grips (much superior to cork in these saturated conditions) the rod need not exceed 16oz. The easy action blends 100 yard-plus fishing with soft baits to the essential option of lobbing just 20 yards if necessary. It is surprisingly difficult to control short casts on a stiff rod when accuracy also is at stake.

Wide open surf beaches encourage you to fish by yourself. Then you can safely afford to reduce leader breaking strain. Twenty to thirty pound high-grade monofilament holds a 4oz cast together and enhances bait action. Sometimes thick leaders deter bass from taking the bait; over-stiff traces also reduce bites. Bass are by no means cunning or fussy as a rule, but where you can afford to cut line diameter without losing control, do it.

Bites and Landing

The mechanics of surf bassing are secondary to picking the right time and presenting good baits. Bass respond to any form of legering, either paternoster or running trace. Bait the hook heavily and work the surf line from twenty yards beyond comfortable wading depth to maximum range. The old theory about bass hunting the third breaker is surprisingly accurate; the wave coincides with a nice depth of water, strong undertow combing food from inshore sand and easy casting range with soft baits. Eighty yards is about right on the majority of beaches. Cast out, tighten up on the sinker and feel for bites with finger and thumb looped on the line. Strike anything that moves.

Slack line or rod-bending bites happen at any time. Mostly, bass pick up the hook and run. A double-tug followed by a steady run is characteristic of bold surf bass. They can also suck in a bait without shifting the sinker an inch. Be ready for a tough fight; no risk of being smashed if you take your time but exhilarating for all that. Keep the rod tip high, set the clutch to medium tension and apply extra pressure on the spool with your thumb.

Never force the issue when the bass rolls into the last line of breaking surf where swells and backwash can pick up a ten pounder and either swill it high up the beach (the object of the exercise) or sweep it out to sea so quickly that the line snaps. Lift the fish on to a wave and let the sea do the beaching. Guide the fish ashore and grab it. Avoid dorsal spines and sharp gill plates.

PART THREE

FLY FISHING

Pat O'Reilly, Bob Church, Charles Jardine and Arthur Oglesby

Introduction

Fly fishing was long considered the nose-in-air end of the angling scene. For many it still evokes images of bewhiskered gentlemen, with attendant gillies, on exclusive stretches of southern chalk streams, fishing the upstream dry fly only to fat brownies from manicured river banks. While there may have been some truth in this, it certainly never was the full picture.

In the burns of Scotland, the becks of the north country, the spate streams and rivers of the west and south-west – waters that never saw a stocked fish – the pursuit of small wild brownies with wet flies and spiders, fished up, down, or across, has always been the sport of the ordinary fisherman. On Scottish lochs, Irish loughs and Welsh llyns trout – and sometimes sea trout – have always been there for the taking for those who will master the necessary skills.

While a deep pocket – and perhaps a long wait – is still needed to gain access to the premier trout streams of the south, more fly fishing is now available in this country than has ever been the case. This is the result of the recent proliferation of stillwater fisheries, mostly water authority reservoirs, being opened to the trout angler. This has made trout fly fishing probably the fastest-growing branch of our sport.

The first water-supply reservoir to be thus exploited was Blagdon lake, in the Mendips, as long ago as 1904. But it is the post-war years that have seen the fastest expansion, with the opening in the 1950s of Blagdon's Mendip sister, Chew Valley Lake, and, in more recent years, of such renowned waters as Grafham, Rutland Water and Bewl. Now there is no part of the country not within easy reach of stillwater fishing at reasonable cost, mostly for the brown trout's emigrant transatlantic cousin, the rainbow, faster-growing and more tolerant of water conditions, but no less sporting and an excellent fish on the table.

These waters extend over hundreds, even thousands, of acres, but smaller, privately run, stillwaters, most of them covering no more than a few tens of acres, are also on the increase. The famous Two Lakes in Hampshire led the way, and its owner and developer, Alex Behrendt, is the acknowledged pioneer of these fisheries. Two lakes has been followed by such famous names as Damerham, Allen's Farm, Dever Springs, Avington, Hucklesbrook and many others. These waters hold fish of large average size, cost more to fish, and call for specialized techniques. For these reasons for most anglers they are probably an occasional treat rather than staple fare.

Salmon fishing is rather more difficult to come by, at least if such classic rivers as Tweed, Dee, Tay and Spey are uppermost in the mind. On these it may be a case of fishing the leaner times of the season and waiting years for access to the prime beats. A case of dead men's shoes. If, on the other hand, you are close to the spate rivers of the north and west, or in Ireland or the Western Isles of Scotland, and if you are able to take advantage of the onset of the best water conditions, there is still top-quality salmon fishing to be had. And, in the light of increasing pressure on the king of fish, the fly is now more than ever the preferred sporting way of coming to grips with it.

Fly fishing for trout, sea trout and salmon is indeed now accessible to all. It is also possible for all. Do not be put off by the myth that it is difficult, put about by those who would keep it to themselves. Anyone can learn to catch a trout in a day or two – though experience does of course increase one's catches in the long term. Fly fishing is an easier sport than coarse fishing. Indeed, many of the finest fly fishers are so precisely because of a long apprenticeship in coarse fishing. As in all forms of fishing, watercraft is paramount. The following chapters provide the proof.

19

River Trout
by Pat O'Reilly

TROUT AND TROUT STREAMS

Brown trout, born and reared in a hatchery and grown on in stew ponds, are stocked into an upper tributary of the River Severn. Each carries a Severn-Trent Water Authority tag. The intention is to supplement the river's stock of wild trout, and to provide improved sport for local anglers. The following spring, on the River Towy in South Wales, an angler lands a sea trout, bright and silver, fresh up on the morning tide. A green tag shows it to have been one of those brown trout stocked into the Severn system, having completed a journey of several hundred miles. What made that fish choose a nomadic existence?

On a small Devon river the final phase of a dam is completed. A new reservoir is formed and the passage of migratory fish up or down the stream is restricted. But sea trout are already up above the dam. What will happen to them after they have spawned? The answer: they survive, eventually toning in so closely with the colour scheme of local resident trout that only an expert eye can identify those individuals which were once sea trout.

A trout, it appears, is a sea fish in the process of evolving into a freshwater fish. (The Atlantic salmon is going through a similar process, but to date its progress is somewhat less than that of *Salmo trutta*.) To the biologist, there is no difference between brown trout and sea trout (the same can be said about the rainbows and steelheads of North America), but to the fly fisher, brown trout and sea trout are quite different. Not only are sea trout generally much bigger, but the two species look so different one from the other . . . usually! In most respects they are a separate 'species', responding differently to a fly and, on being hooked, each behaving in its own characteristic way. A sea trout will leap and cavort on the surface in spectacular fashion, while a brown trout will more often make for deep water, fighting doggedly for the safety of a bolt-hole.

19 River Trout

At any point in time, I suggest, a particular fish may be a resident brown trout or a sea trout, or it may be somewhere between the two – a sort of halfling, bearing some characteristics of each . As anglers, we will do well most of the time if we treat them as separate species. But we should keep in mind the Jekyll and Hyde nature of *Salmo trutta*.

The salmon family includes not only the Atlantic salmon but also grayling and various species of char and trout. River fly fishers are generally most interested in brown trout (*Salmo trutta*) and, occasionally, rainbow trout (*Salmo gairdneri*). Both these species are widely distributed throughout the rivers and streams of North America, where the brown trout was introduced over a century ago. The brown trout is a native of European and Asian rivers, where rainbow trout rarely thrive and have to be supplemented with hatchery stock. Notable exceptions are the River Chess in Buckinghamshire and the River Wye in Derbyshire, where rainbow trout have successfully established themselves on certain stretches. By and large, however, it is safe to assume that rainbow trout found in British rivers are the result of the work of trout farmers.

Brown Trout

Salmo trutta is a versatile creature, adapting its livery to suit its habitat and growing to a size determined by the amount of food available. The trout of a peat-stained spate river may be predominantly olive and gold with bright crimson spots, while its chalk stream brother may take on a coat of light brown and silver with spots of a darker brown, almost black. At one time

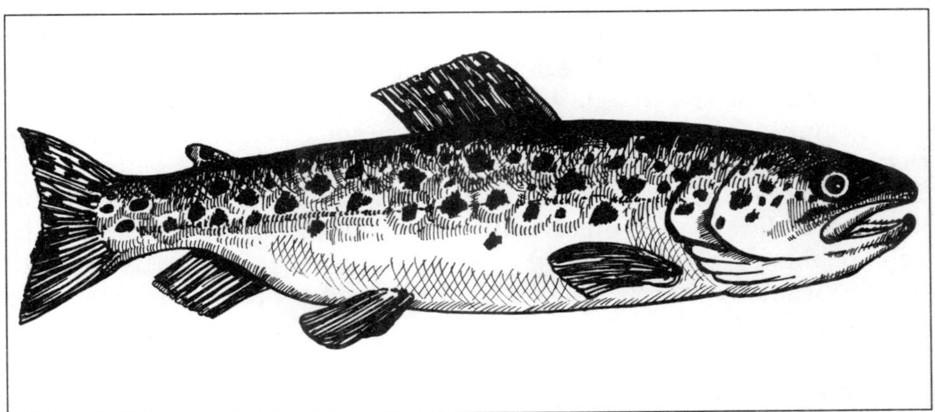

Brown trout.

it was thought that there were many more species of trout. Special scientific names were allocated to the brown trout of Loch Leven, to the slob or bull trout of the estuaries, and to the enormous trout which inhabit the depths of certain of the great lakes of Ireland. All of these, as far as the biologist is concerned, are strains of *Salmo trutta*, differing only in their behaviour. From our point of view, as fly fishers, there is a great deal of difference between the brown trout of a mountain stream, of a lowland brook and of a chalk stream. In this book, they are each treated separately, as different animals sharing only the same name.

Sea Trout

Young trout which yield to some primeval urge to leave the river and run away to sea, will return at a later date to spawn in the same or some other river. (Sea trout cannot match the legendary homing instinct of the salmon, which generally do return to spawn in the rivers of their birth.) It is these returning fish which we call sea trout. There are various regional names for the migratory strain of *Salmo trutta*. Peal (in the West of England), white trout (in Ireland) and sewin (in Wales), are just a few examples. Small sea trout are sometimes referred to as whitling or finnock; large sea trout at the fishmonger's shop as salmon-trout (the prefix is an unnecessary enticement for anyone who has enjoyed the delicate flavour and texture of a freshly caught spring sea trout).

Identification

Large sea trout are sometimes mistaken for salmon. To distinguish a sea trout:

1. The caudal fin (tail) of a salmon is usually forked, while that of a sea trout is more or less straight edged.
2. The upper jaw-bone of a salmon rarely extends behind the eye, while that of a sea trout does.
3. Both salmon and sea trout have between 120 and 130 scales along the lateral line, but in the salmon only ten to thirteen scales are behind the adipose fin (the small fleshy fin on the back of all salmonids between the dorsal and caudal fins) and the tail. Sea trout have between thirteen and sixteen such scales.
4. Salmon have fewer spots than sea trout, and rarely do they occur below the lateral line.

Although any single test may be inconclusive, in practice it is rarely difficult to distinguish the species. Sea trout, even the bright silver dream fish of early spring, have an overall different 'look' about them that is hard to describe. I can only hope that you get plenty of opportunities to learn from first-hand experience the difference between these two great sporting fish.

Rainbow Trout

Rainbow trout (*Salmo gairdneri*), native to the Pacific basin, were imported to European rivers about the turn of the last century. They pose problems to the river keeper because of their tendency to run downstream in shoals. On rough streams liable to flooding it is doubtful whether stocking with this species can be justified. However, in suitable conditions rainbow trout grow much more quickly than brown trout and are less expensive to rear.

Rainbow trout.

They reach maturity earlier than our native trout and, although shorter lived, can attain similar weights. A 2lb wild fish is a very good one on any of the few British rivers in which rainbow trout breed successfully, but pond-reared fish can attain weights of 20lb or more with careful rearing. Rainbow trout have such distinctive colouring that it is difficult to imagine how they could be confused with brown trout, but one certain means of separating the species is by the tail fin. That of a rainbow trout carries numerous black spots, while the tail of a brown trout is without any spots.

TACKLING UP

No waxed cotton coat, no waistcoat with twenty pockets, not even a salmon fly in his hat, but there he was ahead of me, on the stretch of Devon hill stream I had set my mind on fishing. In grubby old jacket and patched wellies,fly fishing was clearly his intention. I stood there, dismayed, as he untied a battered cane rod from the crossbar of his 'sit-up-and-beg'. He was obviously one of the youngsters, up from the village (three miles, but he'd have had a hard pull, up hill all the way).

But what about that rod! Its cork handle sported more holes than the 'twenties' section of a competition darts board – the result, I had no doubt, of securing flies the lazy way. The top joint had a set which, in another limb, could have got a doctor struck off the register for gross incompetence; the spiggot joint was so worn that he had to pack it with not one but two blades of grass. In no time at all he had threaded a line through the rings and was tying on a small dark fly. Curiosity got the better of me and I ambled across.

'What fly? ' I enquired. I could see, now, he was no youngster – middle-aged, more like. He didn't look up, but shook his head vaguely.

'Dunno. Fair copy o' these midges, though. Try one!' He thrust a tiny black and whitefly into my hand. It didn't look like anything in particular, but local knowledge should always be welcomed, so I thanked him, adding, 'What do they eat when they can't get humans?' It was plagiarism, of course but good enough to stand recycling. The urchin paused with a knot half completed. His brow furrowed and he looked straight at me. He was older than I had thought, much older, probably nearer seventy than the seventeen I had credited him with at first sight. His wrinkled leathery face beamed.

'Tolkien?'

I nodded, and he finished the knot. 'These things are no problem, son, once you get going. ' And with that he got going, off across the stream, hopping from one boulder to another until, with the sun on his right shoulder, throwing a long evening shadow on to the far bank, he began fishing. The tired old cane rod flicked gently back and forth, the motion smooth and flowing, seemingly effortless. Periodically, they would alight on a tiny patch of relative calm, searching some eddy or swirl between the cascades of white water. He needed no more than ten minutes to cover the 30 yards that took him round a bend and out of my sight. In that time he had hooked and brought to hand half a dozen yellow-bellied trout which he quickly released to rejoin their brethren. And all the while I could hear his chuckles of delight, so full was he of the joys of fly fishing.

I soon lost the little black and white fly, but I will always cherish the memory, and the lesson he gave me: what matters most about your tackle is how you use it.

19 River Trout

Flies

The most important parts of a fly-fishing outfit are those nearest to the fish. The reel and the rod are of secondary importance, so I see no reason for following tradition and discussing them first. Let's start at the business end with the flies. Be very careful if you buy cheap flies – they are often badly tied from inferior materials and on poor-quality hooks. Even if you tie your own flies, it will pay you to check each hook for temper before dressing a fly on it. Place the hook in the vice and, with your thumb-nail, try to bend the point away from the hook shank. If the point breaks off at

A selection of wet flies and nymphs (above and centre) and a selection of dry flies (below).

the barb, or if the bend unfolds and does not return when you release the pressure, reject the hook. Professional fly dressers know that their reputations depend upon the quality of their flies. They use good-quality hooks and tying materials. Mass-produced flies, the majority of which are imported, are very variable in these respects. Some are excellent, and good value for money, but many are very poor and fall apart.

Winter is the time when many fly fishers get down to stocking their tackle boxes with flies for the coming season, but for those not into fly tying, here is a small 'starter' selection, obtainable at most tackle shops. Alternatively, you could place an order for your flies with a fly tying professional.

Name	Type	Hook Sizes
Mallard and Claret	wet fly	12, 14
Butcher	wet fly	10, 12
Sherry Spinner	dry fly	14, 16
Black Gnat	dry fly	16,18
Greenwell's Glory	dry fly	14, 16
Mayfly	dry fly	10
G and H Sedge	dry fly	12
Daddy-Long-Legs	dry fly	8, 10
Pheasant Tail	nymph	14, 16
Mayfly Nymph	nymph	10

Even with this small selection, and assuming you settle for just a couple of each type and size, that is still quite some investment. An economy list, with which I would be happy to fish the season, would be the Mallard and Claret and the Butcher wet flies, the Greenwell and the Sedge dry flies, and the Pheasant Tail nymph. In later chapters I will recommend some other trout and sea trout flies for particular situations.

Storing Flies

The most important features of a fly box are that it should allow the flies to dry out quickly and should then keep them secure and dry until next required. If flies are stored wet, the hooks are likely to rust and the fur, threads and feathers to rot. Dry flies need to be stored so that they keep their three-dimensional shape, and the special boxes with individual hinged compartments are ideal, although rather expensive, for this purpose. For wet flies and nymphs, boxes with metal clips are available at little cost, and these generally contain ventilation holes to help speed up the drying process. Boxes with plastic foam inserts are suitable for both dry flies and wet flies.

Leaders

The leader, or cast as it used to be known, is the nylon connection between the main line and the fly itself. A properly constructed leader helps transfer power from the line to the fly so that you achieve delicate presentation. The leader has to be long enough to keep your fly line well out of sight of the trout, and it should be fine enough not to frighten the fish as it alights on the water. Usually, this means that your leader must be at least as long as your rod, but there are times when we can get away with less, and others when a leader of twice the rod's length improves results. (Casting with a very long leader is difficult, and certainly not recommended for beginners.)

That part of your leader where it joins the main line must be thick to transmit power smoothly from the fly line. The nylon to which you attach your fly should be very fine and, ideally, invisible to the fish. So the leader must taper down, either gradually or in discrete sections. The ultimate is a factory-made continuously tapering leader, onto which a short length of

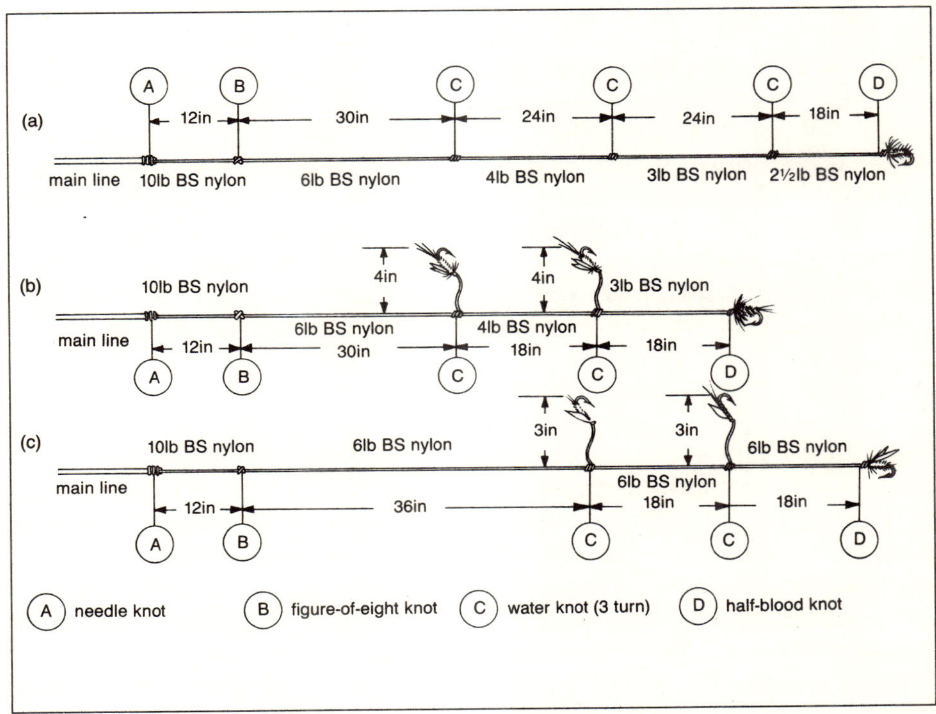

Leader design: (a) dry fly for trout on a small stream; (b) a team of wet flies for spring river trouting; (c) a team of wet flies for summer sea trout.

fine nylon, called the 'point', is attached. If you get your fly stuck in a tree, the leader should break at its weakest link, the point.

There is another reason for using tapered leaders. When fishing the dry fly you will want your imitation to alight gently upon the surface. If it splashes down heavily, followed by a bundle of tangled nylon, no self-respecting trout will give it further consideration. Your leader must, therefore, straighten out just before the fly touches the surface of the water, and the taper helps ensure that this happens. Most river fly fishers make up their own leaders and carry spare nylon to replace the point as required. To make your own stepped taper leaders you will need spools of supple nylon in ratings of 6, 4, 3 and 2lb breaking strain.

Leader Knots

To attach leaders repeatedly to a fly line would cause damage to the end of the line. Instead attach a foot or two of 10lb nylon permanently to the fly line and tie a loop onto the nylon for joining your leaders. Where two or more wet flies are to be used, 'droppers' are required on the leader. Suitable knots for these joints, and for attaching your flies, are illustrated. Once you have formed a knot, wet the nylon before pulling it tight. This ensures that the individual turns bed down fully without melting under the heat of friction.

Some of the cheaper brands of nylon are far too springy for use as leader material. Not only do they have a 'memory' of the radius of their spool, tending to lie in coils on the water, but they may also display marked variations in knot strength. Nylon is relatively inexpensive and it pays to go for good quality. Be wary of cut-price offers on bulk spools. Unless clearly marked with a quality brand name, they are likely to be very poor material and will detract significantly from the pleasure of fishing.

Lines

Most modern fly lines have a braided Dacron core around which there is a flexible plastic coating. By varying the density of the plastic, the lines can be made to float or sink at varying speeds. The floaters are coded F and the sinkers S. Intermediate lines (coded I) have almost neutral buoyancy, and drift through the surface very slowly. They have most of the characteristics of a floating line plus the advantage of minimal surface wake when they are retrieved through the water. Lines with high-density plastic over a few yards at one end are called 'sink-tip' lines, and are coded F/S. I use floating lines for most of my river fishing.

The profile of the line affects its casting characteristics. Level lines are very cheap to produce, but, as it is impossible to cast a fly delicately with

19 River Trout

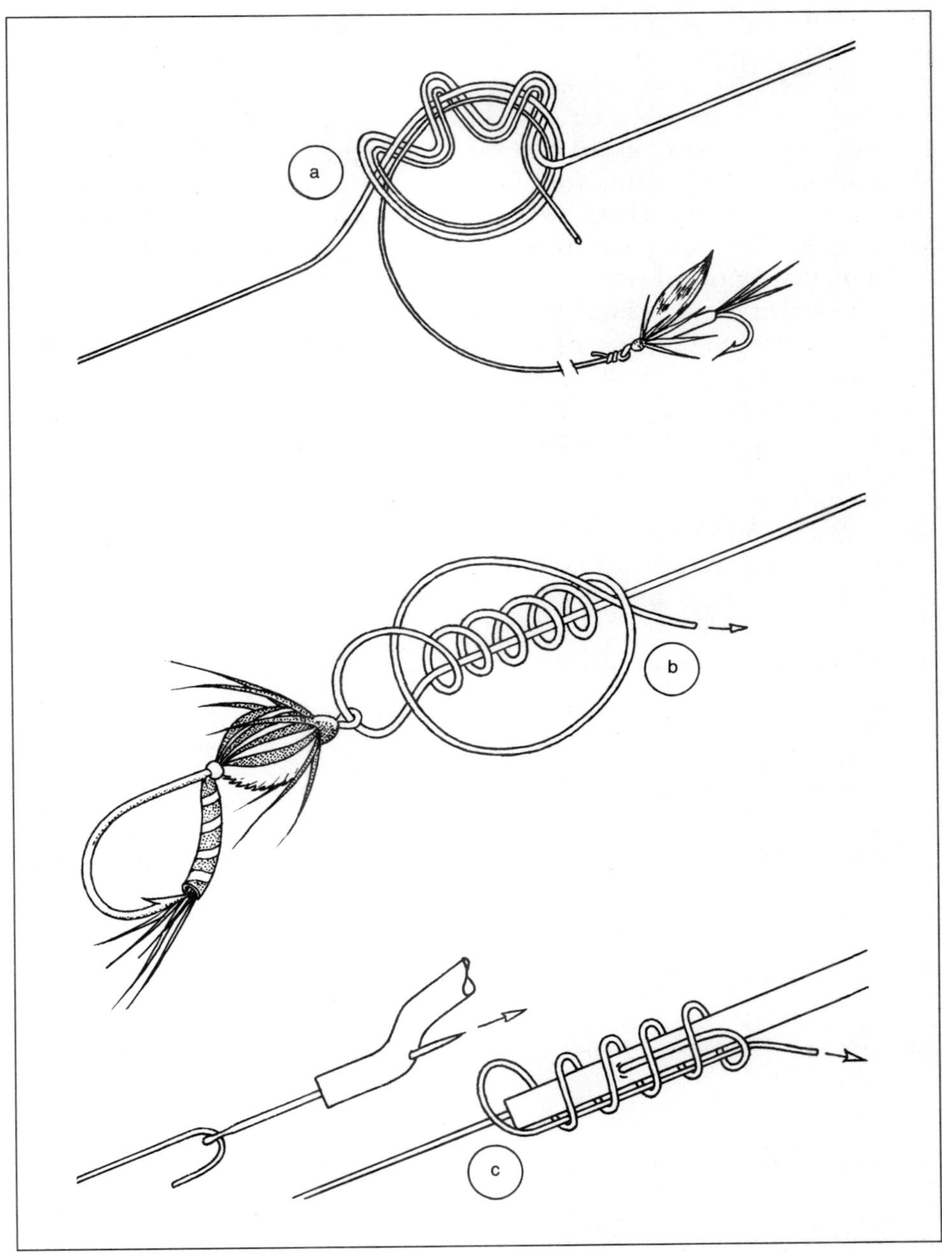

Knots for leader and fly connections: (a) water knot for joining lengths of nylon and for forming droppers; (b) tucked blood knot for attaching flies; (c) needle knot for joining leader to main line and main line to backing.

such a line, they are rarely used in river fishing. The double-taper line (coded DT) provides for delicate fly presentation and is ideal for fishing the dry fly. Weight-forward lines have a shorter belly followed by a long running line. They are better suited to casting on larger rivers. With care, a dry fly can still be presented well using a weight-forward line. Finally, the shooting-taper (ST) or shooting-head line is used when fishing a wet fly at very great distances. There are occasions when you may want to use a shooting head on large spate rivers, but for the present we will concentrate on more conventional river lines – the DT and WF types. So, the overall coding system must include both density and profile information.

Many river anglers have a preference for double-taper lines. For accuracy and delicacy of presentation at moderate range they are unbeatable. However, a weight-forward line allows the beginner to cast a greater distance when his timing and action are less than perfect. It also casts reasonably well with just a short length of line out of the rod tip. More importantly, the weight-forward line flows well through the rod rings when you use the 'double haul' (a casting technique discussed later). With practice, a weight-forward line enables you to turn your fly over at long range with the wind against you.

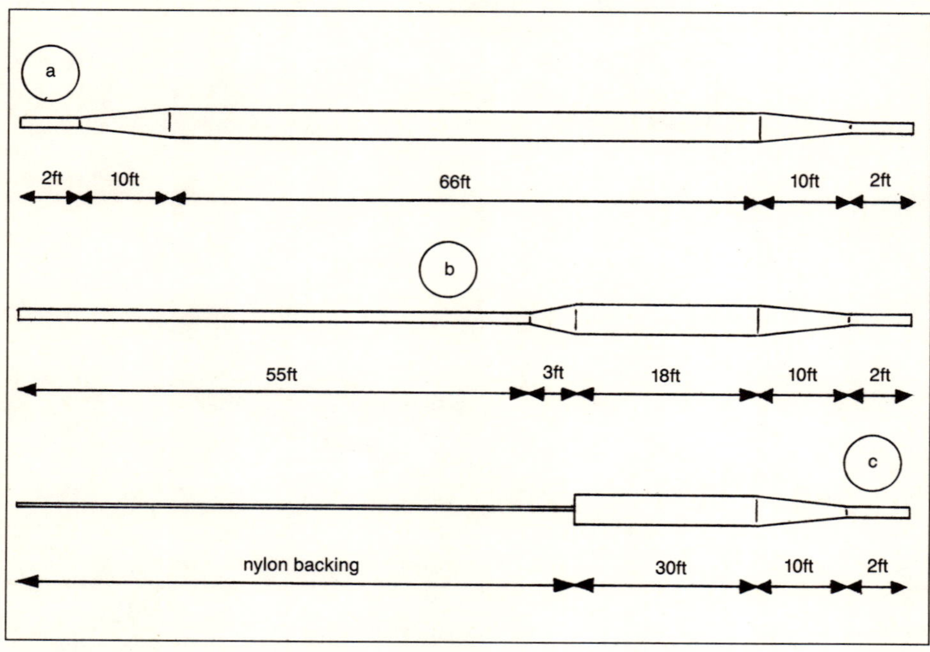

Popular fly line profiles: (a) double-taper; (b) weight-forward; (c) shooting head.

Finally, to the weight of the line. The American Fishing Tackle Manufacturers Association has produced specifications for the weights of fly lines, so that a number 5 line, for example, will have the same weight over the first ten yards of the body of the line irrespective of the brand name. Larger numbers indicate a heavier line, with which a more powerful rod can cast a heavier fly over greater distances. For trout and sea trout fishing, lines in the range 4 to 8 are normally used. So, for instance, a weight-forward floating fly line of AFTM rating number 6 would be coded WF6F.

Line Quality

Modern plastic-coated lines do not rely on surface tension to shy afloat; they are less dense than water. This is achieved by the incorporation into the plastic coating of numerous tiny air bubbles. It is difficult to control the manufacturing process to prevent the air bubbles drifting out to the surface of the plastic coating, and cheap floating lines often have a rough surface finish. The effect is that the line does not slide easily through the rod rings, and in a very short time can cause damage to the rings. I would have nothing at all to do with cheap floating lines. If you need to economize, it would be better to do so when looking for a sinking line, but do make sure that you check any such purchase thoroughly for any flaws in the plastic coating.

Trout will be alarmed by a fly line – whatever its colour – if it splashes anywhere near them. To be successful, you must cast your fly in such a way that the line stays well away from the trout. So, for a floating line you can safely choose a light colour that you can see easily at dusk. (White is ideal.) Sinking lines are thinner than floaters of the same rating and, therefore, make less splash if cast correctly. Nevertheless, they can disturb fish below the surface, and I opt for sinkers of a dark colour to provide some sort of camouflage against the background of the river bed.

Backing

Before winding your line on to the reel, pad out the spindle with 10 yards of wool and then attach at least 50 yards of backing line. This is a monofilament or braided synthetic fibre. It further increases the spindle diameter and also provides extra line length should a fish make a particularly long and powerful run. On the few occasions when the backing is taken out by a strong fish you will want to be confident that the joint between main line and backing is secure and can flow freely through the rod rings.

Rods

A fly-fishing rod is a multi-purpose tool. The choice of a rod is inevitably a compromise, and it must fall somewhere between rods best suited to casting, to hooking a fish, and to playing and landing a fish. Each of these factors is further complicated by the need to consider the size and nature of the river, and of the fish you expect to catch. A 6ft brook rod well-suited to casting for ¼lb trout on a hill stream would be poor equipment for tackling sea trout on the River Dovey, for example.

For ease of casting, particularly in windy conditions, a rod which is stiff, flexing only at the tip, would be the preferred choice. A very stiff rod allows you to set the hook very quickly, but when using a fine nylon leader the risk of it snapping during the strike is a serious one. A softer rod, which flexes through both the middle and tip regions, would be superior in this respect. Finally, when playing a fish which leaps or makes surging runs towards an obstruction, you need to apply controlled pressure. A very soft rod, which flexes from tip to butt, absorbs shocks well, and allows you to apply a larger average level of tension to turn a running fish.

So what is the ideal fishing rod? I suggest that you compromise in favour of safe fishing, and use rods of softer action which reduce the chance of a leader breakage resulting in a trout being left with a fly in its jaws. A satisfactory compromise, then, for river and stream fishing is the middle and top action. Several manufacturers produce carbon or graphite rods to this specification. Built cane rods, which are somewhat heavier and generally more expensive than carbon rods, have a natural tendency towards soft action, and a 6–7ft built-cane rod can be the heart of an ideal brook fishing outfit.

As an indication of the weight of fly line they are capable of casting, modern rods are marked with their AFTM rating. A rod marked AFTM5 is designed to be fully loaded, and hence to cast best, with 10 yards of AFTM5 fly line extended beyond the rod tip. A shorter length of heavier line would give the same loading, and a longer length of lighter line could achieve the same purpose, of course. Thus, if you use a double-taper line, you have the opportunity of varying line length. Most manufacturers now show the recommended range of lines by marking their rods with more than one AFTM number. For example, AFTM4–6 would indicate that the rod would be fully loaded by 10 yards of AFTM6 line extended beyond the rod tip. You could obtain the same loading, and hence line speed, with 12 yards of AFTM5 line or about 14 yards of AFTM4 line. So a beginner should always use a line of the highest rating marked on the rod. Indeed, rarely in river and stream fishing would I choose any other, unless I anticipated the need for long-distance casting, when the lower line rating

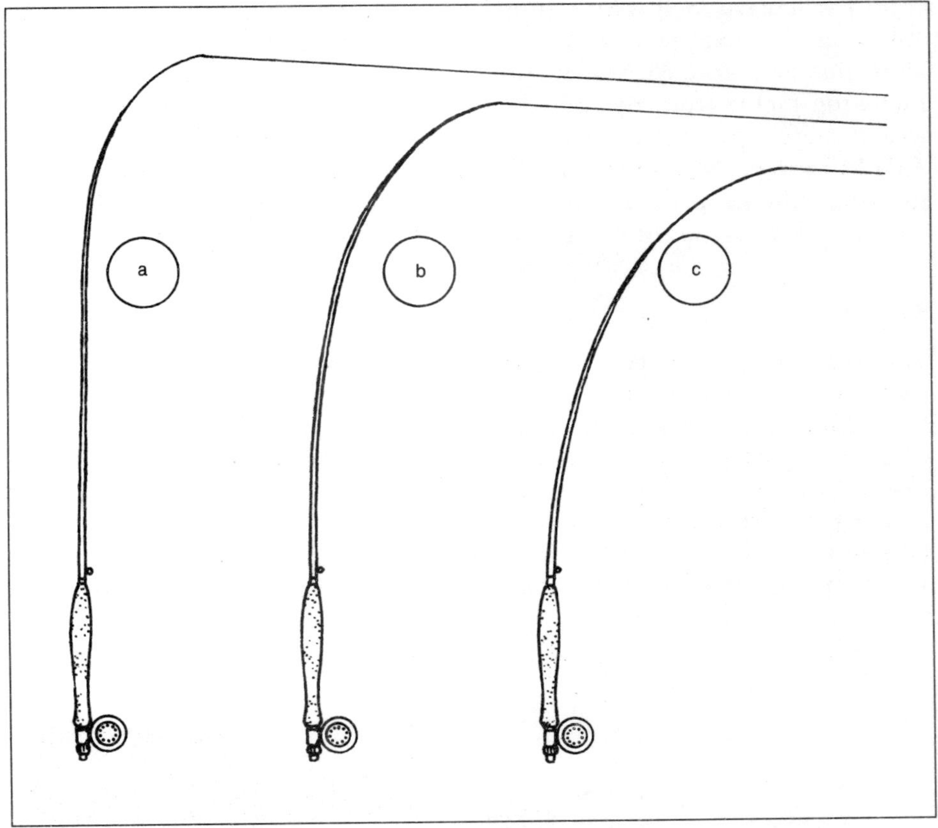

Rod actions: (a) a tip- or fast-action; (b) a medium- or middle-and-top-action; (c) a through- or slow-action. A middle-and-top-action is a good compromise between the needs of casting and fishing.

would allow me to aerialize more line. All this assumes you are using a double-taper line. The situation is more straightforward if you use a weight-forward line. Remember, the weight-forward line has most of its weight in the thick belly of the first 10 yards or so. This is followed by a thin running line. So in our example, extending 14 yards of an AFTM4 weight-forward line beyond the rod tip would not achieve the full loading of the AFTM6 rod. Indeed, you would be likely to damage the running line after a short period, because it only has a thin plastic covering.

Whenever possible, try out a sample rod, with its matching line, before buying, to make sure you can cope with it. Many people buy rods which are too powerful for them This 'try before you buy' suggestion may not seem particularly helpful if you are new to fly fishing, but you might be able to get an experienced fly fisher of similar build to yourself to come along and help you. Most mail-order tackle firms will put together a set of matching tackle (rod, reel and line) to your specification, and they have expert staff who really do understand such matters as 'rod action' and AFTM ratings. Not all small tackle shops can provide this sort of expert guidance (the proprietor may be a sea or coarse angler, for example), so it pays to ask a few questions before spending money on a fly rod.

Reels

Simplicity and reliability are the main requirements of reels. They come in various sizes to suit the line rating. It is usually the width of the spool which the manufacturer varies to produce lightweight, regular and king-size reels of a given pattern. A spare spool is very useful as this will enable you to change quickly from one type of line to another. For small stream fishing a centre-pin reel with a simple drag mechanism or ratchet (to prevent tangles when line is pulled from the spool) will do nicely. On larger rivers you may appreciate the advantages of a multiplying fly reel, particularly

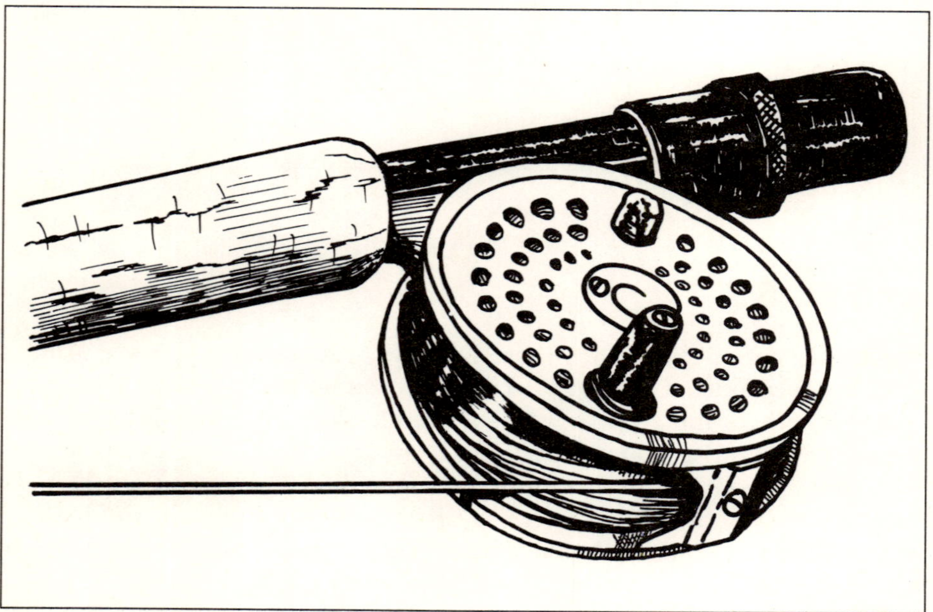

A properly filled fly reel. With backing and fly line, the spool is filled to within ¼in of the lip.

when trying to gather in line quickly in order to follow a running sea trout. On the heavier rods normally used for sea trouting, the extra two ounces in weight is no disadvantage. (It may lessen the apparent weight of the rod in your hand when fishing, since it brings the centre of balance nearer to the wrist.)

Landing Nets

Much of my river trouting is done without a net, but some river banks are so high that it would impossible to lift out or release a fish by hand. When sea trout fishing, a landing net is just about essential, as lifting out a sea trout by hand can be difficult in daylight, and much more so in the dark. Rigid frame nets are simple and inexpensive, but large ones can be more awkward to carry. On 'wilderness fisheries', folding nets can get tangled and refuse to unfold at the crucial moment. On balance, I prefer fixed frame nets, especially when fishing for sea trout in the dark.

Eye Protection

Even an experienced caster can misjudge the effects of the wind on his line. To hear a fly clatter against the lens of your glasses is proof for life that wearing eye protection when fly fishing makes very good sense. I usually wear polarized spectacles which help reduce the effects of reflections from the surface and allow you to see more of what is happening on the river bed.

Essential Accessories

These are few and not costly, and they can all be fitted into your pockets:

1. A tin of leader grease, such as Mucilin. Apply this to all but the last 9in of the leader to help it stay afloat when fishing the dry fly.
2. Fly floatant. Various sprays and dips are available. I prefer the small bottles of light oil because, apart from the concern about the effects of aerosols on the ozone layer, you can see how much is left in a dip and avoid running short of floatant during a day's fishing.
3. Leader sinkant, or simply a wad of soft felt soaked in washing-up liquid. Use it to remove grease from the leader when fishing wet fly.
4. Small, blunt-nosed scissors. Attach these via twine to a ring on your jacket or waistcoat.
5. A priest, or weighted cosh, to kill any trout you decide to keep. Hold the trout (while still in the landing net if you use one) with one hand and strike it sharply above the eyes with the priest.

Clothing

Warm woolly socks and wellies (without holes!) are essential. Waders are not a necessity if you intend to fish chalk streams (where wading is often prohibited), but they do help keep legs warm and dry on wet and windy days. For spate river fishing, waders are extremely useful, as they help you get into position to cover fish which you would otherwise not be able to. For small stream fishing, thigh waders are all you will need, but on larger spate rivers a pair of chest waders would be worth the extra investment if you intend fishing for sea trout and salmon.

How to carry your tackle – either in a waistcoat or tackle bag.

Apart from the quality of materials, waders differ in the design of the sole of the boot. For general use, those with metal studs inserted into rubber soles are very good. They provide reasonable grip on rocky river beds and are sufficiently flexible to avoid undue discomfort when walking across meadows. (Do not walk any distance along made up roads wearing studded waders or you will very quickly spoil them.) Other designs have cleated rubber, crepe or rope soles, all of which allow you to wade with less likelihood of fish being disturbed by the noise of your boots scraping on the river bed. None of these materials is ideal for gripping and it is all too easy to lose your foothold on the kindest of river beds when your attention is on the fishing.

Chest waders allow you to fish from deeper water, but remember that your weight on the river bed will be gradually reduced, and it becomes increasingly more difficult to hold position in a strong current as the depth increases. I would advise non-swimmers not to fish in water where chest waders are required. Another sensible rule is not to wade if the water is so coloured that you cannot see the river bed.

Fishing waistcoats and waxed cotton jackets are good long-term investments. They are designed with numerous pockets, pouches, rings and other fittings to help you keep scissors, priest, landing net, etc. secure and ready to hand. In warm weather I fit everything I need into the pockets of my waistcoat, carrying just my rod and, if the size of my quarry justifies it, a landing net slung behind me. In spring and autumn, I manage to pack all I need into the pockets of my waxed coat. Spare rods and reels have to be left in the boot of the car, of course, but I like the freedom of not having to carry a bag, which I am quite liable to put down and leave behind on the river bank.

Matching the Tackle

No single outfit can be ideally suited to all requirements but, like very other sport, you have to start somewhere. Your quarry and its river environment dictate the weight of line and the size and power of rod you will need. Below are described two outfits which between them should suit most of your river fishing needs. You will probably start with just one of these, chosen according to the waters available to you.

Small Stream Outfit

My idea of the perfect brook and small stream outfit is lightweight and extremely portable. Everything should fit into waistcoat or jacket pockets except the rod itself. Tackling up for small stream fishing is the least expensive way of getting started as a fly fisher, but I should say at the outset that it is a style of fishing which does not suit all temperaments. If you prefer wide open spaces where you can cast with ease, or if you are unable to scramble over rough ground, amongst boulders and through bushes, then do not rush out and buy the outfit described below. It is for the loner, the explorer, the wilderness fly fisher.

Rod 7ft long, middle and top action, AFTM4–5 carbon or built cane.

Line Double-taper AFTM5 floating line.

Reel Simple lightweight trout fly reel for AFTM5 line plus 50 yards of backing.

Leader 8ft long, stepped from 10lb to a 5lb, 3lb or 2lb point according to size of trout anticipated.

Flies A small selection of dry flies and nymphs in a pocket-sized floating fly box.

Priest Essential if fish are to be taken for the table.

Net Rarely required, but a small fixed frame net on an elastic cord is preferable to the folding frame type which tends to get caught in brambles and refuses to open when required.

Spate River Outfit

If you are likely to fish extensively on powerful spate rivers then you would not thank me for setting you up with the tackle outlined above. A longer rod matched to a slightly heavier line will make it easier for you to cover the distances you may sometimes need to cast, although it is surprising how often you can catch good fish within a few yards of where you are standing if you have not already ‘put them down’. With this tackle you will also be equipped for the windy conditions which can prevail in more exposed situations.

Rod 9½–10½ft long, middle and top action, AFTM6–7 carbon.

Reel Single action or (my preference) multiplying regular trout reel for AFTM7 line plus 100 yards of backing.

Line AFTM7 weight-forward floating line (white, moon-glow or ivory). Optional AFTM7 sink-tip or medium sinker on spare spool.

Leader 10ft of level 10lb nylon for spring and autumn (high water) sea trout. 10ft of level 6lb nylon for summer sea trout. Stepped taper leaders with 2lb, 3lb or 5lb point strength to suit size of trout anticipated.

Flies A pocket-sized box of dry flies and a second box containing wet flies for trout and sea trout. Keep these small boxes topped up from a 'master store' kept at home or in the boot of the car.

This outfit would cope with both trout and sea trout and would give you more than a fighting chance of beating the occasional salmon under all but the most adverse of conditions. If salmon from large spate rivers are your main interest then a more substantial rod (and a different book!) will be required.

THE GENTLE ART OF CASTING

It was a losing battle! Try as I would, I could not get my fly to turn over properly in the gusting east wind. Not surprisingly, the trout resolutely ignored a fly which drifted downstream perched upon a nest of curled-up nylon. On this unseasonably cool July morning, very few fish were rising on the tiny lowland rough stream, and I could little afford to make a clumsy cast; today I seemed unable to make any other. I knew this to be the most productive stretch of the beat. I also knew I would have to give it my best. My casting simply was not up to it!

I decided to try the 'dog-leg', a gentle 's' bend where I might just find a rising trout and some shelter from the malevolence of the wind. On arrival, things looked encouraging. Hard against the high east bank a neb broke the surface. It was no steady riser, but I watched it take a couple of olive duns as they skated slowly in the lea of the bank. Fortunately I had a clear back cast, so at a range of some 15 yards covering the fish would be easy. Or so I thought! My first attempt landed amongst weeds on the shingle beach, disturbing nothing but a pair of damselflies which sped off upstream. In half a dozen attempts, using a variety of casting methods, I failed to get my fly within 2 yards of my target. The judge's decision: not near enough!

The wind swirling across the high bank was causing turbulence, and although my line went where I wanted it to, the fly just *would not* follow.

A really slamming cast would have put the fly down in the desired spot; it would have put the trout down, too. This was my last chance, as the sun would soon be too high for serious fishing with the dry fly. I sat and pondered.

Finally, it dawned on me; the answer was simple. I used a slanting cast, neither overhead nor horizontal, to power my line and leader upstream and across so that they bounced off the vertical face of the high bank. As gently as thistledown, they settled on the surface just inches from the edge. Up came the trout, a beautiful quarter-pounder, and the deception was complete. I was delighted, and a bigger fish could hardly have added to the sense of achievement. As so often on river and stream, this was no textbook technique, but a hybrid – a concoction to suit a particular situation. Textbooks and professional tuition can help develop the basic skills – the tools of the trade – but the gentle art of casting a fly on the river is all about *how* these tools are used.

Versatility is the Key

If you have taken up fly fishing recently, or your experience is limited to fishing on lakes or reservoirs with relatively clear banks, then many of the casting techniques described below may be new to you. They are all useful when fishing rivers and streams. Indeed, as you gain the confidence to fish in confined spaces you will further adapt your casting to suit various situations. Often this means departing from 'text book' techniques and improvising to cover fish which have taken up particularly awkward lies.

If possible, get a qualified instructor to help you get started. Professionals qualified via the National Angling Council, the Welsh Salmon and Trout Association or the Association of Professional Game Angling Instructors have to pass stringent tests both on their own technique and their ability to pass on their knowledge and skills to others. At my own fly-fishing school we make extensive use of video cameras and slow-motion play-back to help beginners develop the basic skills of casting, and the self-taught to identify and iron out their problems.

It is easier to start right than to correct faults which have become habits. Unfortunately, some people cannot get away for a few days at a time to attend a course of instruction. They may not find it easy to attend a casting clinic even for a couple of hours. I have, therefore, included here a description of how to make some of the casts which are most useful in river fishing. With a note that the descriptions in this chapter assume a *right-handed* angler, you might like to set up your tackle and try some of the methods described below.

Always practise on a lawn or meadow. Never cast a fly line onto an abrasive surface such as concrete. In place of the fly, tie on a small tuft of wool. Strip off about 8 yards of line from the rod tip and lay it out in front of you. Pick up the rod in the right hand with your thumb along the top of the butt. If, after half an hour's casting, you find this grip uncomfortable, try alternative methods. Some anglers prefer to place the forefinger along the line of the rod, instead of the thumb, while others find it more comfortable to hold the rod in the 'V' formed between thumb and forefinger. Choose the method which affords you a secure grip without causing you any discomfort.

Tuck the butt close in beneath your wrist and position your feet comfortably. For greatest accuracy your right foot should be forward of the left, so that you can aim in the required direction more easily. When distance casting, you may find it easier to keep your balance with your left foot leading. For now, choose the option you find most comfortable, but remember that you may have to use either stance at the river (and a great many others), according to the positions of boulders or other obstructions under foot.

The Overhead Cast

You are now ready to make your first cast. Keep your left hand comfortably by your side, holding the line to prevent more being pulled from the reel as you cast. Start with the rod tip close to the ground. Keeping your right arm and the rod in a straight line, raise the rod slowly at first and then progressively increase the speed from the 10 o'clock position until the butt is vertical. Stop the backward motion at this point and the line will be projected backwards.

As the line straightens out, let the butt break away just an inch or two from your wrist, allowing the rod to drift back to the 1 o'clock position. This is the moment to begin your forward push. Again, make it a smooth, progressive movement. (You *must* avoid snatching.) Accelerate the forward motion until the butt is in the 11 o'clock position, at which point push forward sharply to straighten your wrist, bringing the rod in line with your casting forearm. The rod should now be at the 10 o'clock position where it will straighten, giving up its stored energy. This will further accelerate the line in the forward direction. Your fly line should follow the rod, straightening out in front of you. Finally, as the line falls to the surface, smoothly lower your rod to the horizontal to 'follow through'.

If you have timed your push correctly, the line will land nice and straight in front of you, and the piece of wool should drift down gently at the end of an extended leader. If, after a few attempts at the overhead cast, you are

The overhead cast.

not getting good results, check for one or more of the following mistakes:

1. Using too little effort on the back cast.
2. Using far too much effort and snatching on the forward cast. Once the rod has been 'loaded' (like a spring under compression) on the back flick, all you need do on the forward push is to determine the direction and height at which the line travels.
3. Letting the rod go well beyond the vertical behind you, in which case the line will either hit the ground or will be projected skywards on the forward push to fall all around you in an untidy heap.
4. Pushing the rod too far down in front of you, which causes the line to slam down heavily without properly extending the leader.
5. Not waiting until the line has straightened out behind you. As you cast longer distances, you will have to allow more time before commencing the forward push.
6. Allowing the left hand to follow the rod, thereby losing much of the stored energy. If you find you have this tendency then put your left hand – holding the line, of course – into a pocket, and keep it there while casting.

It helps to have an observer point out the faults in your casting. If you have access to a video recorder and camera then you can be your own critic, analysing your faults on the playback before trying to rectify them. To show how it should be done there are some excellent video films available, illustrating a range of casting techniques.

'Shooting' Line

Gradually extend the amount of line out of the rod tip in order to increase your casting distance. The pause before changing direction will have to be increased as you lengthen the line (just as the period of a pendulum increases with its length). There will come a point, however, probably at between 15 and 20 yards, where any further increase in line length results in disaster. You will have overloaded the rod and will be unable to achieve sufficient line speed to aerialize the line, which will collapse about your ears in an untidy mess. Once you have exceeded the casting potential of the rod, you will have to shorten the line and begin again. Do not wind in this extra line. Instead, leave it coiled loosely beside you on the ground and cast once more. This time, open your left hand to release the coils just as the line is about to straighten out in front of you. If the line is travelling fast enough it will pull on the coils of spare line causing them to 'shoot' through the rod rings, extending your casting distance.

Long-Distance Casting

The distance a stone can be thrown is determined mainly by four factors: the weight of the stone, its shape (which governs the wind resistance), the angle at which it is launched and the speed at which the stone leaves the hand. The same applies when casting a fly line. Heavier tackle (higher AFTMA rating) can be cast further than light tackle, provided that you have the strength to load the spring of the rod fully. But for maximum distance you must also get those other factors right.

As the line travels through the air, you will notice that it forms a loop, the front face of which suffers considerable drag as it cuts through the atmosphere. Weather conditions influence casting distance, but a far more important factor is the loop diameter. A wide loop gives much air resistance, while a narrow loop gives far less. To cast a narrow loop, apply the power as the rod moves through a small arc around the vertical.

A soft, through-action rod has to be moved through a relatively wide arc in order to load it fully, whereas a fast, tip-action rod can be fully stressed by rapid acceleration through a narrow arc. For this reason, distance casting rods are usually quite long and are of fast action. River fishing is not a casting tournament, of course, and in practice the middle-and-top-action rods are, for most purposes, a satisfactory compromise between the ultimate casting tool and the ideal equipment for hooking and playing a fish. Whatever rod you use, the loop size will vary according to your casting technique, with rapid acceleration through a relatively narrow arc giving better results when you reach for distance.

Try to achieve a launch angle of about 45° and, at the same time, to maximize the speed of the line on the final launch forward. As you try for increased distance, you will reach a point where putting more effort into the forward push gives little or no benefit: the rod has reached its limiting velocity and, for the weight of line involved, no further increase in line speed is achievable.

False Casting

Once you are getting reasonable results try keeping the fly line in the air instead of letting it fall to the surface at the end of your forward push. To do this bring the rod forward to the 10 o'clock position and then, instead of following through on the forward push, simply repeat the back flick and keep the line moving backwards and forwards above your head. This is known as 'false casting'. When applied with a very short length of line beyond the rod tip, vigorous false casting is a simple and effective way to dry a fly which has become waterlogged.

False casting has another quite essential role – it enables you gradually to extend the amount of line you cast with. To do this, pull off a foot or so of line from the reel at the beginning of each back-push and let it flow through the fingers of your left hand as the line travels forward. Continue false casting and extending line until you have sufficient to reach the distance you require. With practice you will soon feel the line shooting out under power from the rod. Should you release the line at the wrong moment you will waste most of the rod's stored energy and the line will fall in a heap.

Timing is the essence of good casting, and in due course you will acquire a feel for when the tackle is working properly. Practice and yet more practice are the means to perfecting your technique. Do not worry about distance – that will come all too easily once you have mastered the basics. In any case, river fishing rarely requires a cast of more than 12 yards, and you will very quickly reach that standard. Within your first season you will probably be able to cast up to 15 yards with the lightweight outfit described earlier, and nearer 20 yards with the longer rod. Do not worry if you achieve somewhat less than this, as accuracy and delicacy in presenting the fly are much more important. If you want to become a really accurate caster, practise aiming towards a target such as a dinner plate. When you can land your fly on the target 50 per cent of the time on a calm day, from a distance of 10 yards, you are a fine technician of the art.

It is advisable – especially if you are using the heavier of the two outfits described above – to limit your practice sessions to no more than an hour or so at a time at first. Beginners invariably try to make up for inexperience by putting extra effort into their casting, and this can put quite a strain on shoulder muscles, which are quick to complain. Once you have mastered the basics of casting you will be able to fish for many hours without even noticing a twinge. It is all a matter of timing, not power.

The Double Haul

There is a way of increasing line speed beyond the speed of the rod tip, and this involves using the left hand to further accelerate the line at the peak velocity points on both back and forward casts. Not only does the double haul provide greater distance, but it can also increase casting accuracy at short range, since it enables you to use a narrower loop to cut sharply through the air in windy conditions. When casting in a confined space, this technique allows a tighter loop and hence access to lies which would otherwise be unfishable.

Double hauling demands co-ordination. For each forward and back cycle of the rod, the left hand must make two complete cycles of movement towards and away from the bottom rod ring, so that your hands are at maximum separation when the rod is at its fully forward position *and* at its fully back position. The peak line speed is thus the sum of the speeds of the rod tip and the left hand.

Make a few false casts using the ordinary overhead technique before introducing the double haul action. The most important haul is that made to launch the line on its way to the target, so at this point you should power forward with the rod and pull down line with your left hand. At the end of the haul, open your left hand to allow line to shoot. If you time the haul and the final release correctly, you should be able to shoot several yards of line.

The Side-Cast

Similar to the overhead cast, but with the rod moving more nearly in a horizontal plane, the side-cast is useful when fishing beneath a canopy of trees. It is a means of casting a fly deep under a bush where a trout may be feeding on terrestrial casualties blown in by the wind. There is another important advantage of side casting – with the rod moving just above the surface of the water, it is possible to keep it out of the trout's window of vision.

The principle is essentially the same as for the overhead cast, except that the rod travels almost horizontally. A little extra power and a slight upward lift will be needed on the back cast to clear bank-side weeds, especially when fishing from a river bank well endowed with thistles and the like.

Accurate casting is more difficult to achieve with this technique. Best control of direction is obtained by limiting the angle through which the rod swings so that the line forms a tight loop on the back cast and the fly is less likely to swing to one side or the other before alighting on the water. Watch your line as carefully during the back cast as the forward cast, since the tunnel through which the line must travel may be very narrow.

There will be times when you will want to cast your fly 'round a corner', and the side cast can be used to achieve this effect. To do this you will need to swing the rod through an exaggerated arc, pulling back line slightly with your left hand just before the leader touches down. When you get the timing spot on, the fly will be flicked round to the left in a 'shepherd's crook' form. In practice, accurate casting via this technique is far from easy, but on occasions it can be the means of covering an otherwise unreachable fish.

The Catapult Cast

Through a dense tangle of reeds and branches, you spy a large trout, rising steadily just yards from your bank. You need only get your fly on the water and you *know* it will take it, as long as you keep well back, out of sight. You need a catapult, not a fly rod! Hold the fly in one hand on a very short line, perhaps with little more than the leader projecting from the rod top. Pull back (as with a bow and arrow) so that the spring of the rod is well loaded. Aim towards the required spot on the water and release the fly, which will shoot forward. A fast action rod gives greatest accuracy, but in any case the distance is limited to twice the length of your rod, so you should be able to place your fly close enough to tempt your quarry. One of my very best fish, a six-pounder, fell to this ploy, taking right under the rod tip. Only use this technique if you can see a way of manoeuvring the fish into clear water with enough room for playing and landing.

The Roll Cast

Where the only snag-free space is above the water you can put out a line of several rods' lengths by rolling it across the surface. This technique is ideally suited to wet-fly fishing on rivers whose banks are heavily wooded,

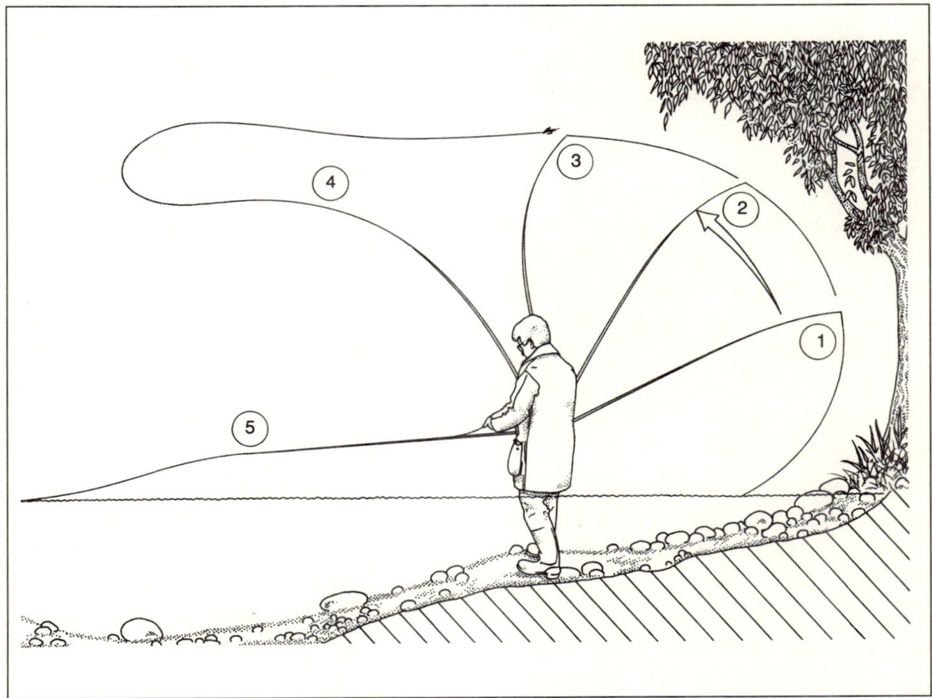

The roll cast – very useful on tree-lined rivers.

but it can also be modified for upstream work with dry fly or for shallow water nymphing.

Assuming you are on the right bank and fishing the wet fly downstream, wait until the line has come round to the 'dangle'. Steadily lift the rod upstream and then back to the 1 o'clock position. Hold the rod still for a second with the line making a gentle curve down to the surface. Now push the rod down sharply towards the surface of the stream. (This is one technique where plenty of brute force *is* an advantage.) The line should roll out neatly across the water.

You will find that a double-taper floating line works very well when roll casting, although a weight-forward line can be effective over short distances. It is all but impossible to roll out a sinking line any distance with normal trout tackle, so don't even try, or you could end up with a broken rod.

The upstream roll is almost as easy to master. Start by flicking a short length of line upstream. Then strip more line from the reel and, as your fly drifts back towards you, simply roll it forward again in the way I have just described. At first, you may need two or three of these false roll casts to work out a 10-yard line, but you should aim to develop this technique to the point where you can put out all the line you want with as little false casting as possible, since inevitably the line will cause some surface disturbance on each false roll.

Spey Casting

A more versatile technique for pushing out a long line across a tree-lined river is the Spey cast. This is a continuous-motion casting technique often associated with the double-handed salmon rod, but Spey casts can also be performed with a single-handed trout or sea trout rod. A right-handed person will generally use the single Spey when fishing wet fly from the left bank and the double Spey from the right bank. A left-handed angler will choose the alternative style in each case. Either method can be used when wading in midstream.

Let us assume that your fly has swung round to the dangle and that you are on or wading beneath, the left bank. You now want to cast out across the river. With the rod held low and pointing downstream, draw in line, taking coils in your left hand, until you have 10 to 15 yards out beyond the rod tip (depending on the size of rod). Raise the rod towards the vertical, peeling line from the surface before pulling it sharply upstream and then in a loop beside you. Now punch the line out across the river. As the line shoots away, release the coils from the left hand. Aim high in your forward punch and you should be able to cast 15 to 20 yards, even with a trout rod.

Wading beneath the right bank you will need the double Spey cast. The action is the same as before, but you must precede it by lifting the rod to bring the belly of the line upstream of where you are standing. The traditional way of practising these casts is to call out a waltz time, 1, 2, 3 . . . 1, 2, 3 . . . 1, 2, 3 through each of the stages of the casting action. Of course, if you are ambidextrous, then you have a free choice of single or double Spey in most situations.

Casting a Wiggly Line

Conflicting surface currents are the number-one enemy when you fish the dry fly. Natural flies swirl in the surface film, pushed and pulled by these currents. Tethered by a leader, your artificial fly is constrained and so cannot behave naturally. Worse still, if part of your line or leader falls across a run of fast current it will cause the line to bow downstream and your fly will skate across the surface. Small trout *may* find this action irresistible, but older and wiser fish are usually suspicious. Casting directly upstream minimizes drag, but this also puts your leader across the fish and may alarm it. In addition, there are many instances in which you need to cast across the stream to avoid wading which might send other fish scurrying upstream to forewarn your quarry. Described below is a technique which will allow your fly to float naturally for a little longer before drag sets in.

Using your normal overhead or side-casting technique, wait until the fly is about to alight on the water and then pull back sharply on the line with your left hand. The line and leader should recoil and fall on to the surface in a series of snake-like wiggles. (Once again, the double haul can help achieve the extra line speed necessary for success.) Practise this cast if you intend fishing the dry fly; it is truly invaluable on both chalk and rough streams.

Other Casting Tricks

The very best wild trout grow big by eating more than (or more of!) their brethren. They do this by taking up lies which provide plenty of food in a small area, and, on a river, it is the current which brings the food supply. Concentrations of current pose the most extreme problems of drag, however, and need extreme remedies in the form of a very much exaggerated 'wiggly line'.

Bounce casting can achieve this. Where a fish lies in fast current against a high bank, you can cast the fly so that it actually hits the bank before falling back into the water with a slack leader. Another method is to cast

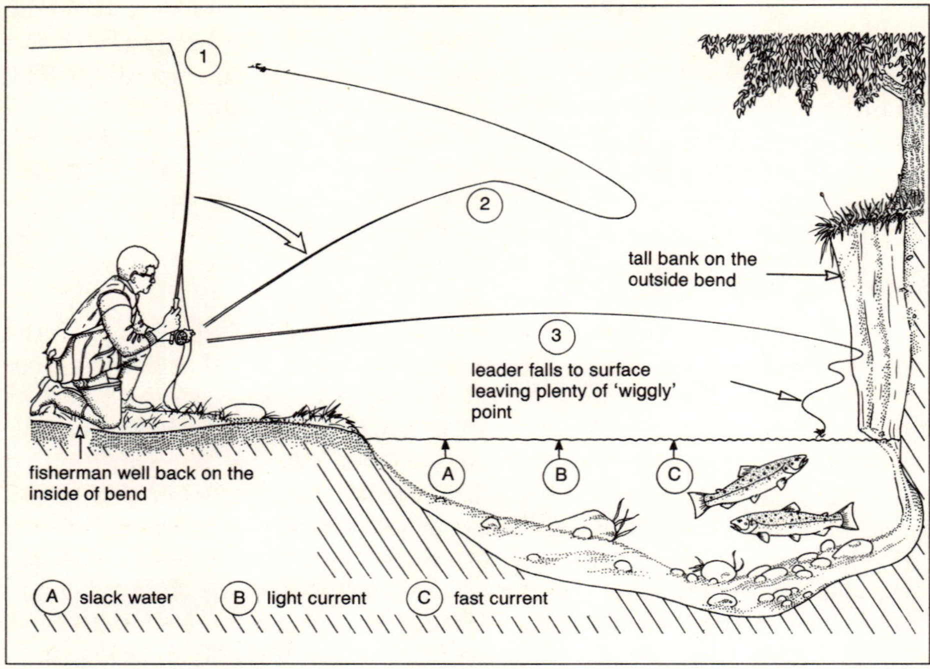

Bouncing a dry fly against a high bank can create enough slack leader to defeat drag for the second or two necessary to deceive a good trout.

too far so that the fly settles on the grass. As the current carries the line downstream the fly should suddenly plop down on to the surface just where you want it! I know that flies do not always do what they are meant to, but when it works, this little trick always leaves me feeling rather smug!

Mending the Line

When the river is high the main problem in fishing the wet fly is that the strong current pulls on the belly of the line. This prevents the fly from sinking and soon brings it skating rapidly across at right angles to the flow. These are just the times when there is likely to be a fair bit of colour in the water, and while early season trout and sea trout are noted for their willingness to chase a fly, you do have to give them the opportunity to see it. One answer is to use a long rod and to cast a very long line. Unfortunately, many good fly-fishing rivers are heavily wooded and long-distance casting is rarely feasible in daylight, never mind after dusk.

A second option, and one which is more widely applicable, is to use a 'mended' line. Having cast out, use the rod to lift the belly of the line and flick it upstream by working the rod tip in a circular motion. You may have to mend the line several times as the fly swings across the current.

Using a floating line, this method of mending is quite easily mastered, but not so if a heavy sinker is needed as, for example, when fishing spate rivers early or late in the season. In fact, many sea trout fishermen are unhappy about mending the line in this way, as every time a fly line hits the water, there is the risk that a fish will be spooked by the disturbance. Mending the line must increase this risk.

A better, though admittedly more difficult, technique is the casting of a ready-mended line. If you are right-handed and fishing from the right bank of a stream then this is what to do. Make a side cast, aiming your fly actually at the water (instead of at a point a foot or so above the surface, which is more usual). Use a little more power than necessary for the distance sought, and have more line stripped from the reel than is needed. At the moment your fly touches the water, release the line from the left hand. This spare line will shoot to create an upstream arc on the surface of the stream. You will need lots of practice to get both the aim and timing right, but it is well worth the trouble if you intend fishing for sea trout.

Many anglers are restricted, through lack of casting skills, to trying only for those fish which can be covered by the basic overhead cast. Once you become reasonably competent in the range of casting techniques discussed above, you will enjoy far more opportunities. With practice, casting will become second nature. Then you will be able to concentrate your attention on the more advanced skills of fly fishing – the selection of effective tactics for deceiving your quarry.

FLY-FISHING TECHNIQUES FOR RIVER AND STREAM

Perhaps in some future age, with increased leisure time and improved equipment, a round-in-eighteen will replace a hole-in-one as the golfer's dream; a maximum break in snooker will go unnoticed; darts matches will be but marathon tests of endurance 180 . . . 180 . . . 180 . . . And what of fly fishing in such an age? Will there still be confidence-sapping blank days, whether due to wrongly identifying the fly on the water, to failing to spot the dimple of a feeding trout hard against the bank, or to approaching a feeding fish from the wrong direction and so putting it down.

Fishing, and fly fishing in particular, is not a sport for the perfectionist. It may be true that certain items of tackle have already been developed to the verge of perfection; that the most accomplished of us can cast dry fly so that it wafts on to the suface with no more fuss than an egg-laying spinner; and that others win tournaments with heart-stopping casts of great distance or extreme accuracy. It is even conceivable that some prodigy might one day combine these achievements of distance, accuracy and delicacy of presentation in 'the perfect cast'. But, now at least, most of us are a very long way from perfection.

What separates the expert from the tiro is their relative skill and knowledge – the techniques and the rivercraft of fly fishing. In these respects, our most respected experts can only be rated fair, and the average fly fisher, appallingly weak. Long may what remains to be learned outweigh what is understood of the techniques for outwitting a trout with a fly.

Wet-Fly Fishing

Shrouded in the mists of time, the origins of fly fishing are obscure. Many believe that wet-fly fishing is the oldest of techniques, and certainly it dates back more than a thousand years, to when materials for making hooks and leaders were crude and ineffective by present-day standards. A heavy iron hook mounted on a trace of horse hair could more readily be concealed in a fly intended to swim submerged in a turbulent race below a weir – ideal wet-fly water. But why do trout take such artificial flies? I have yet to encounter a real fly which can swim against a strong current. There are some aquatic flies which can swim below the surface to lay their eggs amongst plant roots, but even these insects could not cope with the force of current in which wet flies are often successful.

What then does a wet fly represent? Does it imitate an insect or a small fish? And are trout deceived by such crude imitations, or do they take them by some sort of instinctive reaction? I believe we are helped by the opportunism of hungry trout which, seeing something alive and smaller than themselves, assume it is *food*.

As to why a sea trout should take a wet fly, there can be less certainty. Many experienced game fishers believe that the most common reasons are the triggering of an instinct of aggression (since sea trout are predators immediately prior to entering fresh water), or the desire to defend the territory of a temporary lie. I am convinced that there is more to it than this. Neither of these theories can adequately explain why a sea trout which has been resting in a pool for some weeks will follow a fly for several yards before cruising back to its deep-water lie. I suggest that both trout and sea trout will, given no reason to suspect the presence of danger, respond to that primeval instinct which brings about the downfall of so many higher mortals – curiosity.

19 River Trout

Is it sensible to try and find out the reasons for trout or sea trout taking a wet fly? The angler has several needs in common with a river trout. A trout needs shelter and protection from the dangers of predators; humans need that too. And a trout has a distinct aversion to large amounts of physical exertion. It prefers to avoid fast-water lies. Sea trout are an altogether different proposition. They have no real need of food whilst in the river. (They may begin feeding on flies after they have spent many weeks or months in fresh water, but through most of the season the assumption that they feel no urge to feed appears to be generally valid.)

How strange, then, that this wet-fly method, so successful in deceiving the brown trout, will also tempt its migratory cousin. This is the case not only as the migrant enters the first freshwater pool, when memories of the rich feeding grounds of the estuary must still be fresh, but also after many weeks of fasting in the turgid pools of a river in summer drought.

The Basic 'Across-and-Down' Method

In its simplest form, this technique involves casting a fly, or a team of flies spaced along a leader, across the stream so that it swings through an arc beneath the surface. By gradually lengthening the line or pacing steadily downstream, you can thoroughly search a stretch of river for fish which may be invisible due to the depth or colour of the water. Accurate casting is not essential, as the current will ensure that the fly passes the nose of your quarry. In fast water, fish often hook themselves as they turn after seizing the fly, and for this reason some anglers consider this to be a crude way of catching trout. Certainly, when applied indiscriminately it is a method likely to take a high proportion of undersized fish. But, as we will see later, there are occasions where wet-fly fishing can be both effective and selective, provided it is applied skilfully.

An important aspect of across-and-down fishing is timing the strike. Tighten too quickly and the fish will feel the hook before turning its head; too late and the trout might be able to eject the hook. Tightening too quickly is a common failing when fishing for large trout or sea trout, which need to be given plenty of time to turn their heads. Unfortunately, there is no simple rule as to how long you should wait before tightening. Length of line in the water, speed and depth of water as well as the size of both fish and fly must figure in the equation. Fortunately, the larger the fish, the less likely it is to eject the fly if you delay tightening beyond the optimum.

Some anglers prefer to rely on the fish hooking themselves, and there is a simple way of achieving this more often than not. All you have to do is leave an arc of line between the top of your rod and the surface of the water.

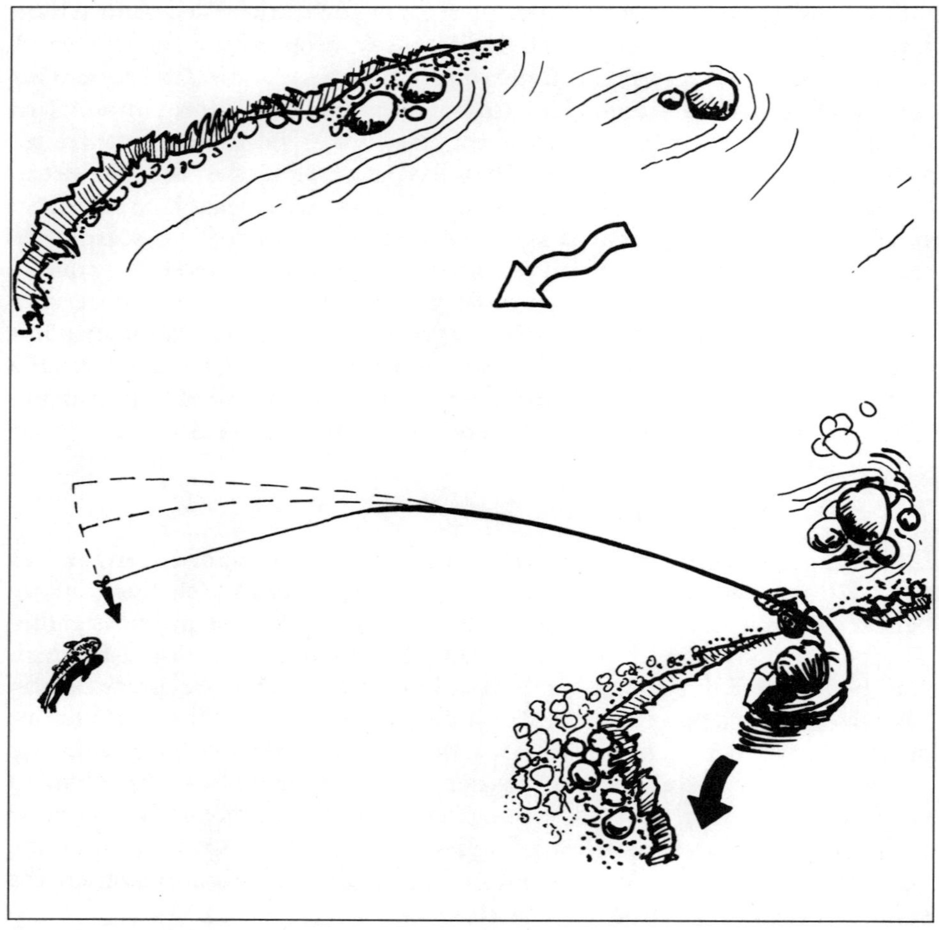

An angler on the river bank casting a wet fly across and down.

When fishing for small trout a few inches of arc will be enough, but for large sea trout you will need to allow at least a foot of arc.

You may prefer to take some positive action in setting the hook. In this case allow rather more line to arc down on to the surface and watch for the initial tightening of this slack line which is indicative of a take. To set the hook, pull down sharply with your left hand before raising the rod to maintain pressure on the hook hold. This method of striking creates far less surface disturbance than the traditional snatching upwards of the rod. It is also faster and, should you fail to make contact, does not send your fly careering out of control into the trees behind you.

For downstream trout fishing, heavily dressed wet flies such as the Peter Ross and Mallard and Claret are excellent fly representations. Sizes 10 to 14 are effective for both spring and autumn trout. They can be fished on a short line when there is plenty of colour in the water, but in clear conditions you will get better results if you fish 'fine and far off'. This will avoid you or your nylon leader giving the game away to your quarry.

Upstream Wet-Fly Fishing

Here you cast your fly upstream and across. After allowing the fly to sink towards the river bed, retrieve line (either by raising your rod or by pulling in line with your left hand) so that you bring the fly towards you across the current. This behaviour is representative of a hatching insect. The problem now is in spotting the take. Provided that you do so and react reasonably quickly, very few fish will be missed, since you are pulling the hook into the scissors of the jaws of the fish.

Lightly dressed wet flies in sizes 14 to 16 are more imitative of hatching insects. Try the traditional northern spider patterns such as Partridge and Orange or Snipe and Purple.

Nymph Fishing

Many aquatic flies spend a year or more in nymphal form, as insects, crawling in the mud and gravel of the river bed, or swimming or darting amongst stones or weed. Many of these nymphs are taken by trout which nose them out of their hiding places. Rather fewer fall victim when, ready to hatch into flies, they make the perilous ascent to the surface. Quite the smallest proportion of a trout's diet consists of flies which have left the water and returned either as duns or spinners.

Nymph fishers attempt to imitate both the immature nymphs and, more often, the adult nymph as it prepares for hatching. An artificial nymph can be made to creep slowly along the bottom, or to rise up towards the surface in a manner which many trout find quite irresistible. A reluctant fish will often respond to this 'induced-take' technique. It is rather like a person who, having taken something for granted, suddenly becomes aware of what they could be about to lose when it is almost too late to prevent the loss.

Nymph fishing is a three-dimensional challenge. The imitation is usually cast upstream, or upstream and across, so that it sinks towards the river bed as the current carries it downstream. By greasing just part of the leader, the nymph can be made to swim at the required depth. Takes show up as a dipping or a sideways pull of the leader, and these indications may be difficult to spot in rippling water. In clear water, where you are stalking individual fish, you may be able to see the trout react as your nymph passes its head. In deep water, you may not be able to distinguish the outline of the trout clearly, but when it opens its jaws to seize your nymph the white of its tongue should be easily spotted. This is the moment to begin tightening your line to set the hook.

Many successful nymph fishers, including the late Frank Sawyer, a famous Hampshire river keeper, and Arthur Cove, who has devised some very successful tactics for use on stillwaters, have asserted that nymph fishing yields trout of larger average size than any other method. I am inclined to agree with them.

Dry-Fly Fishing

A suitably buoyant artificial fly can be made to represent an insect which alights on, or has recently hatched at, the surface of the water. Dry-fly

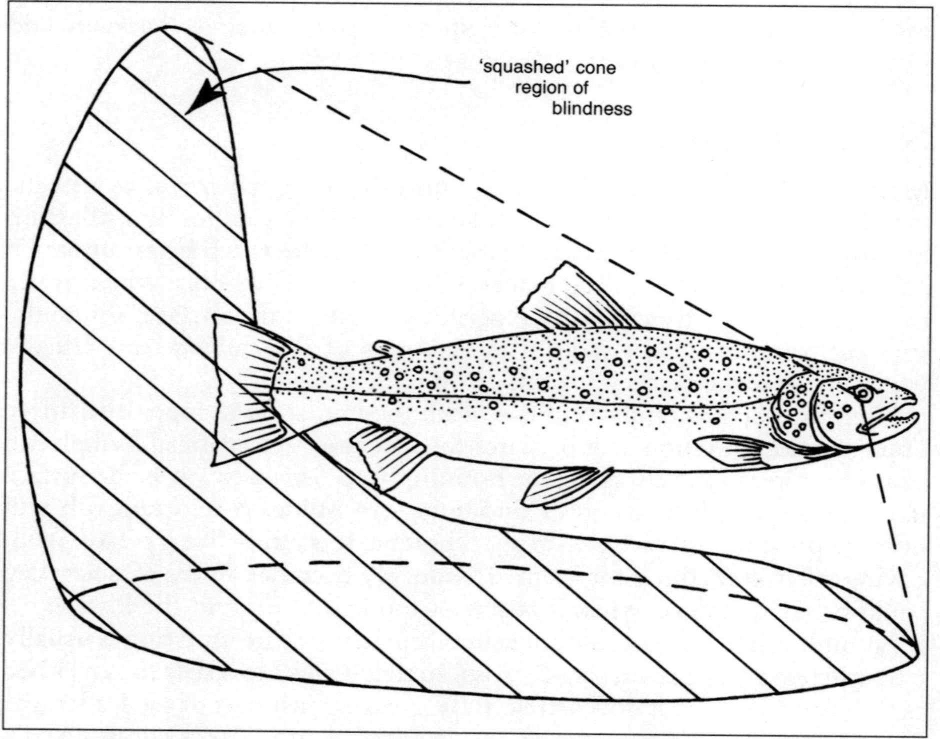

A trout has a very wide angle of vision, with only a narrow region of blindness below and to the rear.

fishing involves casting a fly, usually, but not always, upstream towards a feeding trout. There is something particularly satisfying about casting to and rising a particular fish, and, for me, this makes dry-fly by far the most exciting style of trout fishing. There are times when fish are determined to remain at the river bed, and it is a case of fish a sunk fly or catch nothing, but if there is any chance of enticing a trout with a floating fly, then I readily foresake all other techniques.

The easiest way to fail with the dry fly is to let the fish see you. So, as you walk to the bottom of the stretch you intend to fish, keep well away from the river's edge. Then, moving slowly back up, listen and watch for rising fish. If you cannot see the trout, watch for a while and try to decide whether it is a sizeable specimen or a juvenile fish. When fishing a rough stream, there may be no sign of rising fish. Then you may choose to 'fish the water', by casting your fly into likely lies. (On chalk streams, fishing the water is frowned upon, and on certain beats it is not allowed.)

When you see a fish rise, note the position and give it time to return to its lie, which will usually be a foot or two upstream of where he took the fly. Position yourself so that the risk of drag on your line is minimized and

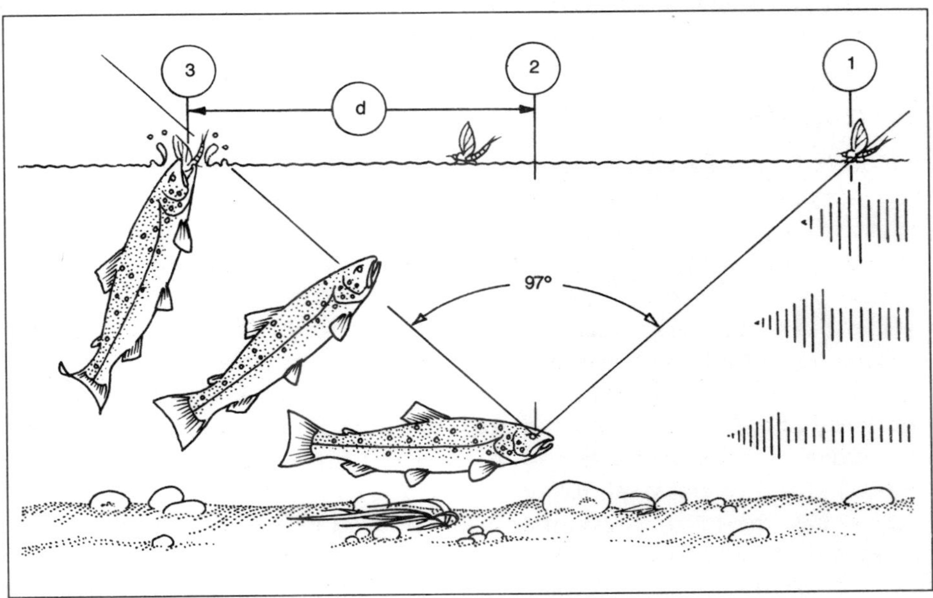

The centre of the rise occurs at a distance, d, downstream from the lie of a trout, depending upon the depth at which the trout lies and the strength of the current. A dry fly should be cast so that it enters the trout's window naturally, at position 1.

make your first cast a little short of the range you judge to be required. This first tentative cast acts as a 'sighter', and allows you to adjust line length more accurately before putting your fly across the trout. It is important to avoid casting too far, as the splash of your fly line falling in its window will certainly put any self-respecting trout down.

Retrieving Line

When fishing upstream wet fly, nymph or dry fly, you must keep in contact with your fly so that you can react quickly if a trout takes it. As your fly touches down, hook the line over a finger of your rod hand so you can clamp the line tightly if you need to strike. Then, as the fly drifts back towards you, retrieve line with your left hand (if your rod is in your right). Avoid allowing too much slack line to lie on the surface, or you will not be able to tighten quickly enough should a trout take your fly. When you lift off to cast again, avoid snatching. Peel the line smoothly from the water to minimize the surface disturbance.

For short-range fishing (on small streams you rarely have the opportunity for anything else) the retrieve can be made by steadily raising your rod as the fly drifts towards you, and then flicking it back gently and recasting in a single smooth action.

Setting the Hook

If your choice of fly is acceptable, and assuming you present it with the necessary accuracy and delicacy, the trout will take it. Tighten into the fish by drawing in line with your left hand. Now raise the rod steadily towards the vertical to absorb any shock as the trout realizes its mistake and dives for the river bed.

There is no need to snatch violently to set a hook. Think of it as merely tightening the line and keeping it in tension so that the fish hooks itself Speed of reaction can be most valuable sometimes, but being able to control the speed of tightening is much more important. For example, you will find that when a large trout takes your fly in slow or moderately flowing water, you will need to delay the strike for perhaps half a second or more so that the fish has time to turn downwards. Then the hook has something to make contact with, and you are not merely pulling it out of the mouth of the trout. In contrast, if you fish the dry fly or nymph for wild brown trout on a mountain stream it is unlikely that your reactions can ever be too fast. These trout are very quick to eject the fly when they detect the deception. It is as if all aspects of their life are played out at an increased pace compared with their lowland brethren.

19 River Trout

A trout being played – the rod is kept well up to absorb shocks.

When fishing for sea trout in spring a rapid tightening is neither necessary nor conducive to secure hooking. In most cases the fish will have moved quite some distance to take your fly and it is better to give it time to turn back towards its lie. Then it doesn't matter if it does open its jaws, since any slack line trailing downstream will pull the fly deep into the scissors, quite the most secure place for hooking. It takes nerves of steel to do nothing at all when you are convinced that a large sea trout has hold of your fly, and perhaps nothing but a few bitter disappointments can convince you that the fish will more often hook itself than be hooked by a hasty strike on your part.

Summer sea trout resting in quiet pools are an altogether different proposition. When the river is very low the sea trout become stale and lazy, only taking a fly if it moves tantalizingly close to their noses. As an indication of the take, all that may register on the line is a tiny vibration, a momentary tightening or slackening. To hook the sea trout you must tighten the line immediately and firmly, keeping it really tight so that as the fish shakes its head the hook is not allowed to come free. Hold the rod high to absorb the impact of that first lunge, for all his lethargy will have been shaken off and your sea trout will use every trick in the book before surrendering to your rod. You must try to avoid letting the line fall slack if the fish runs towards you. You will lose very few trout with a tight line even when fishing with flies tied on barbless hooks.

Playing and Landing a Fish

There must be more riverside stories exchanged on the subject of the one that got away than just about any other fishing topic. And yet, as you may have noticed, some people do seem to be much 'luckier' than others. While there must always be an element of luck in fishing, averaged over the season I believe luck is but a small contributor to results. Good (appropriate) tackle can make a difference, but there is no dismissing the

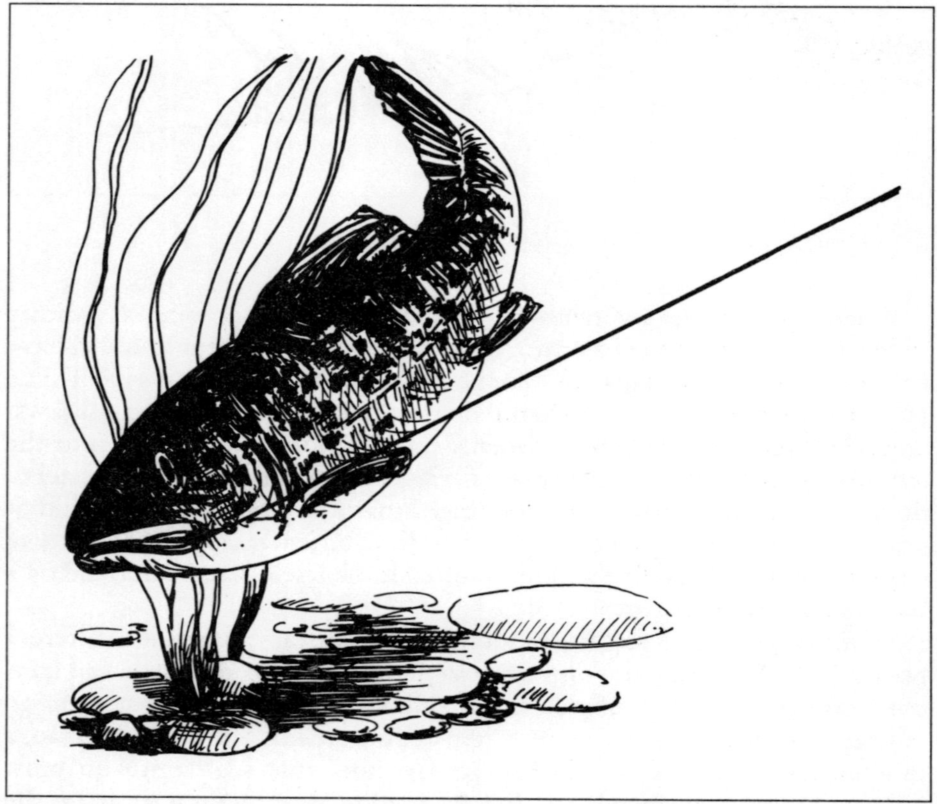

This trout has been hooked in the scissors of its jaws as it turned down after taking an artificial fly.

importance of technique – using the tackle to its fullest potential to present the fly adequately. More good fish are lost within a yard of the net than at any other point during the fight.

It is possible to plan the playing and landing your catch and in so doing ensure that you come off the victor more often. What generally happens the moment you tighten or strike depends on what sort of fish and of what size, and on the nature of the fishery itself. If the fishery holds a variety of species then one thing that will help you decide on tactics is being able to identify your catch early in the fight. Brown trout generally try to bore down to the bed of the river very soon after hooking. The larger specimens are usually solitary fish which will head for the safety of whatever cover they can find. On shallow streams, weed beds and snaggy bank-side holes act as magnets for these trout, while on larger rivers, trout hooked in shallow water invariably head towards the deeper trenches. Their runs follow the contours of the bed of the river, sometimes leaving the line snagged around boulders, submerged tree trunks or other hazards. Keeping the fish up in the water away from these snags must be your top priority on weedy or rocky fisheries.

Playing a Trout in Weedy Glides

On chalk streams it is usually best to play a brown trout on the surface despite the risk of sudden strain on the leader as the fish leaps clear of the surface. I suggest you avoid using very fast action rods for just this reason. A softer action absorbs the transient shocks and allows you to apply a higher average strain with safety. This makes it easier to turn a fighting fish without the leader breaking or the hook pulling free. Rainbow trout, unless hooked in deep water, tend to leap for the first few seconds of the fight, and display less tendency to dive for weed. Large rainbows can be quite determined fighters, however, and may very quickly strip the line to the backing. Their initial runs are often relatively straight, either upstream or down, away from the pull exerted by the line. The traditional advice is to lower the rod tip when you see the fish leap, and at short range this can be an effective method of reducing leader strain. When you have many yards of line in the water, drag prevents the shock transients being transmitted to the rod, so the strain must be borne by the hook-hold and the leader.

Sea Trout in Deep Pools

Sea trout usually leap both at the instant of hooking and also repeatedly during the fight. A tail-walking five-pounder is an awe-inspiring sight and quite enough to strike fear into the most implacable of fly fishers. When hooked in deep water, a sea trout is usually reluctant to leave the pool, and if you play it carefully it can be encouraged to fight in a restricted area, leaving the rest of the shoal relatively undisturbed. You can then increase the pressure as the fish is tiring. A firm tightening is needed to set the hook in the bony jaws of a sea trout. Thereafter, try to keep the line tight without exceeding the strain used during striking. The important thing is not to bully a large sea trout or it will be off into fast water where you will have much more difficulty in keeping the upper hand.

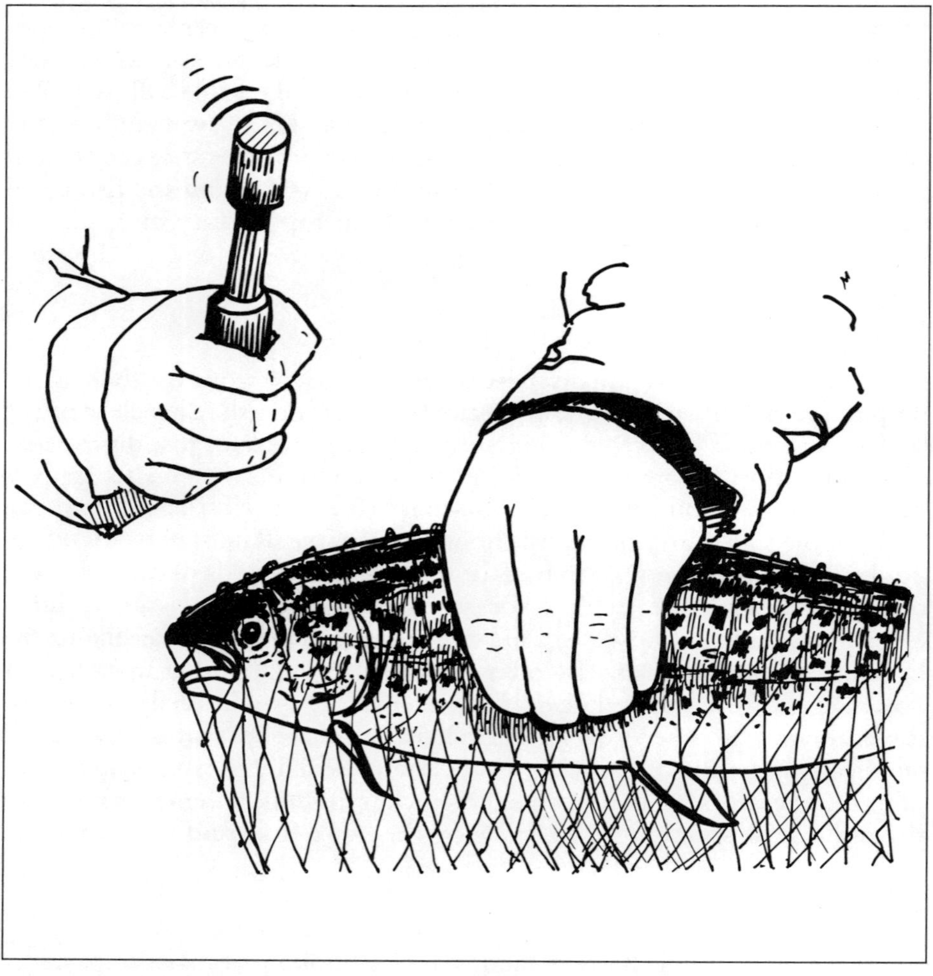

A brown trout, still in the mesh of a landing net, being despatched by means of a priest.

Netting Your Catch

Fish which are to be returned should neither be played to exhaustion nor netted if they can be brought to hand and released while still in the water. It is better to risk the fish escaping than to return it in a condition from which it cannot recover.

A fish can 'let go' at any time, but it does seem that far too many are lost at the net. It is not uncommon to find that the fly has come loose during netting – a fish 'almost lost'! There is a right way to net a large fish. Play the fish until it turns on its side, when it is ready for netting, then raise your rod to the vertical and bring the fish, head-first, across the surface towards you. Keep the net submerged so that the fish is unaware of its presence until it is over the net. Finally, lift the net and lower your rod to let the line go slack. If the fish is to be killed for eating then dispatch it immediately, while it is still in the net. It is not good to see an angler fumbling with a gasping trout which could be cleanly killed if a proper implement were to hand. Never go fishing without your priest. Stones, fixed fence posts, handles of landing nets and the like are *not* effective substitutes. Below are some of the more common ways in which fish are lost at the net.

Chasing

Here the fish is brought in the general region of the net and then the angler or an 'accomplice' scoops wildly with the net hoping to catch the trout rather as if it were a butterfly. What better way to encourage the fish to make a final desperate lunge for freedom?

Gill Netting

Here the net is kept well up so that the fish has to jump over the rim to get in. Instead, of course, he dives below the rim getting tangled by the gills in the meshing. A quick lift of the net and the fish is pulled a foot or more clear of the surface before crashing back, with injuries to its gill cover, causing an almost certain leader break.

Snagged Droppers

There are times when using a team of flies is appropriate, but fish can easily be lost by hooking the net with a dropper fly while the fish on the point is free to swim away. If a trout has taken the point fly, holding the rod well up should help keep the droppers clear of the net. Ensure that the head of the fish is kept above surface as it is brought towards you. Then

A larger-than-life dry fly drifting among a heavy hatch of natural olive duns. It has attracted the attention of a trout, which can dimly be seen below the surface.

it cannot dive beneath the net leaving your leader attached thereto by the dropper.

Just as serious a threat occurs if the trout has taken your dropper. Now the point fly is trailing behind and could easily catch on bank-side weeds, leaving the fish dangling and you quite helpless to control it. If the trout makes a dash for such an obstruction, push the rod tip out across the water to turn your fish away from the snag.

20

Stillwater Trout

by Bob Church and Charles Jardine

THE STILLWATER EXPLOSION

Where did the many thousands of dedicated stillwater fly fishers spring from? Like me, most had a coarse fishing background and this basic grounding in watercraft helped in the conversion to the fly. Those who trout-fish only in the coarse fishing season from mid-March to mid-June may then decide to put their fly gear away and return to tench and carp. This dual affection tends to dwindle after a year or two when they discover just what they have been missing in July and August.

If you must go coarse fishing, do try to fit in a trip or two in between. You will not be sorry as reservoir fish are in the peak of condition in these months. The fly is at its peak too, with sedges hatching in greater numbers as the summer goes on, providing the cream of our sport – casting to rising fish full of life. If you are a devout bank fisher, then try to concentrate on the last two hours at dusk, and pick a sheltered bay where the fly is hatching in profusion in shallow, weedy margins. Then you can fish nymphs, wet or dry flies with confidence. Stay with the trout a little longer. You will not be disappointed.

Make your fly fishing more interesting by travelling around the fisheries. I have a soft spot for the west of Ireland where the immense limestone loughs of Conn, Corrib and Mask beckon me with their beautiful wild brown trout. When I can, I try to enter the World Wet Fly Championships held each year on Lough Mask in August. Around five hundred fly fishers contest four days of eliminators, the final being fished by the surviving hundred and twenty anglers. In my opinion Mask is the most wild and challenging trout water in Europe. Scattered with a myriad of islands, its great depths are punctuated with rocky shoals and reefs lurking just beneath the surface. Drifting over these limestone knife-edges provides the finest fly fishing you will ever experience. If you ever consider a holiday in Ireland it is best to hire a boat and an experienced local boatman. These men

know all the most productive areas and are well aware of the ever-present dangers.

FIND YOUR FISH

American sport fishers, with their plugs and spoons, have developed what they call structure fishing which they employ not only for trout but for other sporting species like small-mouth bass. We should take note of what they do as their style can be easily applied to our own methods. My own results over the past twenty-five years have proved beyond any doubt that this is so.

Their highly successful method is based on the location of any prominent underwater feature. Where do rabbits live? Certainly not in the middle of an open field but in a hedgerow. Thus river anglers look to the head of a pool or to its nooks and crannies where a fish might lurk, and pay scant attention to wide, open, featureless stretches. In a still water, such hidey-holes could be weed beds, submerged hedges and ditches, boat jetties, towers, shallows surrounded by sudden deeps and especially the line where shallows plunge into depths. Locating a trout by seeking out its likely habitat is vital. If you cannot find them you surely will not catch them.

Location is the starting point for all that we do. Boxes stuffed with every fly under the sun will be useless scraps of feather if the fish are not there. Sometimes only quite small areas of even the largest fisheries will hold any trout. In the case of Rutland Water this means the bottoms of the two giant arms where the water is shallow. We are speaking now of the better fish, not the newly introduced stock fish which tend to be found wherever they are put in.

There is definite proof, gained from experiments at Rutland Water, that brown trout feed heavily at night and in the early mornings, on the shallows, before retiring to the depths for the daylight hours. Fisheries Officer David Moore and I became convinced of this feeding pattern after discovering large shoals of brown trout lying quite stationary thirty feet down in seventy feet of water. David first found this concentration of suspended brown trout while experimenting with a new depth sounder. The trout pin-pointed almost to the foot, we took a good number of them to over three pounds and all were stuffed to the gills with the sort of food you would only find on the shallows.

The amount of light is the key factor governing trout movement for much of the season. The more light, the less fish will be found high in the water or on the shallows. Remember that sunlight in June, July and August will have a more adverse effect than it would both earlier and later in the year. The effect on darker, peaty lochs is less than on clear-water lakes. The darker and more overcast the day the higher the all important *Daphnia* will be in the water column. If it is gloomy and windy too then they will be concentrated in great clouds on the downwind shore line. There are no prizes for guessing where the trout will be.

The spawning urge really gets the trout moving from the sanctuaries in the depths on to the shallows. In large natural lakes, trout will move into the mouths of the feeder streams first. Happily this happens at the season's end, in October, and so big catches of spawn-carrying brown trout are avoided. Trying to put one of the really big stillwater trout into the net is an exciting challenge requiring a high degree of dedication. Fishing in April and May probably gives a better chance of connecting with a big brown when they are in tiptop condition.

However, late on in the season, both species behave in a similar manner, turning their undivided attentions to the massive shoals of coarse fish fry. The bank-bound fly fisher's best chance of connecting with one of these big fish is a dawn start. Loch-style fishing can be forgotten and lying at anchor over known fish-holding spots is the boat angler's best bet.

CHOICE OF EQUIPMENT

During the past twenty-five years the popularity of stillwater fly fishing has risen by leaps and bounds and the tackle shops are filled with a bewildering array of gear, all of which the beginner will be convinced he must have. In truth, much of it is designed for special techniques so even if you are feeling financially flush, do not rush out and buy the most expensive rod in the shop. The chances are that it will be designed for a kind of fishing outside your present level of skill or interest. Far better to select versatile equipment at middle-of-the-range prices to begin with. You would be surprised just how many beginners take up the sport and buy on impulse only to regret their rashness when experience has proved their expensive folly.

The First Rod

The choice of the first rod is vital. Assuming you are going to fish the bigger reservoirs in the main, with just the odd visit to smaller waters, I would not hesitate in recommending a medium-actioned rod nine and a half feet long. Forget all the nostalgia about split cane – it is far too heavy. Fibreglass rods too, are not really worth a second thought. The only sensible choice is carbon fibre or those with the addition of boron. I find some Kevlar rods too rigid and breakages have been high, so steer clear of them. It is true to say that even the cheapest carbon rods are better than anything made in glass or cane.

The variations in rod actions are a matter of personal choice. Rods are no more than an extension of your arm, so the one that feels comfortable has to be the one to choose. Rods range from light, crisp-actioned sorts which take very light lines, to specialist eleven and twelve footers used for loch-style fishing from a broadside drifting boat. Both these are not for normal bank fishing however, and will not concern the beginner as yet. It is better to go for something which can handle lines rated between seven and eight. Such a set-up will enable you to make the long casts often necessary for successful reservoir fishing.

If the line is too heavy, the rod will be overloaded and the line will flop down heavily, sending any self-respecting trout running for cover. Most beginners do better with a medium or even a fast-actioned rod. Certainly the stiffer rods allow more line speed to build up when false casting which, in turn, means longer, smoother casts.

The rod bought, you must get down to the business of putting a line on the water. Some find casting difficult to pick up, while others find it quite easy. You do not even need water. A field or your local recreation ground will do fine. The aim is to cast consistently well. A really good caster is not conscious of what is happening. It just happens.

Casting is all about rod power, line speed and timing. The line must straighten out behind then power forward to land smoothly on the water. Sounds easy doesn't it? And so it is, as long as you stick to the basic rules and stay relaxed. The correct stance is with one foot slightly forward so that you can rock backwards and forwards to distribute your weight during the casting sequence. This becomes more important as you cast a longer line. Get the technique right from the start and it's just like riding a bike. It helps if, rather than just thrashing about, you keep what you are trying to achieve firmly in mind, which of course is getting the fly out to the fish.

To begin, draw a few feet of line from the reel and pull it out through the rings. Lifting the rod quickly and smoothly, the short length of line will fly out behind you. Wait for a second until it reaches its full extent before bringing the rod forward at the same speed. The line will fall in a straight line in front of you and that will be your very first cast. It may have been very short, but distance will follow naturally if you stay relaxed and persevere.

Choosing a Reel

The reel is less important in fly fishing than in any other branch of angling. Reels have changed little over hundreds of years. Some may have a more complex drag system but otherwise little has altered. A variable drag is useful when playing big fish but most experienced trout anglers play the fish by holding the line and only use the reel to take up slack line. The single-actioned Rimfly has been the stillwater fly fisher's work horse for decades. They are tough, straightforward and totally reliable. What more could we ask for? The Leeda LC is a great reel too, and will only cost you about £20.

Casting sequence.

It is quite rare to play a fish off the reel as it is far easier to keep a trout rocketing towards you, stripping in the line by hand than winding in, your hand a blur. A danger when using a reel to play a fish, is that it can 'slack line' you by powering away and then, without warning, coming straight back towards you. The sudden loss of tension is quite enough for the hook to fall out. But there are dangers in stripping in line by hand too, as I found out to my cost in a Benson and Hedges match. I had played a trout, of nearly five pounds, close to the boat when it suddenly dived. Swivelling round to keep in contact the loose line caught around my foot. Everything went as tight as a bow string before the nylon parted. So, if you do play fish by hand make a habit of putting the slack line on the reel as soon as it touches the bottom of the boat or the ground.

The Fly Line

The wide selection of lines we have today means that we can reach fish wherever they may be feeding. All the talk about densities and profiles is bound to baffle any beginner but really, there is nothing to it. When I took up trout fishing in 1963 we only had silk lines. If you wanted them to float you greased them up regularly. As soon as you neglected this chore they sank.

Modern lines are about thirty yards long and in either double tapered or weight-forward profile. A cheap one costs about £7 and the best, about four times that amount. The first and most important line to buy has to be a floater. It is more versatile than it sounds as it can be used to fish dry flies, wet flies and nymphs subsurface, and lures in all sorts of ways. A weight-forward Number 7 or 8 is a wise choice. Where you seek distance always go for forward-taper lines. Double-tapered lines are used where accuracy and delicate presentation are the prime considerations.

A slow-sinking line is important in summer when you need to fish three or four feet down to reach the level of fish feeding on nymphs and *Daphnia*, so the beginner will need one of those without any doubt. A line which sinks a little quicker is the one to use in the early season, from the bank when there are good numbers of fish to be caught within comfortable casting distance. So that is another one to consider.

If you can afford it, buy a new floating line at the start of each season. We tend to use them a great deal and they do show the signs of harsh treatment after a few months.

The Leader

Let's begin with those required for general bank fishing. When you are lucky enough to have either a following wind or one blowing from left to right you can get away with a much longer leader than you could in more adverse conditions.

Leader Construction

The only permanent part of the leader is the thicker butt piece – a two-foot-long length of heavy nylon fastened to the fly line with a needle knot. If you form a loop, about two inches long, at its end from then on all the various permutations of leader lengths and strengths can be added with another loop. A typical all-round leader is put together by adding two yards of six-pound nylon to the butt piece and then the same length again, using a water knot, leaving about five inches as a dropper. Then add a further yard with the same knot. You should leave short spurs of nylon about five or so inches long at these joins to form the droppers. With this simple leader you will be able to fish a weighted nymph on the point, something like a Wickham or Invicta on the top dropper and perhaps something drab such as a Pheasant Tail nymph or Stick Fly on the middle position.

You can use exactly the same leader through the summer, the only change being a drop down in nylon strength. The more experienced a fly fisher becomes, the longer the leader he can handle without tangles. It's worth remembering too, that we must shorten everything when attempting to fish into the wind.

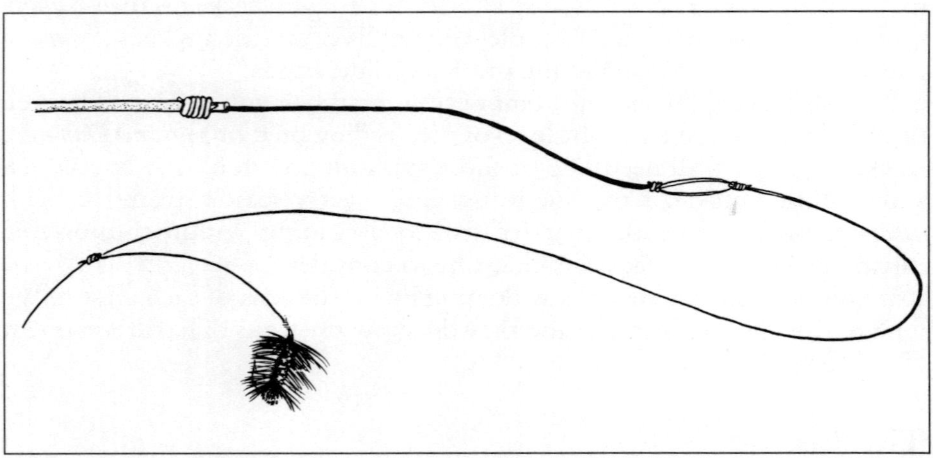

How to connect your leader. Note the permanent loop to which each new leader is attached.

20 Stillwater Trout

THE TROUT'S FOOD AND ITS IMITATION

Let me say from the outset that you do not need to be a genius to evaluate the trout's diet. Indeed, ignorance can be bliss.

There is a simple equation I would like you to consider: water = weed = insects = trout = angler = trout = insect = fly choice. One can even subtract 'weed' but where would we be as fly fishers by subtracting the other parts? So often anglers are content with trout = angler = catch and, laudable as this policy may be, it leaves a gaping hole in our approach with a fly rod and shortcomings when considering tactics. Indeed, far better that we add to the equation 'bait' fish, jointed-limbed creatures such as shrimp and hoglouse and molluscs such as snails.

But how can one deduce the correct candidate? What does it look like? How does it behave? How does the trout react to it? What can the angler use to deceive the quarry? All timeless questions, some of which we have yet to find the answers for. Nevertheless, to give some idea as to, at least, a majority of situations, it would be a good idea to follow seasonal and monthly cycles, offering and highlighting specific species for each. June and September, in particular (but also other months), will be full of variations on one theme, but generally, one type of species will predominate. There may be a variation from water to water so, together with specific insects, I will include at least some local variation.

Lifestyles

Midges

Without question, the most universally important character is the midge or, to give it its fitting title – Chironomidae. There can be few anglers who have not encountered this non-biting mosquito-shaped insect during their angling career. Belonging to the order Diptera (which includes the common house fly), it occurs on probably every water in the land to some degree or other. The family is vast and the variations in size and colour almost infinite.

By and large, chironomids are small. Obviously, one needs a comparison, but sensible and imitative hook sizes start at standard shank 10 going down to as small as 20 and, if one has a penchant or indeed, if confident, 24 and 26. Realistically though, it is seldom necessary to look to sizes lower than 18 in practicable fly fishing situations.

Before progressing, I must just add that many fly fishers refer to this group of insects as 'Buzzers' which is slightly erroneous. They don't all 'buzz' – the noise is generally made when egg-bearing females are making their way back to the water in colonies.

One has to know what one is looking for, however, and indeed, where to find it. In the case of the midge, this is rather less of a problem than with other fauna. Firstly, let me trace its life cycle. The chironomid begins life laid as an egg on the surface. The eggs can be in long strings or globular masses. These, after only a short period, start to contain a tiny worm-like creature which is, in fact, the embryonic larva. These physically wriggle free of the egg and descend to the lake bed. It is here that we, as imitative anglers, enter the scene. This period of development can last anything from three to twelve months, depending on the species.

At this point, the larval life can revolve around many permutations. Generally, it is to be found in waters ranging from three to twenty feet in depth. Here it will carve out one of many varied existences. Some larvae manufacture tube-like tunnels in the silt, often covering one aperture leaving the other for emergence, feeding entirely on the tunnel entrance's webb. Others create cases (rather like caddis), and occasionally, leave this sanctuary on feeding missions. Another variety, and possibly the most important in fishing terms, has a lifestyle which is free-moving and swimming. It is here that many of us have surely cut our entomological teeth, for who has peered into a water butt or perhaps a forgotten watering-can and failed to see the wild thrashing and undulations of bright scarlet worm-like creatures? These are none other than the bloodworm – chironomid larvae. This is rather a misnomer, for not all these larvae are bright red in colour. Indeed, they can vary from very pale buff through browns, encompassing many shades of green, as well as the well-known red variety.

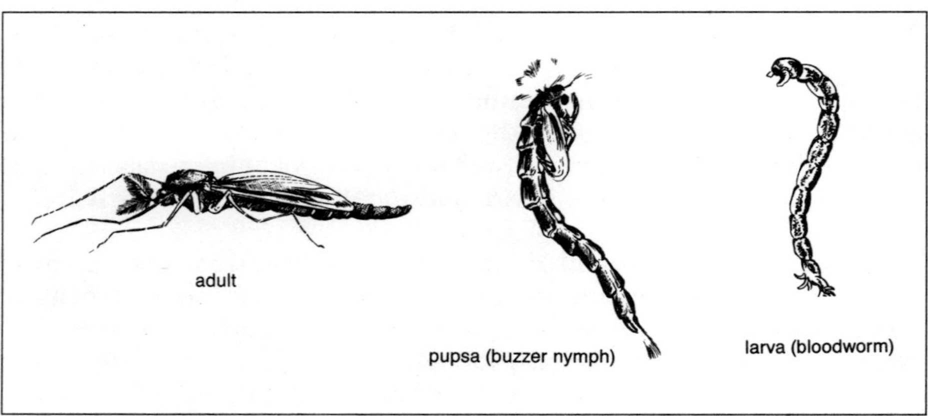

Chironomid (midge, buzzer) stages of development.

Incidentally, the deep redness of many of these larvae types is caused by haemoglobin being present, assisting the creature's oxygen intake allowing it full range of not only a wide variety of habitats but also ones which are both dark and largely devoid of insects. This, in turn, helps the angler as it allows for fishing areas which would possibly prove useless with other insect-based patterns. The one striking feature of this stage of development, even considering its remarkably bright colouration, is its movement – a point Arthur Cove quite revolutionarily embraced, creating his now infamous and lethal 'Red Diddy'. A wonderfully simple concept, it is a thin, curved section of scarlet rubber band, suggesting the wriggling, lithesome figure-of-eight lashings of the natural with almost uncanny realism. Both Taff Price and Peter Lapsley have further elaborated on this theme, utilizing the now commonplace material red or green marabou to achieve the same, perhaps even more sinuous, motion.

Pupae

However, it is the next stage in the insect's life cycle which is perhaps the most important. Certainly, it is the best known – the pupal stage. Yet I believe it is not its sheer volume or colour permutation that makes its appeal so great. Chironomids can be found 'active' for nearly 365 days of the year and on most waters, and it is the pupae that can form the basis of a 'nymph' oriented strategy from the opening of the season to its close. Indeed, it is not unusual, even on quite cold days, to see some evidence of this creature.

Colour

Colours are diverse and sizes almost infinite, yet certain times of the fly fishing year will hold a very definite bias for one or two colours depending on locale. One of the soundest and most enduring axioms in fishing is 'get to know your water', and by heeding it you will most certainly begin to unravel various hatch colour sequences. Over the years, I have developed a modest little theory. Like all ideas, it is fairly generalized, yet it does appear that the colder the weather, the darker the fly; and the coldest part of the spectrum is echoed therein (blacks, blues, dark greens, etc.). April, for instance, sees a predominance of black and grey. As the sun gains more strength, so the dark greens begin to appear until the water temperature begins to rise significantly in mid-May and June, when light olive predominates. In the comparative warmth of, say, July (occasionally June) water, so the fawns, oranges and browns begin to ascend. With the sun at its zenith in late July, August and early September, red prevails, until a point is reached when the colour begins to recede, slipping back into black and greys once more.

Curved or Straight?

Once, when attending a lecture by the entomological enthusiast, Taff Price, I listened in a comparative state of shock as he said he felt midge were often straight and pupae tyings should echo this, as my conception (along with many other anglers), was one of curvature. I now believe he was right – at least in a great many instances. The first thing that one has to bear in mind is that the pupa is a poor swimmer and must feel rather like a paratrooper drifting helplessly into a cauldron of enemy activity, only in reverse, as all the time the pedantic creature is wriggling up from the bottom layers to the surface, it is at the mercy of the avaricious trout.

But, as mentioned earlier, I firmly believe it is weather conditions which suggest when an artificial should be employed to best effect and one occasion which calls for a curved style of dressing is a calm day, particularly when the air is heavy and full of moisture. The water's surface film is extremely thick at such times. I recall a simple test from my formative years, when, at school, we were encouraged to watch a needle floating in a tumbler full of water; of course, the needle was heavier and should have sunk, but the surface tension kept it afloat. It is this factor that makes the surface film the place to be on still, calm or muggy days and evenings if midge are active.

Insects breaking through this barrier, which forms the division between air and water, has been likened to ourselves having to push through four to six feet of earth above us – a prodigious task and one the trout certainly wastes no time in ravenously taking advantage of. Nature is a wonderful arbiter, however, and will create times when midge find airborne transport far easier. These are generally when conditions are rough and the water's surface is broken up with wave action. Then the angler's midge tactics do have to be amended, for the critical depth is no longer the first half inch of surface film, but can be anywhere from two to twenty feet.

As well as being greedy, trout are practised and economic hunters. They will not bother charging after a 'golden fleece' if it is not in their best interests; instead they will dine at leisure during the midges' ponderous ascent to our dimension. This, I believe, is where the straight pupa is at its most effective. I can visualize now, shoals of rainbow scything through the hapless pupae as they rise through the layers. Indeed, there is enormous scope for fishing a very fast-sinking line such as a Wet Cel Hi D Extrafast and a team of pupae, from a boat, in open water, echoing this surfaceward migration. It is during such periods that pupae tactics should also be concentrated in a subsurface two to four foot area.

Often the fish will be cruising without giving the slightest indication of their presence, which leads me to think that certain shoals of trout hunt in different areas, albeit simultaneously. For instance, one concentration of fish may well be following the ponderous climb of the pupae from the lake floor, intercepting them either at this point or in midwater, while a separate shoal will be picking off the straggling survivors in the upper stratas. Hypothetical, I know, but certain instances have definitely indicated these trout feeding divisions to me.

Adult Midges

Finally, we come to the adult. For years this stage of the chironomid's development received little or no attention and what sport we have missed! Indeed, John Goddard, the eminent angling entomologist, felt they were the least important of the cycle, only to reassess the situation totally in *Trout Flies of Stillwater*. Now dry fly fishing is approaching almost cult proportions, the majority of which revolves round this adult stage. In reality, though, the midge's adult life is short-lived. For, on emerging from its pupal shuck, it will rest for only a matter of moments, until its wings are dry enough and transformation is sufficiently complete for take-off – only eight to twelve seconds after splitting its pupal thorax on the water's surface.

One can often see the struggles enacted whilst one is fishing, the shuck being ejected on the water combined with a frantic whirling of movement across the surface of the lake. How could any self-respecting trout not be drawn by the commotion! After skittering for a while, it will then drift up into the air and ultimately mate, the female venturing back to the water to lay the eggs for a next generation, some eight to twelve hours after mating has occurred.

Identifying adults is really quite easy the body is long, fairly thin and clearly banded with a lighter colour. Also, unlike the pupa, it is covered with fine abdominal hair. There are two wings, held closely to and often covering the abdomen and, as with all Diptera, they are flat and hyaline – that is to say, they have an almost clear, shiny quality. The six long legs are quite a noticeable feature, as they protrude from the bulbous thorax or head section, some attaining lengths of a good one and a half times the size of the insect's body. Also issuing from this noticeably chubby thorax (but only in the case of males), are a pair of moustache-like, fluffy antennae. Fortunately, most midges, regardless of colour and size, conform to this shape. The one exception I have found is the large green midge, which has much broader, almost oval, wings, as opposed to the more normal torpedo-like dimensions of other adult chironomids.

Patterns

Over the years, patterns have been developed to accommodate many adult midge instances, especially those of Bob Carnhill and his deadly adult buzzer series which has accounted for legions of trout in many varying situations. However these, by and large, have been fished wet mimicking the drowned insect, sunk by either wave action or vicious bank undertow and related currents. Subsequently, I developed a similar range of patterns, substituting for the soft hen hackle 'high riding' cock hackles, combined with light iron hooks in order to achieve floatability. I was, at the time, blissfully unaware of similar 'minor tactics' being fashioned elsewhere.

This new (to me at least) floating midge exercise worked better than I could ever have dreamed. Not only were rising fish beguiled, these diminutive facsimiles held enough allure to 'ghost up' unseen specimens to the surface. This instance, perhaps more than any other, shows how parallel concepts can evolve almost simultaneously. Grafham, and indeed other, midge-rich waters, have been following this same doctrine in one form or another for a number of years. This proves that the dry midge can be effective, *and* hold very definite attraction for larger than average fish.

Daphnia

During the summer, occasionally even in early-season cold water, one 'animal' can dictate to quite extraordinary lengths, the trouts' location,

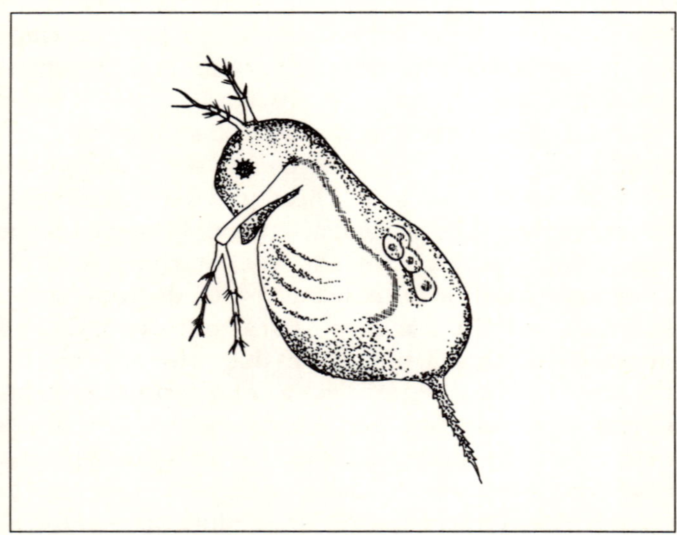

Daphnia *enlarged.*

depth, and even reactions. It is largely inimitable. The humble sounding water flea, *Daphnia* species hold this key. In fact it is a tiny crustacean, the largest being a mighty eighth of an inch long. This diminutive character lends credence to the axiom 'the best things come in little packages', especially if one adds 'when they group together and form vast, glutinous clouds'.

Tactics for Daphnia Feeders

Of course, it has been proven time and time again that trout are eminently catchable feeding on *Daphnia* scything open-mouthed, like basking shark through the hapless concentrations, literally 'souping in' the protein-rich harvest. It is certainly a period very much tailor-made for the lure fisher – a veritable 'orange madness', indeed, a 'green madness' seeming to prevail. This has led directly to the large bright orange and green lures so often used to seduce by colour rather than shape, mimicking the tiny crustaceans' green or orange hues. And yet, as laudable as this policy is, my nymphing philosophies appear not to be compromised, for I have found, by using orange or green thoraxed Pheasant Tails or Arthur Cove's Orange Nymph (indeed, midge pupae in various colours), and the utilitarian Black Long Shank Nymph, one can pander equally well to the trout's dietary fads. The reasoning behind this is quite simple, for I believe that a trout's memory can be triggered, and offering a nymph it may well have fed on only hours previously can bring about a conditioned reflex.

Freshwater Shrimps

The following food forms are nearly found in every water in the land and, without question, sustain trout through the lean, insect-barren months of winter. They are, in fact, a stillwater mainstay.

Two such ebullient little characters are the freshwater shrimp (*Gammarus pulex/lacustris*) and the American resident, *Crangonyx pseudogracilis*. These animals are not 'true' shrimps at all, being amphipods (jointed, limbed beings). Incidentally, the shrimp has fourteen limbs, a number of which are used for a good turn of speed and intricate manoeuvring. The modest difference between the two is movement and colouration. *Crangonyx* flits back and forth in upright mode and is clad in almost transparent blue/grey, whereas *Gammarus* tends to do everything sideways, and its colour can range from dark olive through lighter greens into fawns and browny pinks, even extending to golden yellow/orange. There has been a fair amount of rancour over the last colour scheme. Some say that this is the mating colour, others insist that this tone occurs at the onset of disease and ultimately death.

I tend to favour the former school, for in a lake near my home in Kent, the chalk-rich water gives rise to almost epidemic populations of this amphipod. Strangely, this lake frequently dries up, which manifests several fascinating points. Firstly, the trout's almost total preoccupation with shrimp, there being little other food in the chain. This, in turn, brings about another feature concerning the trout's growth rate which is curtailed by nature's self-imposed drought, then made up for over a shorter span. A fish weighing between one-and-a-quarter to one-and-a-half pounds in April, can increase to two-and-three-quarters to three-and-a-half pounds in September. This is due almost entirely to shrimp feeding.

Almost without exception, these crustacea are a deep golden orange in colour. As the shrimp has no specific mating periods, it may well be that continuous breeding occurs to thwart the ever-present threat of 'dry-up' and the need to produce constant colonies. This is, however, largely guesswork, but it would indicate that the shrimp is very much alive in this golden colour scheme and not in 'death throes'. In any event, trout relish the delicacy.

This invertebrate can be found in just about any weeded area, even in acidic lake crevices. Indeed, it is not uncommon to find innumerable scuttling forms of between half and one inch on pulling up an anchor or bankside weed. This is, of course, the home of the shrimp and leads directly to the correct fly fishing area. So important, I believe its presence to be, that if confined to just one pattern for use on both lake and river, I would, without question, opt for the artificial shrimp, its uses and diversity far outweighing its dowdy appearance.

Shrimp Patterns

There are, of course, a plethora of artificials to choose from. They range from the absurdly, but nonetheless deadly, impressionistic Killerbug of Frank Sawyer (which I endearingly call my 'bedsock fly'), through to the equally persuasive Red Spot pattern of Neil Patterson, which I would never be without, especially on small fisheries, and culminate with the ultra-realistic Marabou interpretation of Peter Gathercole. If fished appropriately, all will catch trout. Their uses are wide and diverse, being general 'search patterns' as well as effective antidotes for cruising or observed trout. The criteria is that somewhere out amidst the lake, there will be a colony of shrimp and a strong possibility that trout, too, will be present.

Hoglice

Though slightly similar, the hoglouse (*Asellus aquaticus/meridianus*) might, at first, appear a poor relation. True, it is lethargic in movement, dull in appearance and, somewhat unsavourily, feeds on rotting lake bed vegetation, yet it has real value to the fly fisher, one that is certainly overlooked on a great many occasions.

This relation to the common woodlouse can be found not only at great depths, but in comparatively large sizes, reaching one inch, further emphasizing the scope for deepwater nymphing techniques. The hoglouse, water slater or (as the Americans call it), sow bug does differ quite markedly, from the shrimp. It is flat as opposed to the rounded, compressed, plated shape of *Gammarus*. The colour differs also, the louse being mottled brown olive on top of a fawny tan base. But similarly to the shrimp, it incorporates two sets of antennae or feelers in the head area and two to the rear aiding its bottom dwelling habits. Size, too, averages that of the shrimp (a third to half an inch).

Fishing strategy should broadly follow that used with *Gammarus*, both lifestyles being similar, only the deep water situation mentioned separating them. It is, however, more normal to seek the shallower areas and is, perhaps, more effective during the insect-sparse early-season period, whilst searching out quiet bays and shallow weeded areas of the reservoir. Trout often forsake the relative safety of deep water in order to harvest the

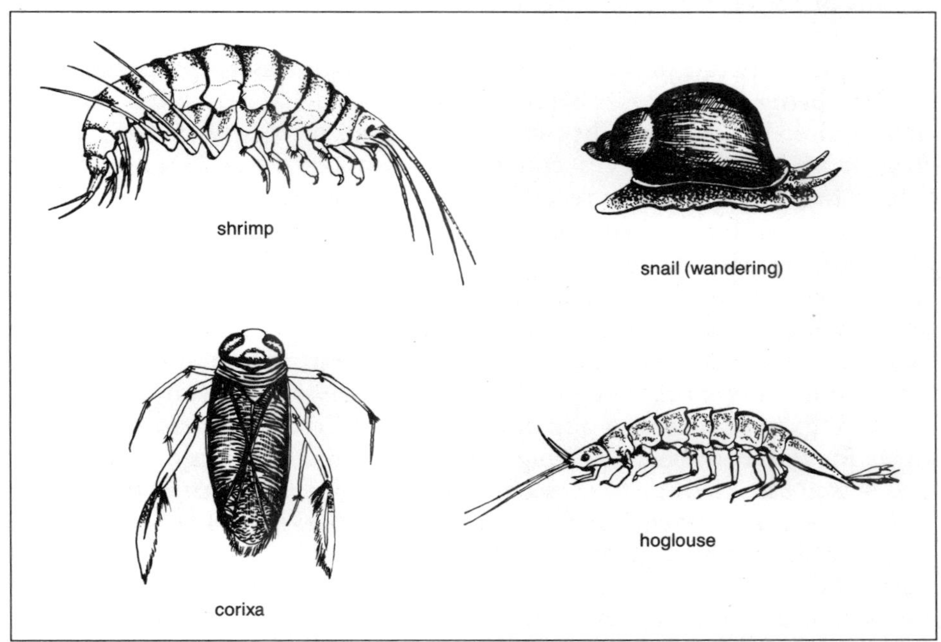

Ever-present food forms.

sometimes dense crops of hoglice. This, of course, fashions our technique, requiring stealth, careful wading (to be discouraged in very shallow water), floating line, long leaders and slow retrieves. Humble though the louse is, be certain always to have at least a couple of patterns in your fly box. It can be a definite case of a pauper turning into a prince. I can recommend Oliver Edwards's pattern as well as Anne Douglas's version.

Corixa

I suspect everyone has 'one of those flies', perhaps two, or, if very unlucky, more! – patterns that simply do not work even given a swimming pool with ravenous trout cheek by jowl. I have several the Dunkeld, Peter Ross and oddly – as this ineffective phenomenon seems to exclude insect based patterns – the corixa. Try as I might, the imitation of this ubiquitous stillwater insect will produce only limited success and then at decidedly odd times. This belies its very real value to the fly fisher. Though outwardly very dissimilar to the previous food forms, it does largely adopt the same habitat, enjoying a wide range of low lying rich reservoirs and relatively acidic upland stillwaters. Colloquially known as the lesser water boatman, it even enjoys the same areas, rejoicing around weeds and in depths of between two and six feet. It is also relatively active throughout the year.

It is probably one of the most readily identifiable reservoir species, most anglers being familiar with the bug's half-inch (and smaller) size and appearance. It has a dark brown mottled shell back (in fact wing cases), pronounced red/brown eyes, creamy white underbody and six legs, two of which being the instantly recognizable oar-like paddles which enable its jet-propulsion from weed bed to weed bed, or surfaceward for necessary stores of oxygen.

Nature has played a nasty trick on the corixa, however, for as fast as its ascent is (and it can resemble a fleeting bolt of silver through the water), in comparison, the descent is both laboured and erratic. Even more hazardous is the bright silver orb-like 'oxygen tank' it brings back from the surface, screaming its presence to any watchful trout. This, conversely, is good news for the fly dresser, offering legion recognition points to copy.

Corixae can often be witnessed flying, which they do over fairly large areas. This generally coincides with the mating periods of late May to early July. We do not know quite why this happens perhaps it is to colonize other parts of the reservoir. However, and importantly for the fly fisher, we do know that the nymph endures as many as five instars (complete moults of nymphal skin) until maturity is finally reached. When these juvenile corixae enter the instar stage, they are a creamy, off-white colour and, as far as I am aware, only Bob Carnhill has noted the significance, especially concerning periods through August and September when, traditionally, great colonies band together along the lake shores. This suggests two things. Either, the juvenile or nymph is joining the adults for the onset of winter or another mating ceremony is entered into. These instances remain hypothetical. One fact does emerge, though. Trout join these gatherings as well, taking full advantage of an almost prepackaged food source.

In summary of the corixa, I can only add that its advantages for the angler, in terms of its ubiquity and valuable fishing opportunities, certainly at specific times of the year, far outweigh my incompetence with this particular artificial. It remains for me a bearable penance which I gladly endure, knowing that if I try long enough, something will happen in the end.

Leeches

Though it may appear unsavoury, this attenuated creature's potential is very real. Trout not only eat it, they appear (in some instances), to be somewhat partial to it. There are, of course, more than one species of leech and it is doubtful if even a ravenous trout would tackle a horse leech which can attain lengths of twelve inches. It is more likely that smaller leeches will be eaten. These will conform, by and large, to either dark brown or dark olive and black shades and all use an undulating, subsurface caterpillar-like movement across their chosen habitat. This is set amid the gloomy surroundings of the lake floor depths. They will venture into upper layers, yet I feel one must realistically see them as a bottom-dwelling creature.

Snails

The last 'constant' major food form in this is, by comparison, mundane. The snail, in its many forms, is vastly important to the reservoir's food chain and diet of the trout. I have caught trout, both in the UK and Ireland, which have rattled audibly, such was the preoccupation with these Pulmonata. There are a plethora of different stillwater-dwelling species in this country, all of which will interest the trout at some point or other. The more common ones include the great pond snail (*Lymnaea stagnalis*), which measures up to two inches and may be of doubtful value, the ¾-inch common wandering snail (*Lymnaea pereger*), which is among the probable trout dietary candidates, the distinctive ramshom (*Planorbis corneus*) and the smaller keeled ramshorn (*Planorbis carinatus*), and the white ramshom (*Planorbis albus*) measuring three-quarters of an inch and a quarter of an inch respectively.

This, of course, is a very small selection of the species, but most conform to similar modes of existence, feeding on algae in and around weed beds, often in quite deep water where they will munch merrily on organic debris, even fish eggs. The shell, though different in construction, does tend to encase a similar shape, the actual gastropod resembling its garden counterpart. It has horns on top of a quite large suction area which it uses rather like a foot to both adhere to objects and vacuum up organic debris into its radula (a toothed, sandpaper-textured tongue), which collects the delicacies to be planted and digested in the mouth.

It is their location, however, which affects our fly fishing approach. So often it is the sole reason for the adage 'slow and deep with a Black and Peacock Spider' during the inhospitable early weeks of the season. For it is, as the aforementioned species, a ubiquitous, seasonal-resilient food item for the trout. There is one exceptional occurrence in its lifestyle which can dramatically mould fly-fishing tactics, and that is the August migration.

We are not absolutely certain as to why great colonies migrate to the surface and drift with the reservoir currents, though it could be due to the need to breathe, absorbing more oxygen at the surface. One might go further and suggest that because this phenomenon coincides with fairly hot weather, it may be an exodus in search of more favourable areas due to their more familiar surroundings shrinking and stagnating through evaporation. Whatever the reason, trout are swift to seize this relatively unexpected feeding bonus, and they can become as preoccupied as when caenis feeding. I have come to the conclusion that this occurrence revolves around the exploits of the wandering snail (*Limnaea pereger*).

Strangely, although accurate floating patterns such as the cork bodied Cliff Henry pattern and Bob Church's Black Deer Hair pattern would both seem perfect remedies, it does appear that, once again, a certain 'orange madness' will prevail. Whether this is due to the mollusc's shell showing an orangy brown when viewed against light, or whether trout merely find the colour synonymous with snail feeding activity, we don't know. However, an orange dry fly or Cove's Orange Nymph can often prove the fish's undoing when 'fished through' populations of snail.

Sedges

This leads us to what can be best described as the 'super hatches' and, though these may at first appear cyclical, I feel that their influence spans a much wider period. Certainly, this is the case of the Trichoptera, colloquially known as sedge and often referred to as caddis. These will probably need little introduction as they are almost the harbingers of long, silken summer evenings, when the adults dance and pirouette across the darkening water's surface and bank-side foliage, fading to indigo in the night shadows. Yet it is during the bleak, inhospitable opening weeks that their journey starts, for, stirring amidst the winter-rotted vegetation, entombed in a cold, grey waterscape, there resides the chameleon of the insect world the cased larvae or caddis.

One would be forgiven for thinking that the familiar homes of tubular construction, dotted with bits of lake bed debris, are common to all species. Not so. Certain varieties of sedge will manufacture residences from different materials. This can give the angler at least an approximation as to certain colonies' locations. For instance, the larvae of the great red sedge will utilize bits of leaf and weed, cemented into a tapered spiral shape; the grousewing favours grains of sand and a slightly curved shape; longhorn species, weed and sand tapered and curved; the brown sedge, two long twigs laid over a fine gravel base, and so on. However, all have one thing in common they move ponderously and painfully slowly, with only the bulbous head section emerging, together with their six stubby, strong legs for propulsion. Some larvae are, to be accurate, free-swimming (*Rhyacophila*), whilst others fashion a silken anchor rope and attach themselves to rocks, posts and other stable underwater constructions. Both these types do tend to be river oriented species, yet observations would

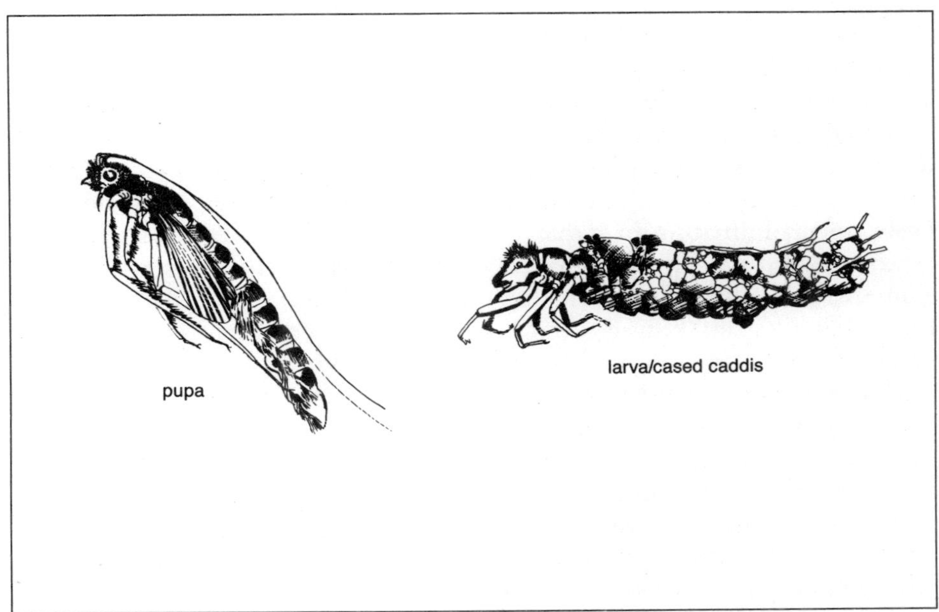

Sedge/caddis stages of development.

suggest at least some form of free-swimming species do exist in stillwater. Both I and Brian Harris, have witnessed large green larvae in Bewl Water.

This may be 'gilding the lily', but what is certain is that caddis imitations such as Stickflies, long-shank Goldribbed Hare's Ear or Harris Marabou-tailed Stick all work during the early months and, indeed, throughout the season. I feel it is lure fishing to some degree, for to mimic the slothful, trundling caddis would require a figure-of-eight retrieve to last some eight to twelve hours! I have not the patience. Thankfully, our erroneous stabs at imitation are met with approval from the trout.

Pupation

On pupation, the larva will spin itself a trapdoor over the case and metamorphose within, changing from the sombre larva into the often brightly coloured pupa. Within this time span, lasting anything from a matter of days to several weeks, wing buds will grow, legs will lengthen and antennae will form. When sufficiently evolved, the pupa will burst free, entering a watery world where it will either crawl along the bottom for hatching on dry land, or, more importantly for the trout fisher, lethargically swim up to the surface in a stop/start mode of rising and falling undulations. It is during such times that the greatest predation occurs.

I wish I could be of some help in identifying pupae with the resultant adult. It appears that this is problematic, even for practised zoologists. Suffice to say, that by carrying a variety of suitably shaped, sized and coloured examples, most situations can be covered. The pupal form has long found favour with the fly dresser, starting with Dr Bell's still effective pre-war pupae pattern, extending to John Goddard's series in the mid-1960s and culminating in, what I feel are now 'state of the art' accurate, renditions by Paul Jorgensen, the great American fly dresser, Gary La Fontaine the caddis aficionado, and our own Gordon Fraser. All three have created lifelike and 'killing' versions which should be carried in hook sizes of std 10 to 18 in colours ranging from pale fawny yellow through to amber, encompassing the greens such as sea-green, and extending to dark olive, also brown.

Generally, sedge emergences coincide with the settled weather conditions; even in rough weather, the hatching period of afternoon and early evening usually combines with moderating wind strength. Thus, the surface tension will be at its most dense, giving rise to the familiar insect struggles for life. I believe it is no accident that James Ogden's perennial Invicta is then at its most deadly – mimicking the natural's state of dishevelment. At this juncture, the pupae splits its sheath-like skin along its entire upper length by internal pressure, resulting in a tangle of unopened embryonic wings, gangly legs and curled antennae. This is echoed perfectly in the Invicta's ragged appearance – a point that Steve Parton has also included in his range of Sienna, Green and Orange Sedges. This ragged tangled appearance is an important recognition factor for both trout and fly dresser.

Adult Sedges

Finally, the adult emerges, laying justifiable claim to its Trichoptera lineage. It is roof-winged, of which there are four – two under- and two marginally longer overwings, slightly hair-fringed. These, in turn, cover a tail-less segmented body, ending in a comparatively small head which is mostly taken up with a hair-surrounded eye. Two noticeably long antennae either sweep forward or curl backwards over the wing, depending on species. Most fly fishers will be familiar with this appearance, but may not realize that some varieties enjoy an afternoon emergence (these tend to be smaller and more hirsute), while others hatch more familiarly, in the evening. This, of course, does have great bearing on tactics, making dry fly fishing viable for a longer period.

There are a multitude of caddis species a flight in this country, a large proportion of which are important to the stillwater fly fisher, but thankfully a 'top ten' does exist. These are the third-of-an-inch grousewing (*Mystacides longicornis*), the great red sedge or murragh (*Phrygania grandis/striata*) measuring a succulent three-quarters of an inch to an inch, the various silverhorns (*Athripsodes* sp.), a third to half an inch, silver (*Odontocerum albicorne*), a half to two-thirds of an inch, caperer (*Halesus radiatus/digitatus*), three-quarters of an inch to an inch. There are, of course, many more, but I believe it would serve little use to extend the list, for I have found that when trout are feeding on these often hyperactive 'V' waking forms, they are decidedly catholic in their tastes, the caddis's airborne struggles proving to be the trigger factor.

This, in my experience, obviates the need for ultra-close imitation. In fact, I now use, almost exclusively, the Troth 'Elk Hair Caddis'. It floats, wakes and masquerades as an adult sedge to a tolerably close degree, and it certainly proves attractive to adult-searching trout in a great many conditions.

The final, or egg-laying stage of the caddis's life, has largely been overlooked, but provides vast scope both, strangely, in the 'wet' sense – some sedge species actually diving under the water to lay their eggs (oviposit) – and the more accepted 'dry' spentwing characteristic, when the female is either in her exhausted death throes or completely vanquished. In the latter cases, the four wings are outstretched and, importantly, *in* the surface film. The first instance of the female's 'last rites' brings about a wonderful contradiction, inasmuch as a leaded streamlined dry fly seems to be the best choice!

My experiments over the years have led me to realize that there are very definite times and places when the second instance of the spentwing should be deployed. I seek out (generally in the dawn period), any build-up of the previous evening's thick surface film. This, in turn, has led me to such places as bays, windward banks and dam walls. The use of fairly accurate spentwing tyings is beneficial and, on some occasions, essential to success. Indeed, having mentioned the impressionistic Elk Hair, I feel it important to add that, at times of flat calms, one should also carry some realistic examples of adult resting sedges such as Tentwings.

Upwinged Flies

I suspect that everyone has a favourite species – one that sends the angler into raptures on its appearance. My pulse quickens when I encounter the first olive of the year. I fully realize that they are not nearly as important as, say, caddis or midge, yet the armada of tiny grey upright, yacht-like wings, setting sail and coursing across the wavelets, somehow seems to herald fly fishing in its purest sense – perhaps it is the river fisher in me. There are, in comparison to other food forms, remarkably few of the Ephemeroptera to interest the trout on stillwaters in this country and, though widely distributed, they emerge in rather small colonies when talking in terms of specific species such as the large summer dun (*Siphlonurus lacustris/ alternatus*), the claret dun (*Leptophlebia vespertina*) or the autumn dun (*Ecdyonurus dispar*), even the regal mayfly (*Ephemera danica/vulgata*). Yet, where the mayfly does occur, notably on the Irish limestone loughs, it does so in vast numbers.

Some species, however, enjoy very wide and dense populations, notably the pond olive (*Cloeon dipterum*) and the lake olive (*Cloeon simile*). For the southern angler, the April appearance of the sepia dun (*Leptophlebia marginata*) must fall into this category, as does an old friend (though you may blanch at its inclusion), the diminutive *Caenis*, collectively known as broadwing, though perhaps more appropriately entitled the 'angler's curse'. Thankfully, all follow a similar emergence pattern: egg – nymph – dun (subimago) – spinner (imago) . The first division between species occurs in the nymphal form, the different shapes pertaining to different lifestyles and species.

20 STILLWATER TROUT

The Nymphs of Upwinged Flies

The mayfly nymph is classified a 'bottom burrower' and is, of course, only useful to the angler when emerging prior to hatching. The stone clingers (autumn dun), again because of their reluctance to move, also belong in this group, as do moss creepers. Laboured swimmers (claret dun) and silt crawlers (*Caenis*), however, can be efficacious although they play a secondary role to the most significant group – the agile darters (large summer dun, pond and lake olives). These, as their name indicates, lead a fairly vivacious existence, generally flitting from weed bed to weed bed, appearing never to stay still for more than a few seconds at a time. Broadly speaking, this particular group conforms to a similar colour scheme of drab browns, through dark olive to almost transparent light olive yellow. In order to determine these various groups, I have provided an illustration which will, perhaps, serve better than words.

I will continue with the agile darters, for they offer true fishing potential. As mentioned, their life revolves around the shelter of weed beds, where they live out an existence which can last between three and twelve months. Just prior to emergence, colonies will become even more agitated and darken noticeably in colour, even the embryo wing pads following suit by expanding slightly in readiness for imminent adulthood. Thus, like all ecloding insects, their perilous surfaceward journey begins. No one is

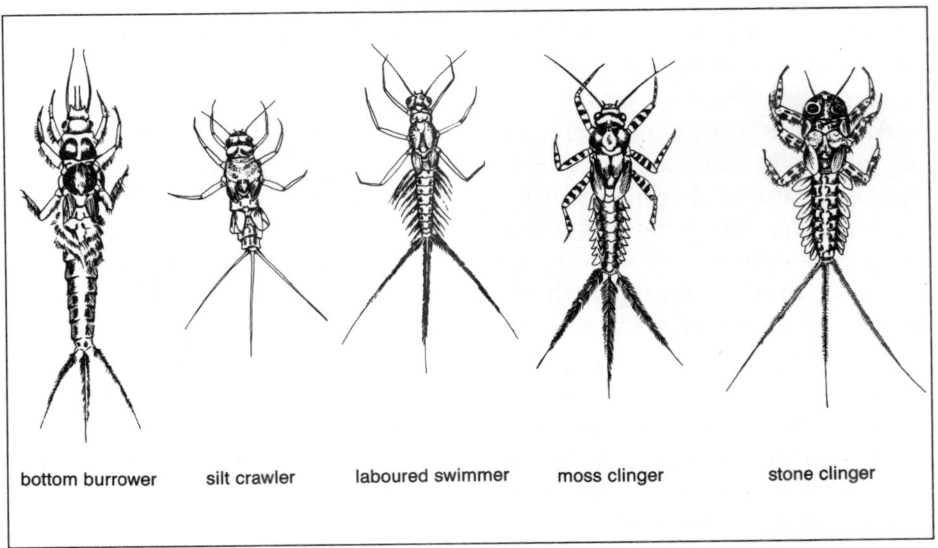

Nymph types. (Agile Darter shown overleaf.)

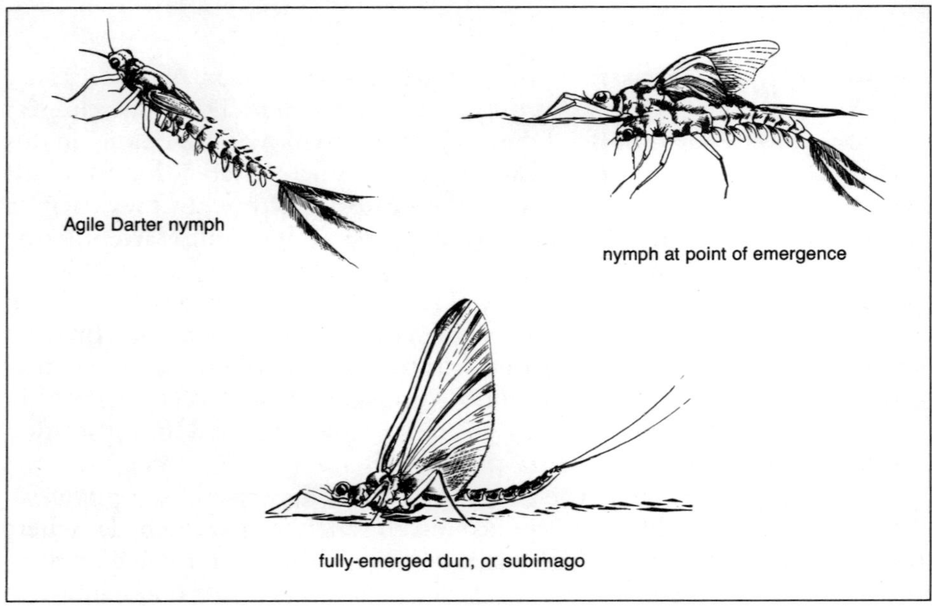

Pond and lake olive upwing stages of development, depicting a typical Agile Darter nymph.

completely certain how the nymph knows when this exodus should begin or why so many should undertake it simultaneously. Perhaps the answer lies in barometric pressure or light intensity. Whatever the reason, they do so with the utmost precision.

All species of upwings seem to have this ability. Thus, hatch sequences are important and one should be vigilant, especially from late May to early-June from about 11 a.m. onwards and then again in September. These times seem to herald the major emergence of both pond and lake olive. (They can occur throughout the season, but these periods are the major instances.) Once again, it is the top inch of water which is the critical fishing area, though a pattern fished in and around weed beds is always a fine strategy.

The nymph of the upwing is not exempt from the rigours of other hatching species, and a floating or emergent nymph is one of the most potent weapons in our armoury. This deadly delay during eclosion can last for what must seem infinite seconds before the nymphal skin splits, due to internal body pressure, and the adult fly emerges, its wings creased and useless along its body. More precious seconds are lost while its wings dry and become erect to enable take off. Trout will, once again, be awaiting these hapless creatures' struggles, ready to accept nature's bounty. Some years ago I was introduced to an American pattern which has become the mainstay of my 'film fishing' and is known as the Floating Nymph.

Duns and Spinners

The wings dry on emerging and the upwing can now lay claim to the title dun or subimago, becoming almost instantly recognizable. It is now that its short 24- to 36-hour adult life begins, which will encompass courtship, metamorphosis and mating (this group only being able to feed in the nymphal form). The change in appearance between subimago and imago is one of nature's masterpieces. The comparatively drab, grey appearance of the dun transforms into the shining, pristine clarity of the spinner. It is at this point that the fly mates (on dry land), the female returning to the water to lay her eggs and ultimately die. This stage is known as the spent spinner and should be among the most important in angling terms. I have found it less so. The *Caenis* apart, both pond olive and lake olive spinner patterns have seldom ever been employed, though I do carry them in my fly box. Indeed, the times when I have used this spentwing pattern could be counted on my hands.

It occurs to me that not everyone will know the difference between the sepia dun and the pond or lake olives. The sepia is very distinctive, being clad almost entirely in chocolate brown colouration. The four wings (two large and two smaller hind ones), are fawn, but appear as dark as the body due to the very heavy dark brown veining. It may also be separated from many species by having three tails which are the same length as the body (half an inch) as opposed to the 'olive's' (both species mentioned) two.

The pond and lake varieties can, at a glance, look almost identical, as both are approximately the same size (a third to half an inch long). Even the body shades of browny-grey olive can look deceptively similar, as can their wings, both being a light, gun-metal grey and, unlike other members of their family, numbering only two, similar to *Caenis*. The tails of the dun are perhaps the most distinguishing feature – in the pond olive these are quite markedly ringed, in the lake variety, a uniform grey. The eyes are another outstanding feature, the lake olive's being soft green flecked with brown, the pond olive (female) quite distinctively showing a faint red line across these oculi. (Males of upwinged species have their eyes, which are quite large, situated to the top of their heads, whereas the females' are smaller and to the side.) It is doubtful, however, that trout carefully note these intricate differences. In the light of this, may I recommend one dry fly pattern to cover both species, carried in sizes 14 and 16 – and a Greenwell will suffice admirably.

Damselflies

The nymph of the damselfly appears to be fashioned from the overzealous imagination of a science-fiction author. Though not present on every water in the land, where it occurs it produces some of the most enthralling fishing of the entire season.

It is most in evidence from mid-June onwards with a cycle running: egg – larva – nymph – adult. The egg, having been stuck to a suitable platform such as a reed stem, hatches into the brief larval stage from where it almost immediately enters an instar (moult), becoming a juvenile nymph. From this point, it begins its twelve-month cycle, gradually darkening as it grows to the familiar slender, stick-like being, moulting ten times in the process. Its omnipresence around weed beds would suggest that it is a suitable candidate for imitation throughout the season, yet it is the bankward migrations starting around May and reaching a peak in July which offer the best opportunities. They are lithe, athletic swimmers, propelling themselves quite quickly via jets of water from beneath their three, large, paddle-like tails (tracheal gills). This has the effect of accentuating its seductive wiggle. The damsel nymph seems to make its bankward exodus during a period from early morning through to midday, often favouring areas lined by grassy meadows or long-stemmed plants, where it can crawl from the water and change into the striking and elegant, winged damsel adult. Of all the species available to the angler, the most universal will probably be the common blue (*Enallagma cyathigerum*) which (in nymphal form) can attain lengths of up to two inches.

Damsel nymph.

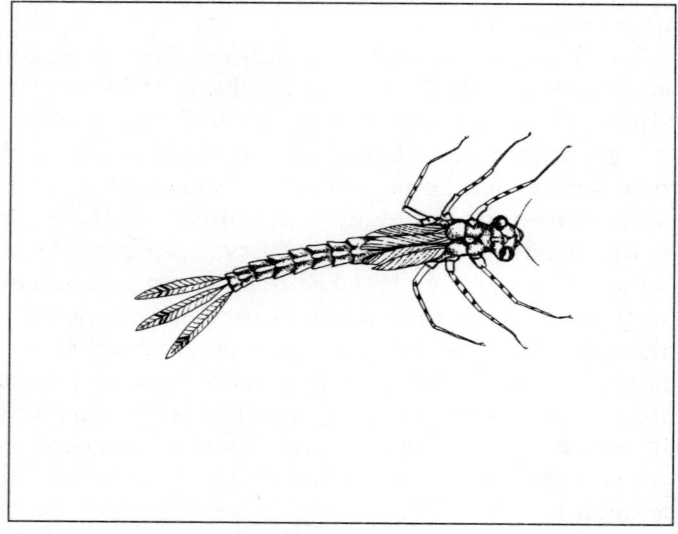

MAJOR STILLWATER INSECT OCCURRENCE

	March	April	May	June	July	August	September	October	Size
Shrimp	A	A	A	A	A	A	A	A	½-¾in
Hoglouse	A	A	A	A	A	A	A	A	½-¾in
Corixa	A	A	I.A.	I.A	A	I.A.	I.A.	A	¼-½in
Snail	A	A	A	A	A	I.A.	I.A.	A	¼-½in
Leech	A	A	A	A	A	A	A	A	½-2in
Fish	A	A	A	I.A.	A	I.A.	I.A.	I.A.	
Daphnia		A (late)	I.A	I.A.	I.A.	I.A.	A	A	
Chironomidae									
Larvae	A	A	A	A	A	A	I.A.	A	
Pupae				(See corresponding adult.)					
Black Midge									
(Duckfly, Blae & Black)	E/H	E/H	A				A	E/H	¼in
Small Black	A	E/H	E/H	A	A		A	E/H	⅛in
Ribbed/Olive		A	E/H	E/H	A	A	E/H	A	¼in
Golden Dun			A	E/H	E/H	E/H	A		¼-⅓in
Brown				A	E/H	E/H			⅛-⅓in
Orange Silver		A	E/H	E/H	E/H	A	A		¼-⅛in
Large Red or Ginger			A	E/H	E/H	E/H	A		¼-⅓in
Small Red				A	E/H	E/H	A		⅛-¼in
Blagdon Grn		A	E/H	E/H	E/H	E/H	A		⅛-¼in
Caddis (Trichoptera)									
Larvae	I.A.	I.A.	A	A	A	A	A	A	
Pupae				(See corresponding adult.)					
Great Red			A	E/H	E/H	A			¾-1⅛in
Caperer				A	E/H	E/H	A		¾-1in
Large Cinnamon			A	E/H	E/H	E/H			¾in
Black Silverhorn				A	E/H	E/H	A		⅓in
Brown				A	E/H	E/H	E/H		⅓-½in
Longhorn				E/H	E/H	E/H	E/H		⅓-⅔in
Small Red			A	E/H	E/H	E/H	A		⅓in
Small Silver			A	E/H	E/H	E/H			⅓in
Grouse Wing				E/H	E/H	E/H	E/H	A (early)	⅓in
Brown					A	E/H	E/H	A (early)	½-⅔in
Ephemeroptera									
Pond Olive Nymph		A	A	I.A.	I.A.	A	I.A.		
Pond Olive Dun			A (late)	E/H	E/H	A	E/H		⅔-¾in
Lake Olive Nymph		A	I.A.	I.A.		I.A.	I.A.		
Lake Olive Dun			E/H	E/H		E/H	E/H		½in
Mayfly Nymph			I.A.	I.A					
Mayfly Dun/Spinner			E/H (late)	E/H	E/H (Ireland)				1-1½in
Caenis Nymph			A	A	I.A.	I.A.	A		
Caenis Spinner				A	E/H	E/H	A		⅓-½in
Sepia (Nymph/Dun)		I.A E/H		I.A. E/H					⅔-¾in
Claret			A	E/H	A				⅔-¾in
Plecoptera (Stoneflies)	Due to very localized emergence and activity must be considered as a bonus and comparative rarity.								
Odonata									
Damselfly Nymph			A	I.A.	I.A.	I.A.	A		¾-2in
Dragonfly Nymph			A	I.A.	I.A	I.A.	A		¾-1¾in
Hawthorn		I.A.	(late) I.A. (early)						½-⅔in
Phantom Midge			A	I.A.	I.A	A	A		⅛-¼in
Ants				A	I.A	I.A	A		¼-⅓in
Alder Larvae		I.A.	I.A	A					¾-1⅛in
Cranefly (Daddy-long-legs)			A	A	I.A.	I.A.	I.A.		¾-1¼in

NB This is an overall average grouping and does not allow for specific occurrences or different regional peculiarities which may be significant to only a few waters.

I.A. = Increased Activity.
A = Active in water thus open to imitation. Sparse hatches.
E/H = Specific hatching period of adult or species.

I have found the adult damsel less than useful, especially on large waters, though it appears to be an ideal trout candidate. However, I am assured by that big fish/small water expert, Bill Sibbons, that trout will take a blue imitation. He feels that fish cannot differentiate between water and air when chasing the blue female adults. His longshank Blue Nymph, fished at very fast rates just underneath the surface, has caught him many a weighty bag which appears to confirm his theory. Before leaving the damsel, it might be important to add that certain waters, even certain areas, seem to bring about both light and dark nymphal variations. Trout can show a marked preference for one or other, so it is a good idea to carry various shades.

A JOURNEY THROUGH THE SEASONS

March

Keep it Simple for Success

Before that never-to-be-forgotten day when he catches his first trout, the newcomer to fly fishing faces what must seem a host of difficulties. Eager to learn any possible short cuts to success, it is quite easy to understand the frustration when he reads that even the so-called experts cannot agree about the best methods and where and when to use them. Lures, wet flies, dry flies or nymphs – which is it to be? Slow sinker, fast sinker, lead core, floating line or sink-tip line? Small fishery, large fishery or gravel pit? Just where does the beginner start? There is also the very real danger that the novice will befriend an experienced trout fisherman and try to copy everything he has seen, ending up with an enormous handicap. For the newcomer even to attempt to imitate the old hand is a sure path to failure.

The first requirement, if he is to be steered along the road to success, lies in the catching of those first couple of trout. These early trophies will provide all the confidence a beginner needs. But how to catch them? It is difficult for someone on his first outing to fish next to an experienced angler, only to watch trout after trout being hauled out before his eyes. There is simply no substitute for experience and this must be understood right from the word go. It helps if he can mix with others on the bank and he must begin to keep a diary which will be invaluable in the years to come. Trout behave in exactly the same way under the same sort of conditions which helps narrow the field of possibilities a great deal.

So now it is mid-March and the majority of fisheries are open. I know it is frowned on in some circles, but I would advise the newcomer to do a bit of touring around the reservoirs in those early weeks as they open their doors. The fishing is usually pretty easy and so a degree of confidence is quickly built up.

Sunk Lures

Even on opening days there are a few things to look out for, however. The first is to avoid a shallow area with a wind blowing from behind. Even if it does hold fish, they will soon move away with the slightest disturbance. With very little weed about, a slow-sinking line can be used with confidence during the early weeks. My own records prove that the lure must be a black one such as the Black Chenille, Sweeney Todd, Viva, Black Zonker, Ace of Spades, Christmas Tree, Black Muddler, or my old favourite, the Black and Peacock Spider.

Whichever one you choose, don't go too big – a size 10 is about right. The correct line will be either a Wet Cel I or Wet Cel II which goes down just that little faster. For the longest casts they should be in shooting-head form but forward-tapered lines are a must if you cannot get on with one. I must stress the need for extra distance, as it really can make all the difference, especially at hard-fished waters.

The first trout will, in all probability, be a stock rainbow of about a pound. If nice and silver, it is worth taking home. Spooning its stomach will reveal a few tiny green and brown chironomid larvae telling us that the fish were grubbing about on the bottom for what they could pick up. At this time of the season, food is pretty hard to find. The very reason that they took the fly in the first place was because it represented the first decent mouthful in weeks. More important is the fact that the small lure was accepted – a large one would have frightened them away or invoked that frustrating, tap-tap sort of take which comes to nothing.

Try the Nymph

By midday or perhaps a little sooner, the fish will have become pretty bored with seeing lures, so the time is right for something totally different. Even the newly introduced stockies wise up a little by the middle of opening day. Now switch to a floating line. At the risk of getting tangles, put a dropper half-way down a nine-foot cast using a water knot. I always use six turns for added strength when using five- or six-pound nylon. Tie on something buggy like a Corixa, Shrimp or a Stick Fly or perhaps a Green and Brown Nymph on the point. The dropper can hold a size 12 or even a size 14 Black Buzzer or standard Pheasant Tail nymph.

Straight away, the fish are seeing something different. Instead of the lures being retrieved in a straight line they are deceived by the rise and fall of the nymphs and if there are any willing fish about they should take without problem. Later on in the afternoon it is often a good idea to take off the dropper nymph and to substitute a Blae and Black, Mallard and Claret, Zulu, Greenwell or even a very much out of season Invicta. If through fishing pressure, the angler has been forced to remain in one spot, it does pay to leave the water for a spell to rest the swim a little. If your neighbour does the same, then the chances are that any fish hovering about at extreme casting range will move in closer now that the disturbance has gone.

For the evening session go back to the lure and slow-sinker for a while, but this time use a white-based pattern, again sticking to the size 10 rule. An old Grafham early season standby is an albino Black and Peacock Spider. Other patterns worth a try are Cat's Whisker, Light Bulb, White Chenille, Missionary or a white Frog Nobbler. Come dusk and packing up time I should be most surprised if the newcomer has not completed his first limit.

On the Move

There are a few pointers I have left until now in the hope that the novice will take them to heart. The first is that if a pitch has been fished for a reasonable time without so much as a tweak, then for Heaven's sake move. The chances are that the fish are just not there to be caught. It is no good whatever staying rooted to a spot unless you know that it is a well-known holding place like a deep gully or perhaps a deepish place with the wind blowing on to it.

With the season seeming to open earlier each year and the banks lined with anglers when you arrive, where do you go? Do you just muscle-in between two others hardly daring to look them in the eye hoping that they will not complain? If you do get away without an argument, the chances are that your cheek will be rewarded with a pound stock fish but certainly not one of the overwintered fish, which will be swimming around in much quieter places. At such times, take courage and head for the wind-lashed shores. Two places on a reservoir that receive the least attention are where the wind blows straight into the face or where it blows across from the right. Casting is awkward and you will need to punch a line under the wind or bring the rod around to keep the line and hook away from your head, but the rewards will often be worth it. If you are left-handed, of course, you have got it made.

The turbulent water attracts the trout to venture close into the bank as it washes hibernating food items out of the silt. Mind you, I am not talking about trying to fish into the teeth of a gale or when the water has become coloured. Trout do not like muddy water, and in any case, they cannot see the fly too well either. What they do, though, is congregate in numbers just on the edge of the coloured water backwash. A concrete bowl reservoir like the well-managed Toft Newton in Lincolnshire opens its doors in March. Even when you have a saucer shape the wind-blown currents need to end somewhere. I suggest that you discover where this happens as this is where most of the trout will be.

Trying to use an extra dropper or lure becomes far too much of a hazard when casting into the wind which is difficult enough as it is. Even using one on a standard twelve-foot leader presentation leaves a lot to be desired because of the blow-back effect. You should shorten the leader to a maximum of ten feet and tie on a size 10 Black Tadpole. This can be a variation on the theme but it must be weighted. Get the line moving really well by double hauling and then make the final delivery low so that it cuts

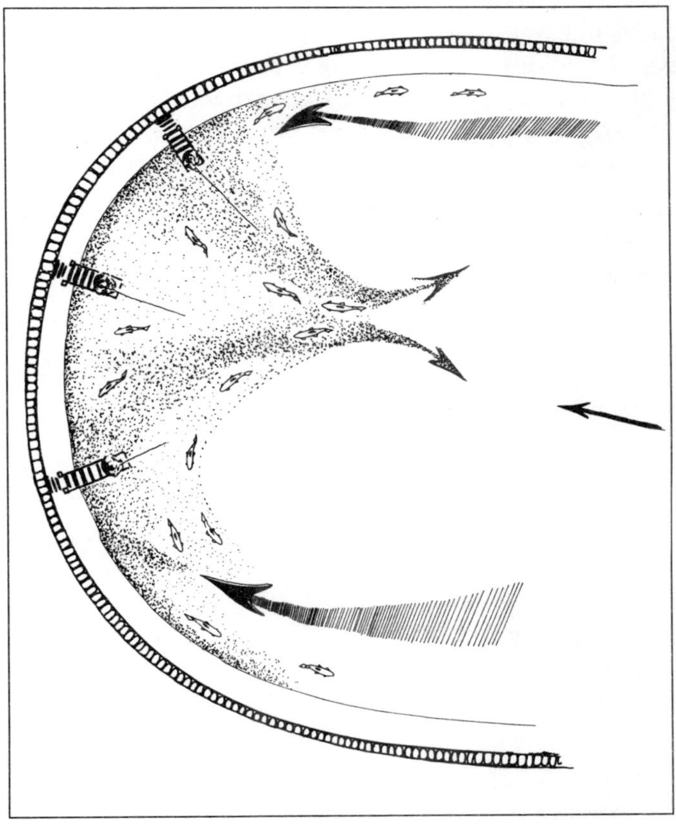

How the wind creates a current in a concrete bowl-type fishery, such as Farmoor II or Toft Newton.

under the wind. As the flat nylon backing shoots out through your left hand, apply the brakes by stopping the shoot, pinching the nylon in your left hand, forcing the lure to flip over ahead of the line and leader. At this time of the year there should be little bottom debris so let the lure sink right down to the bottom. The retrieve should be slow, in longish pulls or a series of twitching hops.

For twenty years my early and late season trips saw me quite happy to fish a standard lure with a small lead shot pinched on the cast next to the hook eye.

Ringing the Changes

At both ends of the season, the trout move into the deeper areas of the smaller waters. Most methods will catch fish now, but do give the deadly two-lure system a trial. I use a medium sinking line, twelve-foot leader and dropper fixed half-way along and a good selection of size 8 marabou-tailed, lead-headed lures in fluorescent orange, lime green, yellow, blue, white and perhaps, olive, red and pink. You will soon see the need for all these colours. You fish one colour for an hour, with success, and then the trout suddenly decide they hate it. The colour switched, back come the fish. All these colour changes only apply to the point lure, the dropper being permanently filled with a size 10 Viva which stays there whatever happens.

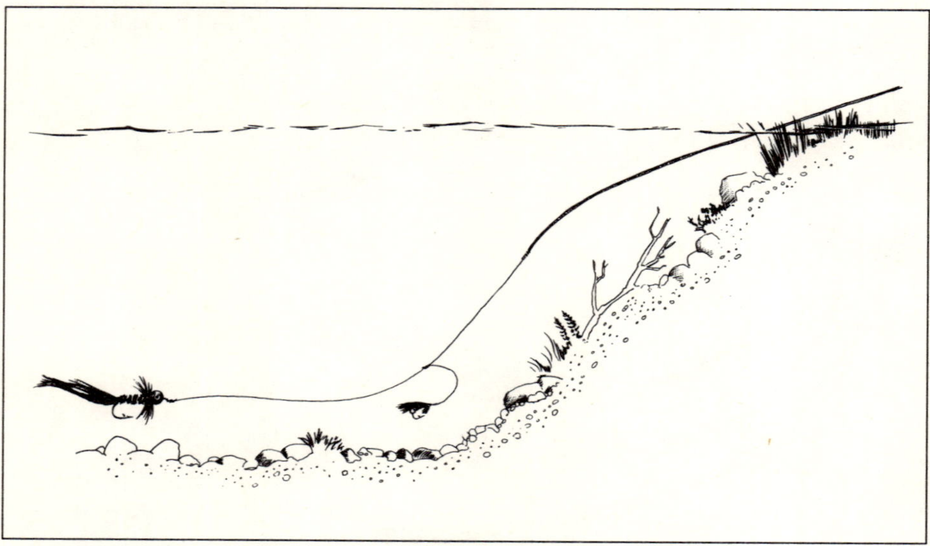

The lead-headed lure and Viva combination at the point of lift.

If you are bank or boat fishing, then make for the deepest part of the lake and if in a boat, drop in the anchor as quietly as you possibly can. Start the session with a fluorescent orange lead head on the point and make a long cast. As the line begins to sink, feel it down through the depths. With time, you will feel it actually touch the bottom. If you start the retrieve then, the lure will stay deep, bouncing along the bottom with the small Viva a couple of feet higher up.

April

Things Start to Buzz!

After the easier early season fishing when he who works harder and casts further catches the most trout, comes the more difficult period when the shell-shocked survivors begin to feed naturally. April on the reservoirs heralds the first small, black midges with the most activity being concentrated in mid-afternoon, extending through into early evening if it is not too cold. The chironomid pupa is better known, I suppose, as the buzzer. Irish anglers call the same creature the duck fly. On waters like Lough Corrib, the first hatches really do stir the brown trout into action.

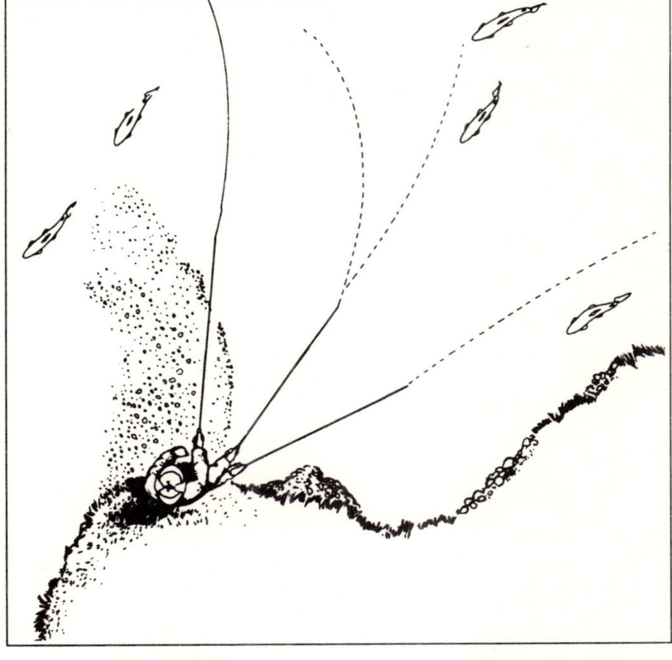

The headland point of a bay gives the angler a great vantage point from which to intercept cruising fish.

There are, however, times when adult, small black buzzers will be seen in profusion and not a trout will rise. This is an indication that the water is still too cold. However, they will still be feeding on the larvae and newly-hatched pupae as they struggle for life in and around the decayed bottom weed. Warmth, then, is the key factor in selecting your fishing spot. A good place to head for is where the water is sheltered from strong wind, yet where there is still enough movement to create a small ripple. The point of a bay where the water is around eight to ten feet deep would be my first choice, providing as it does, the opportunity of covering a wide arc of fishable water. Boat fishers must seek out the same sort of conditions.

Fishing a Team

Anyone contemplating fishing a team of nymphs from a boat must make it as stable a platform as possible. Anchors fixed at bow and stern are a must. One anchor will allow the boat to swing about all over the place. To be really effective, early season nymph fishing must be done very slowly indeed. The less you move the flies, the more you will catch. On mild days, the emerging fly is taken well and only occasionally will the adult, winged creature take their fancy, but a prolific hatch of millions of buzzers of the same colour and size can present problems.

For now, of course, your trio of offerings have just become part of a very large crowd. So how do we turn the odds in our favour? Quite simply by stepping up the size. So when the hatch is in full swing, I would use a size 10 or even a size 8 long-shanked Cove Pheasant Tail. If, however, the

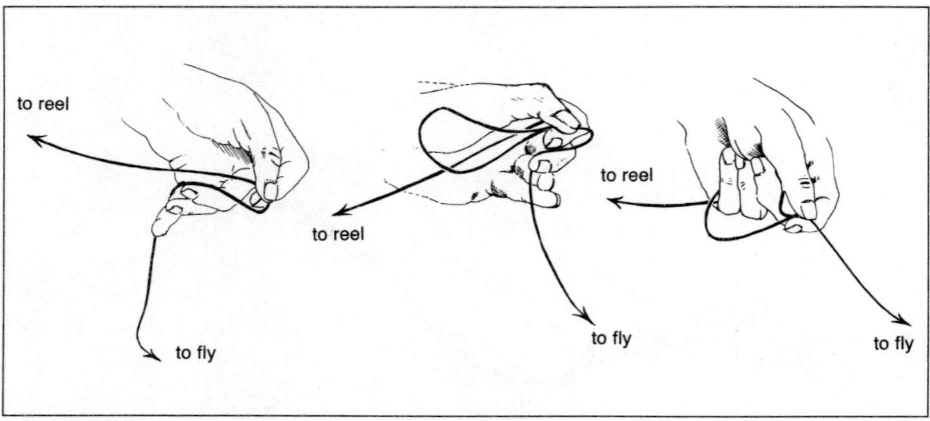

The figure-of-eight constant retrieve is something that must be learned if you are to become a successful nymph fisherman.

hatch has peaked, then a smart switch back to the size 12 and size 14 patterns is in order.

It is worth noting that the pupal stage of the buzzer can last up to three days. It will spend much of this time on the bottom, where the wings take shape. Then the moment arrives for the journey to the surface and freedom. Up they go, in their thousands, only to be met by a 'sticky' surface film which they cannot penetrate. Masses of them twist and wriggle about, a few inches underneath the invisible barrier, only to be scooped up by the trout.

This buzzer behaviour allows us to fish our imitations anywhere between the bottom and the surface. As a general rule of thumb, I would advise fishing the pupae well sunk during the day and then, as the evening rise begins, to grease up and fish the imitations just beneath the surface. If there is a light breeze blowing this last method can be lethal.

Some years ago, I perfected a method while fishing at Pitsford which is nothing more than a size 10 normal-shanked Black Muddler, on the point as a controller, with two buzzers on the droppers. The cast is made across the wind, allowing the team to drift around just taking in the slack. The beauty of the Muddler is that it achieves perfect presentation without any need for greasing the leader (something I am never very happy about doing). I go further, and rub the nylon down with mud before even starting.

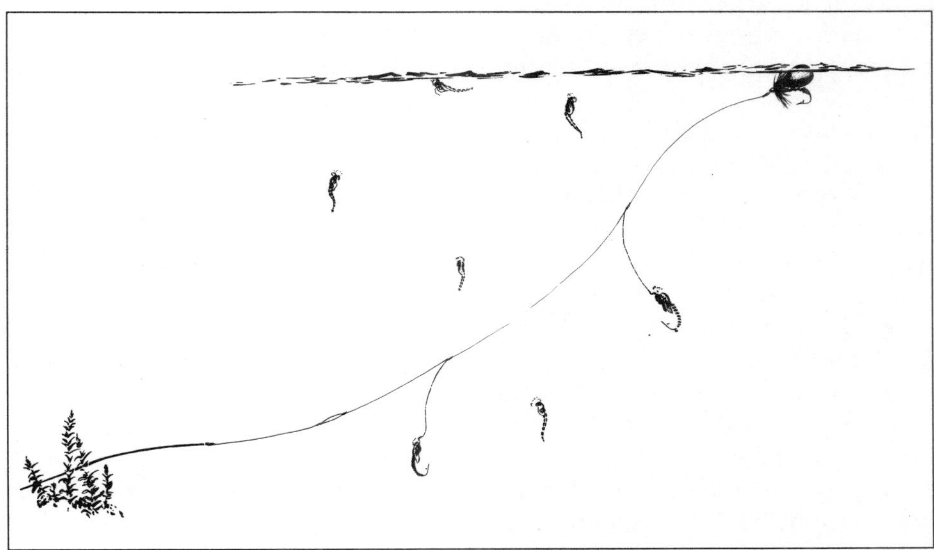

The controller fly method used in conjunction with a fast-sinking line, where a team of two conventional midge pupae dressings are used with an ultra-buoyant tail fly.

The easier, early outings are most often followed by much harder times. One good reason for this is that the general standard of fly fishing is so good when compared to only a few years ago. Constant full houses and good catches certainly deplete the initial stocking more than some managers dare to admit. However, all the waters that enjoy a weekly stocking should now come into their own and these fisheries are the ones to head for now. Buzzer fishing will be the order of the day. Some useful patterns to try include Carnill's Poly Ribbed Buzzer, Peter Gathercole's True to Life pattern, the Suspender Buzzer, Blae and Black, Zulu, Pheasant Tail and Mallard and Claret.

May

The Deadly Drop Back

Any fly fisherman who thinks that he can be successful in the competition context without a sinking line should think again. During April and May a sinking line will be the correct choice ninety-nine times out of a hundred. Don't even begin to think what may happen in a few weeks time. That's another story and more of that time later. When I began competition fishing seriously, about five years ago, I did so purely as a challenge and to see whether I was good enough to make the grade, but before taking part in my first match, I already had the knowledge accumulated over twenty years of fishing other styles to draw on and that has stood me in good stead. Basically, the change required only a few adjustments – the biggest being forced to fish in front of a drifting boat in what were often unfavourable conditions for that style.

I enjoyed some success from the word go, probably because I had that long apprenticeship with an all-important feel for sinking line work. Couple this knowledge with complete confidence and you will catch fish if they are there to be caught – believe me. So what are the factors which must be considered when taking up competitive fishing?

Firstly, one must always know exactly where the flies are in the water and how they are behaving. The long cast has been made and the flies are falling down through the water but the inevitable is happening. The boat is drifting forward towards them quite quickly, despite the action of the drogue. You are now in the unhappy and certainly unwanted position of having an ever-increasing amount of slack line between your retrieving hand and the flies. You counteract this by slowly retrieving the line as the boat progresses forward. In reality, a thirty-yard cast will be halved, but not to worry. You have kept in touch with the flies and that is vital as during the next fifteen yards they will be travelling just where you want

The drop-back technique as used in conjunction with a moving boat either with or without drogue, when the angler is casting to the front with a sinking line (drifting in the traditional manner): (a) indicates the initial long cast; (b) the flies' descent; (c) the initial movement from the lake bed in conjunction with the rod moving upwards; (d) the sweep of flies and where trout may often take; (e) a fish following the flies when near the surface; and (f) the effective sudden downward movement of the rod making the flies fall naturally through the water layers where trout may often take. The shaded arm shows the downward movement that will drop the rod tip to effect (f).

them to be – along the bottom and among the trout. The takes can come at any time during the long, slow and even pulls, but a time to really expect that pull back is when the flies change direction for their swim towards the surface. This all-important change of direction can be exaggerated by lifting the rod slowly and in one long swoop. Now comes the most important moment of all and knowing just what to do next has given me my success in many of the early season competitions.

As you bring the flies to the surface, in the long sweep, watch for the top dropper to appear. Very often a trout will be following close behind, but is not quite sure whether to take the fly or not. Remember that the water will still be cold and that the trout are not yet in the 'up and at 'em' mood. These reluctant trout can be converted into takers by pausing very briefly at this point and then lowering the rod top quite sharply, so that the fly sinks back into the water. Now is the critical moment. Keep a weather eye on the leader and nine times out of ten you will suddenly see the leader form a different angle. It may move to the left, the right or even plunge downwards. Whichever happens, lift the rod and the fish will be on.

Confidence

Having confidence in your tackle is something else to consider. When using the sinking-line method, make sure that you use the right rod and not the long one you will employ later on in the season for floating-line and bob-fly work. For the heavy work, I prefer a ten- or 10½-foot boron to give me that extra power and stiffness on the strike. The longer, softer rods tend to 'nod' like a soft spring while retrieving a sunken line and are clearly unsuitable for the task in hand. Too many fish will be pricked and lost if you persist in using one.

The knowledge that your fly is going down very fast is a great help. After all, you want to fish the bottom not the midwater. The High-speed Hi D and the Canadian lead-impregnated lines are firm favourites, but the Canadian has been replaced by something even better and now sinks faster than ever. Early season stocked trout tend to move to well-known holding spots year after year. These honey pots are usually on the downwind end of the reservoir and have provided some of my best catches. A good wind with waves a foot or so high makes the trout less cautious and, provided you manage the boat properly, catching them should present few problems.

However, just because you have threaded a fast sinker through the rings does not mean that you have to head straight for the deepest water. In fact, you should do exactly the opposite. The whole object of the exercise is to get flies fishing where the trout are, and that is on the bottom. That is something we can do in relatively shallow water. Over deep water it would be impossible in the style we are fishing and the fish will not be there anyway.

A well-known standard pattern for the opening weeks is the mini Viva, but the problem is that everyone uses it. After a week or two of being continuously hurled out by thousands of anglers, country-wide, even this one will have lost its charms, so I suggest that you switch back to patterns of your own. Fish them with confidence and you will be more than half-way there. You can, of course, fish a nymph on a sunken line. Indeed, I often hedge my bets and fish one of each until a clear pattern emerges. A tip worth remembering is to fish two and not three flies. That way they will fish cleanly on an even keel, increasing their attractiveness a great deal.

Enter the Pond Olive

Many reservoirs and gravel pits support good olive hatches. Although this fly is around from the third week of May to the end of June, they reappear in late August and early September. The best hatches occur in the shallows around the weed beds which have been home to the nymph colonies.

Some other useful patterns to try at olive time are a standard length Pheasant Tail with an olive thorax, a Hare's Ear tied with dyed olive fur, the Spring Favourite, Greenwell's (both wet and dry), olive Soldier Palmer, Apricot Spinner and a dry pond olive. Tie them all on size 12 hooks.

Variations on a Mayfly Theme

The mayfly is becoming more abundant with each season and that has to be good news. On the quality Irish loughs the mayfly festival is never in doubt. Hatches continue throughout the summer and sometimes well into September. On the other hand, many lovely English streams have been

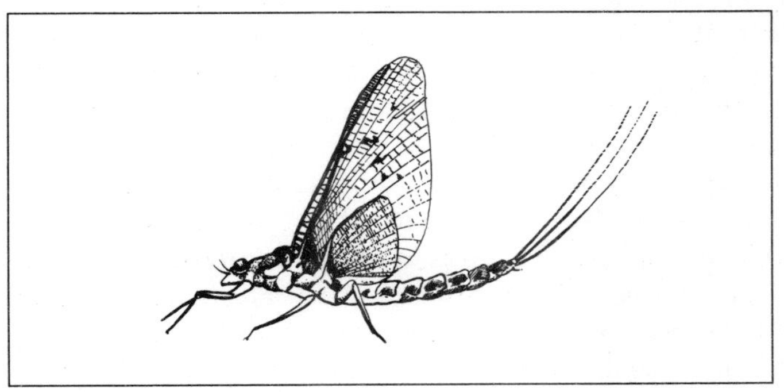

Mayfly adult (subimago).

ruined by abstraction and pollution over the past forty years, killing off their once thriving mayfly populations.

As always, nature has a way of fighting back and now there are more trout waters boasting a hatch than ever before. Many of the gravel-pit fisheries and small waters boast good hatches and some of the larger reservoirs, like Ladybower in Derbyshire and Tittesworth in Staffordshire, are well known for their annual mayfly bonanza.

The Irish Loughs

The Irish mayfly usually begins to hatch in numbers during the last week of May and by the first week of June the hatch is well underway. The fishing on our own English waters would then be over. The best mayfly hatch I ever saw was on Lough Conn. The successful team that day was a size 14 Black Spider on the point, a similarly sized Green Peter in the middle and a size 10 mixed yellow and olive mayfly on the top dropper. The fish did not come too easily at first and it was not until I sprayed up the mayfly that the action really began.

The secret of fishing Conn and the other wild loughs is not to cover the same water twice. Apart from the fish being put down (a line of thought which some boatmen do not follow), there is so much water to fish, so why waste it? Fishing in the traditional loch style, with a good boatman, beats all the other more elaborate styles more in keeping with rainbows. Remember, you are trying to catch wild brown trout and possibly a salmon too and the angler who has served his apprenticeship with rainbows at the small fisheries must have a rethink.

English Reservoirs

The deceptively simple Irish style works well on our own reservoirs where mayfly exist. But how do we take on the evergrowing number of much smaller fisheries which also enjoy a hatch, like the chain of gravel-pit fisheries which stretch all the way from Leamington Spa right across the Cotswolds? Then, of course, there are the superb Hampshire waters to look at too. One such gem is Dever Springs at Barton Stacey near Andover.

I first visited the fishery in 1987, with Conn Wilson. I had wondered why he made the long drive to the water when he had some really good fishing on his doorstep. Spring Lake, the smaller of the pair, is reserved for dry fly or nymph fishing while any methods are allowed on the larger and deeper Willow Lake. Armed with the knowledge that a few mayflies had been seen, I worked on the theory that the nymphs would be active deep down. I set up with a nine-and-a-half-foot carbon rod, weight-forward floater, six-pound leader and a lightly leaded Dick Walker Mayfly Nymph. I could hardly believe the response with a trio of rainbows, all over three pounds, coming quickly to the bank.

Oddly enough, although the fish were quite happy to take the nymph, a few had begun to rise, not to the adult mayfly but to hawthorns being blown on to the water from nearby blossom hedges. Despite this surface activity, I stuck with the nymph and cast towards a clump of rushes where I thought a better trout might be lurking. Lurking he was, and hungry too. Within seconds the fly line had been ripped off the reel. I had to follow the fish, passing the rod over the head of another angler. That trout fought like a salmon and at seven pounds was something to smile about.

After lunch I was persuaded to try the Hawthorns. I found just one in my box which I sprayed and cast across the wind. The fly line bowed slightly with the drift, straightening out as a trout snapped up the dry fly. Keeping a gentle arc in the line is a good idea, as it shows when the trout really does have the fly in its mouth and is not simply trying to drown the fly with big noisy rises.

As on all small waters, trout do become nervous during the main part of the day and head for the middle of the lake and sanctuary. I had spotted a few mayflies being blown across into the deeper water being taken a long way out. My outfit not man enough for the job, I tackled up a No 9 floating shooting head, tied up a five-pound leader and sprayed up a special mayfly pattern. The leader was cleaned with mud.

Double-haul casting with a following light wind gave the essential additional range and my fly was fishing fifty yards or so away. A few just wanted to splash the fly, but not the four rainbows which scaled a score of pounds. That may have been an unorthodox way of fishing a dry fly, but I was satisfied that my end tackle was as sensitive as if I had been using much lighter gear and I shall never be afraid to try the dry fly at long range again.

June

Lessons on Loch Style

As soon as summer arrives, there are sighs of relief all around, for now we can think about fishing on or near the surface at the big reservoirs. One aspect of the style which has captured my imagination is how the top dropper can have such an effect. Fish it well and the fish rise from nowhere but do it badly and you may feel that the fishery needs restocking. Fishing the surface from a boat has gained rapidly in popularity thanks mainly to the upsurge in competition fishing. The majority of clubs now organize friendly events and eliminators for the English team. Even when not actually taking part in matches, anglers are fascinated by the traditional style of fishing from a broadside drifting boat.

Before you even consider what flies and methods to use, to do consistently well, you will require the utmost in concentration. The eyes of a master at the style are never still as he scans the water for signs of fish. The trout's direction and speed computed, the flies will be cast into the projected path and a take fully expected. Ideally, I would prefer a wave off of about six inches or so, but anything up to a foot or a little more is good too. Provided the air temperature is about average, and the sky not too bright, it is a certainty that fish will be well up in the water. If they are not showing do not worry. What they will be doing is moving up the wind about a foot down, on the look-out for food, which can range from minute *Daphnia* particles to buzzer pupae.

If the conditions are good they will rise, fly or no fly. This is where we are really tested as fly fishers. As the wind freshens and the waves get higher, I step up the leader strength and fly size. It is now a good.

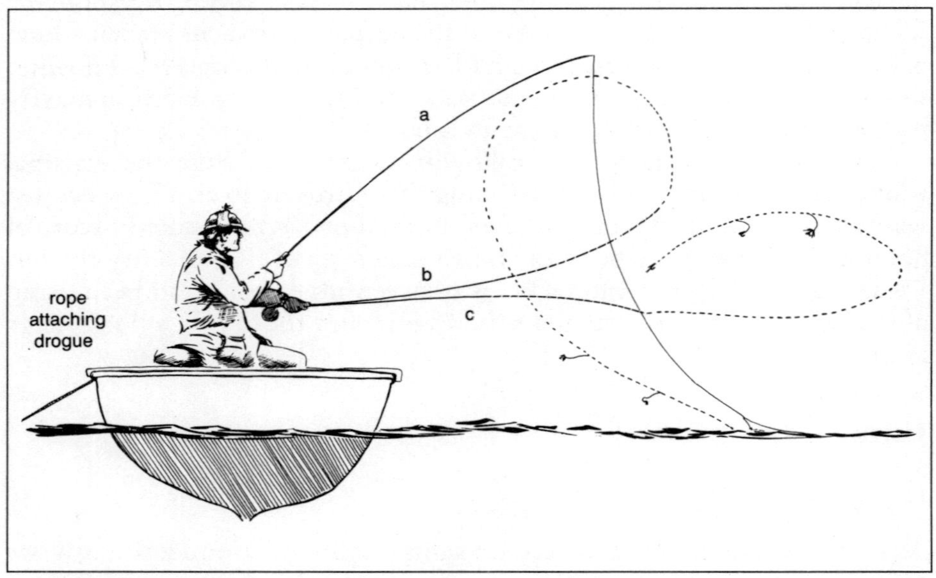

A traditional roll-casting sequence depicting the retrieve of the three wet flies. Rod (a) shows the beginning of the movement when the top dropper or 'bob' fly is dribbled across the surface. Rod (b) shows the movement forward as the tail fly reaches the surface close to the boat. Rod (c) shows the completion of the cast, the shaded arm denoting the power movement coming doward to effect a clean roll cast.

time to try some gaudy patterns to tempt the fish up from deeper down. For the lighter wind, however, my leader is put together with two yards of six-pound nylon joined to one of five-pound stuff using a six-turn water knot. A similar knot joins the further yard of nylon, a pound lighter still. My bob fly choices for a light wind are a size 14 or perhaps a size 12 Black Pennell, Red Tag or wingless Wickham, all of which match a fly skittering along the surface. While the trout may not actually take the bob fly itself, it will often entice it to take the others on the cast.

It is a good idea to try a nymph on the point and sometimes something like a Mallard and Claret or Greenwell's Glory on the centre dropper. When drifting slowly in light winds you will be fishing the deceiver method at its very best. A stronger wind will not necessarily mean a faster drift if you use a good drogue. What you must do is change your leader to something a full pound heavier all the way through to cope with the larger waves and the bigger flies. I always cast a little further in these conditions as it gives the fish a better chance of seeing the fly.

As summer progresses, I try some of my Irish lough flies when the sedges are flying. It is now more than obvious that these Irish patterns work well on our own fisheries. The Green Peter and the brown or claret Murragh are well worth an outing. Talking of sedges, I do tend to take a lot of fish on the Invicta used as bob fly. A new one which I use in mid-season, I call the Thicket, which is a sort of larger than life olive imitation. It works well both in a flat calm and high waves. Another winning bob fly came as the result of a lucky mistake. One day, when changing flies, I tied on a Claret Pennell instead of the ordinary black version. After quickly taking a good brownie, I decided to keep it on. It was a good decision for it produced seven out of the eight fish I caught that day.

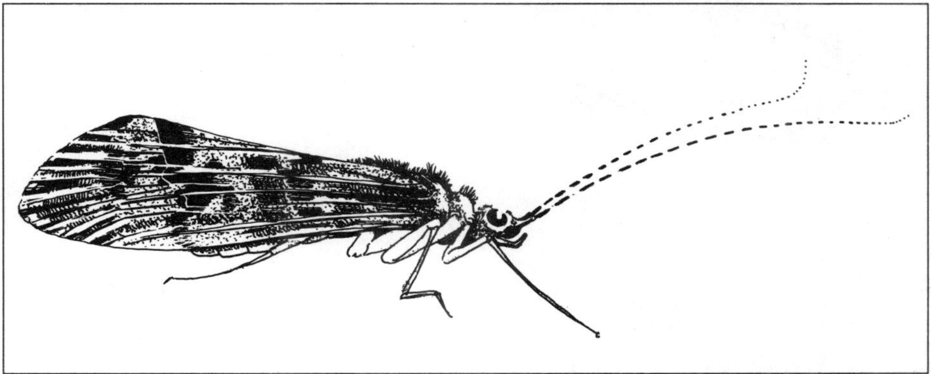

The adult sedge.

A Dry Fly with a Difference

For thirty years, fishing a dry fly on the big reservoirs was always considered to be some sort of a joke – a tactic for the eccentrics. Many would now admit to using dry flies when the suitable occasion arose. But what has happened over the past few seasons has certainly made all reservoir fishers think twice before they call the style an old codgers game. I say dry flies because they were greased to float on the surface, but in many cases they were little more than some kind of emerging buzzer and not a dry fly in the normally accepted sense of the dressing.

The story really began at Grafham with club members such as Dave Barker, Bob Worts, John Moore, Mike Ball and Andy Linwood spending a lot of their time on the water experimenting with various dry flies, and slowly the dry fly nymph was developed. Soon, their catches were beginning to look better than those of their friends, using conventional wet fly, nymph and lure tactics. Not only were there good bags of average fish caught but some very big ones too. The whole thing climaxed with Bob Wort's Grafham record ten-pound three-ounce fish which took him over two hours to bring to the net.

All this happened at a time when fishing was difficult, with less stock in the water than had been enjoyed for some years. A number of important competitions were to be fished later that month and some anglers were giving the new method a try. Dave Shipman from the Rutland club was

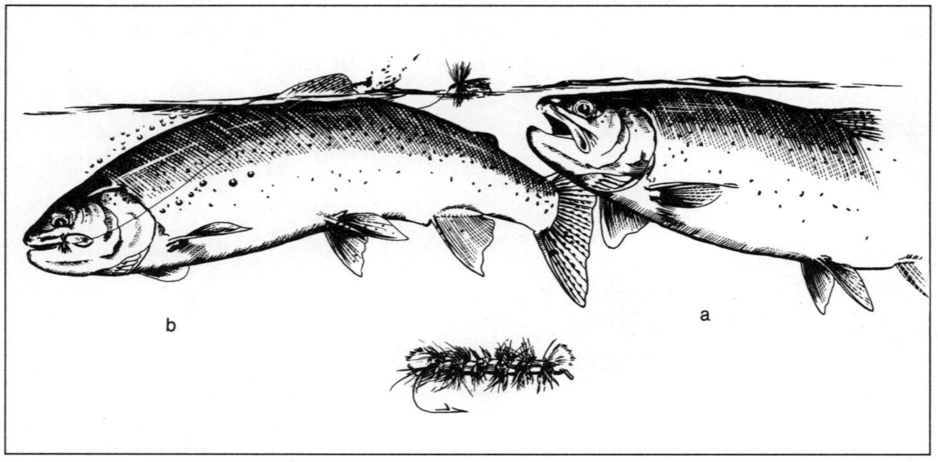

The new dry nymph method. Trout (a) approaches the floating fly; trout (b), on turning down, shows the correct point at which the strike should be made. The inset depicts the Shipman Floating Bozzer.

using the style to great effect. While others were struggling, he averaged nine fish a visit. Then he won three big events in a row the Pro-Am, the Benson and Hedges English National and the Midland Final eliminator for the English National. Dave's tactics were straightforward enough, or so it would seem. He was fishing three well-spaced buzzer nymphs on a five-pound leader. The flies were different from the accepted buzzer dressings, being very rough-looking creations of seal fur of ginger brown, dark olive, red and orange.

It was important to grease up all three nymphs with generous blobs of Gink then religiously to degrease the rest of the leader. He then cast down the wind from a broadside drifting boat. The secret was then to leave the nymphs static as the boat drifted towards them. The retrieve needed to be just enough to remove the excess slack line. The strike must not be too hasty as some trout try to drown the fly before taking it in their mouths.

It was obvious that those who were doing well at Grafham had come to terms with the 'new' method. Some very good surface fishers who judged it to be a flash in the pan failed miserably. To tie up some of the Shipman nymphs, you need seal fur, which floats well and is translucent when wet. A piece of white nylon wool is tied in on top of the hook to leave short breather tufts at head and tail. Then dub on the selected seal fur forming a carrot shape, ribbing through it with gold wire.

Green is Best

Each year, from the beginning of June until the end of July, green is the major colour in the natural food choice and it follows that it is a shade which must be included in our artificials. When using wet flies, the old favourites such as the Olive Quill, Greenwell's and Golden Olive are good, but I have a pattern of my own which beats them all. Results with this pattern, known as the June Fly, have been excellent. If fish are showing in near flat calms during the evening and are being difficult, do try a size 14 on a four-pound leader. You won't be disappointed. Cast close to a rise and then retrieve with a slow figure-of-eight. It is a fairly simple pattern to tie. I use sizes 12 and 14 and sometimes a size 10. A gold lurex tag slopes round the bend. The body is pale green wool left rough but slim, and the hackle, just one turn of dark brown cock. The wing is grey starling. My second green pattern has also proved its worth. It is a nymph called the Spring Favourite. This one has a body of dubbed marabou to give the impression of life. Again, this one works when fish are showing but ignoring all your offerings. Tie it on the same size hooks. The tail is a fine spray of white cock hackle fibres, and the body, olive marabou ribbed with fine gold wire or tinsel. The thorax is built up of the same material and then covered by a grey feather shell-back. The throat hackle is a spray of primrose yellow cock hackle fibres. Tie a suspender-style version for static fishing.

It is not just the small imitative flies that succeed in this midsummer period, and one lure which often produces the goods is the Leprechaun. This pattern was invented by Peter Woods about fifteen years ago. Because of its fluorescent green chenille body it was really only tried as an experiment one June day at Grafham when it was very hot and the water thick with suspended green algae. It had been a difficult day when everything else had failed. Peter set up a slow-sinking line and put on his new creation. What happened during the next hour caused a stir, for he put eight good rainbows in the boat while his amazed partner remained blank.

July

Into the Twilight Zone

What is it about sedge time on the bigger fisheries that makes July and August the most consistent fly fishing time of the whole season? There are a number of factors which make this so. Firstly, the weedy areas close to the bank, where the sedges hatch at their thickest during the evening, bringing the fish into easy range on areas which will have been virtually barren of trout. Rising fish are a common sight at this time too, the trout being drawn to the surface from their feeding close to the bottom by the insect activity.

It is a time for fishing imitative patterns, including the dry fly. There are a couple of exceptions to this rule, but more about those later. It is more than possible, on such sunny days, to slog away for little or no reward. Daytime fishing at this time of the season is best done from a drifting boat but bank fishing can be devastatingly effective during that magical hour before darkness falls. It is now that the crafty regulars appear – just as the anglers who have spent their day thrashing the water are heading for the carpark.

Ninety-nine times out of a hundred, the fishing can be guaranteed to get better as dusk approaches. Even flat calms can be fished with confidence once the sedges begin to appear. The only thing which can kill it stone-dead is a hatch of the dreaded *Caenis*. This has happened to me a few times at Pitsford and the trout switch on to the little horrors every time. Why, I know not.

Whenever you can, it pays to put your adult and pupal imitations into the edge of the ripple. We often see lots of grousewing sedges about but I am not convinced that trout really take to them as we think they might. Stomach contents show plenty of buff sedges and medium brown ones too, but you won't find many grousewings. Frank Cutler has a theory that they taste bitter and he's probably right. He usually is about such things.

Sedges seem to hatch best in the calmer, sheltered bays and this is one time that flat calms don't bother me. This applies to both bank and boat fishing in the evenings. Now the simplest of all methods will put fish in the net. Go straight for a twelve-foot leader holding a size 12 dry bi-visible sedge pattern, making sure that the leader has been thoroughly degreased.

You will see what seem like dozens of trout rising but it is a big mistake to keep lifting off in an attempt to put the fly into the path of a rising fish, odd though that may seem. Although there are plenty of rises, the odds are that the disturbances will be made by only a few, highly mobile trout. With that in mind, it is important not to frighten them away. Far better to be patient and to put your fly out twenty yards or so and then wait for the fish to find it. The fly must be treated so that it floats proudly. The trout are just mooching about sipping in the sedges and will soon come across yours. Remember, no retrieving. Just cast out and leave everything else to the trout.

August

Special Boat Techniques

Trolling on the Oars

It is a fact that the bigger trout seem to be taken in by a lure running at a smooth, even speed. Trolling on the oars gives this movement and there are a few specialists around who have used the technique to put trout into double figures in the boat.

Some of the bigger reservoirs allow trolling on the oars in designated zones. The areas cover quite an expanse and so there is a lot of bottom searching to be done. Many anglers would not dream of trolling, seeing the method as unsporting and needing little skill. Of course, there is trolling and trolling. Done well, it can take fish which normal styles would rarely succeed in catching.

There is far more to trolling than simply hanging a sinking line, complete with big lure, out of the back of a boat. The gear must be purpose-made for the job. A very powerful, ten- or eleven-foot rod is essential. For reels, the old Ariel takes some beating, as does the more modern Line-shooter. Both are free-running and take a lot of backing. The lines range from a full hundred yards of lead core to a ten-yard length of shooting head made from the same line. Fast and medium sinkers are used too. Usually, the leader is a minimum of eight pounds. The lures themselves range from a size 6 long shank to tandems and tubes.

Before setting out on the water you need to make sure that the oars will stay put if, for any reason, you have to let go of them. A thick rubber collar about five inches across fits snugly over the inboard side making them quite safe. Even in the hottest weather, trout don't always sink into the deepest water and for much of the time, running a lure along the 20- to 25-foot contour is about the right place to be.

You need to experiment a little to discover just how much lead core to let out, and the time for doing this can be shortened if the anglers work as a close team. Trolling only works when this happens anyway. It is a wise move to keep the hook points razor sharp, as brown trout in particular have bony jaws and a hook-hold is not always that easy. The angler not rowing should hold one rod all the time but he must, at all costs, resist the tap-tap takes and wait until the following fish really does take a firm hold.

It is best to cover the chosen fishing zone in a zigzag, so combing the area thoroughly. The constant change of direction also gives the lure added life as it accelerates around the curves when the boat changes direction. An

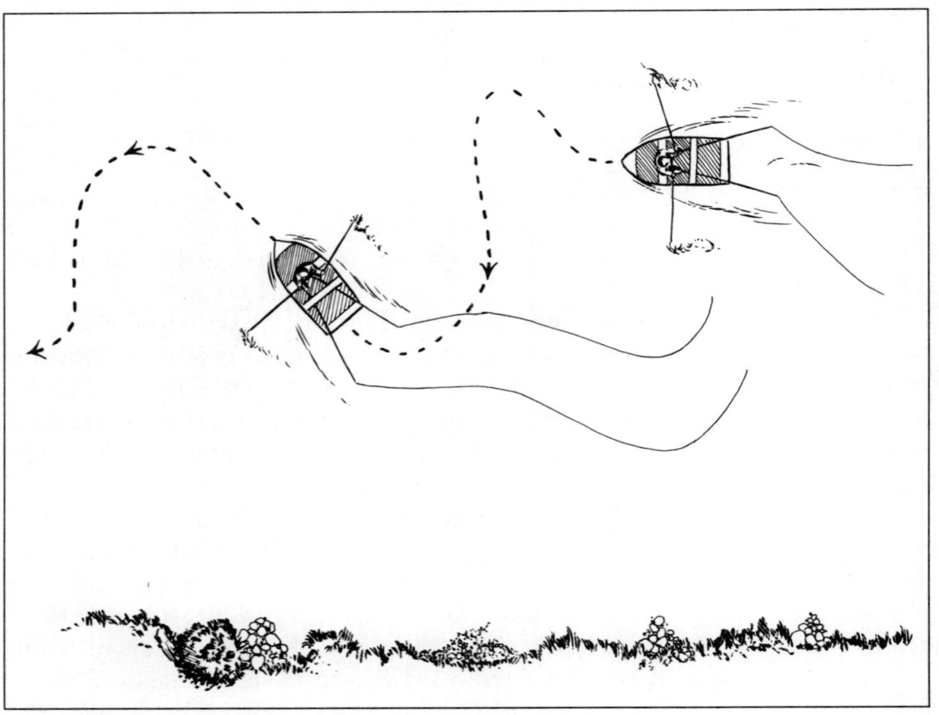

Route taken by an angler when trolling the lure under oar, giving the artificial wide arcing movements at about 150yd from the lake shore.

accurate map of the reservoir is invaluable as it will give you a fair idea where the old roads were, where trees once stood, the location of the ditches and so on – all great places for a trout to live.

Following the Daphnia Shoals

Strong winds and high waves wake up the sulking trout but it is a fact that too many boat anglers waste far too much time trying to get their craft to drift in the desired direction or even to anchor up in the right places. The water movement also ensures that the *Daphnia* billions will be packed into a small area. In Rutland's case this often means that both *Daphnia* and rainbows will be concentrated about three hundred yards from the dam wall.

The correct choice of fly line is critical. The lure must be presented at exactly the right depth and this will most often be within three to four feet of the surface. That is where the fish will be shoaled so that is where our lures must be too. For broadside drifting, I use a very slow-sinking fly line rather than something quicker which will bring the lure back underneath the fish. A floating line will catch a few fish but will be nothing like as effective as the slow sinker.

It is important to slow down the boat with a good drogue and I use one that is five feet square for this job. While the large waves go roaring by, my boat drifts along nicely giving me all the time in the world for good tackle control. A fast-drifting boat with too small a drogue or none at all leaves you in a state of perpetual motion, casting and retrieving, casting and retrieving. A hopeless situation, you will agree. Even though the waves are rough, you may feel like anchoring up some seventy yards from the windy shore having discovered this to be the main fish-holding spot. To do this safely, you need a weighty anchor attached to a long rope with ten yards of meaty chain. When it is rough, always put the anchor out from the bows. That way you won't ship a drop of water, but try anchoring out from the side and you are certain to be in for a wet and uncomfortable time.

Hot orange patterns work wonders at this time and Old Nick, in particular, is really deadly. To dress it, use a size 10 hook and tie in a bunch of hot orange hackle fibres for the tail. The body can be either gold or silver tinsel palmered with a hot orange cock hackle. A further three turns of another hackle are added at the head. I tend to use two and not three flies in this situation and Old Nick has a permanent place on the dropper.

The point fly is another orange one but this time it is one of my own fluorescent Ugly Duckling series. Dress it on a size 10 hook. Tie in a bunch of hot orange cock hackle fibres for the tail, followed by a body built up from gold Candlelite. The wing is fluorescent marabou and the head a ball of hot orange fluorescent chenille.

But just what is happening on the upwind side of the reservoir, away from the wind and the crashing? There won't be much *Daphnia* so forget the orange patterns. It is likely too that the water will be much clearer and the trout that much harder to tempt. There won't be that many flies hatching either, until much later on in the day. Nevertheless, a sedge pattern of some sort must always be on your cast. A Mallard and Claret can be pretty good as can a Fiery Brown on the point position and for the dropper, nothing beats the old Soldier Palmer.

Follow that Muddler!

Muddler fishing from a broadside drifting boat is deadly in July and August. Rainbows are predators and when the water temperatures are high and spawning problems have long been forgotten, they develop this killing instinct to a fine degree. A Muddler Minnow stripped fast across the surface will draw them like a magnet.

If you are to do the job properly your tackle must be more specialized than for normal surface wet fly fishing. The set-up I favour is a powerful ten footer, in carbon or boron, capable of casting a No 9 or 10 floating shooting head with ease. The backing will be thirty-pound flat black nylon which gives that easy added distance, especially if you give it a good stretch before you begin. Storing it on a wide-drummed reel is essential, otherwise you will end up with those nasty tight coils which make tangling a sure thing. For leaders, I use six- or seven-pound stuff for the smaller Muddlers and step up only a pound when using bigger versions. The impact of the take is often so fierce that it is all too easy to get smashed so don't risk light leaders. That would be asking for trouble. We now have an outfit which will put the lures long distances without too much false casting. I have a reel which will cut out the tangles and a rod strong enough to hook and handle good fish at long range.

To be successful, both partners need to fish in exactly the same way. The boat is set to drift broadside on to the wind. If the breeze is only moderate, there is no need to slow down the drift, but if the wind is really blowing and the waves are big, a drogue fixed to the central rowlock will slow things up. Both anglers cast as far as they can downwind, then pause for a second or two. Then the Muddlers are stripped back in long fast pulls. In a big wind you will need a size 6 lure with a large unclipped head. A useful rule of thumb is that the bigger the wave, the bigger the Muddler which we should use. I often use a dropper when fishing the Muddler this way. Something bright like a size 10 Peach Baby Doll is useful a couple of feet in from the lure, as are Old Nick, Goldie, Zulu and Mickey Finn. In the lighter winds I use a size 10 or even a size 12 Muddler. Either way you will

An angler fishing from the boat casting as far downwind as practicable, and stripping back as fast as possible. The inset shows the clearly defined 'V'-wake made by the quickly moving muddler and the pursuing trout.

be certain to get any amount of bow wave follows which fail to come to anything but the action makes the style exciting to say the least.

I like the standard Muddler but it does pay to be versatile. Try the white, black, orange and red versions as well as the more exotic Minstrel, Badger or Texas Rose. As well as the hair-winged patterns I also use them winged with marabou and some using quite a lot of Flashabou. Popping bugs can be used in exactly the same way as the Muddler. They cast well and the pull produces a noise which can be heard quite clearly as the popper skitters and jumps its way back to the boat.

If at the end of the day, you are still a couple of fish light and you have any energy left, there is still a chance to make up the bag. A few sedges will be hatching in the quieter upwind bays and so now you can switch to the size 12 Muddler to imitate a skating sedge. Aim for a much slower retrieve, even as slow as a figure-of-eight.

September and October

Time to Dap the Daddy

The Irish loughs abound with inlets and bays where the professional boatmen moor their boats. The first lesson visiting anglers learn, just as I did, is that when fishing, life over there is lived in bottom gear. You will never believe just how much fun you have been missing until you have spent a day afloat on a lough with a local gillie. When your sides are not aching with laughter at the never-ending tales, he may well be singing a song. A stop for lunch is a must, no matter how good or bad the sport has been. Everything stops for lunch in Ireland and when afloat, this means a trip to the nearest island and a brew from an old black kettle on a driftwood fire. I can smell it now, just thinking about it.

Perhaps the most important lesson I have learned from these men of the lakes is just how incredibly effective dapping the natural insect can be. On every occasion when a suitable wind springs up, the dappers will double the catches made with normal wet fly fishing methods. This has long been considered a fact of life by the gillies, who maintain that a catch of six fish to the wet fly is good but that one of double that to the dap is hardly worth a mention.

The presentation, of course, is so natural that if a trout is up in the water anywhere close to where the dapped fly settles then he will take it with confidence. Most of our reservoirs allow dapping with both natural and artificial flies. That being the case, it amazes me why we have been so slow to adopt the method. Perhaps we are just too lazy to spend time collecting the naturals. The tackle presents little or no problems. You can quite easily manage with a long trout rod or better still a light salmon rod, six yards of floss line joined to a hundred yards of ten- or twelve-pound nylon backing, a short leader and a size 10 or 12 fine wire hook. You can, if you wish, buy some of the hooks specially made for dapping live insects which have a clip to hold the creature without damage.

It is possible to dap on any water if the wind is strong enough. I have seen it done from the bank but it is really a boat fishing method. To get the insect on to the water, simply hold the rod vertically and pay out the dapping line until it clears the tip ring. Now you lower the rod and you are in business. Leave it there for a second or two then just lift the rod again and repeat the process. Jiggling the rod can help too, as it makes the fly skitter across the top in a series of little hops and jumps. Try doing that with normal wet fly gear!

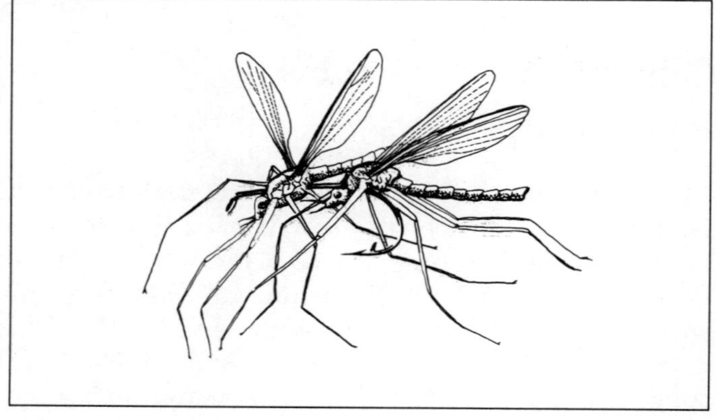

Two live daddy-long-legs (craneflies) ready for presentation on the special dapping technique.

Although, over in Ireland, natural mayflies, sedges, grasshoppers and daddys are used, the latter are by far the easiest to collect from deep grass and outbuildings close to the water. Fish over six pounds have been caught dapping at Grafham over the past few years by those wise enough to use the old method.

Begin the dapping day right at the top of the wind. After all, this is where the natural flies first land on the water before drifting further out on to the lake. Takes can come out of the blue and will either be a confident sipping in of the big fly or else a great splash at the moving fly. When they try to drown the fly like this just wait awhile and the trout is certain to make another and more determined move. Whatever happens next, take your time. The line will straighten out and then it is merely a matter of lifting into the very surprised fish. Playing a good trout without the drag of a fly line is something else, believe me.

Time for the Fry Feeders

The survival rate of coarse fish in bigger reservoirs has been very high indeed over the past few years. And what do trout just love to feed on at this time of the year? You've guessed it – fry. What usually happens at the big fisheries is this. There comes a time when because of falling water temperatures both fly hatches and *Daphnia* dwindle down to nothing. Catches from drifted boats begin to drop, but now is the time when the ever-patient bank fisher comes into his own. Vast shoals of fry now begin to show right in the margins. Their size can vary from a couple of inches to more than twice that as they seek the protection of the weed beds, jetties, moored boats and anything which will give them shade.

I have taken many good rainbows stuffed to the gills with two-inch roach during the last couple of weeks at Rutland Water. These fish have the tendency to feed very close to the bank in the first couple of hours of daylight and again in the last hour before darkness falls. Boat fishers are rarely able to get out on to the water at these killing times but, because they can anchor-up in the deeper water hot spots, they are still in with an excellent chance during the main daylight hours, especially if the day is clouded over.

September is the time of year when the very cautious brown trout of July and August suddenly go a touch silly as they show signs of shoaling together in preparation for their abortive spawning ritual. When this mood is upon them, they are far easier to catch than at any other time of the year. Many will become preoccupied with the fry, nature probably telling them to eat as much as they possibly can before the onset of winter.

Incredible catches of brown trout from Rutland Water and the other large reservoirs have focused a great deal of interest on the stillwater

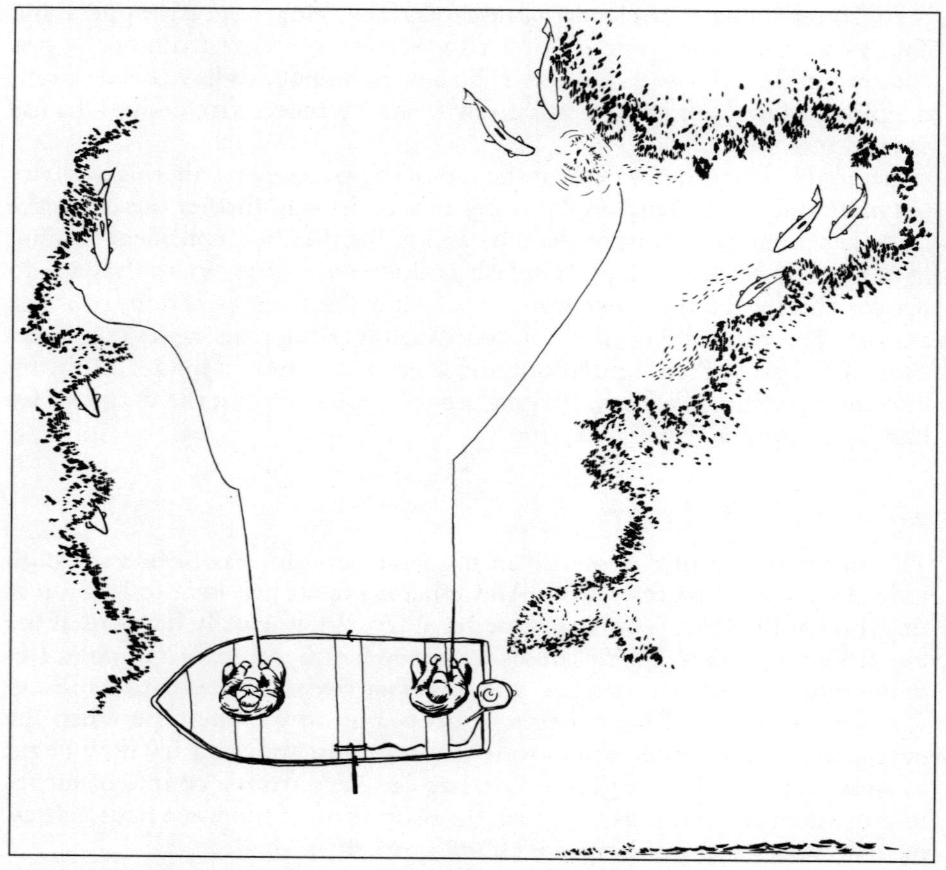

Anchored boat with both anglers casting along the edge of a large weed bed.

fishers' biggest prize. As we all know, brown trout become harder and harder to fool when they top the three pound mark and this fact, along with their relative rarity, makes them all the more valued.

By this stage of the season, the rainbows are in the peak of condition following a summer of heavy feeding. To be quite honest, the fight of a big rainbow which has been loose in a big water for a year or more leaves any brown trout standing for sheer power and speed. These superb rainbows join in the fry-feeding bonanza just as the browns do and it is quite possible to catch a rainbow of just a pound or so crammed with fry.

Don't be impatient if you see fry topping without signs of feeding trout. In my experience, trout fry feed in short bursts of about half an hour or less before retiring to digest. They cannot possibly keep on eating such large food items for hours on end, although I did once find no less than eighty fry in one rainbow.

By mid-September it is all beginning to happen. At Rutland, early morning bank men will be having a whale of a time. Rainbows to four pounds and browns, even heavier, really get the old ticker pumping, I can tell you. What really sets the adrenalin racing is the sight of a massive brown trout leaping clear of the water no more than ten yards from the boat. Brown trout, in particular, will leave the security of summer homes and it is not unusual to see them playing about in the waves. Lures like the hot orange creations, which have worked their charms, should now be forgotten in favour of the fish imitators. Although the old favourites, Appetiser, Jack Frost, White Muddler, Baby Doll and Badger Matuka are well worth a try, do give some of the newer patterns a chance. These are such as the waggy lures, floating deer-hair fry and of course the lead-headed, marabou-tailed lures, big and small.

Make sure you use your most powerful rod which must be strong enough to set the hook in the mouths of those big old brownies. Forget the light leaders of a month or two ago and certainly never use anything less than six-pound nylon with seven or eight pounds being even more sensible. A good surface method is to scrape the waves through with a white or natural-coloured Muddler Minnow alongside the weed beds. The retrieve speed should be varied to suit the conditions and the mood of the trout. Sometimes only a very slow movement will induce a take, at others you must move the lure very sharply indeed.

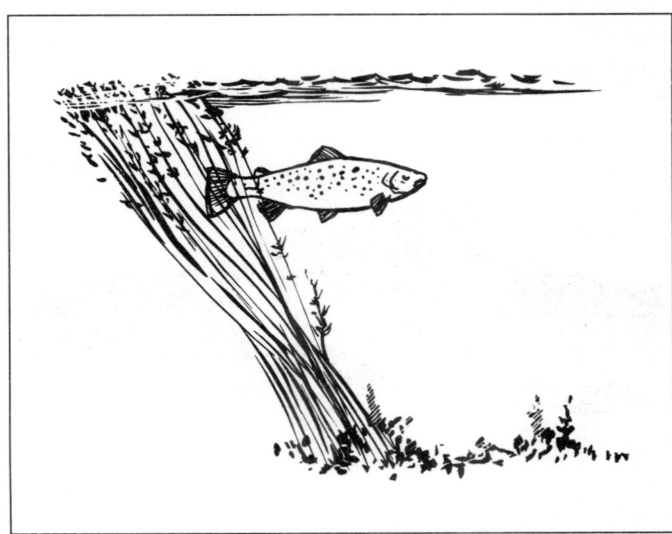

The 10ft-deep feeding area on the edge of the weed bed shown on page 318.

21

Salmon

by Arthur Oglesby

THE FISH

Much more is known today about most of our salmonid species than was known even ten years ago. The Atlantic salmon, *Salmo salar*, the wanderer of the vast oceans and the source of leaping legends, has particularly had its lifestyle carefully and accurately documented. In the past ten years we have learned more about *salar* than we ever knew before. This is due entirely to the commercial fish farmers, who were quick to see an opportunity of rearing salmon in an artificial environment and who, equally resourcefully? saw the vast commercial potential.

The Life Cycle of Salmon

Although I am not a scientist and can only express a layman's opinion it seems reasonable to suppose that all the salmonid species had a similar origin; that environmental changes brought slight behavioural and

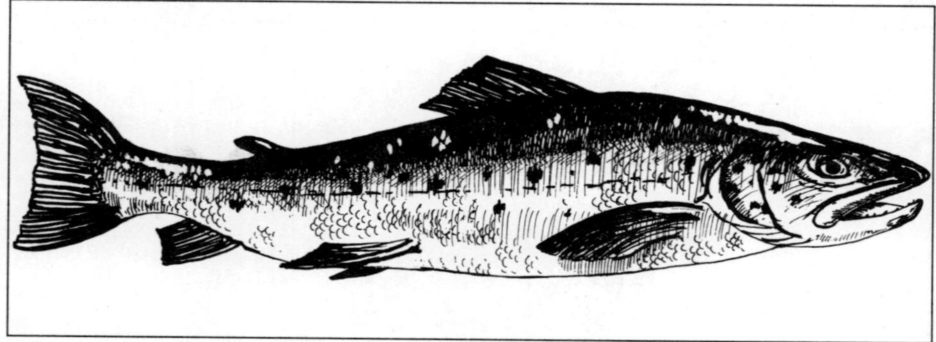

Salmon.

physical modifications and that the salmon, sea trout and brown trout we have today share a common denominator. Indeed, one does not need to be too perceptive to note the hallmarks of the species of *Salmo* – similarly shaped bodies, the adipose fin and the ability to develop spotted flanks as nature or the time of season dictates. All require a similar degree of water purity and all seek the faster-flowing rivers of our uplands for their spawning ritual. All, without exception, rely on a rich protein diet, which they get by preying on smaller fish or on the abundance of aquatic insect life which is still to be found in many of our rain-fed and spring-fed rivers. All survive and thrive best within the narrow confines of a water temperature between 41° and 68°F. Of course, they can exist in temperatures just outside these limits, but their rate of food digestion and metabolism seems to be at its best between 50° and 59°F and many of the species start to show distress at prolonged temperatures much in excess of 68°F.

Salmon also start their life cycle in a similarly highly oxygenated stream to that sought by trout, approximately six weeks after the laying and fertilization of eggs or ova in the nest or redd. This is usually a trough scooped out of the gravel by the female. As she lays her eggs in it, the male comes within close body contact and sheds his milt over them. On completion of the orgasm the hen re-covers the redd with fist-sized stones and it is then left to the vagaries of nature to dictate when the ova or eggs will fracture to permit the young embryo to emerge. Water temperatures have a direct bearing on this, but six weeks seems to be about normal.

Following this the young fish live on a built-in food supply in the form of a yolk-sac. This will sustain them for a few more weeks, but the time will quickly come when they must force their way out between the stones and face the full fury of their new and hostile environment. At this stage they will offer easy pickings for the many predators which abound. They will be expected to face the full onslaught of a flood or whatever else nature has in store for them. Many will not even survive to acquire their first natural meal. Nature is ruthless, only demanding that one spawning pair produce another spawning pair in a few year's time.

For those which are to survive for a while longer there will now be the best part of two years to be spent hiding and escaping from predators in the river while grabbing every morsel of food to come their way. In the wild state, only slowly will they develop their parr markings (faint black bars down their sides) and even more slowly (two years approximately) will they come to that moment when they don a silvery coat and nature will tell them to drop downstream towards the sea. Now known as smolts, the young salmon have at last acquired the migratory instinct and nature ordains that they must proceed to sea to meet whatever fate has in store. During the downstream migrations they may suffer untold hardship and exploitation. Waterfalls and dams must be passed; the turbines of hydroelectric schemes and the ever-increasing filth of the effluent dumped into the river from housing and industrial areas must be negotiated. Indeed, it is possible for the migrating fish to find a downstream environment so hostile that they will not survive the filth and effluent when they reach it. In such a situation you may well wonder how the adult fish make it upstream in the first place. Usually, of course, the adults returning from the sea test the quality of the fresh water they intend to enter. At times of a big flood, for instance, the pollution levels may be sufficiently diluted for the fish to pass with comfort. Then, within hours rather than days, they can press on upstream into the higher reaches of the river where the water quality is generally of a high order. The migrating smolt, on the other hand, has no prior information on the effluent levels awaiting it in the lower reaches (usually around the month of May). It can only drop downstream as nature demands and if it drops into water with a high biochemical oxygen demand it may well succumb and die.

Kelts

Those mature salmon which survive the spawning act are known as kelts. Frequently they may be readily recognized by a lean and hungry look, ragged and torn fins, a distended vent and an abundance of maggots under the gill covers and in the membranes. Some fish may have patches of white fungus on their bodies and all tend to look slightly 'tinny', as if the silvery coat which they were slowly forced to abandon, prior to spawning, is trying to come back. It may be very much a metallic appearance as opposed to the silver freshness of a recently run salmon. Many of the males will stay on the redds, either fighting off other spawning pairs or merely seeking another mate. Most males eventually succumb and die, but a good percentage of the females – those which are soon fully spent but which have the sense to seek rest in quiet water – will survive to make it back to the estuary and resume their sea feeding.

For those salmon smolts of the new generation which survive the trauma of the transfer from fresh to salt water some form of shoaling must take place. Large shoals of smolts then proceed to sea and start a vast feeding spree which will take them from mere fingerlings in one year to fish of about 5lb or over in the first sea feeding year. No one knows just what influences are brought to bear, but the fish may then return to fresh water after only one year at sea. These fish, known as grilse, come back as mature spawning fish. Most do not appear until the first floods of summer and then tend to run the rivers rather quickly and be of little overall value to the angler. Many are caught by the inshore coastal and estuary netsmen, but those which escape this mayhem are regarded by some as the pimpernels of the river – here today and gone tomorrow.

To those fish which prolong their sea feasting beyond a year we can now award the title 'salmon'. These fish may spend up to three or even four years at sea before the urge to spawn comes upon them and they start their wearisome journey back to the rivers of their birth. Just what triggers off this homing instinct and gives them the ability to find the river of their birth is one of nature' s mysteries. As they start the return migration they stop feeding and their stomachs begin to occlude or atrophy. Much speculation has been generated on the question of which comes first. Does the stomach occlude and cause the fish to fast? Or is it the voluntary fasting which causes the stomach to occlude and become inoperative? Many believe that it is the mounting sexual urge which causes the fish to fast and that the occlusion of the stomach is a secondary manifestation.

Return to the River

Those fish which remain at sea maintain a steady growth rate. A lot depends on water temperatures and the availability of food. Many of our salmon are known to migrate into northern Arctic waters, where they may go under the ice. Some go to Greenland, the Faeroe Islands and north Norway. Some may well attain weights in excess of 30 or 40lb, but the big British salmon of bygone days are now more rare while fish in the 10 to 15lb bracket are more frequently encountered. Much is still unknown of the minutiae of the salmon's life cycle, but in all instances the return to fresh water is prefaced by a loss of appetite and a firm preoccupation with the business of survival of the species and ultimate mating.

With its return to fresh water, we know that the salmon's appetite continues to be suppressed. It is perhaps a little ironic that the longer the fish resides in fresh water the less it is inclined to take our lures or any item of food. Of course, other influences might induce a fish to take our lures but the actual consumption of food for nourishment is virtually unknown.

How long it takes a salmon or sea trout to proceed upstream is a source of further speculation. Evidence is strong for the assumption that the early spring and late autumn salmon move only slowly through the lower beats of a river when the water is exceptionally cold. There is equally convincing evidence that later spring and summer fish, in warmer water, may run fast and far. During their sea lives most salmon attract parasites known as sea lice. These can survive for only a short period in fresh water. The actual period varies considerably and in laboratory conditions these parasites have been known to remain clinging to the host for up to seven days. In the hurly-burly of a turbulent river, however, it is assumed that they only survive for up to forty-eight hours. But this is only a supposition and there may be no real way of establishing the truth. On the assumption that sea lice may exist on salmon or sea trout for up to forty-eight hours, however, we may draw some interesting if tentative conclusions. A week before writing this I caught a 7½lb Spey salmon with sea lice on it at least forty-five miles upstream from the estuary. This suggests that my fish had run upstream at a speed of nigh on one mile an hour or twenty-four miles in a day. It also evokes questions such as what might induce it to stop for anything other than a short rest, and when it might regard its upstream migration as at an end until spawning time. Do rivers fill from the top, as some authorities suggest?

UDN

Along with all the other pestilences and trials which salmon and sea trout have to endure, there has been an occasional and deadly plague which strikes them down from time to time. Originally named *Bacillus salmonis pestis* in the late nineteenth century, it now enjoys the more exotic title of ulcerative dermal necrosis, or UDN. No one yet seems any wiser on the origins of the disease, but it broke out with dire effect in the 1880s and again in 1966. In both instances it took nearly twenty years to abate, but it was back again with a very bad outbreak on the Tweed in November 1985 and who might say with any conviction that it will not come back in plague proportions at any time in the future? It is assumed that UDN occurs with more deadly effect in cold water conditions and that it is of viral origin rather than bacterial or fungal. Whatever else it might involve, it seems that the final fungal growth is the last and most deadly symptom in the chain. While it might be only coincidental, the 1966 outbreak came to many rivers at a time when they seemed to have highly abundant stocks. We still had to wait for the main onslaught of the Danish high-seas netting to further deplete our stocks and it may be that the disease was merely nature's way of eliminating an excess. When it hit the Lune in October 1966 I was one of the first anglers to catch a fish with a small patch of fungus on it. Within days there were fish dying in their thousands. It was a sickening sight.

TACKLE

Rods

The subject of tackle is a veritable minefield. Much of the tackle used by our forefathers was heavy and cumbersome, with rods of up to 20 feet in length. In North America the trend has been towards a complete reversal of our traditional methods and expert fishermen such as Lee Wulff declare a preference for diminutive 6-foot rods weighing little more than two ounces. It has to be stated at the outset, therefore, that there is more than one way of killing the cat. Diehard British salmon anglers have been weaned on a diet of long rods whereas most notable American anglers regard any rod over nine feet as unnecessarily long.

For many years I was steadfastly in the British camp and firmly indoctrinated with the notion that only a double-handed fly rod of over twelve feet was of any use for fly fishing for salmon. It was some time before I even acknowledged the other point of view and it was not until meetings with Wulff and McClane, when I was actually able to watch them fish with their short rods, that I saw any logic in what they were trying to achieve. The sad thing is that the traditional British angler is still of the opinion that the average single-handed rod is far too short for salmon fishing, while the uninformed North American angler shares an equal prejudice against anything over ten feet. This is a pity because I am sure that these doctrinaire views are based on little more than bigotry. Most certainly they do not seem to be associated with logic.

It is one thing to be able to cast a long line with any type of rod but quite another exercise maintaining what I call effective water command. It is one thing to have space to cast overhead all day and another to be compelled to do a Spey or roll cast from under trees or with high obstructions behind. In competent hands and by the use of the double-haul technique a single-handed rod can be used to throw a fly over fifty yards (tournament casters are doing it all the time). With a suitably balanced shooting head and a strong double-handed rod, distances of more than seventy yards are not considered spectacular today. But such fantastic distances are just not required in most practical salmon-fishing situations and it is the man who can comfortably cast up to thirty yards of line and then control the action of the fly who will be the most likely to succeed.

Although it can be done, there are not many of us who can throw an entire 30-yard fly line with a single-handed rod shorter than nine feet. The line has to be of a forward-taper design and the elements have to be helpful. It is much better, in my opinion, to rely on a longer double-handed rod and a double-taper line and thus achieve this distance with comparative ease. The other aspect is that of being able to 'mend' the line and keep full control of it while the cast and fly are swinging or 'fishing' round. Another consideration is the space available for an adequate back cast.

Perhaps at this stage it may help to consider the different tactical requirements of the British and North American angler. Fishing for salmon in North America, and indeed in many other countries where *Salmo salar* exists, is largely confined to the months of June, July and August, after the spring thaw has provided enough water for the new run of fish to negotiate the rivers. By the time the floods have subsided it is June – a delightful time for fly fishing with a single-handed rod anywhere. With deep wading or fishing from canoes there is little need for anything but a single-handed rod and with ample casting room there is no reason to be overencumbered with heavy tackle.

In Britain it is possible to do some form of fly fishing from early February through to the end of November, but tactics vary quite drastically from the techniques best employed in February or November and those required for low water in July or August. While I hold no great brief for the ultra-short rod, as used by Lee Wulff, I feel that there are times when an ultra-long rod is merely an encumbrance better avoided. My choice is clear, and in the longer lengths of rod has been dictated by the advent of carbon fibre, or graphite, which has provided me with a 15-foot rod which will easily throw an entire 30-yard fly line with either a Spey or an overhead cast and also give all the water command I could require. Such a rod is the 15-foot 'Walker' by Bruce & Walker of Huntingdon, England. It is Bruce & Walker policy to offer customers a 15-foot rod with two differing actions. Many years ago Jim Bruce decided that he liked a salmon fly rod with a slightly softer action, while his co-director, Ken Walker, opted for one of stiffer or faster action. Their commercial sense told them that there would be a market for both rods and it was not long before we had the option of the 'Bruce' or the 'Walker'. My preference generally is for the 15-foot 'Walker' but I have used the 15-foot 'Bruce' to equally good effect. The 'Walker' feels happier with a No 11 line while the 'Bruce' seems well exercised with a No 10. Bear in mind that a Spey cast is best accomplished with a double-taper line or one with a continuous taper. A forward-taper line will not do!

Such a rod is my constant companion when fishing the Spey in April or May. It is also well suited to casting big flies on heavy sinking lines and shooting heads in the early spring and late autumn. Come to June, however, and the Spey may well be shrinking down to its bare bones. It may be easily waded and covered with little more than the 6-foot rod as favoured by Lee Wulff. With such a rod, however, a useful form of Spey cast is virtually impossible and it may require several overhead casts to work out the required length of line to cover the water properly – in other words, to achieve effective water command. It is for this reason that I opt for a single-handed rod of 10 feet. This gives me all the overhead casting power I need and yet will still permit the occasional Spey cast in confined places. My favourites are the 10-foot 'Light Line' or the 10-foot 'Multitrout' by Bruce & Walker. Both directors would hotly deny that either rod is suited for salmon, but I have caught salmon of up to 14lb on these slender rods and never felt any risk of breakage.

It must be realized that any rod of any length has to perform two tasks. It must act as a spring when you are casting and as a lever when you are playing a fish. Many anglers overencumber themselves with unnecessarily strong rods in the mistaken belief that they will tire a fish more quickly. In some cases it may be true that, provided the leader will stand the strain, a very strong rod will horse in a fish a bit more quickly than a soft, sloppy rod. But more often than not it is the length of the rod that determines the speed with which a fish may be played out. Some anglers who fish on reservoirs also rely on very strong rods to achieve long casting distances but I look for a rod which will be comfortable to use all day and which will play a fish competently. As casting time is likely to represent at least 95 per cent of a fishing day I see little point in fishing with something which is merely going to make my wrists or arms ache. Often the time taken to land a fish on a light rod is only fractionally longer than it is with a heavy, stiff one.

Much confusion has arisen in the minds of some anglers who are diehard traditionalists and who think that split cane epitomizes the very best in rod construction and action. At a sporting dinner a fellow fisherman turned to me and said that he refused to believe that carbon-fibre rods could be better than his trusted split-cane rods. He was, of course, perfectly entitled to a preference for his rods, but to suggest that split-cane rods are better than carbon fibre is to neutralize man's achievements through the history of discovery and invention – a bit like suggesting that he would prefer to cross the Atlantic in a DC3 than in Concorde.

The facts on playing fish with any type of rod are difficult to establish. A great deal depends on circumstances. Are you in contention with your fish in deep water from a boat or are you well away from the river bank and playing it in shallow water? Are you fighting your fish on a long or a short rod? And is the fish directly under the rod point or at an angle of 45°? Very often the last consideration has most bearing on the problem and, although it might not seem logical, I can assure you that, from the pure aspect of playing fish, it is easier to fight a fish on a short rod than it is on a long rod. The fact is, of course, that the lightness of carbon fibre has enabled us to make rods longer than we found comfortable when they were made of cane. It is for this reason alone that some anglers are complaining that playing times with fish are now more prolonged. This has nothing at all to do with the materials used in rod construction, but everything to do with the length of the rod concerned. I have played and landed salmon of 36½lb and 45lb on a Bruce & Walker 10-foot 'Multispin' carbon spinning rod in under fifteen minutes, but I can recall playing a fish of only 28lb on a

16-foot cane rod for over thirty minutes before I could come to terms with it.

In late spring and summer I get great pleasure in salmon and seatrout fishing with a 10-foot 'Light Line' or 'Multitrout' rod. On most occasions either of these rods will bring a fish to the bank almost as quickly as my big 15-foot 'Walker' – they have easily coped with fish up to 14lb.

It is important at this stage not to get the impression that long rods are bad news. The modern, longer carbon rods give great water command and you must never overlook the fact that over 90 per cent of your time is going to be spent casting and 'commanding' water and that less than 10 per cent will be spent playing fish. The combination of lightness and water command offers a greater dividend than anything you might achieve from shorter rod lengths.

The length of the rod does have some bearing in the playing of a fish. Often the most leverage is exercised with a short and rather stiff rod. But this has nothing at all to do with the material used for rod construction, so I have little hesitation in suggesting that modern carbon fibre or graphite – providing it is from a reputable company – is the best rod-building material available today. The long rod comes into its own in the extra water command we get from it; but it does command a fish as well providing that you know the best angles and attitudes for maximum leverage.

Although they filled a great need and will remain popular for many years the snag with all tubular rods – and one that all manufacturers have been reluctant to concede – is that they all have in-built faults. Almost without exception, they all have a spine, or a portion of their circumference which is thicker than another. This is due to the fact that the 'cloth' or matrix of carbon or glass is rolled on a mandrel before heat treatment and ultimate formation. This spine effect may give a stiffer action in one plane than another and in the practical situation of rod assembly on the river bank it is impossible to get the spines of each section running in line. Another snag with any tubular rod is that when it is flexed beyond a certain and critical curve the tubular section bends into an oval shape, with a consequent loss of power and increased risk of breakage. These faults are in-built in any rod of hollow, tubular construction and this may be why some diehard anglers cling to their old-fashioned and heavy split-cane rods.

In order to marry the merits of carbon fibre as a material and the construction techniques of split cane, the Bruce & Walker company some years ago launched a carbon-fibre rod on the tried and tested principles of hexagonal strips cemented together. Gone instantly is the problem of the spine and gone too is the tendency of the rod to adopt an oval shape when under stress and strain. At a stroke this rod has silenced all the possible criticisms of carbon fibre and tubular construction and offers a unique opportunity to have light rods with all the traditional feel and action the diehards have demanded.

Reels

On the question of reels for fly fishing there is not a lot to be said. In most practical situations a rod would cast better without a reel. Some anglers believe that a heavy reel merely balances a heavy rod. The same theory is put forward by those who suggest that it is easier to carry two buckets of water than one. It is a theory which I do not find very convincing. However, I don't much care about how much a reel weighs so long as it is well made, holds the right amount of line and backing and has an adequate check mechanism to offer some resistance to a fast running fish.

Lines

As to lines, I tend to favour those of American manufacture, with Air Cel and Welt Cel my current favourites. I find that the Air Cel double-taper No 11 floating line (DT-11-F) does all and more than I could require of it when used with my 15-foot 'Walker' rod. I use it in conjunction with a No 2 wide-drum 'Expert' reel and sufficient 30lb test backing to fill the reel. Usually I also like to use a long leader of about 14lb test. I do not bother with conventional leaders, which one can buy in the shops, but merely settle for about twelve feet of level 14lb test monofilament taken from a spool. I think that it is important not to overencumber yourself when fishing – particularly when deep wading. Apart from breast waders, which are essential on many rivers, all I carry with me into the water is my rod, reel, line and fly, and a box of flies and a spool of nylon in my pocket. A pair of specs is also an essential item for me, as are scissors tied to my fishing coat. I have yet to find it necessary to festoon my body with fishing vests, wading sticks, nets and tackle bags, but I do acknowledge that a wading stick should be regarded as an essential item for those anglers fishing strange water or those who need the security of a third leg.

For fishing with sinking lines I have come to the firm conclusion that a shooting head is used with much more ease than a full 30-yard line. The beauty of the shooting head is that it may be cut from a full line to just the right length that can be comfortably aerialized, and then spliced to oval monofilament backing of about 30lb test. When casting it is important to have the whole of the shooting head outside the rod point. Then with a suitable length of backing pulled off the reel and coiled it will be possible to make 30-yard casts with ease. Initially I merely cut a 30-yard DT-11-S line in half. I then splice the butt section of the line to the monofil backing with a nail knot and give it some trial. Usually I find that 15 yards is fractionally too long for comfort and experience has shown me that 12 yards makes an ideal length for a 15-foot rod while 10 yards cut from a DT-8-S line (the normally accepted length of a standard shooting head) is better for the shorter single-handed rods. However, I rarely use a sinking line when I am fishing with a single-handed rod. Usually the single-handed rod comes into use in late spring and summer and at this time a sinking line is rarely required anyway.

To cope with the full range of water conditions at least three densities of sinking shooting head are needed. For those rare occasions when the river is very big, in flood even, I like to have a 550-grain lead-cored shooting head such as the Deep Water Express. This I have used to good effect on the gigantic rivers of Norway, though it has to be admitted that it is used only rarely in Britain, as is the Wet Cel Hi-D. Lines more normally used would be the Wet Cel II or the Wet Cel Intermediate – the former for a reasonable height of water in the cold weather of spring or autumn and the Intermediate for those other occasions when the water may be low merely due to frost or lack of rain. This latter line just sinks slowly beneath the surface and is very suitable for many types of wet-fly fishing.

Leaders

Leader strength and length is a question which frequently crops up. My formula is fairly straightforward and is based on such considerations as the strength of the rod I am using, the size of the fly, the depth and strength of the current and the size of the fish likely to be encountered. As already indicated, most of my spring fishing on the Spey is undertaken with a 15-foot rod, a DT-11-F line and about twelve feet of 14lb monofilament

Knots (opposite).
1. The needle knot for joining backing and leader to fly line. The nylon does not have to go through a hole in the end of the fly line; it can simply lie alongside.
2. The double-loop knot is the loop for a level nylon fly leader.
3. The figure-of-eight knot for attaching line to leader.
4. An alternative to the above, using two loops.
5. The turle knot for attaching fly to leader.
6. The blood knot for attaching two lengths of nylon (preferably of similar diameter).
7. The double-grinner knot is a useful alternative to the water knot.
8. The nail knot, an alternative to the needle knot.
9. The water knot for joining two lengths of nylon of differing thicknesses and for producing an effective dropper.
10. The half-blood knot for attaching fly to leader, but not ideal.
11. The tucked half-blood knot is a slightly more secure version of the above.
12. The grinner knot for attaching fly to nylon leader.

21 Salmon

①
a
b
c
trim
d
②a
b
③a
b
④
⑤
a
b
c
⑥a
trim
b
trim
⑦
⑧a
b
trim
⑨a
b
c
trim
d
⑩
⑪
⑫

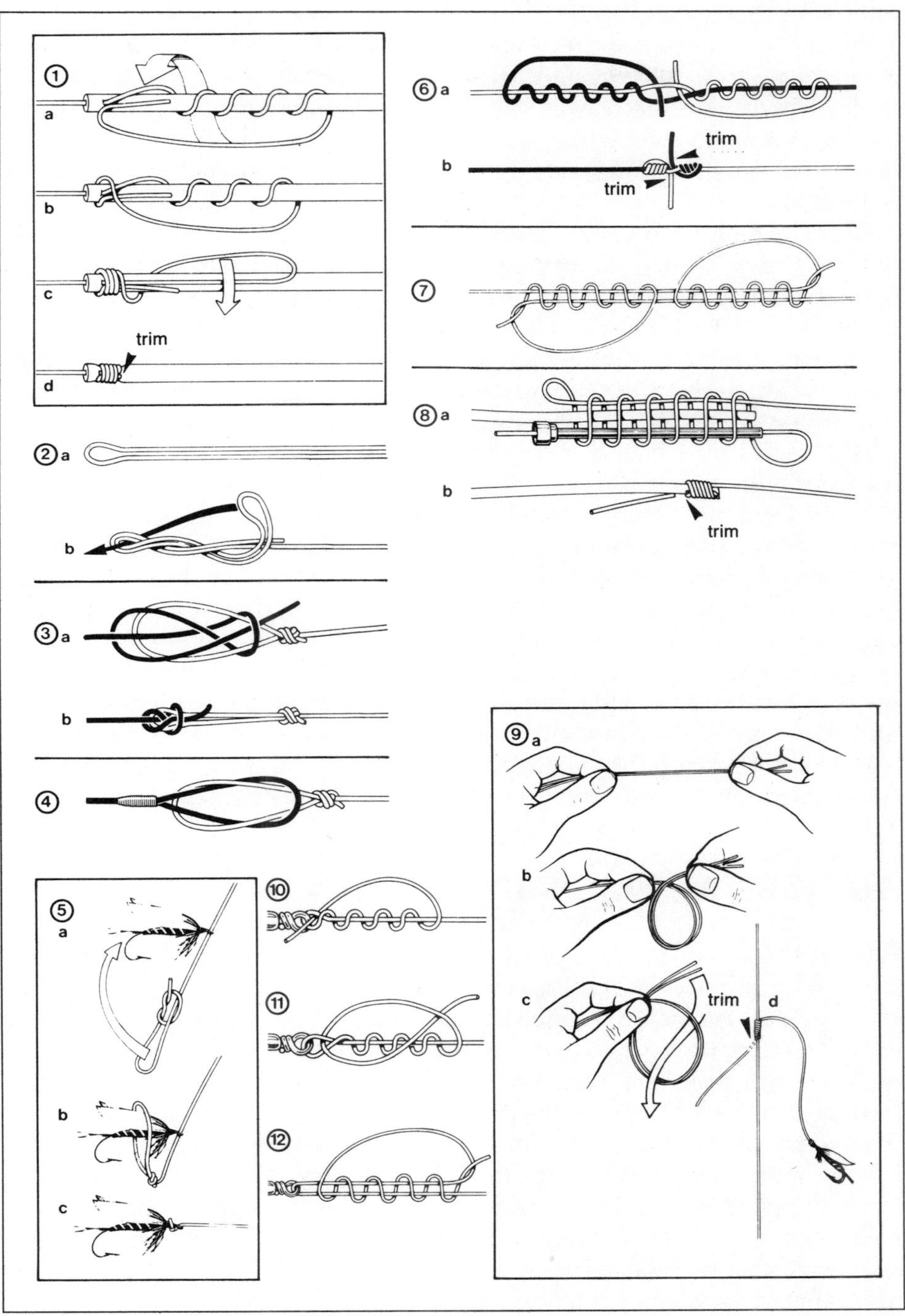

as a leader. Were the river to fall towards summer level, I might opt for the 10-foot 'Light Line' rod, but I would expect the leader strength chosen to be adequate to match the rod. It is of little use using big flies on slender leaders for the simple reason that they will quickly crack off on casting. Nor does it make sense to use small flies on very thick leaders. The fly does not move in a very animated manner and is restricted by the thick monofilament.

When fishing with very big tube flies, however, it is important to have a very strong leader if only so that it can absorb the shock loads of continuous casting. During the early spring and late autumn on such a river as the Tweed I frequently use monofilament of 25lb test in conjunction with the very heavy tube flies. Even then it pays to make a periodic examination of the point where the leader joins the fly. Continued casting can abrade the leader and thus cause an early break when a fish is in play.

Although I have caught salmon and sea trout accidentally when fishing for trout with ultra-light leaders, I do not recommend fishing with leaders of much less than 5lb test. The play has to be prolonged and there is always the risk of the fish getting free with the fly stuck in its mouth. If it really is your intention to catch fish then it demonstrates greater responsibility to use a leader strong enough to achieve this easily. For this reason I am totally opposed to the line/leader strength classes they have in some forms of competitive fishing. For the same reason, take special care with knots. Use the ones illustrated and practise tying them until you do a proper job every time. For every fish caught and landed on ultra-light tackle there are scores that go away with hooks festooned around their mouths. In my view this is the antithesis of good sportmanship. We owe the fish some respect.

ARTIFICIAL FLIES AND LURES

Salmon will occasionally take a wide variety of artificial flies and lures but it has to be admitted that there is very little logic that can be applied to our choice. As I have noted, salmon do not feed in fresh water in the accepted sense, but they do have a history of vigorous feeding in fresh water as parr or immature fish, and another, though less known, history of prolific feeding in the sea. I have already touched on some of the speculation on freshwater taking habits but reluctantly I have come to the conclusion that I really know very little about it at all. This, for me, is one of the great fascinations of fishing for migratory fish – the knowledge that I do not really know for certain what might induce them to take my lures and flies.

This is why the evolution of artificial lures for salmon has been based more on trial and error than on logic. In earlier years the angler watched trout feeding on hatching flies and came to the rather naive conclusion that if trout would take small flies salmon might take larger flies. Back in the late nineteenth century George M. Kelson, in his book *The Salmon Fly*, postulated the theory that salmon actually fed on butterflies and that similar garish-looking creations might make suitable artificial flies. Even some of our modern writers on salmon allow themselves the luxury of claiming not only that fish can tell the difference between subtle changes of colour in our flies, but that the difference really matters and can influence the taking response of the fish. Frankly, I regard this as nothing more than arrogance. It is little short of an inference on the part of these authors that they have some divine information which is denied to ordinary mortals.

Choice of Pattern

In this situation, what are you to do ? On what rule, if any, do we base our choice of the size and pattern of the fly or lure? It could well be argued that one man's opinion is just as valid as any other particularly if that opinion is based on sound and lengthy experience and not merely on whim or fancy. Usually, in any salmon situation, one fishes with a certain pattern and size merely because the word goes round that it does well on such-and-such a water at a particular time of the season. In May 1985, for instance, it was impossible to purchase a size 6 or 8 Munro Killer fly anywhere in Grantown-on-Spey. Local anglers were catching fish on them and the word spread round so quickly that the tackle shops had soon exhausted their stocks. It is my view that the fact that 90 per cent of the fish at that time were caught on Munro Killers had nothing at all to do with the pattern of the fly, but everything to do with the fact that the taking fish in the area were being offered little other choice. Against all the dogma I had a brief cast at that time with a 10-foot trout rod, a 6lb test leader and a small size 12 Greenwell's Glory and caught a lovely fresh salmon of 7½lb.

It is again my view that the choice of pattern of an artificial fly is possibly the least important factor in any tactical appreciation of the game. The size of the offering at any one time might be worthy of study, but it is not so paramount as the question of getting on that collision course with a fish which might be in a taking mood – a subject I shall continue to examine from time to time.

With this firmly in mind, therefore, I shall simply relate what prompts me to use certain patterns and sizes at different times of the season. If other writers suggest differently, who am I to suggest that they are wrong? Their choice of flies may be just as successful on their day as mine, just so long as they don't pretend that their choice is dictated by some superior knowledge denied to the rest of us!

Temperature

Over the years many angling writers have, sought to demonstrate that salmon in cold water require a much larger offering than salmon in relatively warm water. A figure of 48°F has been offered as a base for the water temperature at which a change in behaviour occurs. It has been assessed on the experience and observations of many practical anglers and may be said to be good enough to bear in mind. The fact that salmon may be caught on small flies in water of 42°F or that they will take a 3-inch tube fly when the water is in the sixties does not alter the basic premise, which seems about right.

It was quite early on in my days as a salmon fisherman that I began to experiment with different types of fly. Eventually I constructed a glass-sided tank which, with a flow of water passing through it, provided an ideal test-bed. Various types of flies were suspended in the running water and I filmed many of them with my movie camera. What quickly becomes apparent is that practically all the old-fashioned flies with feather dressing appeared much more inanimate than the modern type of flies with hair dressing. Indeed, some of the larger single-hooked patterns, as used by our grandfathers and great-grandfathers, had little animation at all. Flies constructed on the Waddington or tube principle, on the other hand, with long flowing fibres of heron or squirrel tail, took on the appearance of something alive and vibrant, and the treble hook at the tail bore a strong resemblance to the tail of a small fish.

Certainly in their time the old-fashioned flies were just as successful as the modern ones, but if we are seeking some thread of logic it must make sense to assume that the more lifelike flies should have more appeal to the fish. In the construction of my flies, therefore, I look for those materials which are likely to cause a greater degree of animation when the flies are tethered in running water. This means that I like to use heron fibres, soft squirrel tails, and goat or yak hair. Bucktail works quite well in the larger sizes but is a bit inanimate in the smaller patterns. Squirrel tails offer the most-used materials and these may be dyed in a wide variety of colours to suit your whims and fancies.

If it is generally agreed that in salmon fishing we cannot make exact imitations of flies or small fish as we aim to do in trout fishing, we must seek some peg on which to hang our piscatorial hat. I think that it is dangerous to assume that salmon or sea trout take our offerings merely because they might represent food upon which they have fed in the past. The entire history of the genus *Salmo* demonstrates a highly developed predatory nature, so we might assume that salmon on their return to fresh water need only have their predatory instinct triggered for them to attack anything that suggests lifelike behaviour. Whether in the past they have actually fed on anything similar to what we are offering is not important – we know that they do not attack our flies with the intention of serious feeding. Are we safe in assuming that there will be occasions when they might take anything that merely suggests some form of prey? If so, can we make the corollary assumption that anything we care to construct, within the broad definition of what has become known as a salmon fly, in whatever bizarre colours we care to choose, will occasionally be attractive to the fish provided that it has some semblance of life?

Sadly, this seems to be too vague and too simple a solution. Whatever offering a fish might be induced to take, it does not make aesthetic sense to construct flies which do not vaguely resemble something in nature. Every live object, other than man, is endowed with a way of protecting itself and it does this by what you might call its natural camouflage, colour or pattern. This being so, is it not reasonable to expect the most rapacious animal or fish to be slightly perturbed by the sight of some prey which is so garish-looking that it could not exist in nature?

I think that we can assume that the stronger the current and the colder the water, the larger and heavier the fly or lure should be. Salmon in cold water do not seem to want to move far or fast to intercept a lure. The lure needs to be brought into close proximity with the fish – and this usually means the biggest and heaviest flies, offered on heavy sinking lines. So, how do we construct these lures or flies and in what colour or pattern?

Water Colour

Having noted that it makes sense to be aware of the colours of nature, we have now to consider another aspect of fly selection that of making sure that our offerings are visible in differing situations of water clarity. In perfectly clear water obviously little more is needed than a fly or lure that looks as though it belongs there. It should not stand out like a sore thumb and should take on a similar appearance to many other forms of natural life which rely on their colour to protect them from predators. It might help to consider the overall colour of the particular river we are going to fish. On the Spey, for instance, particularly following a snow melt or recent rain, there tends to be a slight coffee or peaty tinge to the water. This may suggest the use of darker flies, with those containing a smudge of black or brown the most popular. Perhaps this is why such patterns as the Munro Killer, the Stoat's Tail and the Thunder and Lightning find great favour – they look totally natural in that environment.

The Aberdeenshire Dee, on the other hand, tends to have a more clear, sandy colour and this may account for the continuing popularity of the

Blue Charm, along with the Logie and the Hairy Mary. One of the four classic rivers, the Tweed, tends to get more suspended matter in it from time to time – particularly in the high water of early spring and late autumn. In these circumstances it may be desirable to overcome some of the loss of visibility by the use of more garish-looking flies, such as the Garry Dog or Tosh.

In the absence of rigid guidelines, let us start by considering what we might need on the Spey, Dee or Tay in the months of February or March. Over most of this period there will still be a deal of melting snow from the higher mountain slopes. This should keep the rivers well topped up and it may well be that the snow-melt is augmented by fill-dyke rain. With the winter floods having got rid of much of the autumnal debris, most rivers will be running big and fairly clear over well-polished stones. Other than at times of flood it may be safe to presume that there will be little suspended matter and that the water temperature is still in the low forties. Few fish may be showing and we might well have to rely on little more than an assumption that there are any there at all. Most will be well down near the bottom of the river and in those deeper pools where their workload is at a minimum. It may need a good-sized lure in an eyeball-to-eyeball confrontation to spur the fish into taking mood. In these circumstances I would opt for a 2-inch or 2½-inch tube fly on a sinking shooting head. I might not want the fly to look too subdued in colour and particularly on those short, grey, overcast days. I might opt for something with a bit of yellow or hot orange in it to make it fairly easily seen. Dyed bucktail is an excellent material for the construction of these large tube flies.

Tube flies may be used right through to the end of April if it is thought desirable, but it is usually about the middle of that month that water temperatures start to rise towards the critical level of 50°F. From long experiences of the Spey at this time I know that water temperatures may vary by as much as ten degrees in a week. I have known times when the water may be up at 52°F and a week later back down to 42°F. Alternatively, I have known temperatures to rise by ten degrees just as quickly. It is at such a time that many of us are faced with a dilemma on the size of fly to choose. Some anglers may be reporting great success on size 6 flies on floating lines, while others may insist that the large fly on the sinking line or the spinning bait does best for them. The reality is that the rise and fall of temperature is equally confusing to the fish and the question is not so much one of the choice of fly or lure but of the sheer luck of presenting the offering close to a resting fish.

It helps to remember that providing the water is fairly clear a fly moving near to the surface is usually more easily seen by the fish than one fishing close to the bottom. In the first instance we rely on a positive move by the fish to intercept the lure or fly; in the latter instance we attempt to move the lure into a position where it prompts the fish into an attack. Indeed, it is amazing just how fish will sometimes move out of the way of an intimidating lure and not be provoked into taking it. Fortunately, of course, there are other occasional times when the provocation proves too much for it and then a springer is on!

My box of flies contains a wide variety of tube flies for use in the early spring and late autumn. I like to have a selection in a wide variety of colours, from subdued to garish, and in different sizes and weights. Usually I tie them on polythene-lined brass tubes. But it is wise to have a selection on the much lighter aluminium or plastic tubes for when you don't want the fly to fish quite so deep. I think that the length and colour of the fly must be chosen according to clarity and temperature of the water, while the weight should be decided on the volume of water the river is carrying at any one time. Such decisions are not made without experience of the water being fished and, until you know the form, it might pay best dividends to be advised by the gillie or the local tackle shop.

Good Fly Height

In a normal year it is usually about mid-April when such rivers as the Spey and Dee come down to what might be termed a good fly height – that is, they begin to look promising for a trial with a full floating line and slightly smaller flies than we might have been using with the sinking line. Here again the choice may be based on little more than fancy or knowledge of the popular patterns being bought at the local tackle shop. Providing the water is clear and the fly does not seem out of place colour-wise, when suspended in the current, it may be that one choice is as good as any other. I have a great liking for my early-season flies to be tied on treble hooks. Those marketed, by the Esmond Drury Company are superb. In sizes from 2 to 8, they offer a wide permutation of patterns for every conceivable occasion. Often I fish on through April with a well-dressed size 4, but if the water gets low and slightly warmer than normal I might well use a lightly dressed size 8 during the early part of May.

Many writers have suggested a size/temperature chart for the estimation of the size of fly to be used at any given time – usually a steady graph indicating that fly sizes diminish as the water gets warmer. One suggestion is that in water temperatures of from 35° to 40°F you should use a fly of over 2½ inches in length in yellow or with a bright-coloured wing or body, or a gold body ribbed with black. Between 40° and 45°F the fly should be a size 2 or 4 of almost any colour you care to choose. Between 45° and 50°F it is suggested that fly sizes may alternate between 2 and 7 and again be of any colour, while temperatures of between 50° and 55°F might call for a dull-looking fly from size 4 to 8. The final temperature range given, between 55° and 60°F, calls for dirty-grey or brown-coloured flies from size 6 to 10.

As a rough guide I do not find too much to quarrel with in this little package. It makes a basis for trial, but it presupposes that the water is always slightly colder than the air and that the river is running at a normal height without any suspended matter to decrease fish vision. Bear in mind that with any fly fished on a floating line, and providing that the water is clear, the fish are going to have little difficulty seeing it no matter what its size. In most situations in the early season, however, I am sure that it is a mistake to choose too small a fly. There are times when salmon will take exceptionally small flies – trout flies even – but I would rather offer them something more substantial until later in the season.

Trebles, Doubles, or Singles?

The choice of treble-, double- or single-hooked flies is one which exercises much space in the correspondence columns of our angling magazines. I like to have all three on hand, and it is worth considering their relative merits. The advocates of the treble hook rightly claim that it offers wonderful hooking potential. It does not seem possible for a fish to take a treble hook into its mouth and then pull against the rod and line without being hooked. Of course, we know that fish can and do fail to become hooked in such situations, but it may be reasonable to suppose that they do so less frequently than when double or single hooks are used. The snag with the treble, and one of which you might not be fully aware, is that, size for size, it offers much more drag or water resistance when dangling in a current. The smaller treble-hooked flies tend to rise well up in the water and in a strong current they may skate on or too near the surface to be fully effective. A single-hooked fly of the same size, however, may offer less drag and thus swim slightly deeper, offering a more attractive proposition to the fish. On the other hand, a big treble – merely because of its weight and irrespective of its extra drag – may well fish at a greater depth than a lighter single-hooked fly which offers less drag.

This raises the question of the ideal depth at which a fly should swim or move when it is being fished on a floating line. Some writers have attempted dogmatic statements on this score, but I find it all too speculative to be able to deduce anything of meaning. A lot obviously depends on the strength of the current, the weight/drag effect of the fly and the length of the leader in use. Another factor is the buoyancy of the front section of the fly line. Old lines get frayed and the point tends to sink slightly. Most certainly I regard the question as too academic to be worth much practical consideration. Many writers argue, and I am certainly one of them, that in most situations of fishing with a floating line it is desirable to have the fly as near to the surface as possible without it actually cutting the surface and creating visible drag. Lee Wulff, on the other hand, pleads with us to try his method of the 'riffling hitch' when salmon become difficult: the fly is tied on at right angles and is allowed to skate over the fish lies with a pronounced V wake coming from it as it moves.

When fishing with a sinking line, on the other hand, I like to know that my fly is well down. If I feel it scrape the bottom on odd occasions, without continually getting hooked on some obstruction, I have that confident feeling that it may be at or near to an eyeball-to-eyeball confrontation with the fish I am seeking to catch.

Although I have caught fish on very small flies I tend not to fish deliberately for salmon with anything smaller than a size 12 hook. Many times while fishing during the late dusk of a June evening I have caught salmon on size 12 and 14 flies intended for sea trout. There were several years when, during May on the Spey, I would fish for the resident brown trout with size 14 and 16 flies and not be surprised to catch salmon. With

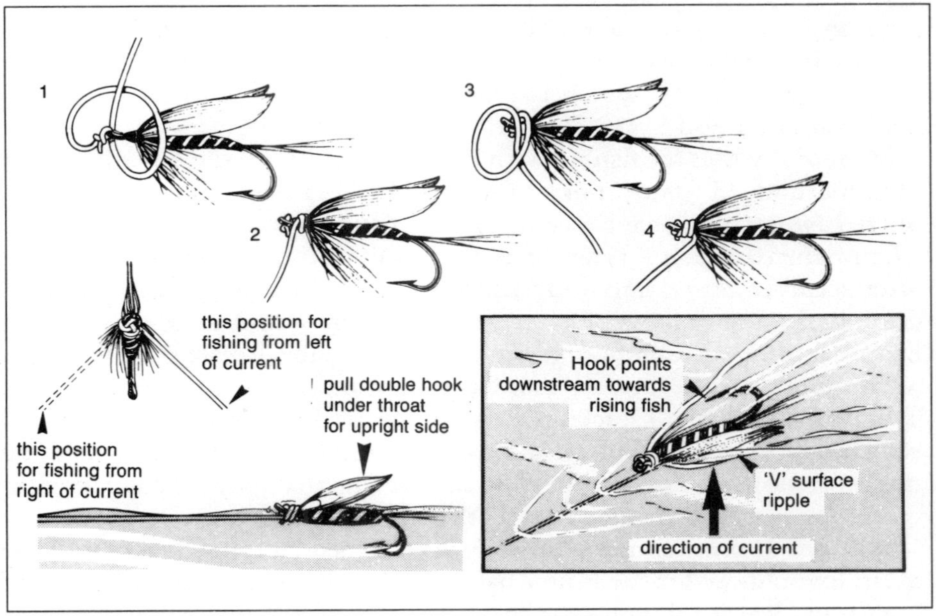

The riffling or Newfoundland hitch. The two lower illustrations demonstrate how the position of the hitch may be varied to give a high or low swim in the water.

such small flies, however, there is a danger of the fish merely mouthing them without being hooked, but when those small singles do go in over the barb, into somewhere like the tongue of the fish, they may need to be prised out with pliers.

My stock of salmon and sea trout flies, therefore, tends to be rather large. When fishing with a floating line, I usually have a specific pattern in sizes from 2 to 12, with some flies lightly dressed and others more heavily dressed. Some will be tied on trebles and others on doubles and singles. Outpoint hooks are preferred, although I do like a sneck-bend for singles. All in all I should have at least half a dozen size variations in one pattern, with a similar number of flies with more or less dressing than is standard.

A useful addition to any tube fly is a piece of valve rubber or polythene tubing, which fits over the base of the tube and prevents the treble curling round and snagging on the leader. This can occur with tubes and all treble-hooked flies and constant vigilance is needed to be sure that the fly is not in fact snagged round the leader and facing the wrong way in the water.

Large tube flies are most often used with sinking lines during the early spring and late autumn. Just occasionally I might try one on a floating line in the low water which follows a freeze-up. At best they are not nice to cast and the very heavy ones may require modified casting techniques to get them any appreciable distance. I have these tubes or lures in many different colours from all-black, for clear water conditions, to garish red, yellow or hot orange for water which is very cold or contains a lot of suspended matter after a flood.

Most of my flies for fishing with the floating line, on the other hand, are of more subdued colour. I like browns and blacks with an occasional flash of red when fish have seen regular patterns or when exceptional circumstances obtain – times of unusual water height or temperature. Red often seems to attract migratory fish and one wonders if there is a link with the colour of natural ova. On rivers, such as those in Alaska, where some fish are feeding on salmon eggs, a touch of red in the dressing of a fly seems to add to its appeal. One fly that has caught me a few fish – one which I have christened the 'Oglebug' – is constructed of nothing more than a black body with mixed black and red goat hair for winging. I tie them on trebles, doubles and singles, but I do not pretend that they are any better (or worse for that matter) than many other fly patterns.

If I have to name some of the long-established patterns that I find I use most, I would opt for the Blue Charm, the Munro Killer, the Thunder and Lightning, Jeannie, Logie and the Stoat's Tail. But if you tell me that you prefer the Jock Scott, the Durham Ranger, the Green Highlander or the Black Doctor, I should not and indeed could not offer any argument at all.

As we have seen, the old theory that you offer smaller flies as the water gets warmer and lower seems to be acceptable to most of us. There is also that other cliché about 'dull for a dull day and bright for a bright day'. If I adhere to any tenet on bright and dull flies, I tend to think of bright flies for cold water and dull flies for warm water, but it is unwise to adopt any firm notions.

I recall fishing the Spey during the month of July. The best of the spring fishing was past and the water temperature was in the sixties, but I was on a beat known as Castle Grant No 3 where that well known pool, Pollowick, was literally full of fish – old and new. On the Monday morning I went down to Pollowick and took the boat over to the right bank. My wife and a friend stayed on the left bank and by lunch time they had three fish between them to my two. It rained heavily that afternoon and we did not bother to go back to the river until the Tuesday morning. By then it had risen an inch or two and was the colour of clear, though dark, coffee. There was a foam on the water which suggested an excess of acidity from the peat in the hills and no amount of fishing with a floating line and a normal size fly would bring the slightest response from a fish. It was the same all day on the Wednesday and Thursday morning, but by lunch time I was totally fed up of my fruitless casting.

I talked the situation over with my wife, she asked me what I thought was the best course of action. 'In my book', I said, 'in circumstances like these I suggested trying the large fly on a sinking line!' 'Good heavens!' exclaimed my wife, 'why aren't you trying that now ? 'I had to admit that it did seem an appropriate moment to take a bit of my own advice and it was not long before I had tackled up with a sinking shooting head and the same garish-looking 2-inch fly I would use on the Tweed in February or November.

I had not been fishing for more than a few moments before a salmon was on, firmly hooked well down in the mouth. Of course, there is a danger of foul-hooking fish when using this technique in the comparatively low water of summer, but I went on to catch a total of five salmon that afternoon and all were firmly hooked in the mouth. By tea time I made way for a companion who had joined me. Seeing my notable catch he tackled up with a similar line and fly and within five minutes he was playing a fish. It fought well in the strong central current of Pollowick and it did not take us long to deduce that it was a bigger than average fish for the river. Twenty minutes later I sank the gaff into a monster of 36lb to give my friend his biggest ever fish.

It was not until the Saturday of that week, and our final day on the water, that I got any more response to smaller flies on the floating line. Fishing with a fly on a floating line is certainly one of the most enjoyable styles of salmon fishing I know, but the days when conditions are perfect are not so frequent as some writers would have us believe.

CASTING AND PRESENTATION

Throughout this chapter you will note that I tend to talk at length about effective water command. *Total* water command comes from the correct use of proper tackle and a full knowledge of all the casting techniques. *Effective* water command, on the other hand, comes from a knowledge of the water, knowing where to wade – or be boated into the correct positions, and superb tackle handling to get the distance and angle required. In any event, it means that you have to be thoroughly competent with your tackle and this necessitates the acquisition of all the casting skills you can muster.

Casting

I have always claimed that it is very difficult to teach casting in a book, that it is a little easier to do it with a film or video, but that the most satisfactory way of teaching anyone to cast is to get him or her on the water and literally spend as long as it takes to get the desired result. Of course, a lot depends on your aptitude and enthusiasm but provided you are enthusiastic – totally dedicated, in fact – and not seriously disabled or one of those rare people who are totally uncoordinated, it should be possible to make you into a competent caster fairly quickly. For the time being I shall attempt to give some instruction through the printed word with the assistance of some drawings and photographs.

Good casting is not an art; it is merely a craft, and can soon be earned by most able-bodied people provided that they maintain sufficient enthusiasm. But in order to fish properly, superb casting has to be allied with proper presentation and, providing you have good tackle, once these two simple techniques are mastered you will soon be on the way to being a better-than-average salmon fisherman. Indeed, there are some rivers and places where the ability to make exceptionally long casts will give you a head start over lesser mortals who have not taken the pains to learn. In this respect it is a source of great amazement to me that a person will spend several hundred pounds buying the best tackle, a similar sum on renting the best fishing beat and hotel, and then resent the time and money spent in learning to fish properly. A few pounds spent with a top professional instructor, preferably a member of the Association of Professional Game Angling Instructors, will frequently do more good than the reading of

100,000 words in print on the subject. Beware of incompetent casting instructors – the blind leading the blind. These self-styled experts abound!

Following my apprenticeship with the late Tommy Edwards, it did not take me long to learn just how important good casting is in order to fly-fish for salmon and sea trout to full potential. But general standards are abysmally low and it was for this reason that, under the leadership of Esmond Drury, a few of us formed the Association of Professional Game Angling Instructors back in the seventies. Other organizations have tried to set the same high standards upon which we insist, but in my experience comparatively few instructors are fully competent to teach all the casts a complete game fisherman might require. Even some expert anglers find it difficult to translate what they do so effectively when fishing into useful tuition. In the final analysis we may not be able to make you into the expert fisherman you might like to be, but we surely can make the average novice into a reasonably competent caster.

Let us assume that you have equipped yourself with two outfits – a substantial double-handed fly rod, such as the 15-foot 'Bruce' or the 15-foot 'Walker' and a 10-foot single-handed fly rod such as the 'Light Line' or 'Multitrout'. To match the 15-foot rod you should have a double taper No 10 or No 11 floating line (DT-10-F for the 'Bruce' and DT-11-F for the 'Walker'). Cut portions of two densities of DT-10-S, or DT-11-S will do for the sinking shooting-head lines, and these should be spliced to oval monofilament backing of about 30lb test. Almost any old reel will suffice, but I like the 'Expert' range marketed by Bruce & Walker, or the Hardy Marquis series. For the single-handed rod I usually opt for a forward-taper line (WF-7-F) spliced to backing of about 20lb test, while for the stiffer 10½-foot rod a No 8 (WF-8-F) might work better.

If you have no experience of casting at all, it may be better to start practising with a single-handed fly rod and a floating line. Line size has direct bearing on the thickness or the weight of the line. The AFTM (Association of Fishing Tackle Manufacturers) rating is assessed on the 30 feet of line which are to be aerialized outside the rod point and it is the weight of this line, and its effect in loading the spring of the rod, that determines the rating of a given rod. Most single-handed trout rods up to about 9 feet require No 6 lines and will hence have the symbol # 6 stamped on them. Rods above this length, or with a stiff reservoir action, may require a 7, 8 or even a No 9 line. Double-handed salmon fly rods, on the other hand, usually call for a No 9 in the smaller sizes, working up to a 10 or 11 for the longer and more powerful varieties of rod.

Your initial lesson, therefore, will begin with a 10-foot carbon-fibre fly rod and a No 7 forward-taper (WF-7-F) floating line. If you are right-handed, take the rod in your right hand and stand with your right foot

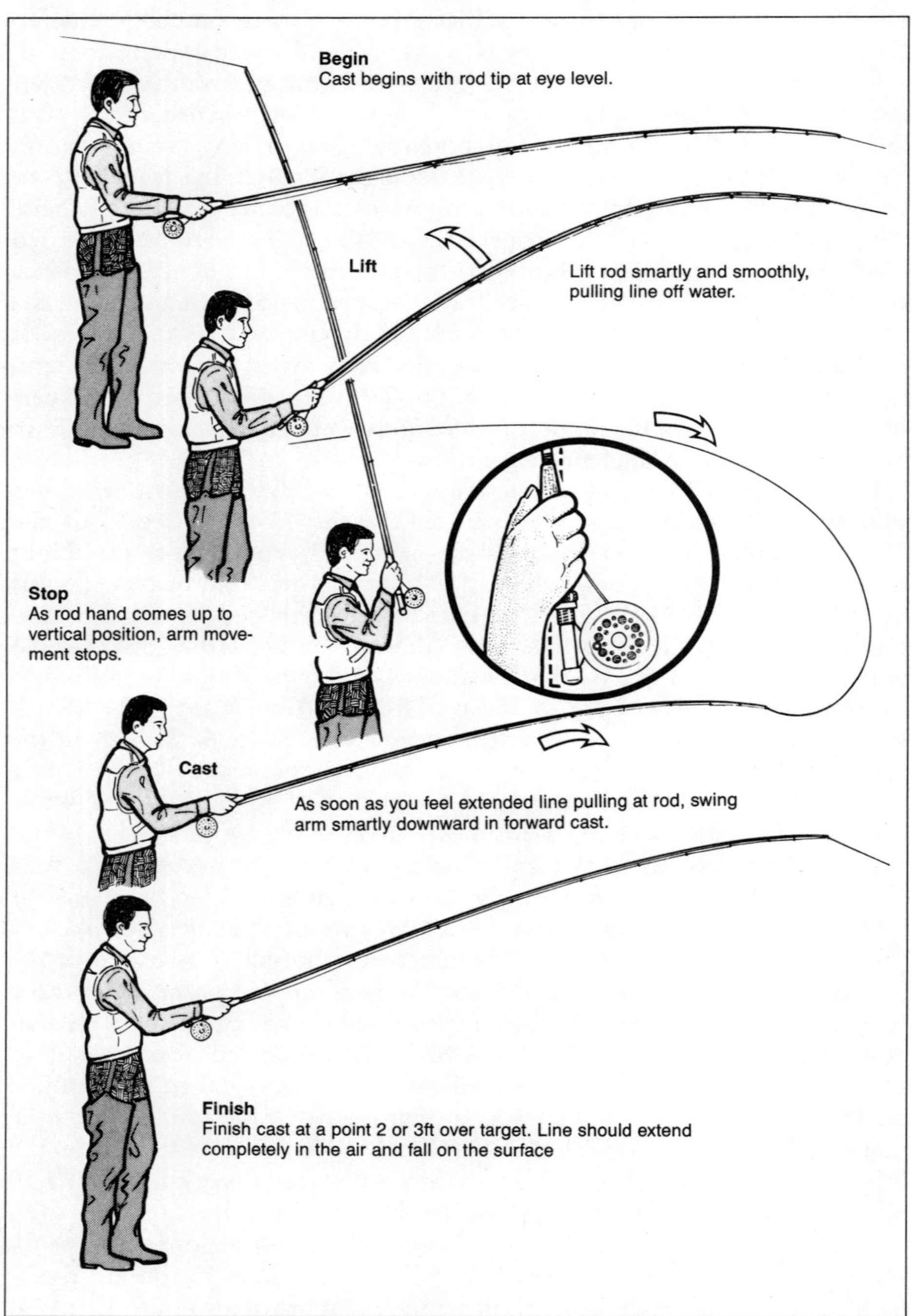
Begin
Cast begins with rod tip at eye level.
Lift
Lift rod smartly and smoothly, pulling line off water.
Stop
As rod hand comes up to vertical position, arm movement stops.
Cast
As soon as you feel extended line pulling at rod, swing arm smartly downward in forward cast.
Finish
Finish cast at a point 2 or 3ft over target. Line should extend completely in the air and fall on the surface

slightly forward of the left foot. Pull off six or seven yards of line and lay it down in front of you. Now, starting at the horizontal and with a snappy flick, raise the rod until it is just past the vertical in order to drive the line and leader up into the air behind you. To achieve this, many instructors suggest that you maintain a stiff wrist. It has become fashionable to teach casting in this style, but I find that novices respond much better to the use of a slightly articulated wrist action and the late Tommy Edwards and Eric Horsfall Turner were so adamant that this was the right technique that they wrote the following in their book *The Angler's Cast*:

The point we stress, heterodox though it may be to accepted opinion, is that wrist action is by far the *most important factor* in any single-handed cast. If the sceptic has any doubt on this point, let him pick up a hammer and drive a nail into a piece of wood. Does he hold the hammer with stiff wrist and forearm? Of course not; he breaks the stroke at the wrist and causes acceleration of the hammer head by a sort of flick. That, precisely, is the action of the single-handed cast.

Returning later to the hammer and nail analogy, they write:

The essential feature of striking a nail so that it penetrates wood is that the hammer head reaches its peak of power at the moment of impact with the head of the nail. The moment of impact, translated into terms of the fly cast, is when the rod point stops to allow the line to travel over the track on which it has been impelled or, in our jargon, allows the line to 'turn over'.

It may help initially to sit on a small stool; place the right elbow on the right knee and merely flick the line back and forth to get the right rhythm. Always assuming that you are right-handed, the rod should be flicked with the thumb coming up to your right eye. But if there is any tendency to go too far back then the rod should be raised and flicked with the thumb coming up to your nose, when, if you are doing it wrong, the rod will bang you on the forehead at the precise point where it should be stopped anyway. A good forward cast requires an equally good and powerful back cast. After some practice casting a modest length of line becomes relatively easy, but you should avoid trying to aerialize too much line as this may cause faults to creep in. You may let the rod and the line go too far back and catch in the ground behind. You may also develop a tendency to 'push' in

Opposite: The single-handed fly cast. Points to note are that the angler does not bring his rod much past the vertical in the back cast, and that there is slight movement to the wrist to obtain the 'hammer' action.

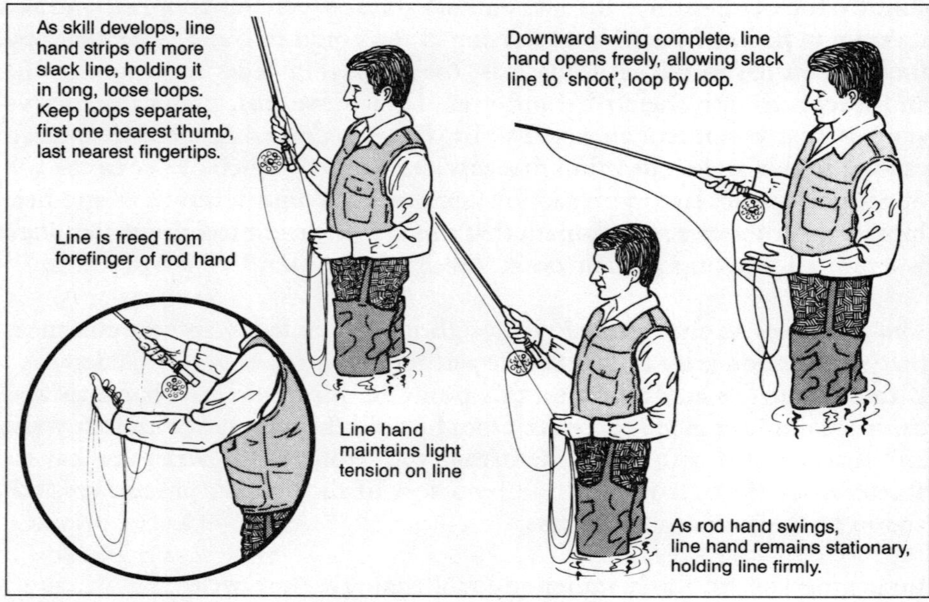

Shooting a line. Greater distances may be achieved by shooting hand-held coils of line at a precise moment, following application of power in the forward cast.

the final cast. This push will do nothing to achieve more power (and thus greater distance), for it merely kills the spring of the rod you have been at such pains to 'load'. Remember that the rod must act as a spring when you are casting and as a lever when you are playing a fish.

Pushing and waving the rod too far back are the common faults in the early days of casting. Once these have been avoided and extra line is required to be cast, this is best achieved by what is termed 'shooting' a line. Here the maximum length of line that can be comfortably aerialized is augmented by coils of spare line held in the left hand and released at the right moment in the forward cast–fractionally after the application of full power. Any tendency to let the coils go before the correct moment will cause the line to collapse in an untidy heap. When precise timing has been attained it is possible to shoot remarkable lengths of additional line. Indeed, if you replace your forward-taper line with a 30-foot shooting head spliced to oval monofilament backing you will, by the use of the double-haul technique, be able to cast thirty yards with ease.

As soon as you are competent in the normal overhead mode you will invariably modify your casting technique to give you a combination of the precise dry-fly action, just described, and the double-haul technique. This will enable wider movements of the casting arm to achieve greater distances with less apparent effort. Other modifications may include altering the plane in which the cast is made. Bear in mind, however, that any variation of the plane from back cast to forward cast will involve circling with the line – a bad practice, which will restrict potential distance as well as causing a crooked lay-down of the line.

Although the forward-taper (FT) or weight-forward (WF) line is best suited to the shooting of line, you may find if you are fishing a river which is overgrown with trees and bushes that a double-taper line is preferable. With this line it will just be possible to do some roll and Spey casts. As the longer rod offers an advantage in this respect, I will defer further comment on Spey casting until I deal with the double-handed rod.

In any event it may take a lot of practice before you are fully competent with the single-handed fly rod. Care must now be taken not to develop too much wrist action. I know of one or two eminent anglers who have a fearful wrist action. They would be horrified if I named them here, but their casting looks bad and their style severely restricts potential distance. Once competence has been attained by the use of modest wrist action it may pay to seek to minimize it and develop more power in the wrist in a shorter stroke. It cannot be overemphasized that it is the flexing or loading

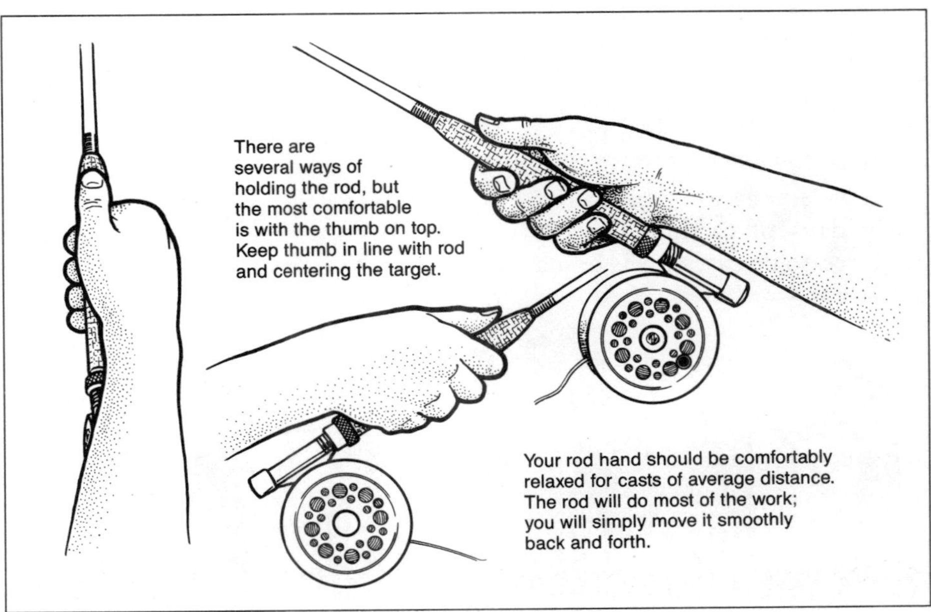

The rod hand.

of the rod that propels the line. Wafting your arms about in wild gyrations and pushing the rod will give you all the work the rod should be doing.

The Double Haul

Exceptional casting distances with a single-handed rod may be achieved only by the use of the double-haul technique. This was developed in America some years ago for tournament casting, but it is a cast which is now widely used on our reservoirs and stillwaters when maximum distance is required to get out to cruising fish. Sadly, there are very few anglers who can do it properly. Some do a modified type of single-haul cast, but I see very few anglers who can do the double-haul as it was intended to be done. The whole idea of the haul is to tighten the loop in both the back and forward casts. This increases line speed and thus the potential distance to be cast.

One snag is that a tight loop in the casting line may result in what has loosely been termed a wind knot – a single overhand knot caused by the leader catching on itself. When tightened, this knot reduces leader strength by at least 50 per cent. It might be all right for tournament casters to come off the platform with a highly knotted leader, but it does not do for a

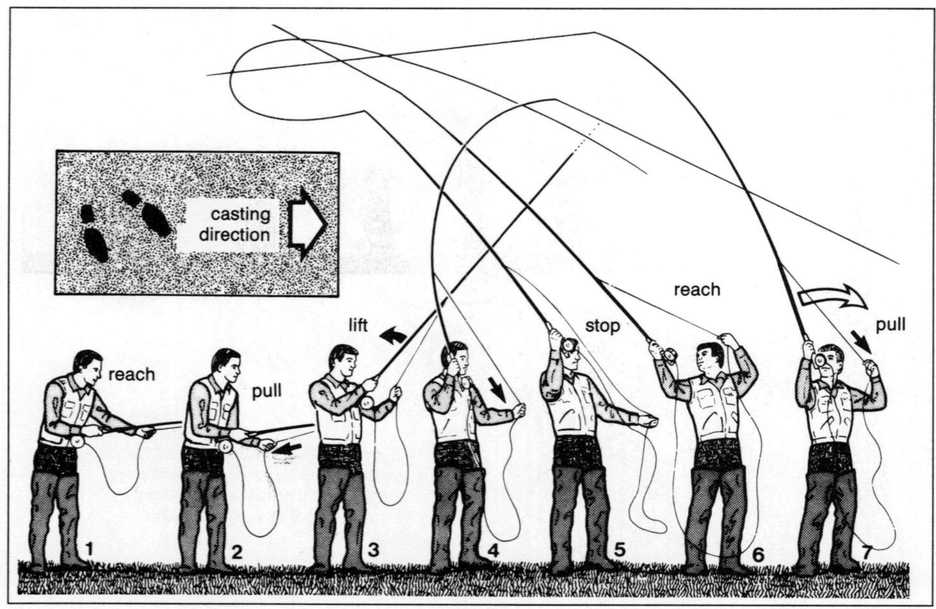

The double-haul cast. With a shooting line, considerable distances may be achieved.

practical angler to have them when he is out to catch fish. There are ways of eliminating the possibility of wind knots in normal casting, but there is still every possibility of their being induced when using the double-haul technique.

Like the Spey cast, the double-haul is yet another cast best learned on the water under competent instruction. It needs constant practice to acquire even modest proficiency. It pays to start with a comparatively short shooting head and with all the line, and the knot joining it to the backing, outside the rod point. The stance should also be entirely different from that adopted with the dry-fly cast. Now you should stand with your left foot firmly forward and with your body facing right-angles to the intended direction of the cast. As you initiate the back cast, pull line down between the reel and the butt ring at the same time as the back cast is being flicked out behind you. This tightens the loop and also produces a bigger load on the rod tip. Some slight drift back of the line may then be permitted fractionally before the forward cast is initiated with the same pull-down action with the left hand. This rhythm is maintained until you feel confident that you are doing it well. Then, with suitable coils of backing already laid out on the ground in front of you, or in a line tray on the water,

The basic principle of this method of casting is to increase line speed by tightening the loop.

release the line with your left hand while aiming as high as possible in the final forward cast. This high delivery point of the cast will leave ample time for the backing to shoot before gravity exerts its final influence and brings it all down on the water. With practice and development of the correct technique it is possible to achieve some remarkable distances. In the world of tournament casting it is barely worth competing until you can achieve a distance of sixty yards or more with a single-handed rod.

Much practice will be required before you acquire a complete marriage of the action of both hands. When properly done, the double-haul looks like poetry in motion, with an apparent minimum of effort. When done by the average reservoir fisherman, on the other hand, it frequently looks clumsy and inept. Many would do far better to forget all about double-hauling and merely rely on their old style.

The Double-Handed Rod

In using the double-handed rod it is important to bear in mind that your right hand, again presuming that you are right-handed, will dominate the casting action and the loading of the power. Initially you should stand with the right foot forward so that you can comfortably pivot onto the left foot

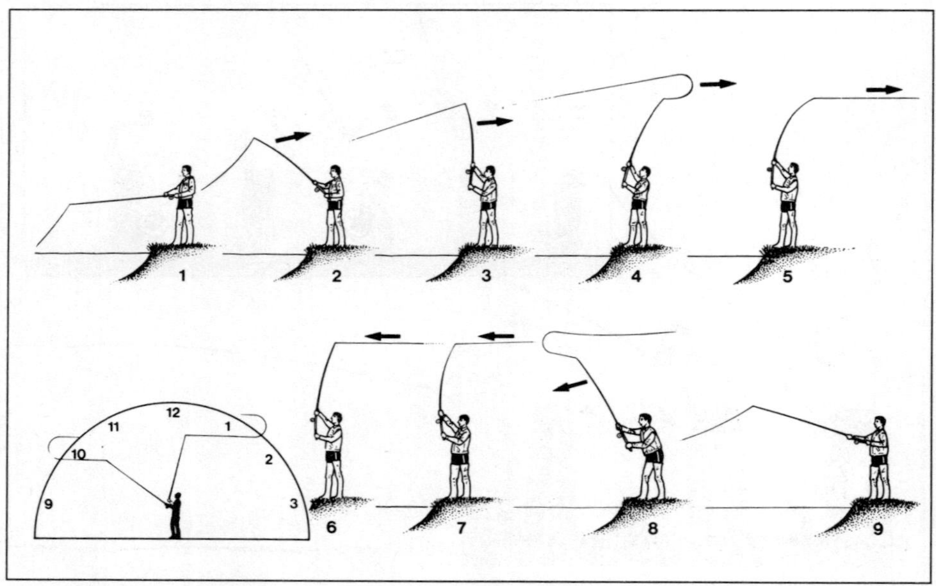

The double-handed overhead cast. As with the single-handed rod, avoid taking the rod too far back in the back cast.

as you swing back and then onto the right foot as you swing forward. This pivoting of the body from the waist upwards will itself impart a short lifting action to the rod. The right hand should be placed well up the cork grip with the left hand merely taking a loose hold at the butt, just sufficient to share the weight load. Then, with a similar backward flick to the one used with the single-handed rod, make the back cast by a combination of transferring the weight onto the left foot and at the same time flicking the line back high into the air behind you. There must be no attempt simply to wave the rod about. This will merely make you do the work the rod should be doing.

With practice and the adoption of a similar technique to that used with the single-handed rod, you will soon find that you are casting a modest distance. In some respects it is easier to learn casting with a double-handed rod than it is with a single-hander. If, in fact, you have had problems with your single-handed casting and many ladies do if the rod is too stiff for them – it pays to put two hands on the rod initially until the proper action is acquired.

As soon as modest competence has been achieved with the double-handed rod you must be ever-watchful for the same faults as afflict the

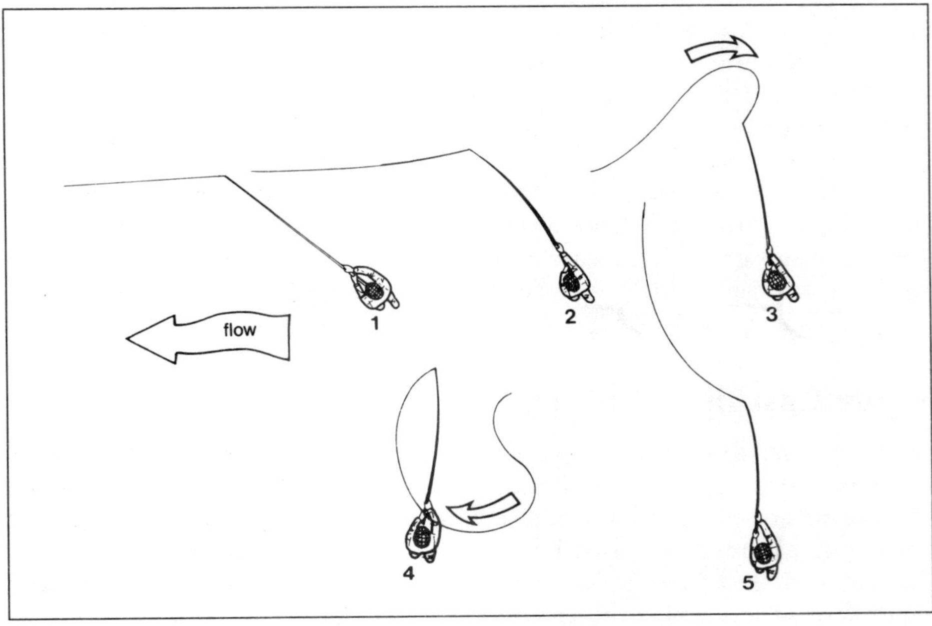

Making a new cast after the fly has come to the dangle involves making a technically bad cast; this may be overcome by making a false cast and then shooting line on the following cast.

unwary in single-handed casting. These include pushing, bringing the rod too far back, or merely waving the rod and not getting that essential loading of the spring. Bear in mind that all casts are best executed in the same plane and that any form of circling with the back cast severely restricts distance and a straight lay-down of the line. This is a particular problem for the salmon angler who has to make his cast across the current and then let the line swing round until it is on the dangle. The initiation of a new cast from immediately downstream automatically entails a circular motion, which means that the next cast will not be as good as it might be.

There are two ways of overcoming this problem. First, with a comparatively short line, it is easily eliminated if you move the rod point from the dangle and point it in the direction where the new cast is to be delivered. Make a back cast from this position, and deliver to its new position in the fore cast, and it will go out with ease. The second solution, effective when a longer line is being fished, is to pull in some coils of line, with the left hand as the line and leader swing into the side and on to the dangle, and then to make a preliminary circling (bad) cast in the direction where the final cast is intended to go. The final delivery can then be made without circling and a considerable length of backing or shooting line can be shot. Some argue that this double casting disturbs the water and this may sometimes be true, but the extra distance achieved by shooting line with this technique usually ensures that the initial commotion caused by the lay-down of the line is nowhere near the fish or the intended final destination of the line, leader and fly.

For really long-distance casting with a double-handed rod it is essential to master the technique of shooting the line. Under normal conditions of wind and weather it will soon be possible to cast an entire 30-yard fly line with a 15-foot rod. Great care must be taken not to lift too much line in the initial back cast. A little may be shot during one false delivery before the balance is shot in the final cast.

Spey Casting

Long overhead casting with a double-handed rod presupposes that you are wading sufficiently far out or that the banks are so low that the fly and leader do not catch in bankside shrubbery or on rocks in the back cast. It does not take much of a brush with the bank or a rock to crack off a fly or, worse still, remove the sharp point of the hook. While the cracking whiplash sound will soon let you know you have lost your fly, you may fish for a long time and be totally unaware of hook damage. It may not be until you have hooked and lost a fish that you think of looking at the state of the fly. In almost all salmon fly-fishing circumstances and certainly with

The angler should develop a nice pendulum action when casting. Any form of 'push' (see example on right) will merely kill the spring of the rod.

a double-handed rod, you would be much better advised to adopt some form of Spey cast. Nowadays there is barely a fishing situation I can bring to mind where I do not use the Spey cast exclusively.

Much of my fishing on the Spey in the springtime is done on water where I have a full quota of paying guests. Naturally they get the best pools and I am left with those places which are difficult to fish or which are overgrown and not very noted holding places anyway. By resorting entirely to Spey-casting techniques I do not have to give a thought to bankside vegetation. I can merely wade down wherever it pleases me and then cast the best part of thirty yards of line without a thought for a back cast. This means that while I am often denied access to the best fish-holding lies I do get opportunities of showing my fly to fish which might not have seen one before. I get to cover water that may have been unfished for weeks. On one occasion I recall going to a short stretch of water under a high overhanging bank. Within half an hour I took two fish out of it and all in full view of another member of my party who was fishing the main pool higher upstream. In the bar that evening I overheard an indignant conversation to the effect that 'Oglesby came down at midday and marched straight in to a place which the gillie had been saving for him all that week. He quickly caught two fish while I did not have so much as a touch.'

The single and the double Spey casts, therefore, are essential techniques if you are to fish to your full potential and hold your head up in any angling company. It pays to spend a large slice of your time mastering these casts for they will surely open up an entire new fishing horizon for you. A friend who is a superb overhead caster and a very fine salmon fisherman came to Grantown some years ago to help me with some tuition. He is a fine caster in every sense and a natural fisherman. I spent a little time showing him the Spey casts and he was not long in mastering them completely, but he went away muttering to himself that having spent a virtual lifetime without knowledge of the Spey casts he now realized how much sport he had missed out on. Although he is now fully competent at Spey casting he is still occasionally to be heard muttering and shaking his head sadly that Spey casting only came to him in the autumn of his life. 'Why did no one show me all those years ago?' he pleads.

One of the snags with Spey casting is that although once the technique is acquired it is simple, gaining the initial competence is not easy. Some instructors insist that a Spey cast is merely a roll cast with a change of direction. As I shall attempt to demonstrate, it is no such thing, but it will help to develop some mastery of the roll cast before proceeding further.

The Roll Cast

A roll cast is the cast you might perform to straighten your line as it lies on the water. This cast should only be attempted on water for it is virtually impossible to do it properly on grass. (In fact all casting practice is better done over water because its 'clinging' effect especially that of running water – helps to load the spring of the rod before the initial back cast. Water is also kinder to fly lines.) Initially the line should be brought feathering back as the rod is raised slowly. There must be no attempt to initiate a back cast. This will ruin a roll cast, for the power is only to be applied in the forward direction once the rod is in a position to be flicked forwards. The greatest difficulty I have with novices is to restrain them from applying any power in the backward movement. This must be a slow, deliberate raising of the rod and arm as the line and leader are maintained on the surface of the water. When the rod reaches a position just backward of vertical, hold it there for some moments while you slowly raise your arm a little more. Then, with a short but snappy flick drive the rod forwards and

Opposite: The roll cast. A useful cast for laying out line under trees when a change of direction is not involved.

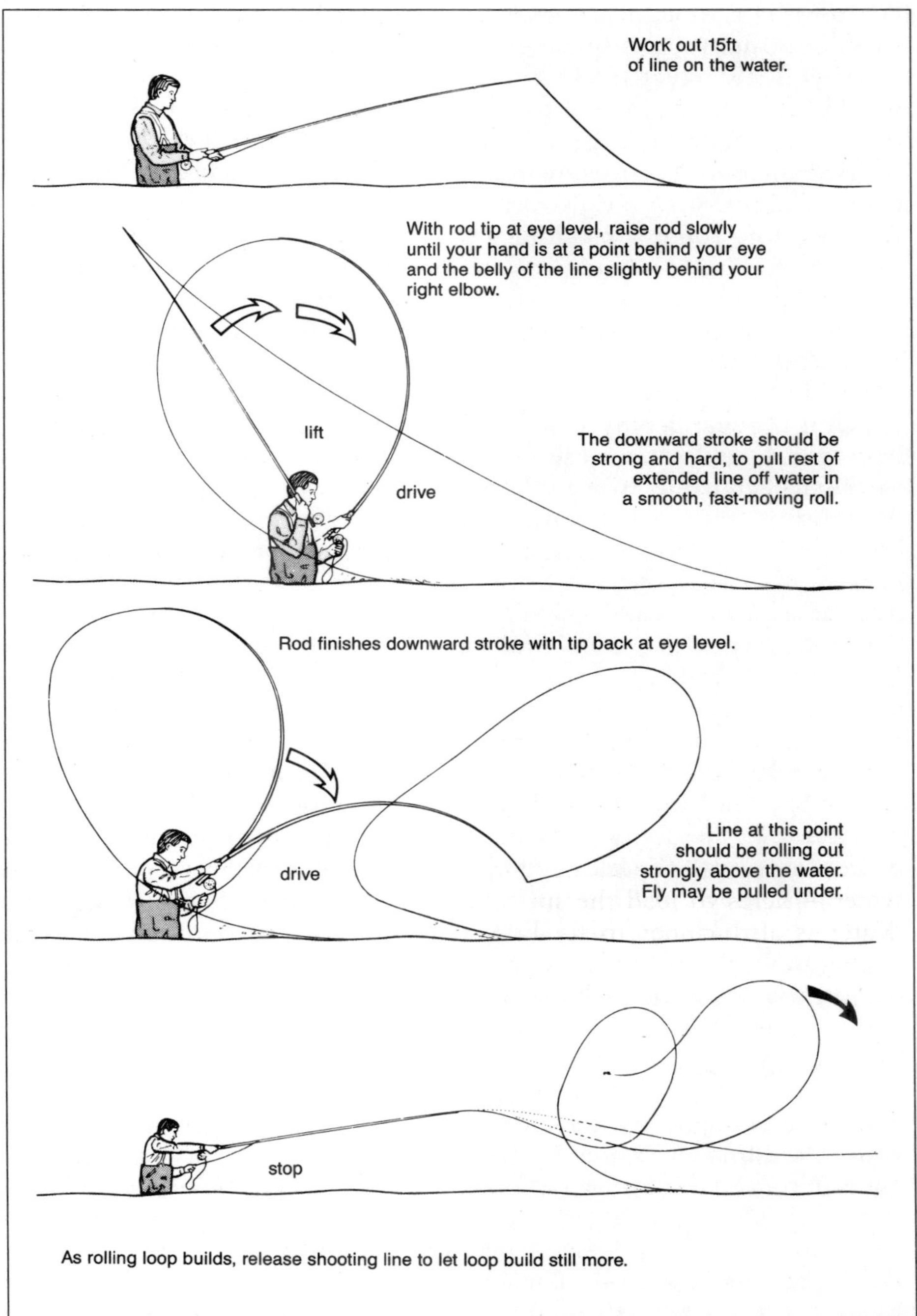
Work out 15ft
of line on the water.
With rod tip at eye level, raise rod slowly
until your hand is at a point behind your eye
and the belly of the line slightly behind your
right elbow.
lift
drive
The downward stroke should be
strong and hard, to pull rest of
extended line off water in
a smooth, fast-moving roll.
Rod finishes downward stroke with tip back at eye level.
drive
Line at this point
should be rolling out
strongly above the water.
Fly may be pulled under.
stop
As rolling loop builds, release shooting line to let loop build still more.

downwards as though you were trying to break it. This causes the line to snake back out to its original position and it may be a very useful cast to work your fly under trees or into little pockets where an overhead cast would get hung up. One of the main snags with the roll cast, however, is that any attempt to change direction usually ensures that the line fouls up on itself and the cast goes nowhere. This is where the ability to do the Spey casts will transform your performance in any location. A word of caution. Do not try to roll cast too long a length of *sunk* line. The rod might not stand the strain. Nor should you attempt to heave too much sunk line from the water in a normal back cast, for the same reason.

One of the greatest criticisms of Spey casting frequently comes from those who either don't know how to do it properly or who have only seen others doing it incorrectly. A roll cast does tend to disturb the water over which it is being deployed and if you were to learn Spey casting on this basis you would soon cause the same water disturbance that gives Spey casting its bad name. In the roll cast you initiate the power stroke slightly downwards towards the water, while in the final movement of the Spey cast the power should be applied upwards so that the line and fly are propelled well out over the water before alighting in much the same manner as in a normal overhead cast.

For all practical purposes I find it easier to teach a novice the double Spey cast before I take him on to the single Spey. The words 'double' and 'single' in this context, in fact, are slightly misleading – the inference being that the double Spey is more difficult to do. Normally the angler who is totally right-handed will seek to do the single Spey from the left bank and the double Spey cast from the right bank (left and right looking downstream, of course). It is perfectly permissible and highly desirable to be able to fish on occasions with the left hand up the rod. In this instance you would do the double Spey cast from the left bank and the single Spey cast from the right bank. Much confusion seems to exist on the whole question of Spey casting and I have seen some videotapes, from supposed teaching authorities, which are little short of a joke.

The Double Spey

For the present purpose therefore, let us consider how you are to modify your roll casting into a double Spey cast. Initially it is important to position yourself on a bit of flowing water and on the bank appropriate to your style (left or right hand up the rod). Being predominantly right-handed, I do the single Spey best from the left bank and the double Spey from the right – although obviously I occasionally have to teach and demonstrate both styles. Let us imagine, therefore, that you are on the right bank of a river like the Spey and that you are wading up to your knees in smooth but easily flowing water. The fly has come round on to the dangle and you now need to get it back across the current for its new swing. There is a high bank behind you and overhead casting is impossible. Of course, it is just possible from this bank that you could fudge a type of roll cast which would get your fly out somewhere near where you want it but with a proper double Spey cast it will go a lot further and with much less fuss and water disturbance.

Initially, the line should be led upstream slightly so that the bulk of what was originally on the dangle is now in a position in front of you, floating on the water. If too much line is led upstream it will be difficult to cast across the water without the line catching on itself. Some prolonged practice will be required in order to lead just the right amount of line into the right spot before the rod is reversed from the left to the right of your body for the final roll or shoot. This last movement has to be performed with a lot of energy and the final punch must be made upwards and not down at the water. This final hit should be a short, sharp, upward jab with such power that again you appear to be trying to break your rod.

In all instances of good Spey casting it is essential to be wading. This enables subtle little movements to be induced which will enable you to cast just that bit further than Mr Average. Ask a casting instructor if he can Spey-cast an entire 30-yard fly line and he will invariably make noises to the effect that the wind is wrong or that his arm aches – any excuse to avoid the crunch confrontation. Of course, it may be impossible to throw even twenty yards if there is a contrary wind or if the tackle is mismatched. Even in ordinary fishing conditions only rarely is it possible to cast more than thirty yards with the double Spey cast, but this is frequently possible with the single Spey. When I was testing a prototype of the new Hexagraph carbon rods in the spring of 1985 I managed a measured Spey cast of 40 yards – albeit in a helpful wind. This is not a distance which is easily achieved and certainly not with a normal double-tapered line in the overhead mode.

The Single Spey

The single Spey cast, therefore, is, in my opinion, the most useful cast throughout a season on a salmon river with a double-handed salmon fly rod. Being more powerful with my right hand up the rod, I tend to use it more on the left bank than on the right. I like to be wading slightly out from the bank so that the first and second movements may be made without any risk of the line catching on the bank behind me while I am executing the cast.

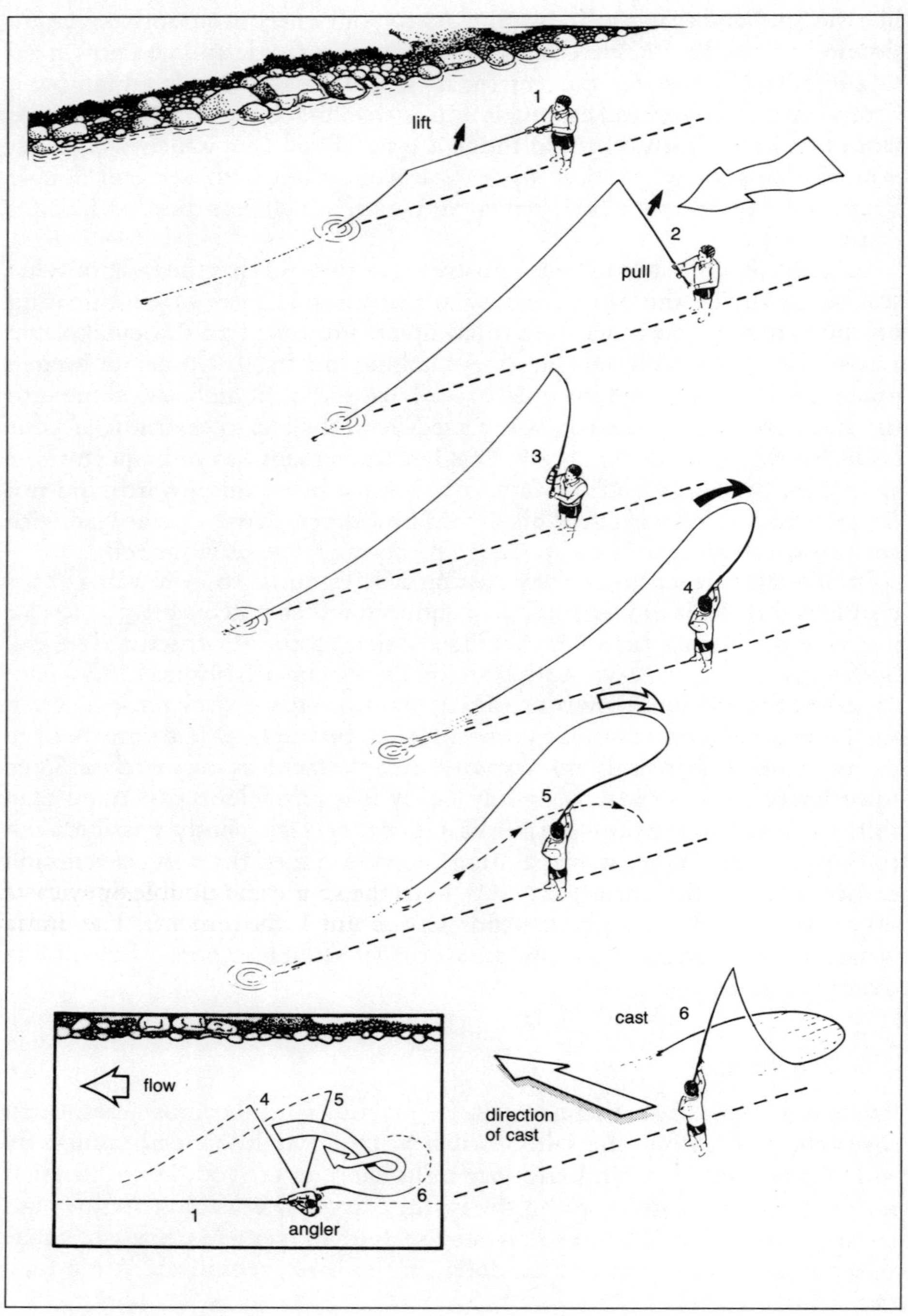
1
lift
2
pull
3
4
5
cast
6
direction
of cast
flow
4
5
6
1
angler

21 Salmon

Let us now assume that I have the entire 30 yards of line outside my rod point and that I am using my 15-foot rod and a double-taper No 11 floating line in a slightly favourable wind – that is, one coming from left to right over my shoulders as I face downstream. With the rod parallel to the river bank, the fly comes onto the dangle, at which point I lower the rod point down near the water surface. I then handline back the reverse-tapered portion of the line until the thick belly portion is just outside the rod point and the rest is neatly coiled in my left hand. I then raise the rod point slowly with just the suggestion of a slight inclination towards my own bank as I do so. At a position where the rod is nearly vertical I pause momentarily and then make a purposeful movement, just like describing a large crescent moon in the sky with my rod point, so that the line which was originally all laid downstream of me is suddenly removed to a position on the water in a large semicircle slightly upstream of where I am standing. This is the crucial movement and it is not achieved without constant practice. With insufficient switch some portion of the line will remain on the water downstream below me and obstruct an effective final cast. If it is all switched too far upstream, on the other hand, it is not sufficiently near to be punched out properly in the final cast. The fly must be just upstream of the angler.

Presuming that the miracle happens for you the first time you make the 'U' movement, you should then let the rod point come a little further back before making the final and important punch out, shooting the hand-held tapered portion of the line as you do so. This final cast is to be likened more to a bait cast than a roll cast. All the force must be directed upwards towards the top of the clouds on the far horizon. Imagine, if you like, that you are immersed up to your neck in water and then try to throw the line upwards at an angle of 45° so that it can all alight as softly as a normal overhead cast. Remember that, with both the single and double Spey casts, force or power is only required in the final movement. The initial movements merely involve a form of carefully caressing the rod and line, coaxing them into a position where the power can best be applied to full effect.

Although distinct pauses must be made between each movement, in a strong current of water only a little time elapses before the position of the line in relation to the water surface changes. In practice it is helpful to try and do the three movements to waltz time, saying to yourself one-two-

Opposite: The single Spey cast from the left bank, with the right hand up the rod. Achieving the effects of examples 5 and 6 seems to provide the most difficulty for novices. The final cast, following example 6, should be aimed high and not like the roll cast.

three, one-two-three, *wham*! In the case of the single Spey cast the first 'one-two-three' will cover the period when the line is being lifted to the near vertical; the second 'one-two-three' to the all-important period when the 'U' movement or the crescent moon is being drawn in the sky; while the wham! describes the power needed to drive the line out and upwards to its new position.

In the double Spey cast, of course, the first 'one-two-three' covers the lift of line horizontally and slightly upstream to get the bulk of the line on the water immediately in front of you. The next 'one-two-three' will relate to the time taken to switch the rod point back to your right-hand side before the final wham ! to send it out to its intended destination. Both casts will need a lot of practice before full competence is attained.

At no time will Spey casting be easy in a contrary wind. Single Spey casting in a downstream wind is not only difficult, it is highly hazardous. Unless great care is taken there is every chance that the fly will catch you in the shoulder or in the ear or neck. A much better idea is to change hands and do a double Spey cast with the left hand up the rod. Similarly with an upstream wind on the right bank. Again, in this instance, it is much easier to change hands and merely do a single Spey cast with the left hand up the rod.

In all salmon casting situations with a double-handed rod it is important to initiate the cast with the rod point down near the water surface. In the overhead mode this allows a slow but purposeful acceleration of the rod point to a position where the flick is initiated to develop full power on the back cast. When you are competent in this mode, but only then, it will be found permissible to allow some slight drift back of the rod point as the line moves behind you. Then, when it is felt – and not imagined that the line is fully unfurled, the new power stroke may be initiated in the forward direction, followed by a slow movement of the rod point back down towards the water. This forward movement of the rod point following the application of power serves two purposes. First, it eliminates any tendency to stop the power stroke with the rod point still in a high position. It is in this high position that the forward-moving line, travelling as it should do in a fairly tight loop, may switch over itself and thus put a wind knot into line or leader. Any tendency to put wind knots in the leader at this stage of the cast, therefore, is easily remedied by lowering the rod point immediately after the power stroke has been completed.

As soon as the cast has been completed, however, it pays to lift the rod point slightly so that it is in what I shall call the *expectant erection* attitude. The higher the rod point and the more it is held at right angles to the river bank, the more line will be kept free of the belly-forming central current.

Although an initial 'mend' may be needed after the cast, the high-held rod will enable your fly to come round more slowly than it would do if you merely kept the rod point in the *despondent droop* attitude or moved the point of the rod in line with the river bank. This latter tactic may be useful in a very slack current, but in a normal flow of water it is more likely to drag your fly round too quickly for it to be of interest to the fish. It cannot be overemphasized that most times you are seeking to achieve a slow movement of the fly over the fish lies.

Good casting will not come without expert tuition, thorough practice and prolonged practical experience. Some will have a natural flair for it while others will need time before competence is developed. Some anglers never seem to reach full potential and there are those who feel that it is not too important anyway. In a boat-fishing situation, of course, the boatman may easily compensate for any lack of skill, but if you are to wade and fish without a gillie at your side it is impossible to be too good at casting. In such fishing conditions it will often be the best caster who will most frequently win the day.

FLY FISHING THROUGH THE SEASON

The Early Season

Let me start by taking you up to the banks of the River Tweed in time for the opening day there on 1 February. Let me assume that you have access to a beat in the vicinity of Kelso; that the water is a few feet above normal, but running clear; that there is an icy chill in the air and that the water and air temperatures are similar at around 35° or 40°F; that you know or can see that the river has a good stock of spring fish; and that, initially, you are going to fish from a boat.

For the first two weeks of the season on Tweed you will be bound by a fly-only rule so there will be no temptation to consider other methods and little difficulty in deciding to put up your 15-foot carbon fly rod, a No 11 sinking shooting-head line and a stout leader of about twenty-five pounds test. You will possibly choose a rather garish-looking tube fly of between two and a half and three inches and, since he will know the strength of the current and the depth of the pools better than you, you may seek your boatman's advice on the weight of this fly and whether it should be mounted on a light, polythene tube or a heavy brass tube. He will then move you out in the boat and when you are positioned on the edge of the current he will suggest that you start casting.

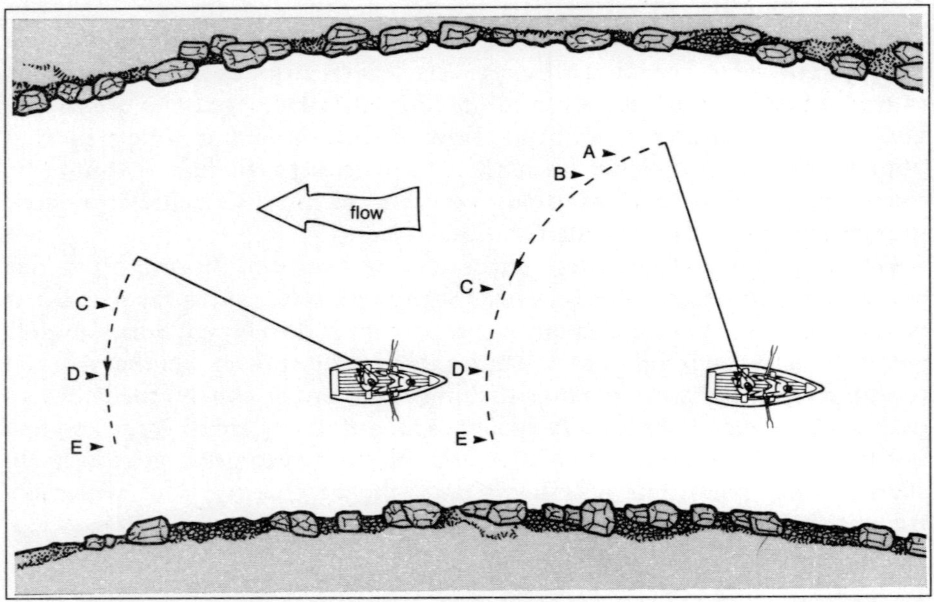

Two casts of equal distance might achieve different results. In cold, high water the boat on the left would present the fly more slowly. In lower, warmer water the boat on the right would search more slowly and still present the fly at a reasonable pace.

Initially it will help to make a few short casts out towards the opposite bank, pulling a yard or two of line and backing off the reel at every cast until your boatman suggests that you have sufficient line out. Always remember, however, that the longer cast will enable your fly to get further down in the water and that holding up the rod point in the expectant erection position, immediately following your cast, will keep more line off the water, as it starts its swing, and thus lets the fly sink further down anyway. Don't be in too much of a hurry to strip the backing in for the next cast. Let the fly dangle for a second or two behind the boat and then only casually pull in the first two or three loops of backing. There may be many instances during the cold weather of early spring and late autumn when fish will slowly follow the fly and only take it as it is being withdrawn back upstream. Sometimes, but more particularly in the autumn, I have had my fly snatched when I have been handlining the backing in at full speed.

All the time you are fishing try to take careful note of how much your boatman moves the boat between each cast. Most times, when you come to the best taking places, he will let your fly cover the area more

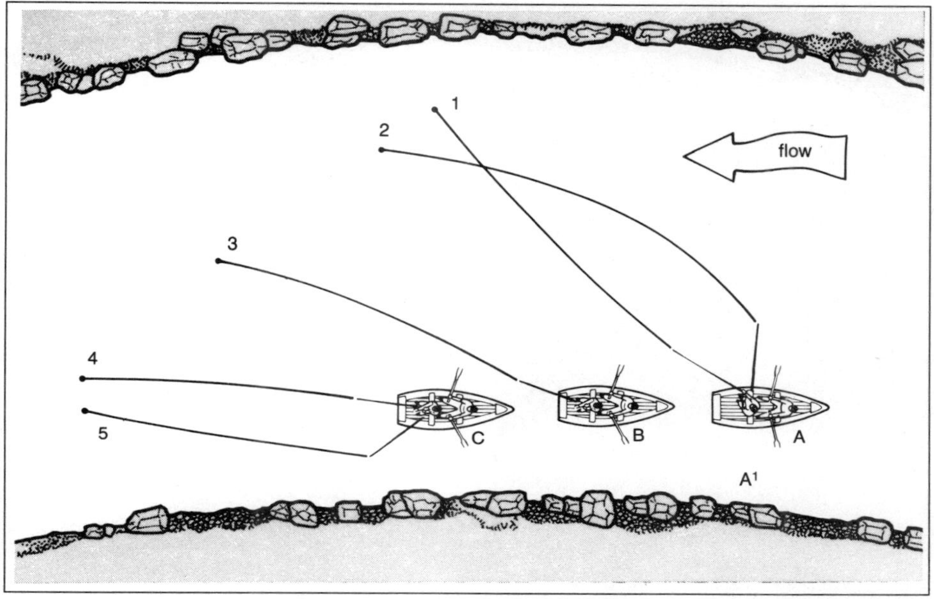

Fishing fast water with a boat requires the boat to drop downstream slightly as the cast is being fished out.

thoroughly. In any event maintain your same rhythm and style and don't forget about the slight pause before you start the retrieve for the next cast.

By 11 a.m. you are getting down to the middle of the pool on which you started, the current is easing a little, and you sense that your fly may be going down a little too deep. Frankly, this won't matter so long as you are not actually scraping the bottom too frequently, but if this does occur then it will be better if you change your fly for one of the same length and colouring as your original choice but tied on a lighter tube.

At the very next cast you feel an exciting tug on the line and a fish is on. It pulls and thrashes on the surface and eventually starts to come towards you with, perhaps, a little greater ease than you might have thought normal. Although quite bright-looking, the fish looks a little lean and your boatman offers the early remark, 'It might be a kelt.' The fish is duly netted and a close look inside the gills reveals that they are covered in maggots. Some of the fins are ragged and torn and the vent is distended. You do not need to be very clever to deduce that it is a kelt and you promptly remove the hooks and put it back.

Bear in mind that not all kelts will be quite so easy to identify. Some may fight with a deal of stamina and may look a lot more handsome than stale

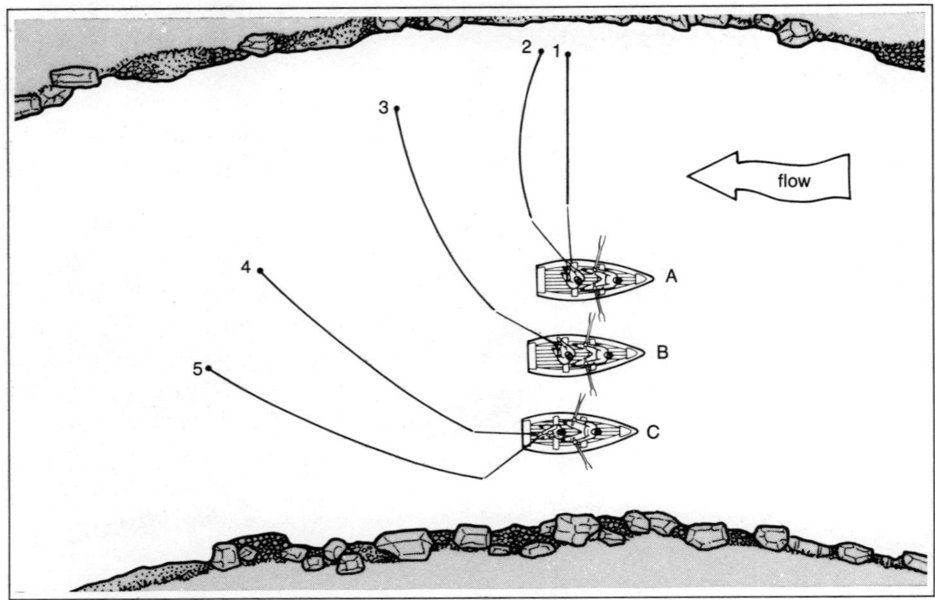

Fishing sluggish water with a boat may involve the boatman manoeuvring the boat back towards the bank as a square cast is fished out.

fish which, although they have not spawned, have been in the river a long time. Take care also to check whether any fish you catch is a baggot or what Tweed fishermen call a kipper. These are respectively unspawned or partially unspawned female and male fish and used to be encountered fairly frequently several years ago when I fished the Tweed in February.

While most baggots are quickly identified by the fact that they begin to extrude eggs fairly quickly when handled, there will be times when they carry sea lice and when the eggs may not be shed until after you have knocked the fish on the head. Kippers (unspawned male fish) are more easily identified and usually have a partial hook or kype uncommon in fresh-run springers. They may also show slight discolouration and some may only be partially spawned and still seeking another mate to complete final and total orgasm. Remember that both are classed as unclean fish and it is unlawful to kill them.

With the kelt safely returned it is not long before you feel another slow draw at the fly. The line just stops rather solidly and you may wonder, as I frequently do when I hook a salmon on the sunk line, whether it is a fish or whether I have merely snagged on the bottom. But you then feel that electric movement as the fish backs away. It may be that there is little initial activity and your boatman will have ample time to row slowly for the shore. In these early months, and particularly on the Tweed, he will know that it is not likely to be a very big fish and that the chances of it taking you a long way from where you hooked it will be slight. Nonetheless, he will maintain the boat just out from the bank until he is convinced that you are in full control. Only then will he row for the shore, tether the boat to the bank and stand by with his waiting net.

At this stage many anglers feel some compulsion to get out of the boat and onto the bank so that they can move up and down the river in order to follow the fish as it moves. Frankly, you will not impress your boatman if you do this. The experienced angler will sit tight and continue to play the fish from the boat. In a dire emergency, when the fish makes a long run, it will be a simple matter for the boatman to get back in and move you to a new position. Far better, therefore, that you remain seated and continue to play your fish from where you are. There is nothing more likely to frustrate a boatman than to have you on the bank running back and forth as the fish moves while he dashes hither and thither trying to net it for you.

Eventually, as your fish begins to tire, it will thrash on the surface in the vicinity of the boat. Don't be in too much of a hurry at this stage and do make sure that your reel can always run free should the fish make a sudden lunge for deeper water.

In a very short while now your fish begins to tire and to flounder onto its side. It is while it does this that you should suddenly take command and lead it like an unwilling dog over the rim of the waiting net. Your boatman will do the rest and he will raise the net the instant you lead the fish, head first if you can, over the net. Hey presto! You have a handsome springer of 8lb to start your season.

After lunch your boatman decides to rope you down a pool which is a little more shallow. There is a nice edge to the current where running fish might choose to lie temporarily. He suggests that you put up an intermediate weight sinking line, but with the same fly you had on when you caught your fish, which will enable your fly to move over the shallower water without getting hung up.

If, as your week progresses, the river drops fractionally, this will be a pool where you might profitably wade. Throughout your week note how the river rises with melting snow or rain or falls after overnight frosts, and how the changing water height affects the tactics advised by your boatman. You should take special note of the places where you actually hook fish, the time of day and the height of the water. This knowledge, stored in a recess of the mind, will eventually make you almost totally independent of your boatman in deciding tactics for any given day. By that time you may even be able to suggest a specific course of action to suit yourself or the prevailing conditions, but it will not be knowledge which is easily won.

During this time you may expect the weather to do all of the most diabolical things it is possible to endure. For instance, the river could be in roaring flood and not worth a cast. Alternatively, it might even be frozen over or so covered in a form of slushy ice, known as *grue*, as to be virtually impossible to fish. Sometimes it is just feasible to make the odd cast in heavy grue, but it may prove difficult to get the line to sink and not continually get fouled up on the moving ice floes. Putting the rod point under the water immediately after the cast sometimes gets your fly clear of the grue and into a position where it might attract a taking fish.

In flood conditions, of course, your fishing activity will tend to be confined to that portion of the river immediately under your own bank. Here again it may be thought that a short cast will suffice, but do always bear in mind that the longer cast will get your fly down further in the water and in times of flood you will want your fly down anyway, despite the fact

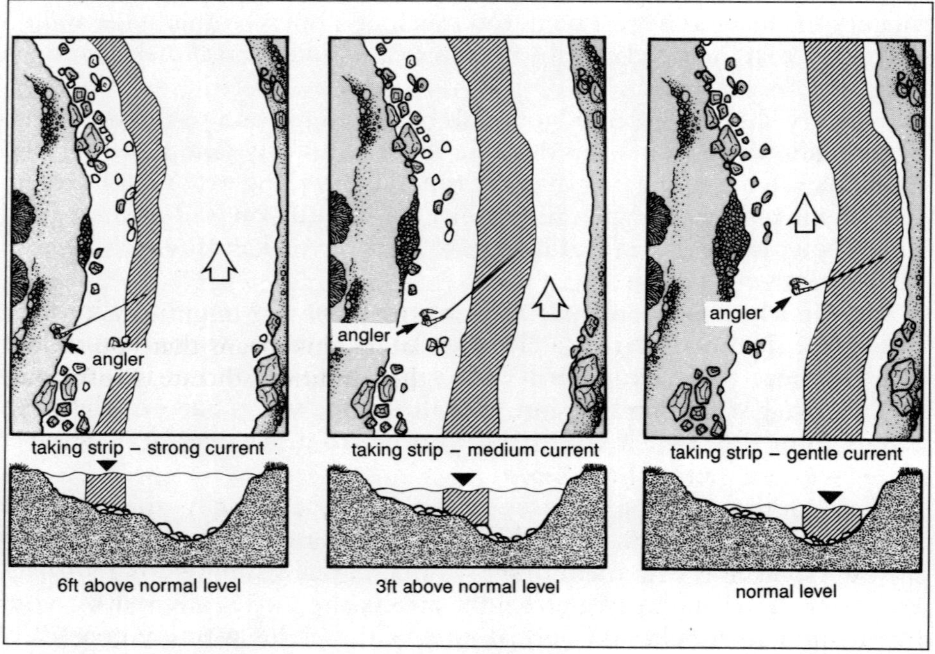

Effective water command. In a high water (left) the fish may be close into the bank and the angler will achieve EWC from the bank. In a normal water (centre) some wading may be necessary. In a very low water fish will be confined to the main channel and deep wading may also be necessary.

that the fish you hope to catch may be only a few feet out from the bank. Effective water command is one thing, but at times of very cold and high water you also have to think in that third dimension – the depth of the water.

Spring

On your return from the Tweed with a nice catch of fish for your deep freeze, you begin to get excited about the real spring – when you hear the dawn chorus of birdsong and when daffodils spread their colours into the warming winds. You have planned a visit to the Spey in late April or early May. It is on a good beat downstream of Grantown and your gillie advises you, from long experience of his piece of water, to bring a 15-foot double-handed fly rod with both floating and sinking lines, and a wide variety of fly patterns and sizes, as well as a 10-foot trout fly rod with appropriate line, leaders and flies.

Unless the river is running big from melting snow, which it could well be at this time of the year, you will be fishing in breast waders and you might also need a wide variety of clothing to cover rapidly changing weather conditions. In the April of 1984, for instance, there were several days when Strathspey, with a shade temperature running into the seventies, was the hottest place in Europe. During late April 1985, on the other hand, we still had to suffer some bitter north-east winds with heavy snow showers.

You must also be aware of the wide range of water temperatures at this time of year – as much as ten degrees in a week. One day it could be down to 42°F and seven or eight days later it could be up to 52°F. By the same perverse law, as devised by Mr Sod or Mr Murphy, it might equally have moved from 52°F back to 42°F a week later. This means that you should be constantly ready to change tactics as the conditions dictate. Most times you may prefer to start with your 15-foot carbon-fibre fly rod and a No 11 floating line. This will certainly simplify your Spey casting and enable you to cover all the likely water without too much effort. You might have to share the services of your gillie with four or five other rods on the beat, but he will allocate a section of the river to you and then show you the best taking lies. At lunch time you will change places with another rod and fish his piece of water in the afternoon. These changes will continue all week so that you get an opportunity of fishing all the water available on the beat at least once during your week.

Having been prepared for a wide range of water and air temperatures, you must also expect the river to rise or fall as a consequence of the effect of temperature or rain on the deep snow-ridden corries of the Cairngorm mountains. A warm wind or rain can materially affect the amount of water released into the river, as can nothing more than a strong south-westerly wind putting a wave on Loch Insh and forcing the water into the river. All these factors may cause water temperature and height to fluctuate quite markedly. You may find that you are fishing quite comfortably with your floating line one day and then, the day after, you are fishing in exactly the same style as you did on the Tweed in February. Unless there is a gauge on the river, it might not be too easy to take a mental note of the rapidly changing conditions. The fish too will tend to be very unsettled by any change in temperature and water flow and it will be the angler who is prepared to fish hard in the most appropriate manner who will do better than the casual fisherman who likes to potter.

Having been allocated a pool for the morning you should be at pains to study exactly where you are to wade. Ask the gillie or a person with wide experience of the water to give you any hints on exact lies for a particular height of water. Make sure that you know the best wading and entry and exit positions and don't take any chances. I have yet to lose one of my spring guests on the Spey, but it is an ever-present threat to the unwary.

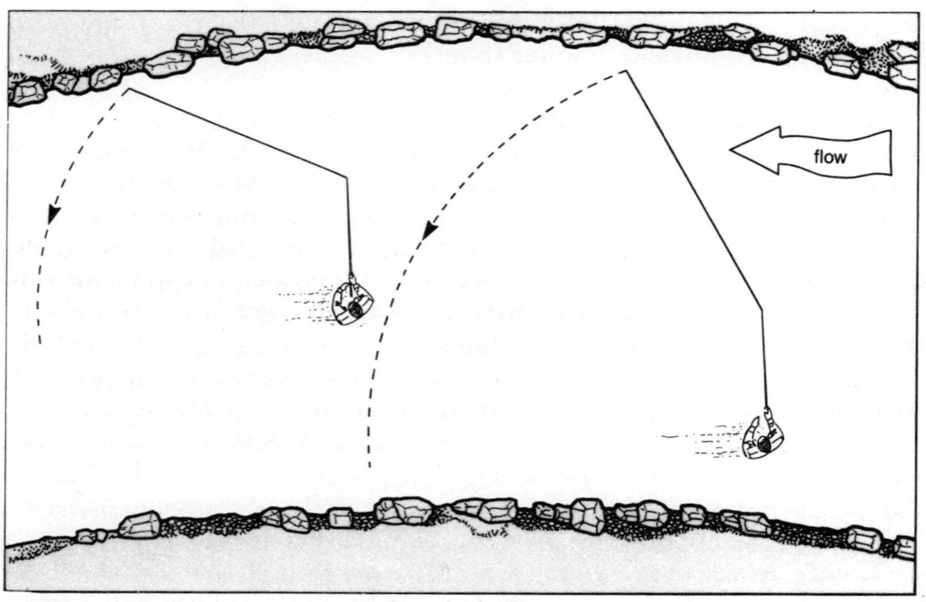

Knowledge of the river bed and fish lies is essential to achieve effective casting range. Deep wading may frequently be essential to get the best water coverage.

Whenever the water gets exceptionally cold or higher than average, consider trying the sunk line. Don't be too worried about neglecting the traditional small fly of the spring. Unless the weather is very warm and the river very low, even when fishing with a floating line it is a mistake to fish with flies that are too small. Show the fish something that is readily seen. Most of them will be fairly fresh-run and the ability (or the sheer luck) to cross a resting fish will be much more important than your choice of fly. Stick with size 4s or 6s on the floating line and with little less than 2-inch tubes on the sinking line.

Your day-to-day tactics for fishing at this time of the year may only be governed by your experience or the advice of the gillie. Most Spey gillies prefer the floating line to the sinker and they despise anyone who wants to spin. It brings to mind that lovely quotation from the Good Book which urges us to 'Consider the lilies of the field, they toil not neither do they spin.' My corruption of this delightful verse might read: 'Consider the gillies of the Spey, they toil not neither do they spin.'

It took me many years to come to terms with the fact that the Spey is essentially a fly water and that over a season the floating line will do better than the sinker – but there have been notable exceptions. I dare not predict from one day to another, let alone over a week or a season, just how the spring will be in Strathspey. I am there every year from mid-April to the end of May and I cannot recall any two years when the climate has followed the same routine. But it is a time when you might serve a useful apprenticeship to salmon fly fishing on the Spey.

Meanwhile, let me run through the form on a hypothetical late April day on, say, the Polchraine Pool of the Spey on the No 2 Castle Grant beat. Let me assume that there is a light breeze from the south-west and the sky is partially obscured. A cock chaffinch chants cheekily from a nearby branch, wheeling plovers, oystercatchers and curlews add their chorus to the spring symphony, and up the strath you notice a solitary osprey hovering high over the river near Cromdale bridge. The river gushes round the central arch at Cromdale and the gauge registers one foot ten inches.

Consulting your gillie, you ask from which bank at Polchraine you might have the better chance. Traditionally, as the river bends slightly to the right, you may think that the right bank and the inside bend will offer the best chances. Indeed, there is some superb water in both the neck and the tail at this side, but there is a lot of slack water in the middle which may be best fished from the left bank and it will be difficult to decide for the best. You must also consider the direction of the wind and the light, should the cloud clear and the sun emerge. Usually you will try to avoid fishing with the light at your back. In this position it will surely be shining into the eyes of the fish you hope to tempt.

With water height as described, I would not mind too much from which side of Polchraine I fished. The right bank offers slightly better casting positions and helpful prevailing breezes, while the left bank demands Spey casting with limited wading. There is little doubt, however, that the right bank offers easier fishing for the novice and you quickly opt for that.

It is 10 a.m. before you are fully clad in breast waders and ready with your tackle. The water is at 48°F while the air has already made it to 52°F. You have chosen a No 11 double-taper floating line and the same 15-foot carbon-fibre fly rod you used earlier in the season. A 12-foot length of level 14lb test monofilament serves as your leader and you soon select a size 6 double- or treble-hooked Munro Killer as being the fly most popular at this time of the year. You wade out slowly into the neck of the pool and make a few short casts. Slowly you lengthen these until you are covering a nice section or arc of the water at your side of the river. As soon as effective water command has been attained (about twenty-five to thirty yards) you maintain that casting distance and merely take a pace or two downstream between each cast.

As you move out of the fast current, where your chances of a fish might be better in a lower water with a higher temperature, you note that your fly is now swinging round very nicely into a portion of deeper water as it comes almost onto the dangle from where you stand. You cover this area most carefully and are excited to see a quiet head-and-tail rise just a few yards downstream of where your fly is moving. Two casts later, when your fly is in the vicinity of where you saw the fish, you momentarily feel something check your fly as it swings round to the dangle.

More than likely the fish you saw was the one which made a pass at your fly. Without serious thought or consideration you make the same cast again, hoping for a firm take. Most times, following such action, nothing happens and you just move on downstream, cursing your luck but hoping for another fish which will take more boldly. Sometimes I adopt this procedure myself, but there are times when I am in an inquisitive mood and then I rest the fish which apparently pulled my fly. I strip in the line without altering the amount held on the reel, which – provided that I don't move my feet in the meantime – will enable me to instantly place the fly exactly where it was before. More often than not I will do little more than rest that fish for five minutes and then try again with the same fly. Occasionally I might change the fly for one a size bigger and then make it move a little faster over the lie of the fish by handlining or with a downstream mend. The fish has already demonstrated that it has all the hallmarks of a taker and you should not give in too easily and presume that it will be uncatchable.

21 Salmon

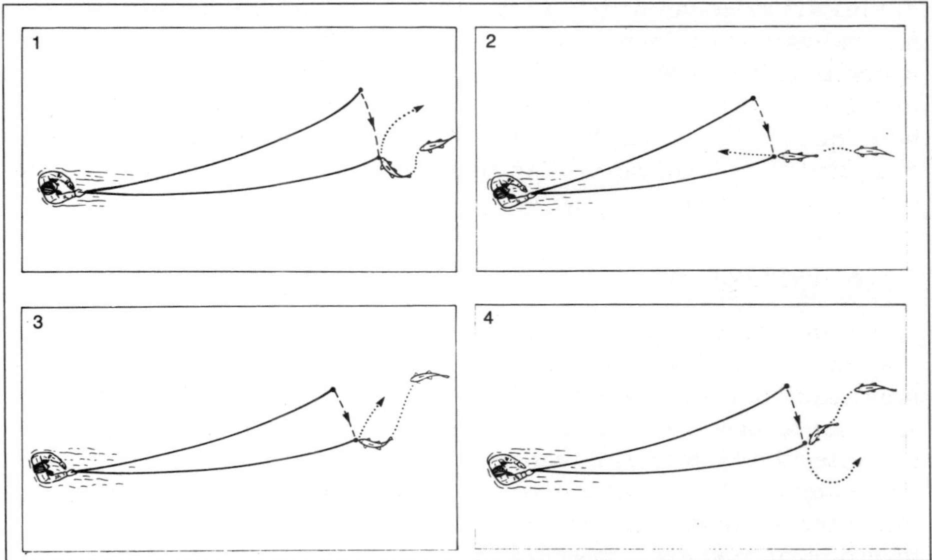

The take. Various ways in which a salmon might take your fly, but in most instances the angler knows nothing until the pull is felt.

After several changes of fly and odd periods of waiting you eventually conclude that the fish is no longer interested. You continue on down the pool and you are just coming to that portion where the water goes fairly slack on the right bank, and you are perhaps wading more deeply than you enjoy, when the line tightens and your rod arches over into a tight bow – a springer is on ! Initially the fish does little more than let you feel its weight. It backs away in the current while you quietly maintain the bend in the rod and ease yourself out towards the bank. Far better that you make the bank as soon as you can. This way you will be able to move with more haste should the fish run your line down to the backing.

Once on the bank you should not give ground downstream unless forced to do so. Maintain a steady strain on the fish and only let it take line when you feel that the tackle is being strained to near limits. At all times seek to be winning back line from the fish and never let it rest or lean on your tackle, so to speak. Constant pressure and harrying will tire it all the more quickly, but be ever ready to yield line when you have the fish coming in fairly close to you. Many a fish gains its freedom in the final stages of play when the angler is overconfident that all is nearly finished.

Slowly the fish begins to tire and it starts to wallow on or near the surface. This may be the time to wade back into the water and stir up some of the mud or gravel with your feet to reduce visibility in the water. You must now maintain a constant pressure to pull it into the area of turbid water. Eventually the fish lies on its side more frequently and it is during one of these moments that you ease it into the edge and then, when it is lying quietly on its side, lift it up by the tail and heave it onto the bank. Your first fish of the season on the floating line, a lovely thirteen-pounder, has become a reality.

Late Spring

If you find that mid-spring fishing is too unpredictable it may pay to delay your visit to the Spey until late May or June. Most certainly the pools will now be full of resident spring salmon and there will be a sufficient head of sea trout to make fishing for both species well worth while. Most of the snow on the Cairngorms will also have melted and the river will be beginning to settle down to normal summer level. In most situations you can now put your sinking lines to one side and concentrate entirely on the floating line. Initially it might make sense to continue with your double-handed rod, but you should be ever watchful for the water to drop away, when, with deep wading, the single-handed rod with a lighter line and smaller fly could be more effective.

Often on the Spey the river begins to fall away by mid-May and air and water temperatures start to move into those levels more associated with summer. I am thinking of times when the water temperature gets into the low fifties and air temperatures stay in the mid-sixties Fahrenheit for a long portion of the day. Now most of the salmon that were running a month ago will have settled into the main holding pools and catching them begins to sort the men from the boys. The best of the fishing may now be restricted to the periods between dawn and lunch time, and again, a more interesting spell, between dinner time and the onset of full darkness. Even then it is important not to conclude that afternoon fishing is always a waste of time. One may afternoon brought me four fish when all my guests had gone back to the hotel for an afternoon siesta.

Summer

After your spring visit to the Spey you are faced with several summertime possibilities. In most situations June will bring a start to the dog days of fishing, but it will offer superb opportunities for sea trout at dusk and on through the short hours of darkness. Many of the salmon will be getting slightly past their best and it may need rain to lift the river out of the metaphorical doldrums and back into life. You may alternate with double-

and single-handed rods as the conditions dictate and there may be times, following a summer flood, when it will pay dividends to resort to the sinking line and fly used back in February.

But June is a lovely time to be on such a river as the Spey and there were many years when I literally had to tear myself away in order to swan off to Norway for my annual pilgrimage to its famous Vosso river. By the time we get into July we really are into the dog days of British fishing. Good alternatives are still to be found in Norway, Iceland and Canada and if you can get access to some of their good rivers you will be there at the best time of the year.

However, July does offer good opportunities in the smaller spate streams of the west coast and the Hebrides. I have had great fun at Amhuinnsuidhe Castle on Harris during early July though the sport may vary with salmon and sea trout and from year to year. It is a fascinating time of the year to be in such a paradise – although one may never dare predict the ferocity of the winds or the horrendous level of the rainfall. Perhaps we should invent a special inclemency scale for Hebridean weather, with zero representing a zephyr-like calm under cloudless skies and semitropical temperatures, and 100 representing twenty-four hours of continuous rainfall with storm-force winds and freezing temperatures.

August

There are many years when I pay an August visit to the Spey, but this can be a very dour time for fish and when we confine most of our efforts to the early mornings or late evenings. Invariably I fish with a floating line on a single-handed rod but there are times, as the river rises after rain, when the sport goes flat. While a slight rise of water in midsummer, particularly after a fairly long spell without rain, might bring some fish, it is quite likely to bring down some peat water from the hills which will increase the acid level of the water and make the fish a bit reluctant to take. When foam on the water suggests excessive acidity, you may on occasion revert to the sinking line with advantage. One July afternoon produced five fish for me when the rest of our party, myself included, had drawn blank for the previous three days.

In August few rivers in Britain offer regular sport. Oh, there will still be good opportunities in the Hebrides and on some of the west and north-coast lochs of Scotland, but almost everywhere else will be dependent on new rain to lift the rivers and give them a veritable shot in the arm.

Depending entirely on rainfall, many of the smaller rivers should now be getting their main runs of summer salmon, grilse and sea trout. In those halcyon days when I had regular access to the Lune and the Yorkshire Esk it was great fun to have the boot of the car loaded with tackle and to be hanging on the end of the phone waiting for the word that all was right. Many a time I have been hightailing it over the Whitby moors or the Pennines just on dawn so as to be well in time for what a keeper or a friend had predicted as being the magic moment. Usually it was important to down tools at the precise moment as instructed, for the river could be back down to summer level again in a matter of hours rather than days. Usually I made arrangements to stay near the river for as long as it held up and the good conditions lasted. There is little doubt that the ability to do this gives you a head start over those who have to adhere to the disciplines of an appointments book or routine business.

There was one memorable occasion when I went to the Lune just as quickly as I could. It was at a perfect height and I quickly caught three fish weighing 18, 9 and 8lb. 1 stayed over that evening in the local pub to await guests joining me on the following morning. Sad to relate, they missed the magic moment and fished all that day for not so much as a pull.

Autumn

While all salmon fishing is a bit of a lottery, it is never more so than in summertime, when we rely on flash floods to bring some of our rivers into trim. September is a more predictable month – the dog days are virtually over – but on the classic rivers it often means catching stale fish that have been in the river for some months. On a little river like the Yorkshire Esk, however, which frequently does not get its first fish of the season until July or August, September might well provide an opportunity of intercepting a run of fresh fish. Sadly, most of my Esk fish were caught on baits and spinners. It was never a good fly river following a flood.

October is a great month to be on one of the lower beats of the Tweed. Once again, a fly-only rule applies. Because of the residual heat left from the sun's prolonged spell in the northern hemisphere, daytime temperatures may be higher than in the spring, while the hours of darkness and daylight resemble those of late February or March. This suggests that, while you may still fish with the floating line, you might not be so concerned with very small flies as you were in July, August and part of September. Indeed, if there is good October rainfall and a few overnight frosts, you might well resort to the sinking shooting head and the same large tube flies you used in February and March. Always bear in mind that water temperatures must be related to air temperatures. In no circumstances do I like a day when the water is warmer than the air, but even then there may be a chance of fish if you resort to the sinking line and the large fly.

21 Salmon

In late October and early November I journey north for my annual visit to the Upper Floors beat of the Tweed just upstream of Kelso. This water is regarded by many as the finest beat on the whole river but, as with any other piece of salmon water, it is possible to spend a week there and catch nothing. We need the river to be at the right height and to know that there has been a run of fish. In 1980, the first year I had access to this lovely water, I fished hard all week for nothing. My wife managed one fish, but the river was at flood level over most of the week and fishing was almost a complete waste of time. The following year we did slightly better, but it was not until 1982 that I hit a mild bonanza.

On that Wednesday morning even Bob Paterson, my boatman for the day, asked me just how many fish I would like. By lunch time I had five on the bank and he suggested that I should get another five that afternoon. My last fish of the day took my fly in the failing light and at 22lb it was my biggest fish of the day. It brought my total to ten fish weighing an average of 14½lb. All were caught on my 15-foot 'Walker' with a sinking No 11 shooting head and one of the large tube flies so popular on the Tweed in early spring and late autumn. The river fell a little more during the rest of the week and I caught quite a lot more fish. But that day produced the most magic moments and, following the rise of water we had endured three days before, it was almost predictable.